GREAT
TRUTHS
OF THE
BIBLE

A BIBLE STUDY FOR
THE LAY PUPIL AND LAY TEACHER

ALAN B. STRINGFELLOW, LIT. D.

I

GREAT TRUTHS OF THE BIBLE

This book was originally published as the third in a series, however each volume is written as to be independent within itself.

Through the Bible in One Year is an overview of each book of the Bible — the structure.

Great Characters of the Bible is a study of God's use of people (the divine and the human), to carry out His sovereign will and purpose.

Great Truths of the Bible adds spiritual sinew to the study of the structure and characters of the Bible.

Dedication

This work is dedicated to Dr. Jess C. Moody, a brother beloved and co-laborer in the ministry of our precious Lord. His intimate friendship has been an abiding inspiration to me for thirty-five years. Jess Moody's incomparable preaching has brought multitudes to Christ as he has exposed the "great truths" of the Bible.

A.B.S.

ISBN 1-56322-047-4

HENSLEY
PUBLISHING
6116 E. 32nd St.
Tulsa, OK 74135

What This Study Will Do For You

You are about to begin an exciting adventure into the Word of God, an adventure involving the great truths (doctrines) of the Bible.

Can a lay person comprehend the great truths of Scripture? This is a question that will be asked by a large percentage of the pupils beginning this study.

The answer is "yes."

Paul was in Thessalonica less than a month. Yet he taught that group of babes in Christ the great truths he knew they would need. He taught them the richness of the doctrines of God as recorded in I Thessalonians, such as:

- Election, (1:4)
- Holy Spirit (1:5-6; 4:8; 5:19)
- Assurance (1:5)
- Trinity (1:1, 5, 6)
- Conversion (1:9)
- Second Coming of Christ (1:10; 2:19; 3:13; 4:14-17; 5:23)
- Walk of a believer (2:12; 4:1)
- Sanctification (4:3; 5:23)
- Day of the Lord (5:1-3)
- Resurrection (4:14-18)
- The tripartite nature of man (5:23)

Paul taught these eleven great truths and the young believers understood.

So if you are a Christian, you can learn the great truths of the Scripture. Because, as Jesus said ". . . the Comforter, which is the Holy Spirit, whom the Father will send in my name, he (the Holy Spirit) shall teach you all things, and bring all things to your remembrance, whatsoever I have said unto you" (John 14:26).

In addition to giving you the greath truths of God's Word, this study will

- build your confidence in the truth of *all* Scripture;
- cause you to understand the so called hard subjects of the Bible;
- make you grow spiritually by consuming "the meat of the Word";
- produce unquestioned confidence in your Christian life;
- give you "blessed assurance" in your daily walk;
- provide you insight into subjects rarely taught or preached;
- take you completely through the Bible by focusing on the great truths of Scripture

The "great truths" of this study were selected from hundreds within the Scriptures because of their particular importance to the Christian. They are doctrines every Christian can and should learn. Be diligent in your study and place complete dependence on our great teacher, the Holy Spirit.

Introduction For Students and Teachers

To receive maximum knowledge and inspiration during the next 52 weeks, heed the following suggestions. They are designed to help you become a disciplined disciple of God's Word.

"MUSTS" FOR THE STUDENT

— Attend every class session for 52 weeks.

— Read the assigned portion at the end of each lesson.

— Review your notes from the previous week's study.

— Mark your Bible with key references from one Scripture to another.

— Take notes in class.

— Search the Scripture and mark references in class. Write in the Scriptures in this notebook where lines are provided.

PUBLISHER'S STUDY NOTE

It is important to note the author's premise in developing this course of study; namely, that *the Bible is the divinely inspired Word of God.* Nothing can take it's place.

Thus, GREAT TRUTHS OF THE BIBLE should be read neither *in place of* the Bible nor as a study *about* the Bible. Rather you should use it as a guide that takes you *into* the Bible and involves you in the study of God's Word, resulting in your understanding it better and appreciating it more.

You will also note that the text of this manual appears in outline rather than exposition. This permits quick coverage of the controlling thoughts of the book under study along with the key verses, the central message and the major themes.

Because your manual is in this form, you will get maximum benefit if your study is under the direction of a teacher. The teacher in turn should be prepared by attending weekly teachers' meetings taught bay the pastor or other capable assistant.

Another major advantage of the outline form is that it allows the teacher far more latitude than does straight exposition.

In a few instances, you may find that the text differs slightly with your own theological beliefs. Please do not allow these occasions to over-shadow the overall value of this excellent course. Instead, use these differences as a point around which to further refine your own theology. This adds still more value to the program, for it enables you to see denominational differences.

In your study and discussion, always be guided by the Holy Spirit, and you will profit immensely from this work, despite differences in interpretation.

The publisher feels that GREAT TRUTHS OF THE BIBLE is the inspired work of a devoted man of God.

— Promise the Lord at least two or three hours each week for reading the assigned Scripture for the lesson and doing your homework.

Why these "musts?" Because we have expected too little from our Bible students the past several years. The time has come for Christians who mean business for the Lord to devote themselves to the study of His Word and to learning the basic principles that we all should know. Promise yourself and promise God you will live up to these "musts."

"MUSTS" FOR THE TEACHER

First you must prepare yourself spiritually by reading
— I Corinthians 2:12-14
— Ephesians 1:17-18
— John 14:26
— John 16:12-16

These Scriptures will assure you as the teacher that the Holy Spirit will guide you and teach you as you study His Word and impart it to your pupils.

If you are in a church, the program is best taught to teachers by the pastor, minister of education, Sunday School superintendent or a specially selected teacher. This should be done on a weekday evening prior to the coming Lord's Day.

Part of the discipline of this course of study is that you attend each session each week without exception.

You must read the entire assignment for the next lesson, found at the close of each lesson study. The author has suggested that you read the chapters to be taught the following week; he has also listed key verses for pupils if they are unable to read a chapter in its entirety.

You must take notes and search out Scripture references. You must also be prepared to answer questions, add to or take away from the questions as you feel is necessary for your age group.

What's more, you must . . .
— Stay with the subject of each lesson.
— Not be afraid of being too elementary for your pupils.
— Stay on the major points, not minor ones.
— Keep the lesson teaching as simple as possible with all age groups.
— Not change the lesson outline. You may add illustrations and ideas, but do not change the major points of the outline.
— Use your own personality and let the Holy Spirit use you as you teach.
— Expect your pupils to do their part.

You should teach at least 55 minutes every lesson. Even if you have to revamp your class schedule to teach for 55 minutes, it can be done. The assembly periods can be made shorter. It isn't necessary to have a devotional before going to Bible Study. One song and a prayer is sufficient for the assembly period. Class absentees and other business should be handled at class meetings. Make your Bible study period an hour of concentrated Bible study.

May God bless you, pupil or teacher, as you begin your study in *Great Truths of the Bible.* Let the Holy Spirit teach you both.

FOREWORD

I Peter 2:2 says, "As newborn babes, desire the sincere milk of the Word, that ye may grow thereby." In Hebrews 5:12 we read, "For when for the time ye ought to be teachers, ye have need that one teach you again which be the first principles of the oracles of God: and are become such as have need of milk, and not of strong meat." Then, in Hebrews 5:14, "But strong meat belongeth to them that are full of age (spiritually mature), even those who by reason of use have their senses exercised to discern both good and evil."

This study has been written with the layperson in mind. They are not deep theological presentations, but they do require Scripture searching and dependence upon the "Teacher," the Holy Spirit, for complete understanding.

It is good to *know* the great truths of Scripture. It is better if these truths become a *living reality* in the lives of all who study this series of lessons. By *knowing* God's truths, one can *become* "doers" of the Word and not hearers only" (James 1:22-25).

The King James Version of the Bible is used (since it is one most people have) in the writing of these lessons. If another version is used, it will be so stated.

The lessons are not necessarily presented in chronological order. However, the 52 lessons will take the student through the Bible as the great truths from Genesis to Revelation are presented.

May the Holy Spirit of God use these studies for His glory as His Word is magnified, Jesus glorified and His church amplified.

"Whom shall He teach knowledge? And whom shall He make to understand doctrine? Them that are weaned from the milk, and drawn upon the breast. For precept must be upon precept, precept upon precept; line upon line, line upon line; here a little, and there a little" (Isaiah 28:9-10).

Alan B. Stringfellow, Lit.D.

INDEX

About Photocopying This Book

Lesson 1
"The Canon of the Scripture"

GREAT TRUTHS
OF THE
BIBLE

(Where lines are provided, look up the Scripture and write in the Scripture or its main truth.)

I. INTRODUCTION

"Canon" means a "rule, a measuring line, a standard, a model." The word is most unusual because it is the same word with the same meaning wherever found—in Latin, Greek, Hebrew or English. A book entitled to a place in Scripture is canonical—has met the standard, or rule, as the inspired Word of God

II. BASIC SCRIPTURES:

Luke 24:27,44; Matthew 23:35; II Timothy 3:16; II Peter 1:21; Hebrews 1:1-3.

III. THE NUCLEUS OF THIS TRUTH

The 66 books that are in our Bible and how they became a part of the Word of God. Look at II Timothy 3: 16 _____

_____

IV. THE GREAT TRUTH: "THE CANON OF THE SCRIPTURE"

A. THE 39 BOOKS OF THE OLD TESTAMENT CANON OF SCRIPTURE.

1. **The Old Testament Is A Prophetic Statement From God.**

   We start with the paramount idea expressed in II Peter 1:21, "For prophecy came not *at any time* by the will of man, but *holy men of God* spake as they were moved by the Holy Spirit.

   A prophet was one who spoke for God—not only "fore-telling" but speaking as God inspired him. They were the mouthpiece of God. (Refer to "THROUGH THE BIBLE IN ONE YEAR," Vol. I, page 75). In the Greek the word "prophet" means "one who speaks in place of another." Thus, the Old Testament was written by those men of God who declared and wrote the truths of God, predictive and non-predictive. There were those who were called "prophets" and there were those who possessed the "prophetic gift" such as Aaron (Exodus 7:1) and David (Acts 2:30).

2. **The Old Testament Is The Inspired Word of God.**

   The second premise is found in II Timothy 3:16, "All Scripture is given by the inspiration of God, and is profitable for doctrine, for reproof, for correction, for instruction in righteousness."

   The Old Testament claims to be the inspired Word of God. Look up only a few of the Scriptures declaring the inspiration (meaning "God Breathed") of God:

   In Genesis I count the number of times you find the phrase, "and God said."

Genesis 2:7 and 3:15 could only be recorded by the inspiration of God.

Look at Exodus 32:16 _____

_____

Write in Leviticus 1:1 _____

_____

Also Numbers 36:13 _____

_____

Also Deuteronomy 4:2 _____

_____

Also Joshua 24:26 _____

_____

All through the Old Testament you will find the same basic truths of the inspiration of God.

3. **Jewish Tradition Ascribes the Old Testament Canon to Ezra and the Men of the Great Synagogue.**

Their tradition is based upon the fact of Ezra's zeal and ability. He was "a scribe of the words of the commandments of the Lord, and of His statutes to Israel" (Ezra 7:11). He was a man who "had prepared his heart to seek the law of the Lord, and to do it, and to teach in Israel statutes and judgments" (Ezra 7:10).

These men were well qualified to take the oracles of God and determine their authenticity. That they arranged the inspired Word in substantially its present form, we have no good reason to doubt.

Jewish tradition may be more than tradition. There is abundant evidence that Ezra and the Men of the Great Synagogue played *the* vital role in establishing the canon of the Old Testament.

4. **History Confirms the Old Testament Canon of Scripture.**

Josephus, the famous Jewish historian, confirms the books of the Old Testament canon when he wrote his work in 90 A.D., "Against Apion 1:8." He says,

"For we (meaning the Jews) have not an innumerable multitude of books among us, disagreeing with and contradicting one another (as the Greeks have), but only twenty two books, which contain the records of all the past times; which are justly believed to be Divine; and of them, five belong to Moses, which contain his laws and the tradition of the origin of mankind till his death. This interval of time was little short of three thousand years; but as to the time from the death of Moses till the reign of Artaxerxes, king of Persia, who reigned after Xerxes, the prophets, who were after Moses, wrote down what was done in their times in thirteen books. The remaining four books contain hymns to God and precepts for the conduct of human life. It is true, our history hath been written since Artaxerxes, very particularly, but hath not been esteemed of the like *authority* with the former by our forefathers, because there hath not been an exact succession of prophets since that time; and how firmly we have given credit to those books of our own nation is evident by what we do; for during so many ages as have already passed, no one has been so bold as either to add anything to them or take it from them; but it becomes natural to all Jews, immediately and from their very birth, to esteem those books to contain

2

Divine doctrines, and to persist in them, and, if occasion be, willingly to die for them.''

The books which constituted the Old Testament canon were written in 22 books dating from Artaxerxes, king of Persia. In Ezra 7:11-26 is recorded the decree of Artaxerxes on behalf of Ezra. In Nehemiah 2 is recorded the decree of Artaxerxes on behalf of Nehemiah. So the writings of Josephus tell us the number of books in the Old Testament canon and the end of the prophets (inspired speakers for God) came to a close with Ezra and Nehemiah.

No book was admitted to the Jewish canon which was not in existence at the time of Ezra and Nehemiah.

5. The Twenty Two Old Testament Books Are the Same as the Thirty Nine Books In Our Testament.

5 BOOKS OF MOSES	13 PROPHETICAL BOOKS	4 HYMNS TO GOD
(1) Genesis	(1) Joshua	(1) Psalms
(2) Exodus	(2) Judges & Ruth	(2) Proverbs
(3) Leviticus	(3) Two Books of Samuel	(3) Ecclesiastes
(4) Numbers	(4) Two Books of Kings	(4) Song of Solomon
(5) Deuteronomy	(5) Two Books of Chronicles	
	(6) Ezra & Nehemiah	
	(7) Esther	
	(8) Isaiah	
	(9) Jeremiah & Lamentations	
	(10) Ezekiel	
	(11) Daniel	
	(12) Books of 12 Minor Prophets	
	(13) Job	

a. The original Jewish canon, as named by Josephus, contained the books listed above. These are the 39 books that now make up our Old Testament—not one addition nor subtraction.

b. The reason there are 39 books in our Old Testament is
   - The Minor Prophets are 12 books, not 1 (from Hosea to Malachi)
   - Samuel, Kings, Chronicles are 2 books each, not 1
   - Ezra and Nehemiah are 2 books, not 1
   - Ruth and Judges are separate
   - Jeremiah and Lamentations are separate

   With these separations there are added 17 books to the 22 books, or series of writings, making a total of 39 books. Who divided the books?

c. When the Hebrew Scriptures were translated into Greek, known as the Septuagint, they divided the original Hebrew Scriptures into:

        5 Books of Moses—Law
       12 Books of History—(Joshua to Esther)
        5 Books of Poetry—(Job to Song of Solomon)
       17 Books of Prophecy—(Isaiah to Malachi)

Total: 39 Books in the Old Testament Canon

The Greek translation, made in Alexandria in the 3rd century B.C., became the Bible at that time because Greek had become ''the tongue'' in the then known world.

So, the same 22 books named by Josephus, translated into Greek, are the 39 books of our Old Testament.

6. **Jesus and the New Testament Affirm the Old Testament Canon of Scripture**

   a. Look up Luke 24:44 _____

   _____

   b. The testimony of Jesus and the New Testament fulfill all that had been promised in the Law, Prophets and Writings. The entire Old Testament is Christ centered. Look up Luke 24:27 _____

   _____

B. THE 27 BOOKS OF THE NEW TESTAMENT CANON OF SCRIPTURE

   1. **The New Testament Was Inspired by God, the Holy Spirit.**

      The valid test of a writer's inspiration in the New Testament was his relationship to the Lord Jesus. Jesus is the great central fact of the gospel and through Him God made Himself known in the form of humanity. Jesus selected men divinely qualified to teach and record without error the facts and doctrines of His gospel. Look at Hebrews 1:1-2 and underline in your Bible.

   2. **The New Testament Books Were Written by an Apostle or a Companion (Amanuensis) of an Apostle.**

      a. Jesus promised the apostles that the Holy Spirit would reveal to them what they could not understand while He was still on earth. Look at John 16:12-15 and underline in your Bible. Also Matthew 10:20. Look up John 14:25-26.

      b. These, and other promises, were given *primarily* to the apostles for a special assignment. They were also given to the church through the teaching of the apostles (Ephesians 2:19-22).

      c. The apostles spoke and wrote with divine authority. Look at 1 Corinthians 2:9-13 and underline verse 13 in your Bible. Paul declared his authority again in Galatians 1:11-12 _____

      _____

      Now look up Ephesians 2:20 and underline in your Bible.

      d. Examples of books written by companions, known as an amanuensis (secretary), of the apostles can be found in Mark and Luke. Mark was the companion of Peter, and Luke was the companion of Paul.

      Underline 1 Peter 5:13 in your Bible.

      Luke wrote the third gospel and was a companion of Paul during his journeys as Luke records in Acts.

      Look up Romans 16:22 and underline in your Bible.

   3. **All the New Testament Books Had Apostolic Authority.**

      All 27 books of the New Testament were placed in the canon after they had been treasured by the churches. The churches exchanged letters and copied them, and sent them to other churches. Only letters with apostolic authority were accepted as a part of the canon.

      The Council of Carthage, 397 A.D. said, "Nothing shall be read in the churches except the recognized canon." They then named the 27 books of the New Testament. The canon, or rule, guiding them was simply, "A New Testament book must be written by an apostle or an amanuensis (companion) of an apostle."

The Bible is the inspired Word of God, written by men of God, preserved by the keeping power of the Holy Spirit and has been accepted through the ages by the people of God. WE HAVE THE ENTIRE WORD OF GOD!

V. WHAT THIS BIBLE TRUTH TEACHES US TODAY

This lesson teaches us that the Canon of Scripture is inspired by God—written by men of God, (prophets and apostles)—reveals the truth of God—is kept and preserved by the Holy Spirit of God—and is accepted and loved by the people of God.

''Faith comes by hearing and hearing by the Word of God.'' (Romans 10:17).

YOUR NEXT ASSIGNMENT:

1. Read Psalm 119; 1 Corinthians 2:9-13; Isaiah 28:9-13; Isaiah 40:6-8; II Timothy 3:16; I Peter 1:23-25; II Peter 1:19-21.

2. Review the Old Testament and New Testament books in your lesson notes.

3. Mark your Bible where new truths are learned.

Lesson 2 "The Bible – The Inspired Word of God"

(Where lines are provided, look up the Scripture and write in the Scripture or its main truth.)

I. INTRODUCTION

Every word of the Bible is inspired or "God-breathed." In II Timothy 3:16 you read, "All scripture is given by the inspiration of God." Two words used in this text present for us the apostolic view concerning the inspiration of the scriptures. The first word is "GRAPHE," which means "writing," and the second word is "THEOPNEUSTOS," which means "God-breathed." It is the writing, the scriptures, that is "God-breathed," that is inspired. The inspiration came from God to human personalities and human minds to give to us the Bible.

The word "Bible" comes from the Greek word *"biblos"* with its plural form *"biblia."* The modern English form comes from the Latin and OldFrench *"biblia"*—meaning "writings." It is one book, the Bible.

II. BASIC SCRIPTURES:

Psalm 119; Isaiah 28:9-13; Isaiah 40:6-8; I Corinthians 2:9-13; II Timothy 3:16; I Peter 1:23-25; II Peter 1:19-21.

III. THE NUCLEUS OF THIS TRUTH

All of the Bible is inspired of God. Over 40 different men spoke, over a period of 1,500 years, as they were moved by the Holy Spirit. The words they wrote were inspired of God. Look at II Peter 1:21 _____

_____

The fallible men have passed away but the infallible words they wrote abide forever.

IV. THE GREAT TRUTH: "THE BIBLE—THE INSPIRED WORD OF GOD"

A. THE BIBLE IS ITS OWN WITNESS TO ITS INSPIRATION.

1. The Claims the Bible Makes About Itself.

a. No other book or writing could make such claims—only the Word of God. Look up Exodus 31:18 _____

_____

_____

Underline Psalm 119:89 and also verses 105, 152, 160. Look up Isaiah 40:8 and compare with I Peter 1:23-25.

b. The Bible claims to be the Word of God because it says no less than 3,808 times in the Old Testament, "And God said . . . ," or "The Word of God came, saying . . ." The

7

prophets always introduced their message with the statement, "And the Word of the Lord came unto . . ." The prophet delivered the message which was, and is, the Word of God. For example, turn to I Peter 1:10-11 and read slowly. Peter said that the prophets wrote what God told them to write. They did not originate their message. The message came from God.

God said to Moses in Exodus 4:10-12 _____

_____

_____

Forty years later Moses said to Israel in Deuteronomy 4:2

_____

Underline II Samuel 23:1-2.

Turn to Jeremiah 1:6-9 and write in verse 9: _____

_____

On and on we could go with examples. You now see that the Bible claims to be the Word of God.

B. THE HOLY SPIRIT INSPIRED THE AUTHORS OF THE BIBLE.

1. The Holy Men Spoke As They Were Moved By the Holy Spirit. Turn again to II Peter 1:21.

The Holy Spirit inspired the men God selected to give us the Bible. God used different methods in originating the message: the word of angels, the voice of God, the writings of the apostles. In many ways God spoke and what He spoke is in the Bible. Turn to Hebrews 1:1-2: _____

_____

2. The Divine Source and the Human Instrument.

In the Bible there are several passages where the divine author and the human instrument are mentioned. Write in Matthew 1:22 _____

_____

Underline Acts 1:16 in your Bible.

3. The Bible is a Miracle.

As the words were written through the ages, one can see that it was necessary for the Holy Spirit to guard and guide so that a true and perfect message would be recorded. The writings attest to one great theme, Christ, point to one true God, and offer to us one plan of salvation.

C. THE GREAT THEME OF THE BIBLE.

1. The One Great Theme of the Bible is Jesus Christ.

By a creative act God broke the chain of human generation and produced the supernatural One—Jesus, the Son of God. Look at Galatians 4:4 _____

_____

2. The Great Theme, Jesus, Binds the Bible Together.

The theme was proclaimed in the Old Testament like this, "There is Someone coming." In the day of the incarnation it was announced, "Someone is come." In the days of the endtime it is prophesied like this, "Someone is coming again." Jesus is the one great unifying factor who binds the Bible into one

message—God's plan of redemption for us. Underline Galatians 1:1-9 [handwritten]
4:5-6. Also Ephesians 2:4,5,8. _____

_____

D. THE REVELATION AND INSPIRATION OF THE BIBLE.

1. The Difference Between Revelation and Inspiration.

a. Revelation refers to something God has made known; He has unveiled, uncovered something.

For example, it was a revelation when Moses wrote the first chapter of Genesis. Moses was not there when God created the heavens and the earth. No human eye saw that. So God made it known by revelation.

Another example is found in the New Testament. It was a revelation when John wrote the Apocalypse, the Book of Revelation. No man can see the end of the age—looking ahead thousands of years into the future known only to God. But God revealed that future to John and John wrote it.

b. Inspiration refers to the transmission, or the writing. It refers to the method that kept this writing from error or mistake.

For example, when Moses wrote of the crossing of the Red Sea, that was an inspired writing. God kept him from error. He wrote as the Holy Spirit directed him. Moses had seen with his own eyes the crossing of Israel through the Red Sea. The transmission, the writing, was by the inspiration of the Holy Spirit and kept from error.

Another example is found in John 19. When John (the same John who wrote Revelation) wrote the account of the crucifixion of Jesus, it was by inspiration. John was there and witnessed the death of our Lord. He wrote, without error, according to the Holy Spirit.

(There are many theories of revelation and inspiration. This study is for the lay person and arguments should not be a part of our study. The presentation has been written in understandable terms so that the pupil can know the primary meaning of revelation and inspiration.)

2. Inspiration Produced the Bible, A Document of God's Self-Revelation.

a. When we speak of the inspired authors of the Bible, we refer to the inspiration of the writings and not of the men. The inspiration is in the Word of God. It is what the men have written that is inspired. Moses, David, John, Paul *were not always and everywhere inspired.* As men they erred in conduct but their fallibility and errancy were never transmitted to the sacred writings.

b. Each Biblical author yielded his entire personality to the will of the Holy Spirit. Therefore, what they wrote was inspired of God. The truth of inspiration concerns the miracle by which the Spirit of God produced the Bible—a document in human language which reveals God and His plan of redemption for us.

The Bible does not contain God's Word; it is God's Word.

E. HOW CAN WE KNOW THE TRUE WORD OF GOD?

1. There are Many Books Claiming Inspiration of God.

There are some claiming to be "an addition" to God's Word.

There is much being said in our day about "The Lost Books of the Bible."

Then how can we know the truth concerning God's Word?

2. We find the Answer in the Bible.

Out of a multitude of tests we could follow, we shall consider only three that are mentioned in the Bible.

a. The first is found in Deuteronomy 18:21-22. Read and underline in your Bible.

So, the *first test* is whether a prophecy comes to pass as foretold by a prophet of God. Prophecy is not prediction. True prophecy is above manmade forecasts. True prophecy is from God.

For example, eight hundred years before Christ, Micah, the prophet, said that Jesus would be born in Bethlehem (Micah 5:2). This literally came to pass (Luke 2:1-7).

One thousand years before it happened, David said, "They part my garments among them, and cast lots upon my vesture" (Psalm 22:18). Now, turn to Matthew 27:35 and see the fulfillment of this prophecy.

Thousands of years in advance, God prophesied things through His prophets that came to pass. This is the first test of the true Word of God. Man cannot tell the future one hour from now but God reveals the future thousands of years in advance.

b. The *second test* is found in Psalm 119:160: "Thy Word is true from the beginning: and every one of thy righteous judgments endureth forever." The Bible is truth. It has been true from the beginning. From the creation to the consummation of this age is found in God's Word. He knows all things and has given us His Book of Truth.

c. The *third test* is that the Word of God accomplishes its purpose. Look at Isaiah 55:10-11 and write in verse 11: __

_____

_____

God's Word does for God what He has willed for it. The purpose of God's Word is that we might be delivered from the penalty and judgment of sin. It will not return void when it is taught and preached and studied. God's will for His Word is: "it shall accomplish that which I please, and it shall prosper in the thing whereto I sent it" (Isaiah 55:11).

That is God's Word. The 66 books are the inspired Word of God.

3. Then, if That be True, What About the "Lost Books" of the Bible? (We can only mention this briefly.)

The Apocrypha means "hidden or concealed" and is a group of 14 books. These books were written after the time of Ezra and Nehemiah. (Refer to Lesson 1 on the Canon of Scripture.) They were great writings but were not inspired.

The Apocrypha can be found in the Greek Septuagint—the translation of the Hebrew Scriptures made in Egypt about 270 B.C. Jerome, who translated the Septuagint into the Latin Vulgate, also included the Apocrypha. Jerome said the 14 books were inferior to the canonical books.

Remember the rules for the Canon of Scripture. The Old Testament was written in Hebrew and ended with Ezra and Nehemiah.

The New Testament was written in Greek and had to be written by an apostle or an amanuensis of an apostle. The 66 books of our Bible are canonical. The Apocrypha does not meet the qualifications—yet they are in some Bibles, but not the Protestant Bible. The Apocrypha did not appear in a Bible until the Council of Trent in *1546 A.D.*

The books have not been lost. They are not a part of the Canon of Scriptures.

The Bible you hold in your hand is God's inspired Word. Be assured of that fact. Love it, study it, teach it, live by its teachings.

V. WHAT THIS BIBLE TRUTH TEACHES US TODAY

This lesson teaches us that the Word of God is His inspired Word to us. All 66 books speak to us and present for us God's redemptive plan. Read again I Peter 1:24-25.

Write in John 20:31: _____

_____

_____

The longest chapter in the Bible is about the Word of God. Every verse extols the excellence of the written word. That is Psalm 119, and it has 176 verses. Read the chapter and underline verses that touch your heart.

"Forever, O Lord, thy Word is settled in heaven" (Psalm 119:89).

"Thy Word is a lamp unto my feet, and a light unto my path" (Psalm 119:105).

YOUR NEXT ASSIGNMENT

1. Read Matthew 5:17-19; 19:4-5; 22:29-32; 26:54-56; Luke 24:25-32; Luke 24:44-45; John 10:35; Romans 15:4; 16:26; Galatians 3:8; I Timothy 5:18; II Timothy 3:16.

2. Digest this lesson. Underline the scriptures. Make notes in your Bible.

(There was a vast amount of literature written called the "Pseudepigrapha" meaning, *pseudo* "false," *epi* "upon" *Graphi* "write" or "to write upon falsely." This literature was written between 200 B.C. and 600 A.D. It was written under the name of another man (false) such as Prophets, Kings or a New Testament name. There are 18 Old Testament false writings talked about occasionally (the actual number is not known). There are at least 280 Pseudepigrapha of the New Testament. There are many "Gospels" such as "The Gospel of Mary, of Thomas, of Peter, of the Twelve," and others. Much of the writing was Apocalyptic. No canon or council recognized these writings. Eusebius said these writings were "totally absurd and impious.")

Lesson 3 "The Bible: The Authoritative Word of God"

(Where lines are provided, look up the Scripture and write in the Scripture or its main truth.)

I. INTRODUCTION

The authority of the Bible *is in the Bible*. One of the most important evidences of authority is also the simplest because the Bible is its own proof. There is no higher authority. The Scriptures never need to be defended. The Bible defends itself. God the Father, and the Son and the Holy Spirit bear witness to the authority of the Bible. For instance, just as the Holy Spirit bears witness to every believer that he is a child of God (Romans 8:16), He also bears witness that the Bible is the Word of God (II Peter 1:20-21). Therefore, the final *authority* for our faith and practice (daily life) is the Word of God.

II. BASIC SCRIPTURES:

Psalm 119; Isaiah 40:6-8; Matthew 5:17-19; 19:4-5; 22:29-32; 26:54-56; Luke 24:25-32; 24:44-45; John 10:35; Romans 15:4; 16:26; Galatians 3:8; I Timothy 5:18; II Timothy 3:16.

III. THE NUCLEUS OF THIS TRUTH

The teachings of Jesus are our highest authority in reference to the Bible. No word of criticism can be leveled against His integrity. Even Pilate said, "I find no fault (crime) in this man" (Luke 23:4). Jesus taught the Bible with authority (Matthew 7:29). If the authority of Jesus is denied at this point, the entire foundation of God's plan of redemption falls with the Son of God.

The Bible is the authoritative Word because God, the Son, Jesus Christ has set His stamp of authority upon the entire Book.

IV. THE GREAT TRUTH: "THE BIBLE: THE AUTHORITATIVE WORD OF GOD"

A. THE TESTIMONY OF GOD THE FATHER.

    1. The Speaker and the Hearer in the Old Testament.

        a. The Bible is the authoritative Word of God because He settled the Word in heaven (Psalm 119:89) and "His Word is true from the beginning" (Psalm 119:160). Phrases such as "And the Lord spake unto—," "And God said—," "The Word of the Lord came unto—" can be found 3,808 times in the Old Testament.

        b. Phrases we accept and often overlook give the Bible its authority. For example, let us take 35 examples in one book and see the words, "And the Lord spake unto Moses, saying—." Underline these in your Bible:

13

Leviticus 1:1
Leviticus 4:1
Leviticus 5:14
Leviticus 6:1,8,19,24
Leviticus 7:22,28
Leviticus 8:1
Leviticus 10:8
Leviticus 11:1
Leviticus 12:1
Leviticus 13:1
Leviticus 14:1,33
Leviticus 15:1
Leviticus 16:1
Leviticus 17:1
Leviticus 18:1
Leviticus 19:1
Leviticus 20:1
Leviticus 21:16
Leviticus 22:1,17,26
Leviticus 23:1,9,23,26,33
Leviticus 24:1,13
Leviticus 25:1
Leviticus 27:1

   c. The speaker is the Lord God—the hearer is Moses. You will find this throughout the Old Testament. God speaks—the writer records "the Word of the Lord."

2. God Spoke His Plan of Redemption Into Being.

   a. Some of the most important words ever spoken by the Lord God are found in Genesis 3. In this chapter the fall of man and God's plan of redemption are recorded. Underline Genesis 3:14 and write in Genesis 3:15: _____

_____

_____

(This is in each of the "Through the Bible In One Year" series. It is imperative that the redemptive plan of God be taught and studied. See Vol. I, page 6, and Vol. II, pages 2 and 7.)

   b. In the sovereignty and will of God, He made a way whereby we can be saved and we can know Him. He spoke into being the plan of redemption—knowing His Son would have to pay the price.

B. THE TESTIMONY OF THE BIBLE.

1. The Internal Evidence of the Authority of the Scriptures.

   a. The Bible declares itself to be the Word of God.

Read Deuteronomy 6:1-9. Write in verses 5 and 6: _____

_____

_____

Underline Joshua 1:8 and Joshua 8:32-35 in your Bible.

   b. The Word is sure, perfect, endures forever, is true.

Look at Psalm 12:6.

Underline Psalm 19:7-11. Notice the words of authority.

   c. The Word is eternal.

Write in Psalm 119:89: _____

_____

Underline Psalm 119:152 and 160.

Look at Isaiah 40:6-8 and write in verse 8: _____

_____

d. The Word is effective—it is the Gospel.

Underline I Thessalonians 2:13.

Read again I Peter 1:23-25—note the words, "being born again . . . by the Word of God."

C. THE TESTIMONY OF THE HOLY SPIRIT.

1. **The Holy Spirit Bears Witness That The Bible is the Word of God.**

   a. Look again at II Peter 1:19-21 and pay special attention to verses 19 and 21. Note "holy men of God spoke (wrote) as they were moved by the Holy Spirit."

   b. Underline I Peter 1:10-11 in your Bible. Peter is saying that the prophets wrote what they were told to write. They did not originate the message. The message came from God.

2. **The Holy Spirit of God Gave the Message to the Writers.**

   a. Turn to II Samuel 23:1-2 and write in verse 2: _____

   _____

   _____

   b. Jeremiah felt his own weakness in speaking the message of God to Israel. The Lord said He would put the words in the mouth of Jeremiah. Read Jeremiah 1:6-9 and underline verse 9 in your Bible.

   c. In Daniel 12:8-9, Daniel wrote words given to him by divine inspiration which he could not understand. The words were from God.

3. **God Used Many Ways to Reveal His Message.**

   a. He used "the voice of God," "the angels," "the prophets." Look at Hebrews 1:1-2 and notice how God still reveals His message.

   b. Underline Zechariah 4:6 and write in the last part of the verse: "Not by might _____

   _____

   c. The Holy Spirit bears witness to the believer that he is a child of God. Write in Romans 8:16: _____

   _____

   The Holy Spirit reveals the truth and the false.

4. **The Words of the Scripture are Divinely Taught by the Holy Spirit (I Corinthians 2:9-13).**

   a. Underline verses 9 and 10 of I Corinthians 2 in your Bible.
   Write in I Corinthians 2:13: _____

   _____

   _____

   b. Spiritual things are taught in words given by the Holy Spirit. This is accomplished by "comparing spiritual things with

15

spiritual things," actually "comparing Scripture with Scripture."

    c. Notice Paul's own testimony in I Corinthians 2:4 and underline the last phrase of the verse

D. THE TESTIMONY OF JESUS CHRIST.

1. The Authority of Jesus.

The testimony of Jesus Christ is the highest authority to which we can turn for the authority of the entire Word of God. If we accept the teachings of Jesus, we must accept His teachings concerning the Bible.

2. According to Jesus, Divine Revelation is in the Word of God.

    a. What the Scriptures say, God says. Jesus authenticates this in Matthew 5:17-18. Write in verse 18: _____

_____

Also in Matthew 19:4.

Jesus also stated in John 10:35—"the Scripture cannot be broken."

    b. When a person receives the Son of God, the question of authority of the Scriptures is settled. If we accept the teachings of Jesus, we must accept the entire Word of God.

3. Jesus Regarded the Bible as Divine Authority.

    a. Look at the following passages as proof:

Matthew 22:29: _____

_____

Matthew 24:37: _____

_____

Mark 7:13: _____

_____

Luke 24:44: _____

_____

_____

John 5:39: "Search the Scriptures; for in them ye think ye have eternal life: and they are they which testify of me."
John 5:46: _____

_____

    b. The way Jesus used the Scriptures proves His love and reverence for the Word.

The way He quoted the Scriptures was amazing. In answering those around Him, He constantly referred to questions such as, "Have you never read?" and "It is written," and "Search the Scriptures." (Refer to the Sermon on the Mount in Matthew 5 through 7, and notice how many times He uses the phrases mentioned above.)

In Matthew 4, Jesus used Scripture to defeat Satan. Notice verses 4, 7, 10.

4. Jesus Claimed Divine Inspiration for His Teachings.

    a. Jesus spoke the doctrine of God (John 7:16; 12:49). "My doctrine is not mine, but His that sent me."

Write in John 12:49: _____

_____

_____

b. Jesus spoke divine, inspired words.
   Underline John 6:63.
   Write in John 8:28: _____

_____

_____

Underline John 8:42-43.
Write in John 12:50: _____

_____

_____

Jesus spoke as the Spirit of God told Him to speak.
Underline Luke 4:18.

5. Jesus Began His Public Ministry by Quoting the Scriptures.

a. Read the context of His message in Luke 4:16-21 and underline verse 21. Here Jesus was quoting Isaiah 61:1-2.

b. From this point, Jesus lived, taught and preached the Scriptures.

6. Jesus and the Scriptures After His Resurrection.

a. It was after the resurrection of our Lord that he set His seal on the entire Old Testament. If there was any doubt about His knowledge of the whole truth in the days of His flesh—there could be no question of his absolute knowledge after His resurrection (Luke 24:27).
   Write in Luke 24:44: _____

_____

_____

Underline the next two verses 45 and 46.

b. The Jews divided the Bible, our Old Testament, into three parts—the Law, the Prophets and the Psalms or "the writings." Notice that after His resurrection, Jesus recognized the three divisions of the Old Testament and set His stamp of authority upon each one.

7. Jesus Promised that the Apostles Would be Holy Spirit Directed in Their Writing and Teaching.

a. Jesus placed His stamp of authority upon the New Testament by anticipation. There was not a book of the New Testament written when Jesus ascended to glory. How did He authenticate the New Testament written by the apostles?
   Jesus promised the guidance of the Holy Spirit in what the apostles would say and write about Him (Matthew 10:19-20).
   Underline verse 19 and write in verse 20: _____

_____

_____

(Remember that this was just after the twelve were commissioned to go forth and preach, Matthew 10:7.)

b. Jesus reiterated the same promise in Mark's account of the Olivet Discourse (Mark 13:11).

17

c. Jesus promised the apostles that they would have the Holy Spirit to teach them all things and to bring to their remembrance all the things Jesus had taught them (John 14:26). Underline in your Bible.

d. The affirmation is repeated in John 16:12-13. This is one of the most important passages in the New Testament.

Underline John 16:12 and write in verse 13: _____

_____

_____

e. The New Testament was given by the Holy Spirit, based upon the authority of Jesus Christ. They contain the *truth* Jesus would have us know after His departure (John 15:26-27). Underline verse 26.

V. WHAT THIS BIBLE TRUTH TEACHES US TODAY

The entire Bible is the authoritative Word of God because of the testimony of God the Father, the testimony of the Bible itself, the witness of the Holy Spirit and the testimony of Jesus Christ. The Bible is the Word of God, and "cannot be broken" (John 10:35). "In the volume of the book it is written of me," said Jesus (Psalm 40:7); Hebrews 10:7).

Therefore, it is for us to bow to the authority of God's Word and to obey its teachings. It is God's message to man—total and complete for faith to live victoriously. It assures the believer of life everlasting.

YOUR NEXT ASSIGNMENT

1. Read Genesis 1 through 3; Genesis 11:1-9; Genesis 18:1,2,33; Exodus 20:3; Psalm 2:7,12; Psalm 110:1; Isaiah 6:8; 11:1-2; Isaiah 48:16; 63:8-10; Matthew 3:16-17; 28:19-20; John 1:1; John 8:54; 14:16-17; 15:26-27; 16:7-15; Chapter 17; I Corinthians 1:3; II Corinthians 13:14; II Thessalonians 2:13-14; Titus 3:4-6.

2. This lesson is one of the most important in this series. It is the foundation of our study. Make notes when a new idea or truth is revealed. The Holy Spirit will teach you as you study.

3. Mark your Bible.

Lesson 4
"God the Trinity"

(Where lines are provided, look up the Scriptures and write in the Scripture or its main truth.)

I. INTRODUCTION

A *complete detailed* understanding of the Trinity is not possible because we are finite while God is infinite. The truth of the Trinity is found throughout the Scriptures—therefore, we know that the Bible is the Word of God. If the prophets and apostles had not been inspired by the Holy Spirit, they would have left out the Trinity. It is too difficult for the "natural" man to fathom but the child of God accepts the Trinity by faith.

The word "Trinity" is not found in the Bible—while the truth of the Trinity is found from Genesis through Revelation. The word came from the Latin, *"TRINITAS,"* meaning "threefold"—the threefold manifestation of God.

The statement of the Trinity became common in most statements of Christian faith as far back as 160 A.D. The word "Trinity" was first placed in the vocabulary of Christian writings in 317 A.D. in Alexandria. From that time until this era, all of the "creeds" have included the Trinity—the Nicene Creed, 325 A.D.; the early Church of England Creed; the Apostles Creed (used in our day), and many other creeds not here mentioned.

II. BASIC SCRIPTURES:

Genesis 1 through 3; 11:1-9; 18:1,2,33; Exodus 20:3; Psalm 2:7,12; 110:1; Isaiah 6:8; 11:1-2; 48:16; 63:8-10; Matthew 3:16-17; 28:19-20; John 1:1; 8:54; 14:16-17; 15:26-27; 16:7-15; Chapter 17; I Corinthians 1:3; II Corinthians 13:14; II Thessalonians 2:13-14; Titus 3:4-6.

III. THE NUCLEUS OF THIS TRUTH

This truth of the Bible is a pure revelation from God. There is only *one* God—not three. God the Father, God the Son, God the Holy Spirit. God, the eternal Father did not make the Son and Holy Spirit as His creations at His set time. In other words, God the *eternal* Father, the *eternal* Son and the *eternal* Holy Spirit always have been. The Godhead is a Trinity in Unity.

Some have tried to explain the Trinity in different ways such as water in liquid form; when heated, vapor; when frozen, solid.

This is not as clear as the illustration given in Scripture in I Thessalonians 5:23—"I pray God your whole spirit and soul and body be preserved blameless unto the coming of our Lord Jesus Christ." We are not three persons, but a three-in-one person. God is Three in One.

IV. THE GREAT TRUTH: "GOD THE TRINITY"
A. THE TRINITY IN THE OLD TESTAMENT.

1. The Truth is Revealed in Names in the Old Testament.

    a. "In the beginning God (Elohim) created the heaven and the earth" (Genesis 1:1). This name "Elohim" is a plural noun. Plural, in English, means two or more. In the Hebrew, we have three terms refering to the grammatical number: *singular,* meaning one; *dual,* equaling two; *plural,* meaning three or more. Therefore, "Elohim" is a plural moun meaning three or more.

So, in the first verse of the Bible we see God, Elohim—three or more in the act of creation. The three were God the Father, God the Son, God the Holy Spirit.

Moses used this name, "Elohim," 500 times in the Pentateuch.

b. "And God (Elohim) said, Let *us* make man in *our* image, after *our* likeness—so God (Elohim) created man in *His* own image, in the image of God created He them—" (Genesis 1:26-27).

This is another use of the plural noun indicating the Trinity at work in the creation of man—yet indicating one God in the phrase, "in His own image." The Godhead *is* a Trinity in Unity.

c. "The man is become as one of *us*" (Genesis 3:22).

Notice the name of the One who spoke, "The Lord God said."

Here the name "Lord" is used (English form). In the Hebrew the name is "Jehovah." "Jehovah" is the *personal* name of God because it means "Redeemer" and was used only after the fall of man. "Jehovah" always relates in a redemptive way to man.

d. "Let *us* go down and there confound their language" (Genesis 11:7).

Here the name "Lord" (Jehovah) is found. This is God speaking to God—the Trinity is involved.

Look at Isaiah 6:8: _____

_____

_____

2. The Scriptures State the Trinity.

a. The Holy Spirit is stated in Genesis 1:2: _____

_____

Also in Isaiah 11:1-2 you will find the Holy Spirit named.

b. The Son, Jesus Christ, is stated in Psalm 2:7: _____

_____

_____

Again in verse 12: "Kiss the *Son,* lest He be angry, and ye perish from the way—."

c. The Trinity is revealed in Genesis 18:1-2. Read and underline verse 2.

The Trinity is also revealed in Isaiah 48:16: _____

_____

_____

Again, the Trinity is seen in Isaiah 63:8-10. Underline in your Bible.

B. THE TRINITY IN THE NEW TESTAMENT

1. A Declaration of the Trinity in the New Testament.

a. A truth depicted by the prophets in the Old Testament, but not fully understood, can usually find illumination in the New Testament.

The Trinity is declared in the New Testament by the fact that the names of Father, Son and Holy Spirit are used separately as well as together.

b. The Father, Son and Holy Spirit are declared in the following Scriptures:

John 5:36: _____

_____

John 5:37: _____

_____

Underline John 7:37 (Prophecy of the Holy Spirit).

Write in John 8:18: _____

_____

Underline John 8:42:

Write in John 1:1: _____

_____

Underline John 1:32.

Finally, write in John 3:34: _____

_____

_____

c. The Lord's Prayer (not the model prayer) is found in John 17. In this chapter Jesus is praying for His own. Read and underline the references to the Father and the Son.

2. The Lord's Birth Gives Testimony of the Trinity.

a. Underline the Trinity in Luke 1:35.

Read the account of the Lord's birth in Matthew 1:20-23, and underline the Trinity in this passage of Scripture.

3. The Lord's Baptism Proves the Trinity.

a. The baptism of Jesus is one of the greatest proofs of the Trinity. Read Matthew 3:13-17 and notice:

- Jesus was baptized (verse 16).
- the Spirit of God descending as a dove (verse 16).
- the Father speaking (verse 17).

Here we see the manifestation of the Trinity.

b. God the Father spoke the same words about the Son in Matthew 17:5 at the transfiguration.

c. Mark describes the baptism of Jesus in Mark 1:9-11. Luke describes the same in Luke 3:21-22. Compare these two writers with Matthew and you will find the Trinity in all three accounts. (Don't forget that the first three Gospels are called the Synoptic Gospels, meaning "a like view.")

Why didn't John record the baptism of Jesus? John wrote of the *inner, divine* and *private* aspects of the life of our Lord. (See "Through the Bible In One Year," Volume I, page 119.)

4. Jesus Announced the Trinity in the Baptismal Formula.

a. Before Jesus ascended back into glory, He gave us some

specific instructions. These were His last words to the eleven and to the Body of Christ.

b. The Great Commission of Jesus is in Matthew 28:16-20.

Write in Matthew 28:19: _____

_____

_____

c. The formula for our baptism is in verse 19. Note "baptizing them in the *name* (singular) of the Father, and the Son and the Holy Spirit." He did not say, "in the *names* of." Jesus declared *one—singular* name but three Persons: Father, Son and Holy Spirit.

The church, His body, has used the formula ever since, regardless of denomination or label.

5. Paul's Epistles are Filled with References to the Trinity.

a. Paul in his epistles states the fact of the Trinity in so many places that we cannot list all of them in this lesson.

Without the writings of the Apostle Paul, we would have little knowledge of the early church. We would have little Biblical authority for our church order today.

b. Paul declares the Trinity in the following:

Underline Romans 1:3-4.

Write in Romans 8:1: _____

_____

_____

Underline Romans 8:3.

Underline Romans 8:11.

Write in Romans 8:16-17: _____

_____

_____

_____

Read I Corinthians 1:3-4; 2:10-13; 12:4-6.

Write in II Corinthians 3:3: _____

_____

In II Corinthians 13:14 the famous apostolic benediction is found.

Write in Galatians 4:6: _____

_____

Underline Ephesians 2:18.

Notice the Trinity in Ephesians 4:4-6 and again in Ephesians 5:18,20.

Write in Colossians 1:9: _____

_____

Notice I Thessalonians 5:18-19 and underline.

Underline II Thessalonians 2:13-14.

Write in I Timothy 3:16: _____

_____

Underline Titus 3:4-6.

Many other Scriptures could be mentioned. These are sufficient to indicate Paul's teaching of the Trinity.

6. **The General Epistles and Revelation Declares the Trinity.**

a. Peter gives the Trinity in I Peter 1:2: _____

_____

_____

Underline I Peter 4:13.

b. The Apostle John affirms the Trinity in I John 4:2: _____

_____

_____

Again in I John 4:12-15—underline the Trinity.

Write in I John 5:7: _____

_____

c. Jude gives the Trinity in verses 20 and 21.

d. John declares the Trinity in Revelation 1:4-6.

V. WHAT THIS BIBLE TRUTH TEACHES US TODAY

God is God the Father, Son and Holy Spirit. The three are described as distinct Persons. The Son and the Holy Spirit were in the beginning with God the Father.

The Son, Jesus, is second in the Godhead. He came as a manifestation of God. He distinguished the Father from Himself in John 5:26, 27, 30, 36, 37.

God is the Father who sent His only Begotten Son (John 3:16; Galatians 4:4).

The Holy Spirit, the third Person of the Godhead, came as the Agent of the Father and the Son (John 14:16-17). The Holy Spirit was *sent* by the Father and the Son. He was the ascension gift of Jesus to comfort and teach and testify of the Son (John 14:26; 15:26).

The three Persons are equal. God is Father, Son and Holy Spirit. We are a trinity, having body, soul and spirit—yet, one person. The body is not the person—the soul is not the person—the spirit is not the person, alone and separate. All three are *one*.

So, it is with the Trinity. All Three are God. He always existed. His existence is within Himself. God was in the beginning (Genesis 1:1), which means that the Son was also in the beginning (John 1:1), and the Holy Spirit was in the beginning (Genesis 1:2). The name "Elohim" is a plural noun meaning three or more.

So God made us like Himself (in His image and likeness). We are three in one. He created us; sent His Son to redeem us; sent His Holy Spirit to seal, teach and fill us—to convict and guide us.

Note: We shall study each Person of the Trinity separately in the next few lessons. These will help you understand this lesson).

YOUR NEXT ASSIGNMENT:

1. Read Genesis 1 through 3; 6:5-8; 11:10; 12:1-8; 15:1-6; Exodus 3 and 4; 15:2; 20:2; Deuteronomy 6:3-5; 29:29; Psalm 9:10; 14:1; 33:6-9; 34:7; 90:2; 99:9; Job 37:16; Jeremiah 32:17-18; 23:6,24; Malachi 3:6; Luke 24:39; John 1:1, 14, 18; 3:16; 4:24; 13:13; 14:16-17; Acts 14:15; Acts 15:18; Ephesians 1:19-21; 4:6; Colossians 1:15-19; I Timothy 3:16; Titus 2:12-13; Hebrews 12:29; James 1:17; 1 John 1:5; 3:20; 4:8-16; I Peter 1:20; 5:10; Revelation 19:6.

2. A lot of Scripture, yet not all that could be assigned on "God the Father." Read the assignment and underline the Scripture.

3. Review your study on "The Trinity."

24

Lesson 5
"God the Father"

(Where lines are provided, look up the Scriptures and write in the Scripture or its main truth.)

I. INTRODUCTION

"God the Father" is a vast and overwhelming assignment. The lesson is written for the "lambs" and not for the "giraffes" who will study the contents of this volume. It is not a theological dissertation, but a simple outline with Scriptural background. After all, we are trying to reach people with "what the Bible has to say."

The word "theos" is Greek, meaning God. Therefore, theology is the study of God. Before anything came into being, *He* was—and is—and shall always be—for He, God, is eternal, meaning "no beginning and no ending." He is the Existing, Abiding, Eternal One. He was "in the beginning." When that beginning was, no one can know. We live by the years, months, weeks and days. We live by the watch, by the hour and minute. To the average person, with finite ability to comprehend, everything must have a beginning and ending. NOT WITH GOD! He created the seasons, years and days. "In the beginning (no one knows when that was) God created the heaven and the earth" (Genesis 1:1).

II. BASIC SCRIPTURES:

Genesis 1 through 3; 6:5-8; 11:10; 12:1-8; 15:1-6; Exodus 3 and 4; 15:2; 20:2; Deuteronomy 6:3-5; 29:29; Psalm 9:10; 14:1; 33:6-9; 34:7; 90:2; 99:9; Job 37:16; Jeremiah 32:17-18; 23:6,24; Malachi 3:6; Luke 24:39; John 1:1,14,18; 3:16; 4:24; 13:13; 14:6-7; Acts 14:15; 15:18; Ephesians 1:19-21; 4:6; Colossians 1:15-19; I Timothy 3:16; Titus 2:12-13; Hebrews 12:29; James 1:17; I John 1:5; 3:20; 4:8-16; I Peter 1:20; 5:10; Revelation 19:6.

III. THE NUCLEUS OF THIS TRUTH

The existence of God is within Himself. He is Self-existent. He caused us to be, but nothing caused Him to be. He always was and ever shall be God. God the Father is the creator of man, but *only the Father* of those who have accepted His Son. We who are Christians call Him Father. All mankind are creations of God, but not all are children of God. The supernatural birth causes a person to be a son— "and if a son, then an heir of God through Christ" (Galatians 4:7). When Jesus was on the cross, He cried, "My God, my God, why hast thou forsaken me?" (Matthew 27:46). He called God "God," not Father, because He was taking the place of the sinner—all our sins—the Just dying for the unjust. Therefore, He could only use the title "God." He is the God and Father of our Lord Jesus Christ (Ephesians 1:3).

IV. THE GREAT TRUTH: "GOD THE FATHER"

A. THE NAMES OF GOD HAVE MEANING.

1. The Names of God Reveal His Character.

    a. "Elohim"—God's official title—revealing He is God (Genesis 1:1). "Elohim" is a plural noun. In English, plural is two or more. In Hebrew, plural is three or more: singular, meaning one; dual, equaling two; plural, meaning three or more. So, in Genesis 1:1 the Trinity was present—three or more. In Genesis 1:26-27 the Trinity is again found in the words "us" and "our."

b. *"El"* is the singular form of Elohim. You find it in the names of the Bible such as:

"Beth *el*" meaning "house of God" (Genesis 12:8).
"Dani *el*" meaning "God is my judge" (Daniel 1:6).
"*El* i jah" meaning "my God is Jehovah" (I Kings 17:1).
"Immanu *el*" meaning "God with us" (Isaiah 7:14).

Notice the times "el" is used at the beginning or ending of a name. Always it means "God."

c. *"Jehovah"*—the personal name of God. The name means "Redeemer" and is always used in connection with redemption and/or deliverance by God. "Jehovah" told Moses to lead the children of Israel *out* of Egypt—to "deliver" them from bondage. God told Moses to tell the people, "I AM THAT I AM—I AM hath sent me unto you" (Exodus 3:13-14). "Jehovah" is the eternal "I AM." In Exodus 20:2 and many other places you read, "I am the Lord thy God—." It means "I am Jehovah thy God." There is only one Jehovah (Deuteronomy 6:4). Using the correct Hebrew words, the passage reads: "Hear, O Israel, Jehovah our Elohim (three or more) is one Jehovah."

d. *"Adonai"* means "Master" or "Lord." It is used in the Old Testament for both deity and man. It is found the first time in Genesis 15:2. When the King James Version uses the word, it is capitalized for Deity—for man, the capital is omitted.

2. Compound Names Reveal God.

(We would call these "double names." The compound names can be found using *"El"* or *"Jehovah."* We list only a few.)

a. "El Shaddai"—"Almighty God" (Genesis 17:1).

b. "El Olam"—"Everlasting God" (Genesis 21:33).

c. "Jehovah Elohim"—"Lord God" (Exodus 34:6).

d. "Jehovah-jireh"—"the Lord will provide" (Genesis 22:14).

e. "Jehovah-shalom"—"the Lord our peace" (Judges 6:24).

f. "Jehovah-shammah"—"the Lord is there" (Ezekiel 48:35).

3. Jehovah is Revealed in the Names of Others.

a. Wherever you find a name ending in "iah" in Scripture—it means "Jah" or "Jehovah."

Look at some of the famous names ending in "iah":

Isaiah means "the salvation of Jehovah."
Jeremiah means "whom Jehovah hath appointed."
Uzziah means "the might of Jehovah."
Zechariah means "whom Jehovah remembers."

Look all through the Scripture and notice the names ending in "iah."

B. THE NATURE OF GOD.

1. God is a Spirit.

a. Look at John 4:24: _____

_____

b. He is invisible (Colossians 1:15).   26

c. John the Baptist said in John 1:18: _____

_____

d. He has revealed Himself in different ways.

To the leader, Moses, He manifested Himself in a Burning Bush (Exodus 3:4).

He revealed Himself as a Pillar of Cloud and a Pillar of Fire'' (Exodus 13:21).

He revealed Himself in His Son, Jesus Christ (John 1:1,14).

Also look up Galatians 4:4: _____

_____

Underline John 1:18 and 32. Also John 5:37.

There are other ways God has revealed Himself. These examples should set you on a course of searching the Scripture.

2. God is Light.

a. Write in I John 1:5: _____

_____

b. Ponder the wonderful words of John 1:4-5.

Now, write in John 1:9: _____

_____

c. Jesus, the God-Man said He was Light (John 8;12). Remember the study on the Trinity at this point. Jesus was God in the flesh (incarnate).

d. The last passages of the Revelation reveal that God is Light (Revelation 21:23).

3. God is Love.

a. Write in I John 4:8: _____

_____

b. The great verse in all Scripture proves the love of God (John 3:16).

c. Underline Hebrews 12:6 and Revelation 3:19.

d. Read the passage in I John 4:7-21 and underline the word "love." Now on to the next Chapter 5:1-3.

4. God is a Person.

- He not only loves (Scriptures above).
- He grieves (Genesis 6:6).
- He hates (Proverbs 6:16-19).
- He provides (Matthew 7:7-11).
- He cares (I Peter 5:6-7).

This indicates He is a Person with a personality. He created love. He also gave us free will to choose. We are made in His image and likeness.

God is more than a "first cause," "a force," "a power."

In John 17, Jesus who is God the Son prayed to God the Father. Notice John 17:5, 11 and 13. Jesus talked to the Father, a Person.

C. THE ATTRIBUTES OF GOD.

1. God is Omnipotent.

The Latin word *"omni"* means "all." The word Omnipotent

means "all powerful." He is the Almighty God (Revelation 19:6).

 a. God has power over men and nations (I Kings 11:11).
  Underline Daniel 4:17 and the last part of verses 25 and 32. Also II Timothy 2:13.
  Write in Matthew 19:26: _____

  _____

 b. God has power over all nature.
  Notice Job 28:5,6,25,26; Psalm 33:6-9.

 c. God has power over angels (Psalm 103:20). Write in Psalm 104:4: _____

  _____

  Underline Psalm 91:11 and Hebrews 1:14.

 d. God has power over Satan and death (Job 1:12; 2:6).
  Underline Romans 16:20 and Revelation 20:2,10.
  Death shall be destroyed (Psalm 110;1; Revelation 20:14).

2. God is Omniscient (omni- "all"—science- "knowledge").

The word means "all knowing." He is perfect in knowledge— He knows everything (Job 37:16).

 a. He knows all about nature (Isaiah 40:28).
  Write in Psalm 147:4: _____

  _____

  Underline Matthew 10:29.

 b. He knows all about man (Matthew 10:30).
  Read Psalm 139:2; 94:11; Acts 1:15.
  Underline Hebrews 4:13.
  Write in I John 3:20: _____

  _____

 c. He knows the past, present and future (Acts 15:18).
  Read I Peter 1:20.

3. God is Omnipresent.

The word means "everywhere present." God is everywhere present at all times (Jeremiah 23:24).

 a. God is everywhere present but He is not *in* all that takes place (Acts 17:24-27).

 b. He dwells in heaven (Ephesians 1:20; Revelation 21:2).

 c. He is in every believer in the Lord Jesus (John 14:16-17; 15:26-27; 16:12-14).

4. God Never Changes (Immutability of God).

Immutability means "unchanging." He is always God.

 a. He never changes toward His own (Romans 11:29).
  Underline Malachi 3:6.

 b. He never varies (James 1:17).

 c. He is immutable (Hebrews 6:17).

V. WHAT THIS BIBLE TRUTH TEACHES US TODAY

Jesus clearly stated in John 8:41-47 what is meant by "God the Father." The meaning is the same for all of us today. To know the Father we must first know the Son. Look at John 8:18-19. Then, in verse 42 Jesus

28

said, "If God were your Father, ye would love me—." Jesus minced no words on this subject. In verse 44, He said, " _____

_____

_____

Underline verse 47.

What does all this mean? A child always has the nature of his father. The nature of the Adamic race is sinful. All of us are born with the Adamic nature. So, by the natural birth we are sinful and we serve sin and Satan.

When we accept the Son, Jesus, as our Redeemer, we experience the new birth—the supernatural birth. Then, and only then, is God our Father.

The world is divided into two identifiable groups—the unsaved are identified with Adam; the saved are identified with Christ. All people are identified with Adam by the natural birth; saved ones are identified by the spiritual birth in Jesus Christ.

"As in Adam all die, even so in Christ shall all be made alive" (I Corinthians 15:22).

To call God, Father, you must accept His plan of redemption (meaning "to be bought with a price"). Jesus paid the price of our redemption on the cross.

It is a privilege to pray, "Our Father."

Can you?

YOUR NEXT ASSIGNMENT:

1. Read Genesis 1 and 2; 18:1,22; 22:11-13; 26:2,24; 32:24-32; Exodus 3:1-14; Deuteronomy 18:15-22; Isaiah 6:1-13; 7:14; 9:6; 52:13 to 53:12; Zechariah 3:1-10; 6:12-15; Matthew 27 and 28; Luke 1 and 2; John 1:1-14; 4:6; 6:35; 7:37; John 8 and 17; Acts 1:8-11; Galatians 4:4; Philippians 2:6-7; Colossians 1:15-29; 3:1-14; Revelation 5:5; 22:13,16.

2. Review your notes on "God the Father."

3. Mark your Bible—especially if a new truth has been learned.

Lesson 6 "God the Son: His Past"—Part I

(Where lines are provided, look up the Scriptures and write in the Scripture or its main truth.)

I. INTRODUCTION

The study of "God The Son," the central figure of all Scripture, shall occupy four lessons in this series. We shall consider *"His Past"* in two lessons, taking us back to "In the beginning"—His Old Testament appearances, His names, His birth, death, resurrection and ascension.

We shall then consider "His *Present* Priestly Ministry"—and then "His *Future* Kingdom and Glory." The four lessons shall present Jesus Christ our Lord as simply as possible.

Jesus appeared in the Old Testament in pre-incarnate manifestations. This means *He appeared in visible form before the incarnation—*before His birth in Bethlehem. These are called "theophanies"—*a visible manifestation of deity.*

As we enter this study you should pray for the Holy Spirit to teach you all truth. Search every Scripture reference given and have a heart receptive to the Word.

II. BASIC SCRIPTURES:

Genesis 1 and 2; 18:1,22; 22:11-13; 26:2,24; 32:24-32; Exodus 3:1-14; Deuteronomy 18:15-22; Isaiah 6:1-13; 7:14; 9:6; 52:13 to 53:12; Zechariah 3:1-10; 6:12-15; Matthew 27 and 28; Luke 1 and 2; John 1:1,14; 4:6; 6:35; 7:37; Chapters 8 and 17; Acts 1:8-11; Galatians 4:4; Philippians 2:6-7; Colossians 1:15-29; 3:1-4; Revelation 5:5; 22:13,16.

This is a small portion of Scripture to be read. The Scriptures are too numerous to mention all of them.

III. THE NUCLEUS OF THIS TRUTH

God the Son, the Lord Jesus Christ, was co-eternal with God the Father and the Holy Spirit. Christ was with the Father in eternity past (Genesis 1:1). John declared the same thing, "In the beginning was the Word (Jesus), and the Word (Jesus) was with God, and the Word (Jesus) was God. The same was in the beginning with God" (John 1:1-2).

In eternity past the omniscient (all knowing) God, in His foreknowledge, knew that man would sin and require a plan of *redemption*—(the price required to be paid for sin).

A Saviour, spotless, sinless, was to come as "the Lamb slain before the foundation of the world" (Revelation 13:8). God The Son knew the consequences of man's sin and willingly came to earth in the form of humanity to pay that price (Philippians 2:6-8).

The church, which is His body of redeemed souls, was "chosen in Him before the foundation of the world" (Ephesians 1:4).

The nucleus of the lesson simply stated is—Jesus was in the beginning. The prophets saw One who was to come. As the time approached the vision grew so clear that it would have been possible to describe the life of Christ from the Old Testament. Jesus said of the Old Testament, "They testified of Me." He was revealed throughout the Old Testament—He came into the world exactly as the Scriptures had said—lived, died and came out of the grave to ascend back into glory.

This lesson covers only "His Past," Part I, from eternity past up to His incarnation.

IV. THE GREAT TRUTH: "GOD THE SON: HIS PAST" PART I

A. APPEARANCES OF JESUS IN THE OLD TESTAMENT (THEOPHANIES).

1. His Manifestation to Abraham.

   a. One of the three angels was Jesus who promised Abraham a son in old age (Genesis 18:1-10).

   b. The "Angel of the Lord," who is none other than Jesus, pre-incarnate, spoke to Abraham at the offering of Isaac (Genesis 22:11-12). Underline verse 8.

   c. The "Angel of the Lord" (Jesus) confirmed the covenant with Abraham because of his faith (Genesis 22:15-16).

2. His Manifestation to Isaac.

   a. He appeared to Isaac and directed him; confirmed the Abrahamic Covenant to Isaac (Genesis 26:2-5).

   b. The Lord "appeared" to Isaac and gave assurance of blessing (Genesis 26:24-25).

3. His Manifestation to Jacob.

   a. The "Angel" wrestled with Jacob and the Lord changed his name to "Israel" (Genesis 32:24-32). The "man" of verse 24 was "the Angel of the Lord" (Hosea 12:3-4). The concept of seeing God, as is indicated in verse 30, is not always the same in Scripture. In Exodus 33:20, God said, "No man shall see me and live." When Jacob said he had seen the Lord, he meant he had seen a divine Personage, the Angel of the Lord, Jesus Christ (II Corinthians 4:6). God is Spirit. Jesus was the only visible manifestation of God.

   b. The "Angel which redeemed me" was not just another celestial being (Genesis 48:15-16).

4. His Manifestation to Moses.

   a. "The Angel" appeared to Moses in a flame of fire out of a burning bush which was not consumed. Moses hid his face—therefore, there was a visible appearance of deity. The "Angel" gives us the answer. Moses saw a "theophany" (Exodus 3:2-14).

   b. The Rock in the wilderness was more than a mere rock (Exodus 17:6). Now look at I Corinthians 10:4 and write the words of Paul " _____

   _____

   _____

5. His Manifestation to Joshua.

   a. Jesus appeared to Joshua as the Divine Captain (Joshua 5:13-15).

6. His Manifestation to Isaiah.

   a. Underline Isaiah 6:1, 5, 8. In verse 1 notice, "I saw also the Lord."

7. His Manifestation to Zechariah.

a. The appearances in this book are numerous. Look up some of them (Zechariah 1:8-13; 2:1,9; 3:1-10; 6:12-15).

8. His Pre-Incarnate Ministry all Through the Bible.

a. "The Angel of the Lord"—"the Angel of the Covenant"—"The Angel of His Presence" are names most Bible scholars identify as the pre-incarnate Christ. We list some—(Psalm 34:7; Genesis 31:11; Isaiah 63:9; Malachi 3:1).

b. Other Scriptures intimating His pre-existence—(Psalm 110:1; Daniel 3:25; Exodus 14:19; John 1:15; Colossians 1:15-19).

B. PROMISES AND PROPHECIES OF THE MANIFESTATION OF CHRIST.

1. The Witness of the Prophets.

(Space allows us to get only a glance of what the Old Testament says about the first coming of Christ.)

a. The oldest prophecy is found in Genesis 3:15. He was to be the "Seed of woman" indicating the virgin birth. The term is used in Genesis 3:15 and not found elsewhere. The blood principle, in conception, is the contribution of the man. If Jesus *had not* been born of a virgin by the conception of the Holy Spirit—then *Adam's seed* would be mentioned in this first prophecy of Christ.

Write in Genesis 3:15: _____

_____

_____

b. The "Seed" continued through Abel, Seth and Noah (Genesis 6:8-10).

c. God selected *a nation* who would produce the Seed (Genesis 9:26). He would be a descendant of Shem. Notice the genealogy from Shem back to Abraham (Genesis 11:10-26).

The nation was to be the Hebrew nation (Israel).

d. He would be the Seed of Abraham, the first man to be called a Hebrew (Genesis 12:2-3; 14:13). The Abrahamic Covenant was an unconditional covenant of God to bless Israel through Abraham's Seed—and to the church in Christ (Galatians 3:16,29).

Read Galatians 3:14 through 29 and notice that Jesus is the *Seed.*

e. He would come through Isaac (Genesis 17:26).

f. He would come through Jacob (Israel) (Genesis 28:10-15).

g. The tribe to produce the Seed was Judah (Genesis 49:10). Compare that Scripture with Hebrews 7:14 and Revelation 5:5.

h. He was to come from one family, the house of David, and be heir to David's throne (II Samuel 7:12-15).

Write in Romans 1:3: _____

_____

i. His birth was to be in Bethlehem (Micah 5:2).

j. He would be the Son of a virgin (Isaiah 7:14). Isaiah foretold this to the entire "house of David" and not to Ahaz only (Isaiah 7:13).

Write in Isaiah 7:14: _____

_____

_____

_____

    k. Isaiah depicted the manifestation of Jesus (visble appearance of deity) so vividly in Isaiah 53:1-12.

    l. It is impossible to give all of the witness of the prophets. The theme from Moses to Malachi is the Messiah.

2. The Witness of the Angels.

    a. The Angel Gabriel announced to Zacharias the miraculous birth of a son, John the Baptist. He would be the forerunner of Jesus to prepare the way of the Lord Jesus (Luke 1:11-19). Underline verse 13. Now underline Luke 3:4.

    b. The Angel Gabriel announced to Mary that she was to bear a Son and call His name Jesus (Luke 1:26-33). Read and underline verse 35.

Write in verse 31: _____

_____

_____

    c. The angel announced to Joseph the virgin birth of Jesus (Matthew 1:19-21). Notice verse 25.

C. HIS NAMES INDICATE HIS ETERNAL BEING.

1. Jesus, the Personal Name of our Lord.

    a. Jesus is the name given by the Angel Gabriel to Joseph (Matthew 1:21) and Mary (Luke 1:31). Jesus was given this personal name before He was born.

    b. "Jesus" is the Greek form of the Hebrew name "Joshua." Both mean "Jehovah Our Saviour." The name "Jesus" is more prominent in the Gospels—before His death, burial and resurrection. It is His earthly name, the name of humiliation and suffering.

Write in Matthew 1:21: _____

_____

_____

The name "Jesus" was used mainly before salvation was completed.

2. Christ, the Title of the Son of God.

    a. The name "Christ" means "the Anointed One." It means the same as the Hebrew word "Messiah" (Daniel 9:25).

Write in John 1:41: _____

_____

_____

    b. Christ is the name prominent after Calvary. The Epistles spell out the doctrine of salvation by faith in the sacrifice on the cross. Jesus was "made both Lord and Christ," Peter said, in Acts 2:36: _____

c. We get our name from Christ—we are called *Christ*-ians.

3. Lord, the Title of Deity and Authority.

   a. The word ''Lord'' in the New Testament comes from the Greek word *''KURIOS,''* translated in our Bible as ''Lord, God, Master.'' In the Old Testament all three names of God are compounded into the one name ''Lord.''

   b. Read Romans 10:9, ''If thou shalt confess with thy mouth the Lord (Jehovah, God, Master) Jesus . . .''

4. ''I AM''—The Name Which Includes All His Names.

   a. Jesus said, ''Before Abraham was, I Am'' (John 8:58). Twenty times in the Gospel of John, Jesus declared the same words: ''I am the bread of life,'' ''I am the light of the world,'' ''I am the good Shepherd,'' ''I am the resurrection and the life,'' etc.

   b. Write in John 14:6: _____

   _____

5. The Son of God—His Title of Glory and Deity.

   a. Jesus is *the* Son of God and has been throughout all eternity. We become *a* son of God by the new birth.

   b. Underline Luke 1:35 and John 19:7.

6. Emmanuel—''God With Us.''

   a. Jesus is ''God with us'' and fulfilled Isaiah's prophecy (Isaiah 7:14).

   b. Write in Matthew 1:23: _____

   _____

7. The Word—The Living Word.

   a. Jesus is the Word and was in the beginning (John 1:1-2).

   b. The Word, in the flesh, reveals God in visible form (John 1:14,18).

8. Saviour—He Was Born to Save From Sin.

   a. Look up Matthew 1:21; Luke 2:11.

9. The Lord Jesus Christ—The Full Title.

   Underline Ephesians 1:3.

10. Other Names.

   a. There are 207 names for our Lord in the Scriptures. We have only mentioned a few.

   b. For your individual study, look up the following names— only a partial list:

   > ''The Only Begotten Son''
   > ''The Alpha and Omega''
   > ''Lord of Glory''
   > ''Wonderful''
   > ''Counsellor''
   > ''The Mighty God''
   > ''The Ancient of Days''
   > ''Son of Abraham''
   > ''Son of David''

"The Last Adam"
"Rabbi"
"Master"
"Good Shepherd"
"Great Shepherd"
"Chief Shepherd"
"Great High Priest"
"Door"
"Branch"
"Stone"
"Redeemer"

V. WHAT THIS BIBLE TRUTH TEACHES US TODAY.

Jesus was in the beginning—eternity past. He was with God and He was God (John 1:1-2). His preexistence is established in the New Testament with an abundance of Scripture. He was before all creation because He was Creator. "All things were made by Him and without Him was not anything made that was made" (John 1:3). In Ephesians 3:9 you read, "—God, who created all things by Jesus Christ."

Write in Colossians 1:16-17: _____

_____

_____

He appeared throughout the Old Testament. The prophets spoke of Him and His coming. His names speak of His eternal being (Revelation 22:13).

He declared, "In the volume of the Book it is written of Me" (Hebrews 10:7 quoting Psalm 40:7).

We have found Jesus in the Old Testament. All Scripture, history, Psalms and prophecy converge toward one central Person: Jesus Christ.

Now, we are ready to consider His coming in the flesh, His life, death, resurrection and ascension in the next lesson.

YOUR NEXT ASSIGNMENT:

1. All Scripture assigned in Lesson 6 and the following: Romans 1:3-4; 8:3; I Corinthians 15; II Corinthians 8:9; I John 1:1-7; 5:20; Revelation 1:5-6; 3:20).

2. Memorize the definition of a "theophany."

3. Review your notes on this lesson.

4. Mark your Bible and note the important truths you have learned.

Lesson 7
"God the Son: His Past"—Part II

(Where lines are provided, look up the Scripture and write in the Scripture or its main truth.)

I. INTRODUCTION

The second part of "God the Son: His Past" shall begin with the incarnation—God manifest in the flesh; His virgin birth, His two natures, His death, His resurrection and ascension. These are foundational truths which fulfill all the prophecies of the Old Testament. We base our faith upon the truths of this lesson. By faith we accept what God's Word says about these great doctrines of the Christian faith. The Bible presents the facts and the Holy Spirit shall "guide us into all truth" (John 16:13).

There is no room for argument when God's Word speaks. We are entering holy territory and human reason must be cast aside. The "natural man" cannot understand the things of God "because they are spiritually discerned" (I Corinthians 2:14).

II. BASIC SCRIPTURES:

All the Scripture assigned in Lesson 6 and the following: Romans 1:3-4; 8:3; I Corinthians 15; II Corinthians 8:9; I John 1:1-7; 5:20; Revelation 1:5-6; 3:20.

III. THE NUCLEUS OF THIS TRUTH

God was made flesh when Jesus was born of a virgin. This was prophesied throughout the Old Testament. The incarnation fulfills all the prophecies exactly as was foretold from Genesis 3:15 on through Malachi. Jesus gave personal testimony concerning His death, resurrection and ascension by quoting Scripture. The birth and death of Christ were planned before the foundation of the world (Ephesians 1:4). He gave Himself to be sin for us so that we might be made the righteousness of God in Him (II Corinthians 5:21). He came into the world to die. "Thou shalt call His name Jesus: for He shall save His people from their sins" (Matthew 1:21).

IV. THE GREAT TRUTH: "GOD THE SON: HIS PAST" PART II

A. THE FACT OF THE INCARNATION.

    1. The Meaning of the Incarnation

      a. The word "incarnation" means "in-flesh-ment." When we speak of the incarnation of the Son of God, Christ Jesus, we mean God in the flesh—God manifest in the flesh. The word "manifest" means to "make evident, visible."

      b. Write in John 1:14: _____

_____

_____

37

2. The Purpose of the Incarnation.

a. Jesus was made flesh to reveal the invisible God. God is a Spirit.

Look up John 4:24: _____

_____

_____

b. The only visible form of God is revealed in His Son.

Look at John 1:18: _____

We want to see God. Jesus reveals God to us in human form because He is God. The only God we shall ever see is Jesus (John 14:9).

c. Jesus was made flesh to fulfill the covenants of God.

For example, to Abraham. Underline Galatians 3:8,14,16, and compare with Genesis 12:1-3 and Genesis 13:15.

To fulfill the covenant with David (II Samuel 7:12-16). Notice "the throne of David" in Isaiah's great prophecy concerning Jesus (Isaiah 9:6-7). Peter confirmed this in his sermon on the day of Pentecost (Acts 2:29-30). Underline verse 30.

d. The incarnation was necessary to provide a Sacrifice for sin.

Write in I John 3:5: _____

Notice Hebrews 10:10; Acts 13:38-39.

3. The Mystery of the Incarnation.

a. Write in I Timothy 3:16: _____

_____

_____

b. The incarnation is a mystery to mere human beings. God revealed in His Word all we need to know, to "understand."

Write in Colossians 2:2-3: _____

_____

B. THE VIRGIN BIRTH OF JESUS

1. The Meaning of the Virgin Birth of Jesus.

a. Human reason rejects the virgin birth while spiritual discernment is given by accepting and believing in the *Son of God*. The virgin birth is contrary to the laws of nature. If the incarnation means what it implies—then this birth was the birth of God in the flesh. It could not be according to nature but according to God.

b. The virgin birth was prophesied by Isaiah 750 years before it came to pass (Isaiah 7:14).

c. The virgin birth was announced to Mary, a virgin (Luke 1:26-32). The same was announced to Joseph (Matthew 1:18-25).

d. Who was the father of Jesus? God, the Father! Even Mary said, "How shall this be, seeing I know not a man?" (Luke 1:34). Underline verse 35.

Note the last phrase of Matthew 1:20: _____

_____

e. The conception was the work of the Holy Spirit (Matthew 1:20; Luke 1:35). This is called the "immaculate concep-

38

tion" by some. It does not in any way refer to the "immaculate conception" of Mary—which would mean that Mary was without sin. Jesus is the one to be emphasized, not Mary. She was a virgin and had found favor with God, but she was of the Adamic race.

2. The Seed of Woman?

a. Yes, Jesus was to be the "Seed of Woman" as foretold in Genesis 3:15.

b. Jesus declared His incarnation and source of humanity (John 16:27-28).

c. Paul confirmed the Seed in Galatians 3:16: _____

_____

_____

Again, Paul emphasized that Jesus was sent from God and "made of a woman" (Galatians 4:4).

d. God made His Son in the form of humanity without the seed of man—just as He made Eve without the help of a woman—just as He made man (Adam) without the reproductive elements of either man or woman.

C. THE TWO NATURES OF JESUS CHRIST.

1. He Became the God-Man.

a. Jesus Christ had a divine nature and took upon Himself a human nature—both complete in every way. Christ was not God and man but He became the *God-Man*. John 1:14 says, "The Word was *made* flesh"—not "The Word became a man."

b. We become partakers of His divine nature when we accept Him. We have a human nature and at the time of our "new birth" there is added a divine nature (II Peter 1:4).

2. His Humanity.

a. Jesus had a human physical body (Matthew 26:12).

b. Jesus had a soul (Matthew 26:38).

c. Jesus had a spirit (Luke 23:46).

d. Paul says that man possesses a body, soul and spirit (I Thessalonians 5:23). Write in the Scripture: _____

_____

_____

e. Jesus had a childhood and He grew and became strong in spirit, wisdom and stature (Luke 2:40,52).

f. Jesus had human needs:
- He became hungry (Matthew 4:2).
- He became thirsty (John 19:28).
- He became weary (John 4:6).
- He became sleepy (Matthew 8:24).
- He experienced sorrow (Matthew 26:38).

You can find other needs Jesus experienced by searching the four Gospels.

3. He was Without Sin.

a. In His humanity He was the only one who never had a sinful nature. (With the exception of Adam, before the fall into sin

39

in Genesis 3.) Write in II Corinthians 5:21: _____

_____

_____

b. Then the question is always posed, "If He had no sinful nature and could not sin, then the temptation of Jesus was not real—it was a mockery. The answer is evident. He *could not have wanted* to yield being the Son of God. He was not tested to see if He would sin. He was tested to prove He *would not* sin. (The author has heard theologians argue this question for hours. The answer is simple if one does not forget He was *God-Man*.)

4. His Deity.

a. We have covered His deity in His birth and His names. Now we see His deity in His ministry.

b. He was equal with God the Father (John 17:5).

c. His deity and humanity are set forth by Paul in that great passage (Philippians 2:6-8). Notice, "thought it not robbery to be equal with God" (verse 6). Jesus was deity—He was God-Man.

Notice verse 7: "But made (emptied) Himself of no reputation, and took upon Him the form of a servant, and was made in the likeness of men." Did he empty Himself of deity? No! Jesus emptied Himself into the form of a servant. He poured His deity into the form of a servant and was made in the likeness of men.

He was made man to humble Himself and give Himself on the cross for us (verse 8).

Underline the entire passage in Philippians 2:6-8.

D. THE DEATH OF CHRIST ON THE CROSS.

1. His Life Was Given—Not Taken.

a. He came into the world to die (John 12:32-36).

b. He prayed for us in John 17. Notice His references to His death in verses 1,4,5,11,13,24.

c. His death was of His own volition (John 10:17-18).
Write in verse 18: _____

_____

_____

2. Jesus Died for Our Sins According to the Scripture (I Corinthians 15:3).

a. He was the *Sacrifice* for our sin. He is our *Passover* (I Corinthians 5:7).

b. He *reconciled* us to God (II Corinthians 5:19).

Reconciliation means "to cause a restoration, a harmony, a friendship." It means Jesus, in His death, reconciled (caused a change in man) us to God.

c. He became our *Offering* (Hebrews 10:10,14).

d. Other Scriptures give additional meaning to His death:

- I John 2:2, "*Propitiation*" means "Mercy Seat" and satisfaction (Exodus 25:22).
- I Timothy 2:5-6, "*Ransom*" means "the price paid."
- Ephesians 1:7, "*Redemption*" means "to deliver, save,

40

by paying the price." Also look up I Corinthians 6:20.

- Romans 5:1, "*Justification*" means "just as if I'd never sinned" (Romans 3:21,26).

3. His Death Offers Everlasting Life to All Who Will Believe.

a. Write in John 3:16: _____

_____

b. Write in Romans 5:6: _____

_____

Underline Romans 5:8.

c. Write in John 3:17: _____

_____

E. THE RESURRECTION AND ASCENSION OF CHRIST.

1. The Resurrection of Christ.

a. The resurrection of Jesus Christ is the cornerstone of the Christian faith and proves His deity (Acts 2:24,31,32).

b. Christ arose to give resurrection life to all who will believe (John 11:25-26).

c. The resurrection was victory over sin and death (I Corinthians 15:54-57).

d. The resurrection confirms our faith and victory in Him. He was the firstfruits of the resurrection (I Corinthians 15:14-26).

e. Jesus always told of His resurrection when He spoke of His death (Matthew 16:21; 17:22-23; 20:17-19; Luke 9:22; 18:-31-34; John 2:19-22).

f. Proof of His resurrection can be found in the seventeen appearances of Christ in His resurrected body. He was recognized and He talked with people. Some of the scriptures are given (John 20:11-17; Matthew 28:9-10; Luke 24:34; Mark 16:12-14; I Corinthians 15:6).

2. The Ascension of Christ.

a. Jesus spoke of His ascension (John 14:2-3).

b. Jesus promised the Holy Spirit, sent by the Father, in the name of Jesus. He, the Holy Spirit, would be the Comforter and would teach all truth (John 14:16,17,26; 15:26-27).

c. The ascension marked the end of His earthly ministry (Luke 24:50-51; Acts 1:9-11). Jesus, in His glorified living body, ascended back into glory, signifying that the work of our redemption was finished. Underline Acts 1:9-11 and note that "He shall so come in like manner."

V. WHAT THIS BIBLE TRUTH TEACHES US TODAY

Jesus was made flesh and dwelt on this earth. This was a manifestation of God in the flesh. He was born of a virgin. He had no earthly father. He was divinely conceived in the womb of Mary by the Holy Spirit—deity and humanity together—to give the world the Lord Jesus Christ, the God-Man. He was the "Seed of woman" as prophesied throughout Scripture.

His humanity was real. He grew and had human needs. He did not have a sin nature. He had divine and a human nature. He changed His likeness and His position to come as our Redeemer.

He gave His life for all sin. He died to save all who will believe. He came out of the grave to conquer sin and death, and to assure us of the resurrected life.

He ascended back into glory to signify the finished work of redemption and to send the Holy Spirit to abide in us, to teach us and to comfort us.

YOUR NEXT ASSIGNMENT:

1. Read Matthew 22:44; Mark 12:36; Luke 20:42-43; Acts 7:55-56; Romans 8:34; Ephesians 1:20; Philippians 2:9-11; Colossians 3:1; Hebrews 1:3-13; 7:22-28; 8:1; 10:12-14; 12:2; I Peter 3:22.

2. Review your notes on this lesson. This lesson is vital because of the ''Great Truths'' it teaches. These are the foundations of the Christian faith.

3. Mark your Bible where new truths are learned.

Lesson 8
"God the Son: His Present Ministry"

(Where lines are provided, look up the Scripture and write in the Scripture or its main truth.)

I. INTRODUCTION

This third lesson on "God the Son" covers His present ministry among us. After the crucifixion, the resurrection and ascension, the Lord's work did not cease. He is directing His own from His place in glory. His work was not finished and His great movement proceeds on and on until the end of the age.

The only thing Jesus finished in His earthly life was the plan of salvation. When He ascended back into glory He was the same Jesus who was "made flesh and dwelt among us." He had paid the penalty for sin and His life in the flesh had been completed.

Now, His ministry continues through His body—all who believe in Him as Lord and Saviour.

II. BASIC SCRIPTURES:

Matthew 22:44; Mark 12:36; Luke 20:42-43; Acts 7:55-56; Romans 8:34; Ephesians 1:20; Philippians 2:9-11; Colossians 3:1; Hebrews 1:3-13; 7:22-28; 8:1; 10:12-14; 12:2; I Peter 3:22.

III. THE NUCLEUS OF THIS TRUTH

Jesus died to "save His people from sin." He died to provide *the* sacrifice necessary for us to be forgiven of sin. He died to provide a way of salvation—a way to approach God through the blood of Christ. He died (past) to make us clean; He lives (present) to keep us clean. The marvelous ministry of our Lord never ceases. He lives in glory to act *for* us and to act *on* us and *in* us by His Word and Spirit. He speaks to God for us and He speaks to us for God. He is "the one Mediator between God and men, the man Christ Jesus" (I Timothy 2:5).

IV. THE GREAT TRUTH: "GOD THE SON: HIS PRESENT MINISTRY"

A. THE EXALTATION OF CHRIST

  1. The Restoration of His Glory.

    a. The glory Jesus possessed "before the world was" is restored to Him. Write in John 17:5: _____

    _____

    _____

    b. Underline John 17:1.

  2. The Exaltation of Christ by God, The Father.

    a. After Christ came to the earth, humbling Himself, as Paul describes in Philippians 2:5-8, there follows the exaltation of Jesus in verses 9-11. Notice the seven steps upward:

- wherefore *God* also hath highly exalted Him,
- and given Him a name which is above every name:
- at the name of Jesus every knee should bow,
- of things in heaven,
- and things in earth,
- and things under the earth;
- that every tongue should confess that Jesus Christ is Lord to the glory of God the Father.

3. Jesus Is Seated At the Right Hand of God.

a. All power is given Him in heaven and in earth (Matthew 28:18).

b. The right hand of God implies ''authority and power.'' Jesus had finished His work of redemption and His proper place was at the right hand of God.

Write in Stephen's account in Acts 7:55-56: _____

_____

_____

_____

_____

Write in Romans 8:34: _____

_____

_____

c. In His place of authority, Jesus has power over angels, authorities and powers (I Peter 3:22).

d. The place and position of our Lord was resumed after He ascended back into heaven. He had tasted humanity and had been touched with the feeling of our infirmities. ''He was in all points tempted like as we are, yet without sin'' (Hebrews 4:15).

B. JESUS IS PREPARING A PLACE FOR HIS FOLLOWERS.

1. A Great Word of Comfort

a. Jesus said, ''In my Father's house are many mansions: if it were not so, I would have told you. I go to prepare a place for you. And if I go and prepare a place for you, I will come again and receive you unto myself; that where I am, there ye may be also'' (John 14:2-3).

b. We are to share His glory'' (John 17:24).

C. CHRIST IS OUR GREAT HIGH PRIEST.

1. He Was Called of God A High Priest.

a. The Epistle to the Hebrews abounds with the Priesthood of Jesus as compared to the Old Testament high priest, Aaron. The priesthood of Aarom was only a type, a shadow of Christ's priestly ministry. Aaron had to offer sacrifices for his own sin, as well as the sins of others (Hebrews 7:26-27).

b. Jesus, the Son of God, is our Great High Priest.

Write in Hebrews 4:14: _____

_____

_____

c. No man could make himself a high priest—only one that is

44

called of God, such as Aaron (Hebrews 5:4). So Christ glorified not Himself—but was called of God a high priest (Hebrews 5:5-10).

Write in verse 10: _____

_____

2. Jesus Was Made Like Unto His Brethren.

a. Read Hebrews 2:9-18 and write in verse 17: _____

_____

_____

_____

b. Therefore, consider Jesus! Write in Hebrews 3:1: _____

_____

_____

Jesus is called an Apostle (one sent forth) and He is called High Priest (one who represents His own before the throne of God). This Apostle and High Priest is Christ Jesus—the One the ''holy brethren'' (Christians) had confessed as Lord.

3. His Priesthood Is Unchangeable.

a. The earthly priesthood changed because of death. Aaron, the high priest, and his sons had a temporary priesthood. They passed away (Hebrews 7:23).

b. The priesthood of Jesus never changes. Because He lives forever, He has an unchangeable priesthood (Hebrews 7:24). Underline in your Bible.

4. Jesus Lives To Make Intercession For His Own.

a. One of the exciting truths of Scripture is the fact that Jesus is ever living in the presence of God for all of us who have trusted Him. His ministry is for us and to us—always there speaking to the Father for us, in our failures, in all our sins. He intercedes for us.

One of the most important Scriptures is Hebrews 7:25. Note in that verse ''He ever liveth to make intercession for us.'' Now, write in the complete verse: _____

_____

_____

b. Our prayer life is affected by this truth. Why do we always pray, ''In Jesus name''—''For His Sake''? Because He is our intercessor. We pray to God through Him. We do not need someone earthly—nor anyone else—to confess our sins. We confess to Him. Jesus is the only *One* between God and man. We are sustained by His precious ministry every moment. He knows our needs and He knows the promises of the Father. We are perfectly safe in His sovereign will (Hebrews 10:19-20).

Write in John 14:13-14: _____

_____

_____

c. All believers *have* (present possession) a High Priest in Jesus Christ. Write in Hebrews 8:1: _____

_____

_____

Underline Hebrews 8:2.

d. Jesus obtained redemption for us ''by His own blood'' which He shed once and for all (Hebrews 9:11-12).

Write in Hebrews 10:10 and 12: _____

_____

_____

_____

On the basis of His sacrifice on the cross, we can have eternal life. No other sacrifice is needed. He keeps us and sustains us. He hears every prayer. The fellowship between Christ and a believer can only be broken by the believer. We are to confess our sins and He cleanses (I John 1:9).

5. Christ Is Our Advocate.

a. An advocate is one who pleads the case of another—a counsellor. In our society we would think of a lawyer.

Jesus is our Advocate with the Father. Write in I John 2:1:

_____

_____

This was addressed to believers. The believer sins—none is perfect. In our Advocate, Christ, we have assurance and forgiveness.

b. Write in Hebrews 9:24: _____

_____

c. Christ is our Advocate against Satan who is ''the accuser of the brethren.'' As Christ is pleading for His own, Satan is there accusing all who belong to Christ (Revelation 12:10). Look up Revelation 12:9-10 and underline.

6. We Are Sustained By His Ministry.

a. Jesus Christ gives us the ability and makes us able for His service. Write in Matthew 28:20: _____

_____

_____

_____

(Note: ''Lo, I am with you always, even to the end of the world.'')

b. We are to do a ''greater work.'' This greater work is the spreading of the Gospel through preaching and teaching the Word. Note the words of Jesus (John 14:12).

c. We are to do His will and that which is well pleasing in His sight (Hebrews 13:20-21.

D. THE ATTRIBUTES OF CHRIST (SEE ATTRIBUTES OF GOD, LESSON 5).

1. Jesus is Omnipotent.

a. Jesus Christ is ''all powerful''.

Write in Matthew 28:18: _____

_____

_____

b. He has power over nature (Colossians 1:16-17).

c. He has power over death (John 11:25-26). Underline. Also underline Revelation 1:18.

2. Jesus is Omniscient.

a. Jesus Christ is "all knowing."

Look up John 16:30: _____

_____

b. Peter said, "Thou knowest all things" (John 21:17).

c. Jesus knows our thoughts (Matthew 9:4).
Look up Matthew 12:25.
Write in John 7:15: _____

_____

3. Jesus is Omnipresent.

a. Jesus Christ is "everywhere present."
Write in Matthew 28:20: _____

_____

_____

b. Write in Matthew 18:20: _____

_____

V. WHAT THIS BIBLE TRUTH TEACHES US TODAY

Jesus "ever lives to make intercession for us." We have an Advocate who speaks to the Father for us in all our faults, failures and sins. His love is boundless. He is always with us. We can pray and He hears us. He knows our needs. How are we lifted up when we fall? How are we restored into fellowship with the Lord? The answer is the main theme of this lesson. It is "He ever lives to make intercession for us."

Since Jesus is our High Priest, all believers are priests. Look at Revelation 1:6; 5:10; 20:6. The priesthood of the believer is a truth which encourages the people to pray, learn, teach and win. We, as priests, can enter into the "holy of holies," beyond the veil, and pray to God in the name of our Lord Jesus Christ.

We have _freedom_—but we also have a _duty_ and an _opportunity_.

The present ministry of our Lord is His love and concern for you.

YOUR NEXT ASSIGNMENT:

1. Read Matthew 24 and 25; I Thessalonians 4:13-18; 5:6; Romans 8:19-23; Philippians 3:20; I Corinthians 15:51-57; Hebrews 13:14; Colossians 3:1-3; Revelation 20:9-20.

2. Review your notes on this lesson.

3. Mark your Bible where new truths are learned.

Lesson 9
"God the Son:
His Future Ministry"

(Where lines are provided, look up the Scripture and write in the Scripture or its main truth.)

I. INTRODUCTION

This fourth lesson on "God the Son" encompasses the future ministry of Christ. We must remember that He is the "Alpha and Omega, the beginning and the ending, who is, and who was, and who is to come, the Almighty" (Revelation 1:8; 21:6; 22:13). His past and present ministries are only a part of His supernatural mission. His plan of redemption was known before the foundation of the world. The Bible is abundantly clear from Adam to Christ. "For in Adam all die, even so in Christ shall all be made alive" (I Corinthians 15:21-22). The mission and work of Christ was connected to the covenant with Abraham. "In thy seed shall all the nations of the earth be blessed" (Genesis 22:18). Paul confirms this in Galatians 3:17. The Mosaic Covenant ends in Christ (Galatians 3:25). All of the Old Testament revelations God made to men, from Adam to Malachi, presents the plan of God to redeem completely all who accept Christ as Lord and Saviour.

In John 5:17-29 the astounding claims of Jesus are given. His position in glory brings us to His threefold ministry as Prophet, Priest and King.

II. BASIC SCRIPTURES:

Isaiah 61:1-3; Matthew 24 and 25; I Thessalonians 4:13-18; 5:6; Romans 8:19-23; Philippians 3:20; I Corinthians 15:51-57; Hebrews 13:14; Colossians 3:1-3; Revelation 20:9-20.

III. THE NUCLEUS OF THIS TRUTH

Jesus has a threefold ministry as Prophet, Priest and King. These were the three Old Testament offices fulfilled in Christ. In the Old Testament era there were three chief anointings ordered by God. The anointing oil was to be upon the prophet, the priest and the king. In the Old Testament, His office was foreshadowed by the prophetical order in Israel; by the blood sacrifices offered by Aaron and the priests; by the throne of David as a throne forever.

The necleus is:

> Jesus is Prophet, Priest and King.

He holds these offices by the appointment of God. The exalted offices He holds attest to the official title He bears, the authority of His words, the character of His work.

IV. THE GREAT TRUTH: "GOD THE SON: HIS FUTURE MINISTRY"

(Note: In order to understand the future ministry of Christ, we must study His threefold ministry in one lesson. The greater portion of His future ministry will be studied near the close of this volume.)

A. THE ANOINTING OF CHRIST.

1. **The Divine Title "Christ."**

   a. The title "Christ" is the official title of the Son of God. "Christ" means "the Anointed One."

   Look up Matthew 16:16: _____

   _____

   _____

   b. When the Anointed One is mentioned, our mind turns to Isaiah 61:1-3 (Read and underline). Jesus came in fulfillment of the Old Testament prophecies. Simon Peter said, "let all the house of Israel know assuredly, that God hath made that same Jesus, whom ye have crucified, both Lord and Christ" (that is, the Messiah, the Anointed One) (Acts 2:36).

2. **In Christ, the Offices of Prophet, Priest and King Find Their Highest Fulfillment.**

   a. The early Christians lifted their voices to God in prayer as they quoted David in Psalm 2:2 (Acts 4:26-27).

   b. Peter declared the anointing of Jesus with the Holy Spirit and power (Acts 10:38).

B. CHRIST THE PROPHET.

1. **He Was Prophesied By Jehovah.**

   a. Fourteen centuries before the birth of Christ, Jehovah spoke to Moses about *the Prophet* (Deuteronomy 18:18).

   Write in Deuteronomy 18:18: _____

   _____

   _____

   b. Almost fifteen centuries later, Simon Peter proclaimed the fulfillment of Jehovah's promise (Acts 3:18,22,26).

2. **The Meaning of the Word "Prophet."**

   a. The term "prophet" means "one who speaks for God." This is exactly what Jesus did (John 12:49-50).

   b. The words and works of Christ are those of the Father (John 14:9-10).

3. **Jesus Was Anointed As Prophet**

   a. Jesus read the passage from Isaiah 61:1-3 in the synagogue at Nazareth. These words are recorded in Luke 4:18-19 and definitely state, "He hath anointed me to preach the Gospel."

   b. Peter preached in the house of Cornelius of the anointing of Christ (Acts 10:38).

   c. Where did the anointing take place? At the baptism of Jesus (Matthew 3:16-17). Read and underline in your Bible.

   Christ officially entered the office of Prophet.

   d. The importance of this truth is imperative. As a Prophet, Jesus authenticated the Old Testament (Luke 24:44). Jesus spoke for God and as God. He set His seal upon the Word (Matthew 5:18; 24:35; John 10:35).

   e. Jesus called Himself a Prophet (Luke 13:33).

   f. He spoke with authority as a Prophet (Matthew 21:11; Luke 7:16; 24:19; John 4:19).

4. **As A Prophet He Foretold the Future.**

   a. The Old Testament prophet possessed insight and foresight. Jesus, as God's Prophet, foretold what was to come (Mark 13:23).

   b. The future was vivid in His speech just as much as the past and present. In Matthew 13, Jesus made predictions concerning "seed sown," "tares and wheat." In Matthew 24 and 25, Jesus foretold events to take place before His return.

   He was the true Prophet of God. His prophetic ministry began officially at His baptism and ended at the cross when He became the sacrifice for sin.

C. CHRIST THE PRIEST (LESSON 8 COVERS THIS THOROUGHLY).

   1. **A Priest Is A Mediator**

      a. Jesus intercedes with God on behalf of guilty sinners. He is our Great High Priest (Hebrews 4:14-15).

      b. He is the only mediator between God and men (I Timothy 2:5).

   2. **He Fulfilled the Scriptural Pattern of a Priest.**

      a. The Old Testament priesthood had a threefold pattern:
      - to offer sacrifices for the people.
      - to go within the veil to make intercession for the people.
      - to come out to bless the people.

      b. These are the acts of reconciliation, intercession and benediction. Look up Hebrews 7:27; 8:3; Ephesians 5:2.

   3. **He Is A Royal Priest.**

      a. He was a Priest after the order of Melchizedec (Hebrews 7:21). As Melchizedec was both priest and king, so our Lord's priesthood is a royal one.

      b. Underline Zechariah 6:13.

      (For His Ministry of intercession, refer to the last lesson, Number 8.)

D. CHRIST THE KING.

   1. **The Nature of His Kingship.**

      a. As the Eternal Word, He authenticated the Old Testament Scriptures, revealed the Father to men and foretold what was to come. As a priest, He offered Himself without blemish to God and entered into the Holiest to appear in the presence of God on behalf of all believers. Just as He filled the offices of prophet and priest, it is required that He fill the office of the king.

      b. The Father will establish Him as King. Write in I Timothy 6:15: _____

      _____

      _____

      c. Jesus is not now King of the *world*. The time of His Kingship has not yet come. Jesus said there was another in control until He returns again. The one Jesus spoke of is mentioned in John 14:30: _____

      _____

      _____

Paul tells us he is "the prince of the power of the air, the spirit that now worketh in the sons of disobedience" (Ephesians 2:2).

    d. Jesus was born "King of the Jews" (Matthew 2:2). He died as "King of the Jews" (Matthew 27:37). His crucifixion marked the world's total rejection of God's anointed Ruler (Hebrews 10:12-13).

Jesus is awaiting "the times or the seasons, which the Father hath put in His own power" (Acts 1:7). Just prior to His ascension into glory, His disciples came to Him asking, "Lord, wilt thou at this time restore again the kingdom to Israel?" Jesus gave an answer according to His repeated teaching—the time was God's secret. Write in Matthew 24:36: _____

_____

_____

Underline Matthew 24:42,44; 25:13.

2. Prophecies of Jesus As King.

    a. The Word of God is filled with prophecies of Messiah as King.

Jacob, on his deathbed, said, "The scepter shall not depart from Judah, nor a lawgiver from between his feet, until Shiloh come; and unto him shall the gathering of the people be" (Genesis 49:10).

"Shiloh" means "to whom it belongs"—"rest." "Shiloh" means Jesus Christ.

    b. Balaam, forced against his will to utter prophecies of blessing upon Israel, predicted Christ as King.

Write in Numbers 24:17,19: _____

_____

_____

_____

_____

    c. The first Messianic Psalm is given by God the Father.

Write in Psalm 2:6-8: _____

_____

_____

Underline Psalm 2:12.

    d. Read the prediction in Psalm 110.

    e. Isaiah 9:6-7 speaks of this King. Underline verse 6 and write in verse 7: _____

_____

_____

_____

This is in reference to the Davidic Covenant in II Samuel 7:8-16.

    f. Read and underline the prophecy of Jeremiah 23:5-6. Jeremiah wrote, "David shall never lack a man to sit upon the throne of the house of Israel'' (Jeremiah 33:17).

    g. Write in Luke 1:32: _____

_____

_____

3. The Subjects of the King.

    a. In a special sense Christ is to be King of the Jews. God in His own time will cause all Israel to return and Jesus shall truly be King of the Jews (Romans 11:26).

       Equally true is the fact that Jesus Christ will be King over the nations. His dominion will reach unto the ends of the earth.

    b. Write in Psalm 72:11: _____

_____

    c. Christ, in His Kingly character, is depicted in Daniel 7:14:

_____

_____

_____

       Also in Revelation 5:1-7. Read the passage and write in verse 5: _____

_____

_____

       All of the world will be under the King, Jesus Christ.

4. The Blessed Hope.

    a. There is coming to this world a golden era, not ushered in by the church. It will be inaugurated by the return of Christ and it will be ushered in by His establishment of His throne and kingdom. This age, as all past ages, is a record of man's failure (Ezekiel 21:26-27).

    b. There is only one hope for the Christian as we live in the power of the world. We are ''looking for that blessed hope, and the glorious appearing of the great God and our Saviour, Jesus Christ'' (Titus 2:13).

       We stand gazing toward the heavens waiting for the return of our Lord to receive us unto Himself (I Thessalonians 4:17).

    c. Then with His glorified saints, Christ will return to this earth as "King of Kings, and Lord of Lords" (Revelation 11;15; 19:16).

       Write in Zechariah 14:9: _____

_____

    d. This is the future ministry of Jesus Christ.

V. WHAT THIS BIBLE TRUTH TEACHES US TODAY.

God is always faithful in keeping His Word. We have seen prophecies and covenants coming to pass. Since he has been faithful in keeping His promises in the past, we can be assured that the prophecies, yet to be fulfilled, shall come to pass.

Jesus is the center of all Scripture. He *was our Prophet* (we have His Word)—He *is our Priest* (He ever liveth to make intercession for us. Therefore, we pray ''in the name of Jesus.'')—and He *shall be King* over all the earth. He is now Head of the church. He is never called King of the church. He shall come for His bride, the church, and we shall return and reign with the King in His Kingdom.

The Psalms witness to the ministry of Christ in His offices as Prophet, Priest and King. The trilogy is in:

Psalm 22	Psalm 23	Psalm 24
PAST	PRESENT	FUTURE
Crucified Prophet	Risen Priest	Reigning King
Suffering Saviour	Living Shepherd	Exalted Sovereign
Good Shepherd	Great Shepherd	Chief Shepherd
John 10:11	Hebrews 13:20	I Peter 5:4
The Cross	The Crook	The Crown

YOUR NEXT ASSIGNMENT:

1. Read Genesis 1:2; 6:3; Exodus 28:3; 31:3; Numbers 11:17,25,29; 27:18; Isaiah 11:2; 32:15; 42:1; 61:1; Joel 2:28-29; Zechariah 4:6; 12:10; Matthew 1:18,20; 3:16; 10:20; 28:20; John 14:16, 17,26; 15:26; 16:7-15; Acts Chapters 1 and 2; 13:2,4,9,10; Romans Chapter 8; I Corinthians 2:4,11,12; 3:16; 12:3-13; II Corinthians 1:22; 3:3,6,8; Galatians 4:6; 5:5-25; Ephesians 1:13,14,17; 2:18; 4:3,4,30; 5:9; 6:17; Titus 3:5; Hebrews 3:7; 9:8; 10:15,16,29; I Peter 3:18; 4:6,14; I John 4:2,6,13; 5:7,8; Revelation 1:4,10; 2:7,11,17,29; 3:1,6,13,22; 22:17.

2. Review your notes on this lesson.

3. Mark your Bible where new truths are learned.

Hebrews 11:1

Lesson 10 "God the Holy Spirit" — Part I

(Where lines are provided, look up the Scripture and write in the Scripture or its main truth.)

I. INTRODUCTION

What about the personality of the Holy Spirit? This is a strange question, yet it is one most people cannot answer nor comprehend. Perhaps the name has caused great confusion. In our English language the words "Spirit" or "Ghost" take on the connotation of "an evil spirit who possesses a person" or "a ghost is one who haunts a house; an inhabitant of the unseen world who might appear in a bodily likeness"; "a demon" etc. (Elaborate)

The Holy Spirit is the Third Person of the Godhead. He is God the Holy Spirit—*a Person*. He is the Triune God. The Scriptures unfailingly represent God the Father as a Person (Genesis 3:8-9; Exodus 33:11).

The Second Person of the Godhead, the Lord Jesus Christ, is both God and man. In the account of the ascension (Luke 24:50-53), the Lord Jesus extended His hands to bless the disciples who worshipped Him *as God*. He was God. He was a Person.

But what of the Person of the Holy Spirit? There is no question but that the Bible presents the deity of the Holy Spirit. Jesus confirmed this in a few short statements which we shall study. Jesus referred to "the promise of the Father" (Luke 24:49) in His Upper Room address to His disciples on the night He was betrayed.

II. BASIC SCRIPTURES

Genesis 1:2; 6:3; Exodus 28:3; 31:3; Numbers 11:17,25, 29; 27:18; Isaiah 11:2; 32:15; 42:1; 61:1; Joel 2:28-29; Zechariah 4:6; 12:10; Matthew 1:18,20; 3:16; 10:20; 28:20; John 14:16,17,26; 15:26; 16:7-15; Acts Chapters 1 and 2; 13:2,4,9,10; Romans Chapter 8; I Corinthians2:4,11,12; 3:16; 12:3-13; II Corinthians 1:22; 3:3,6,8; Galatians 4:6; 5:5-25; Ephesians 1:13,14,17; 2:18; 4:3,4,30; 5:9; 6:17; Titus 3:5; Hebrews 3:7; 9:8; 10:15,16,29; I Peter 3:18; 4:6,14; I John 4:2,6,13; 5:7,8; Revelation 1:4,10; 2:7,11,17,29; 3:1,6,13,22; 22:17.

III. THE NUCLEUS OF THIS TRUTH

The Holy Spirit is a Person. He is the ascension gift of Jesus Christ. He could not have descended had Christ not ascended (John 16:7). The Father sent the Holy Spirit in the name of Jesus Christ.

The Holy Spirit abides *in* every believer. Prior to Pentecost He dwelt *with* the disciples but not *in* them (John 14:17). In this era of the church—the age of grace—the age when Jesus Christ is calling out for Himself a Body—the Holy Spirit abides in a new temple—*YOU* (if you believe). He takes up His abode at the time you accept Jesus Christ as your Lord and Saviour (I Corinthians 12:13).

Handwritten margin notes:

GREAT TRUTHS OF THE BIBLE

Godhead refers to the divinity or substance of the Christian God, especially as existing in three persons—the Father, Son, and the Holy Spirit.

Heaven

Can we have one without the other?

Car:
1. Body
2. Engine
3. Fuel/source of power
—Can't see with the human eye.

Spirit (Like faith)

Gift!

Examples of people stating a past love one is still with them. why?

(dwelleth with you)

Place of residence

If you, a pupil, a learner, can comprehend this central truth, you can better comprehend the total teaching of the Bible in reference to the Holy Spirit.

IV. THE GREAT TRUTH: "GOD THE HOLY SPIRIT" PART I

A. THE HOLY SPIRIT IN THE OLD TESTAMENT.

1. The Holy Spirit Was in the Beginning.

Holy Spirit was in the beginning.

a. The Holy Spirit, being a Person, the third Person of the Trinity, was active in the creation.

Write in Genesis 1:1-2: _____

_____

_____

Inf

The name "God" in verse 1 is a plural noun meaning God the Father, God the Son, God the Holy Spirit.
The Spirit is named in verse 2.

b. The breath of God is the Spirit of God. The Psalmist refers to the creation in Psalm 33:6-9. Underline verse 6.

Write in Job 26:13: *Reference Breath*

_____

_____

_____

c. The Holy Spirit was active in the creation of animal life (Psalm 104:24-30).

Write in verse 30: _____

_____

_____

d. The Holy Spirit was active in the creation of man (Genesis 1:26-27). Here the plural words "us" and "our" refer to the Triune God.

Here someone read 26 in Genesis on "us" and "our." "After (our) likeness"

Note Genesis 2:7 and underline: *26 Our likeness!*

Write in Job 33:4: _____

_____

2. The Holy Spirit Possesses Divine Attributes.

a. He is Omnipotent.

The Holy Spirit is "all powerful." He shared in the work of creation (as seen above). Refer again to Psalm 33:6 and Genesis 1:2.

b. He is Omnipresent.

The Holy Spirit is "everywhere present." Read the words of David (Psalm 139:7-10).

Write in verse 7: _____

_____

c. He is Omniscient.

The Holy Spirit is "all knowing." Underline Job 32:8

Read Psalm 139:1-6 and write in verse 4: _____

_____

3. The Manifestations of the Holy Spirit in the Old Testament.

a. He *came upon* men. Read Numbers 11:17 and write in verse 25: _____

_____

Read Numbers 24:2 and Judges 3:10, 6:34; 11:29; 13:25; 14:6. Underline I Samuel 10:6 and 10.

b. He was *poured out* upon men. Look at Proverbs 1:23.

Write in Isaiah 32:15 _____

_____

_____

Underline Isaiah 44:3; Ezekiel 39:29; Joel 2:28-29; Zechariah 12:10.

c. He *rested* upon men. Underline Numbers 11:25-26.

Write in Isaiah 11:2: _____

_____

_____

4. **The References to the Holy Spirit in the Old Testament.**

a. The Holy Spirit is mentioned some 88 times in the Old Testament. These are widely spread over the canon, found in 22 of the 39 Old Testament books.

b. In the Pentateuch (the first five books) we find 14 references and these are found in only 4 of the books. Leviticus has no references.

c. Two of the prophetic books, Isaiah and Ezekiel, have 15 references in each.

d. The other books, Judges and I Samuel have 7 references each; II Samuel, 1 reference; Psalms has 5. This leaves 24 references in the other 11 books.

e. In these Old Testament references, the Holy Spirit never indwelled individuals. He came upon them, and he left them as He willed (Judges 14:6;16:20-21). The Old Testament contains predictions of a future pouring out of the Spirit upon Israel (Ezekiel 37:14; 39:29) and upon all flesh (Joel 2:28-29), but remember, this was future and did not occur in the Old Testament era.

B. THE HOLY SPIRIT IN THE NEW TESTAMENT.

1. **He Was Active in the Revelation of the Word of God.**

a. The Holy Spirit, in the Old Testament, was active in the inspiration and transmission of the Word of God. This is verified in the New Testament Scriptures.

Write in II Peter 1:21: _____

_____

Read II Timothy 3:16. Underline Acts 28:25.

b. The New Testament attributes many Old Testament Scriptures directly to the Holy Spirit.

Look up and underline Matthew 22:43; Mark 12:36; Acts 1:16; 4:25; Hebrews 3:7; 10:15-16.

2. **The Difference Pentecost Made.**

a. Before our Lord's ascension, He was assembled with His apostles and told them of "the promise of the Father" (Acts 1:4-5 and 8).

Handwritten margin notes:
— Why?
— Old Testament Referencing Future
— Can't talk about the Holy Spirit without discussing "Pentecost"

57

b. The Lord's own words speak of something entirely new and different. These are the most important statements concerning the descent of the Holy Spirit.
Underline John 14:16 and write in verse 17 _____

_____

Write in John 14:26: _____

_____

Underline John 15:26.
Write in John 16:7: _____ *Example of sports or achievements*

_____

Underline John 16:12 and write in verse 13: _____

_____

_____

Underline John 16:14.

c. Three things comprise the difference in the work of the Holy Spirit before the Lord's ascension and after His ascension into heaven.

- *First,* the Holy Spirit entered into a new temple and that new temple is built on the foundation of Christ out of living stones which are the regenerated believers in Christ (I Peter 2:5). On the day of Pentecost, the Holy Spirit came to indwell His Bride, *the Church* of God, the Body of Christ.
  At Pentecost, the Holy Spirit took up residence in believers (Ephesians 2:19-22; I Corinthians 3:16-17).

- *Second,* not only did the Holy Spirit come to indwell the church as a corporate body, but He also came at Pentecost to indwell all believers. Jesus had said in John 14:17, "Even the Spirit of truth—ye know Him; for He *dwelleth with* you and *shall be in* you."
  In the Old Testament the Holy Spirit did not indwell believers as He does in the present day of Grace. He was a gift to a few individuals as He willed and then it was for a special purpose of God.
  Jesus spoke of one He loved. John the Baptist was called a "great" person by the Lord (Matthew 11:11). John the Baptist was before Pentecost. Jesus said, "he that is least in the kingdom of heaven is greater than John the Baptist."

- *Third,* the Holy Spirit personally indwells the believer in Jesus and is never withdrawn. The personal indwelling of the Holy Spirit guarantees our Spiritual discernment. He is our teacher and He recalls to our memory all that we need (John 14:26).
  In the Old Testament the Holy Spirit could be withdrawn. One example is found in the life of Israel's first king,

3 points to Holy Spirit Remember!

58

Saul. Turn to I Samuel 10:9-10 and there you read, "God gave him another heart—and the Spirit of God came upon him, and he prophesied." That is not the end of the story.

A tragic word is written about Saul (I Samuel 16:14). Write in verse 14: _____

_____

_____

In the age in which we live, Jesus said the gift of the Holy Spirit is personal to every regenerated child of God. With all the faults and sins and vices of the Corinthians, Paul could still write to them: "What? know ye not that your body is the temple of the Holy Spirit which *is in* you, which ye have of God—?" (I Corinthians 6:19).

3. The Meaning and Significance of Pentecost.

a. Pentecost came 50 days after the Feast of the Firstfruits. The Feast of the Firstfruits was a type of the resurrection of Christ (Leviticus 23:9-16).

Pentecost means 50. (For study in reference to the feasts, refer to "Through the Bible in One Year," Volume 1, pages 18-20).

b. The significance of Pentecost is found in the fact that the Holy Spirit descended 50 days after the resurrection of Jesus from the tomb. He had died on the cross, was buried, came out of the grave and yet people recognized Him. He was seen in the glorified body for *40 days*.

Write in Acts 1:3: _____

_____

_____

_____

c. Just before His ascension, Jesus told the apostles to "wait for the promise of the Father" (Acts 1:4). The "promise of the Father" was the coming of the Holy Spirit (Acts 1:8).

d. The length of the waiting period is never mentioned directly, but it is easy to figure. If Jesus was seen for 40 days after His resurrection and Pentecost means 50, they waited 10 days.

e. The Holy Spirit came on time. The Old Testament feasts taught the group, and us, the meaning of Pentecost (Read Leviticus 23). The Holy Spirit could not have descended at any other time.

f. The Feast of the Passover was fulfilled at Calvary. There will be only one Calvary—one death of Jesus. "He is our Passover" (I Corinthians 5:7).

The Feast of Pentecost was fulfilled by the coming of the Holy Spirit. There will be only one Pentecost.

g. Two things happened on the day of Pentecost:

- the believers were *baptized* with the Spirit because Jesus had told them earlier (Acts 1:5). The word "baptism" is not found in Acts 2.

- they were *filled* with the Holy Spirit (Acts 2:4). The baptism was one thing—the filling another. Notice that they spoke in tongues because they were filled with the Spirit, and the tongues were understood in their own language (Acts 2:6,8). This was not an "unknown tongue." It was the way the Holy Spirit began to spread the Gospel of Jesus Christ.

(Note: The next lesson will be on the Holy Spirit and we shall continue this important study.)

V. WHAT THIS BIBLE TRUTH TEACHES US TODAY.

The Holy Spirit is a Person indwelling all believers in Christ. He is the Teacher, the Comforter, the Paraclete (the one by our side), the Guide in our lives.

The Holy Spirit was sent by God the Father in the name of Jesus Christ. Therefore, the Holy Spirit is an ascension gift of Jesus Christ.

The Holy Spirit always magnifies Jesus Christ. The Holy Spirit is "the promise of the Father." There are more than 3,000 promises in Scripture, but only one is called "*the* promise of the Father" (Acts 1:4; Luke 24:49).

This truth assures all believers that the Holy Spirit indwells them and never leaves them.

What a thrilling truth—He abides in us!

YOUR NEXT ASSIGNMENT:

1. Read the same Scripture as given in this lesson. The next study shall also be on the Holy Spirit.

2. The three lessons, Numbers 10, 11 and 12, are vital to our faith. Do not miss a lesson.

3. Mark the Scriptures in your Bible. Especially, the words of Jesus in reference to the coming of the Holy Spirit.

Lesson 11 ``God the Holy Spirit'' — Part II

(Where lines are provided, look up the Scripture and write in the Scripture or its main truth.)

I. INTRODUCTION

In our study of the Holy Spirit we have seen only a part of His ministry. In this lesson we shall explore the references in the New Testament concerning the Holy Spirit—the names of the Holy Spirit in His relationship to the Father and the Son—the work of the Holy Spirit in the church—the characteristics of the Person, God the Holy Spirit—the teaching of our Lord concerning the Holy Spirit—finally, the fruit of the Spirit.

These will help you understand a little more concerning the Holy Spirit. There is no way to cover the entire work of the Holy Spirit in three lessons, but we have a good beginning—a foundation. Personal study will be easier in reference to this great truth.

II. BASIC SCRIPTURES:

Real all the Scriptures listed in Lesson 10.

III. THE NUCLEUS OF THIS TRUTH

The Holy Spirit, the third Person of the Trinity, abides in the hearts and souls of believers in Christ. He is in the body of Christ, the church. This is the age of the church, and since Pentecost, the Holy Spirit has been the power in the church to spread the Gospel of Christ and to call out a people for His name.

In this age of grace and the church, the Holy Spirit is not greater, He is later. He came after Jesus ascended. He could not come until Jesus left the earth. Jesus said, ``If I go not away, the Comforter will not come unto you; but if I depart, I will send Him unto you'' (John 16:7). This is the age in which the Holy Spirit teaches the believers all the truths of Scripture (John 14:26). He, the Holy Spirit, is the Spirit of truth and He testifies of Jesus Christ (John 15:26).

One significant thing about the Holy Spirit should be observed by the student. The Master said, ``When He, the Spirit of truth, is come, He will guide you into all truth: for *He shall not speak of Himself*—He shall glorify me'' (John 16:13-14).

IV. THE GREAT TRUTH: ``GOD THE HOLY SPIRIT'' PART II

A. REFERENCES TO THE HOLY SPIRIT IN THE NEW TESTAMENT.

    1. There Are 262 Passages in the New Testament Which Mention the Holy Spirit.

        a. These 262 passages are found in 24 of the 27 books of the New Testament. The only books in which the Holy Spirit is not mentioned are Philemon and II and III John.

b. The four Gospels, Matthew, Mark, Luke and John contain 56 passages referring to the Holy Spirit.

c. The Acts of the Apostles (known also as The Acts of the Holy Spirit) contain 57 references to the Holy Spirit.

d. Paul's Epistles contain 113 passages referring to the Holy Spirit.

e. The other books, General Epistles and Revelation, contain 36 references to the Holy Spirit.

2. In Both Testaments, Old and New, There Are 350 References to the Holy Spirit.

The subject is of paramount importance to be mentioned so often in Scripture. The Bible places great emphasis on the Person of the Holy Spirit. We should allow Him to teach us all truth, including the truth concerning Himself.

B. THE TEACHINGS OF JESUS CONCERNING THE HOLY SPIRIT.

1. The Testimony Jesus Gave to the Holy Spirit.

a. The first testimony regarding the Holy Spirit and the first definite teaching about the Holy Spirit came from the Lord Jesus.

b. His teachings were spoken before Pentecost and this should be remembered.

2. The Specific Teachings of Jesus About the Holy Spirit.

(The teachings are not chronological but are listed to obtain some order of doctrine.)

a. Jesus claimed that He was led by the Holy Spirit and taught by the Holy Spirit in all He did. In His opening sermon, Jesus said, '' _____

_____

_____ (Luke 4:18).

Write in John 3:34: _____

_____

b. Jesus taught that the Holy Spirit spoke in the Old Testament and, in fact, caused it to be written (Matthew 22:43:44).

c. Jesus taught that salvation is due to the work of the Holy Spirit (John 3:5-6).

d. Jesus taught the abundant life to His disciples.
Write in John 7:37-39: _____

_____

_____

e. Jesus taught of the quickening power of the Holy Spirit (quickening means ''make alive'') (John 6:63).

f. Jesus gave the baptismal formula naming the Trinity. Notice, ''the *name* (singular) of the Father, and the Son and the Holy Spirit'' (Matthew 28:19).

g. Jesus promised the presence of the Holy Spirit in the work of His disciples—the actual words they were to speak (Mark 13:11).

h. Jesus had a message to the church in reference to teaching and the Teacher (John 16:13-16). Here we have His name—''The

62

Spirit of Truth." Here also we have His function—"He shall glorify Christ." In John 16:8-11, He names the three great themes of the testimony of the Holy Spirit. What are they?

- "of sin" because of unbelief.
- "of righteousness" which God requires.
- "of judgment" already declared upon the cross.

i. So Jesus announced the truth by which the Holy Spirit convicts the word:

- My sin
- Christ's righteousness
- God's judgment

j. As the Son spent His earthly life in seeking to glorify the Father, so the Holy Spirit spends His time in seeking to glorify the Son.

C. THE NAMES OF THE HOLY SPIRIT IN THE NEW TESTAMENT.

1. Names Expressing His Relationship to the Father.

a. "The Spirit of God" (Matthew 3:16).

b. "The Spirit of the Lord" (Luke 4:18) (In Acts 5:9 and 8:39 the expression "Lord" may refer to Christ).

c. "The Spirit of our God" (I Corinthians 6:11).

d. "The Spirit of the living God" (II Corinthians 3:3).

e. "The Spirit of your Father" (Matthew 10:20).

f. "The Spirit of Glory and the Spirit of God" (I Peter 4:14).

g. "The Promise of the Father" (Acts 1:4).

2. Names Expressing His Relationship to the Son.

a. "The Spirit of Christ" (Romans 8:9).

b. "The Spirit of Jesus Christ" (Philippians 1:9).

c. "Spirit of Jesus" (Acts 16:7).

d. "The Spirit of His (God's) Son" (Galatians 4:6).

e. "Another Comforter" (Paraclete) (John 14:16).

3. Names Expressing His Own Essential Deity.

a. "One Spirit" (Ephesians 4:4).

b. "Seven Spirits" (the complete perfect Spirit) (Revelation 1:4; 3:1).

c. "The Lord the Spirit" (II Corinthians 3:18).

d. "The Eternal Spirit" (Hebrews 9:14).

4. Names Expressing the Gifts Which He Bestows.

a. "The Spirit of Life" (Romans 8:2; Revelation 11:11).

b. "The Spirit of Holiness" (Romans 1:4).

c. "The Spirit of Wisdom" (Ephesians 1:17).

d. "The Spirit of Faith" (II Corinthians 4:13).

e. "The Spirit of Truth" (John 14:17; 16:13).

f. "The Spirit of Grace" (Hebrews 10:29).

g. "The Spirit of Adoption" (Romans 8:15).

h. "The Spirit of Power, Love and Sound Mind" (II Timothy 1:7).

This variety of names tell us something of His deity, His power, His influence, His ministry among us and in us, His Person.

D. THE WORK OF THE HOLY SPIRIT IN THE CHURCH.

1. The Church Became A Spiritual Organism.

a. Jesus had promised the ''baptism of the Holy Spirit'' (Acts 1:5).

When the Holy Spirit descended, He dwelled in the hearts of believers and they became a unified spiritual organism, called the body, with Christ as the Head (Colossians 2:19).

Write in Ephesians 1:22-23: _____

_____

_____

b. The Holy Spirit forms the church. When does one become a part of the body of Christ? At the time we accept Christ as Saviour—we accept His forgiveness and atonement. He, the Holy Spirit, baptizes us into the body of Christ, the church.

Write in I Corinthians 12:13: _____

_____

_____

c. When one receives Christ, he is sealed by the Holy Spirit in Christ (Ephesians 1:13).

2. The Results of The Work of The Holy Spirit In The Church.

a. On the day of Pentecost, the Holy Spirit came upon and filled the 120 people in the Upper Room (Acts 2:1-4).

b. The *two* operations of the Holy Spirit are distinct and are identified. ''Baptism,'' as mentioned by Jesus in Acts 1:5 and ''filling'' (Acts 2:41).

c. Peter preached the message from Joel 2:28-29 and 3,000 souls were saved (Acts 2:41).

d. Under persecution, the preaching of the Gospel caused 5,000 men, plus women, to accept Christ (Acts 4:4).

e. In Acts 8 the Gospel spread from the Jews to the Samaritans and the Ethiopian eunuch.

Then in Acts 9 to Saul of Tarsus, Paul.

Then in Acts 10 to Cornelius, the Gentile.

f. The spreading of the Gospel was according to the outline of Jesus Christ in Acts 1:8.

3. The Holy Spirit Still Does His Work In The Body.

a. The Holy Spirit came to indwell and administer the church of our Lord.

b. He is to abide ''with you forever.'' He never leaves us.

c. He came to teach us about Jesus. He does that work in and through believers, His church.

E. THE CHARACTERISTICS OF THE PERSON OF THE HOLY SPIRIT.

1. In A Personality, Four Characteristics Are Obvious.

a. A person is one who can think (he has mind, understanding).

b. He can feel (he has emotions).

c. He can choose (he has will, volition, purpose).

d. He can do (he can act).

2. All Four Characteristics Can Be Seen In The Holy Spirit.

a. The Holy Spirit can think—He has mind and understanding. He is presented as such in Acts 15:28 and I Corinthians 2:10-11 and Ephesians 1:17.

b. He, the Holy Spirit, can feel (Ephesians 4:30).

c. The Holy Spirit can choose; He has will (I Corinthians 12:11).

d. The Holy Spirit can do, can act. He is the author of Scripture (II Timothy 3:16; Acts 1:16; Hebrews 10:15-16).

He convicts of sin and is the instrument of our salvation (Titus 3:5-6; I Thessalonians 1:5).

He is the Teacher of truth (John 14:16; Romans 8:14).

He helps us and sustains us (John 14:16-18; Romans 8:26-27).

F. THE FRUIT OF THE HOLY SPIRIT.

1. The Fruit of The Spirit Reveals Christian Character.

a. The fruit of the Spirit is found in Galatians 5:22-23: _____

_____

b. The "fruit" is singular. One can know Christ will produce some "fruit" of the Spirit by the indwelling Spirit.

2. Fruit Comes From the Spirit Filled Life.

a. The Lord Jesus is the great example of the fruit of the Spirit. He possessed all the qualities of Galatians 5:22-23.

b. One cannot bear the fruit of the Spirit by his own activity or goodness—but by yielding to the Holy Spirit.

G. THE WORK OF THE HOLY SPIRIT IN CHRISTIANS.

1. Walking In The Spirit.

a. Write in Galatians 5:16: _____

_____

b. The Holy Spirit will lead our walk. He will direct our paths.

2. Renewing of The Spirit.

a. Write in Titus 3:5: _____

_____

b. This refers to a renewing of the Spirit to live a victorious Christian life.

3. Leading of The Spirit.

a. Write in Romans 8:14: _____

_____

b. The Holy Spirit is always present to give guidance in our lives. The secret is found in "*As many as* are led—."

4. Indwelling of The Spirit.

a. Write in I Corinthians 6:19: _____

_____

b. Read and underline John 7:37-39.

5. The Hearing of Faith.

a. Write in Galatians 3:2: _____

_____

b. Underline John 3:6-7.

V. WHAT THIS BIBLE TRUTH TEACHES US TODAY.

The importance of the Holy Spirit is expressed in the many times His name is found in Scripture—262 times in the New Testament and 88 times in the Old Testament. Jesus taught before Pentecost about the Holy Spirit and His work in all who believe. All of the fundamental truths concerning the Holy Spirit were given by our Lord. Jesus knew He would have to ascend in order for the Spirit to come.

The Holy Spirit is one of the most important subjects in Scripture—yet He is used and abused more than any other subject. Why? Satan works hard at this point. However, the subject is abused because of misunderstanding and little study.

Therefore, we shall give a third lesson to this subject.

YOUR NEXT ASSIGNMENT:

1. Add to the Scriptures in Lesson 10 the following to be read: Romans 4:11; I Corinthians 12:1, 8:11; 12:28-30; II Corinthians 13:14; Galatians 6:7-8; Ephesians 3:16; 4:11; 5:18; Philippians 1:19; II Thessalonians 2:13-14; II Timothy 2:19; I Peter 1:2.

2. Reread lesson 10 and then, this lesson.

3. Mark your Bible where new truths are learned. (Mark the new truths in your notebook in class. Transfer them to your Bible at home. Write very plainly in your Bible. It will be there for many years.

Lesson 12
"God The Holy Spirit" — Part III

(Where lines are provided, look up the Scripture and write in the Scripture or its main truth.)

I. INTRODUCTION

There are so many different teachings in reference to the Holy Spirit. The Bible is the only source of truth. The Holy Spirit is the Teacher of that truth. Then, why all the controversy over the subject? Satan, "the accuser of the brethren," is constantly dividing the members of the body of Christ." We allow Satan to rule and not the Word of God.

In this lesson, the final lesson on the Holy Spirit, we shall consider some of the difficult subjects. We shall study only what the Bible has to say about the Person or power of the Holy Spirit, the ministering gifts of the Spirit, the sealing of the Holy Spirit, sins against the Holy Spirit and the emblems of the Holy Spirit.

II. BASIC SCRIPTURES:

All the Scriptures in Lesson 10. Add the following Scriptures to be read: Romans 4:11; I Corinthians 12:1,8-11; 12:28-30; II Corinthians 13:14; Galatians 6:7-8; Ephesians 3:16; 4:11; 5:18; Philippians 1:19; II Thessalonians 2:13-14; II Timothy 2:19

III. THE NUCLEUS OF THIS TRUTH

There is a tendency to think of power or force as an "it." It is easy to fall into the error of looking upon the Holy Spirit as an "it," an influence, an energy, a power, a force. When we separate the Person from the power of the Holy Spirit, we are in danger of making the Holy Spirit an indefinite mysterious "it." We lose all thought of Him as a Person.

The means of the Holy Spirit doing His work in us is the Word of God. The church, the body of Christ, is our school. In the school there are two things—the textbook (the Bible) and the Teacher (the Holy Spirit) who makes us understand. The Teacher is a Person, not an "it." The Holy Spirit uses "the Sword of the Spirit," the Bible, to explain, comfort and teach the truths of God. For us to learn and grow, we must believe "the Word of God is living, and powerful, and sharper than a twoedged sword" (Hebrews 4:12). We must also believe that the Holy Spirit "will guide us into all truth." To take one without the other is to take the Teacher without the Book—or the Book without the Teacher.

The Person of the Holy Spirit keeps us, helps us, seals us and gives gifts to be used for the glory of God.

IV. THE GREAT TRUTH: "GOD THE HOLY SPIRIT" PART III

A. THE HOLY SPIRIT—A PERSON—A POWER.

    1. When Did The Holy Spirit Descend in Power?

        a. Many learned scholars separate the coming of the Holy Spirit from the power of the Holy Spirit. They arrive at this conclusion from the Scripture in John 20:22, "And when He had

67

said this, He breathed on them, and said unto them, Receive ye the Holy Ghost.''

Such fundamental writers as Arthur Pink expressed the idea of separating the Holy Spirit's coming from the power of Pentecost. Arthur Pink, in his exposition of the Gospel of John, Volume III, page 287, writes: ''What happened at Pentecost was the baptism of power not the coming of the Spirit to indwell them.''

b. There are some difficulties in this theory if we compare Scripture with Scripture and seek the real meaning of the words of Jesus.

c. Before His Ascension, our Lord expressly said that the promise of the Father was still in the future. Look at Luke 24:49-53 and write in verse 49: _____

_____

_____

These words were spoken *after* the words He spoke in John 20:22 and just before His Ascension into heaven (Luke 24:51 and Acts 1:4-5).

d. The instructions were repeated in Acts 1:4 by our Lord. The apostles were to *wait* for ''the promise of the Father.'' The ''promise of the father,'' according to John 14:16-17 was the Holy Spirit Himself.

On the day of Pentecost, Peter said, ''—and having received from the Father the promise of the Holy Spirit—'' (Acts 2:33). This confirmed the words of Jesus.

e. What happened, then, on the day of Pentecost was the coming of the Holy Spirit, which the Father had promised to His Son, the Lord Jesus Christ.

f. Paul called the Holy Spirit ''the Holy Spirit of Promise'' (Ephesians 1:13).

2. Why The Difficulty?

a. The difficulty lies in the fact that one word was not translated correctly. In John 20:22 you find the word ''receive.'' ''Receive ye the Holy Ghost.'' The word John used is ''labete,'' which can be translated in two ways—''take, accept'' or ''receive.''

The same word is used in John 18:31: ''Take Him—and judge Him.''

The exact word is translated in two different ways in John 10:18: ''—I have power to *take* it again. This commandment have I received of my Father.''

In Matthew 26:26 at the institution of the Lord's Supper, the Lord said, ''*Take*, eat.''

b. Therefore, in John 20:22, when Jesus breathed on the disciples, they were quickened in faith and hope. It was not the coming of ''the promise of the Father.'' Jesus gave them the earnest, the guarantee of the mighty gift. Jesus gave first the promise, the breath, then the presence, Pentecost.

3. The Coming of the Holy Spirit.

a. When we say ''the Holy Spirit was given'' in John 20:22, and ''the power came at Pentecost'' in Acts 1:4, we separate the Person from the power as though they were two different things.

68

b. The Holy Spirit could not have come in power until Jesus had ascended. Jesus said so in John 16:7: _____

_____

_____

c. Jesus "breathed" on the disciples to signify that the Holy Spirit had been the Breath of His life. He had lived *in* and *by* the Spirit—He had been conceived in Mary by the Holy Spirit. (See Genesis 2:7).

d. The Holy Spirit, the promise of the Father, came in power at the exact time, at the exact place, to the exact people as Jesus had instructed.

They were ready to <u>take</u> the Holy Spirit, by the hand of faith, on the day of Pentecost; not before. Jesus had said to wait for the promise at Jerusalem. At the end of the ten days they were ready to "take." (Read again John 14:17 and note the words "with" and "in.")

B. THE EMBLEMS OF THE HOLY SPIRIT.

1. The Bible Contains Similitudes (Resemblance, Likeness, Image).

a. The Bible is a Book of similes, metaphors, allegories, parables, types, symbols and emblems. To better understand Scripture, we must understand these similitudes:

- *simile* is a figure of speech in which one thing is compared to another. (Example—Psalm 102:6).

- a *metaphor* is a figure of speech in which one thing is called another. (Example—John 1:29).

- an *allegory* is a prolonged metaphor. (Example–Judges 9:1-21).

- a *parable* is a truth illustrated by a factual story—an earthly story with a heavenly meaning. (Example—Matthew 13 where you find seven parables of Jesus).

- a *type* is an object or event used to prefigure another object or event. (Example—John 3:14)

- an *emblem* is a visible sign of an idea; an object symbolizing another object or idea. (Example—Luke 3:22).

- a *symbol* is a thing or act representing something spiritual. (Example—Genesis 9:12-13).

b. With these words in mind, we are better able to understand the Word of God as we discuss the "emblems" of the Holy Spirit.

2. The Emblems of The Holy Spirit Named.

a. *The dove*. In Matthew 3:16, Luke 3:22 and John 1:32 we read of the Holy Spirit descending upon Jesus "like a dove." The Spirit never descended on another in this manner. Underline these passages in your Bible. The dove rested upon Christ, "abode upon Him" (John 1:32). The Holy Spirit rested upon Christ, abode upon Him and through Him upon all of us who believe.

b. *The anointing oil*. When the priests in the Old Testament were anointed with oil, it was applied first to the ear—he was to hear God's Word; his thumb—his actions were to be done with holy hands; his big toe—he was to walk with God (Exodus 29:20-21).

The oil is one of the most characteristic of all the emblems of the Holy Spirit. Look up Acts 10:38.

Write in I John 2:20: _____

_____

c. *The wind*. The word "breath" has the same meaning as "wind" in both Hebrew and Greek and both mean "Spirit."

Write in John 3:8: _____

_____

_____

Underline Acts 2:2.

d. *The fire*. Fire signifies the Spirit of God. It is fire which purifies, consumes, tests, illuminates and energizes.

Underline Isaiah 4:4 and 6:6-7.

Write in Acts 2:3: _____

_____

_____

e. *The clothing*. The clothing of power is another emblem of the Holy Spirit. Look up Judges 6:34, "the Spirit of God clothed Himself upon Gideon." The same thing is said again in II Chronicles 24:20.

In Luke 24:49 Jesus said, "ye shall be endued with power from on high." The word "endued" literally means "to put on," "to be clothed." The Holy Spirit is our protection. Clothing is for protection.

f. *The seal*. We belong to God (if we are saved) and the Spirit seals us. Underline Ephesians 1:13.

Write in II Corinthians 1:21-22: _____

_____

_____

_____

_____

Underline John 6:27 and Ephesians 4:30.

The Holy Spirit is the seal and the seal signifies ownership (II Timothy 2:19).

g. *The earnest*. An "earnest" is a guarantee, a pledge. Three times in the New Testament the Holy Spirit is referred to as an "earnest" that God gives to the saints.

Read II Corinthians 1:22 again and note the word "earnest."

Write in II Corinthians 5:5: _____

_____

_____

Write in Ephesians 1:14: _____

_____

_____

The "earnest" is the pledge and token that God will give all He has promised. The Holy Spirit is the "earnest."

C. THE COMMUNION OF THE HOLY SPIRIT.

1. The Holy Spirit Enters Into Partnership With Believers.

a. Paul gives the great benediction, naming the Trinity. Write in II Corinthians 13:14: _____

_____

_____

b. The word "communion" is better translated "fellowship" and these two words are best summed up in our word "partnership."

c. The Spirit enters into a partnership with us rather than take us into partnership with Him, and we have here a great fact in the life of a Christian. When we accept Christ, He, the Holy Spirit enters and indwells us and He establishes the partnership on the basis of our acceptance of Christ—not on the basis of our past record. He is always with us as a partner. We do have fellowship with Him.

3. The Difference Between His Communion and That of the Father and Son.

a. The same word for "fellowship" is used in I John 1:3, "Our fellowship is with the father, and with his Son Jesus Christ."

One striking thing stands out in that Scripture. It is the absence of any reference to the Holy Spirit. There are possible reasons. Observe how the language differs: it is "*our* fellowship with the Father—," but it is "*the* communion of the Holy Spirit."

In I John 1:3 we are partakers with the Father and Christ. In II Corinthians 13:14 the Holy Spirit is a partaker with us.

b. Another thought—the Holy Spirit directs attention away from Himself; therefore, He does not cause His name to be recorded in I John 1:3.

3. The Partnership Is With A Person.

a. His partnership is limited by us. He cannot be a partner in schemes that might have the appearance of sin. His partnership should keep us close to the Lord Jesus.

b. This partnership is with the Person, the Holy Spirit. The Holy Spirit shares a common thought with us. "*Communion*" rises out of "*Union*", and the "*Union*" is the "*Union of the Believer with Christ*."

c. Jesus spoke of our relation to the Father through Himself. Underline John 17:21. Note the words, "that they also may be one in Us." This relationship is the common ground of the Holy Spirit's communion with us. The cross is in the background; where the Spirit finds Christ in us, He finds the root of *Union* and *Communion*.

Pages could be written at this point. Perhaps your soul has been touched to investigate your Partner and your relationship with Him.

V. WHAT THIS BIBLE TRUTH TEACHES US TODAY.

The Holy Spirit is a Person, now.

The Holy Spirit is a Power—coming to indwell believers at Pentecost.

One cannot separate the Person from the power.

The Bible is a Book of similitudes and it teaches us through similes, metaphors, allegories, parables, types, symbols and emblems.

We have a Partnership if we are Christians. Our Partner is the Holy Spirit.

The *Communion* rises out of *Union* with Jesus Christ.

This lesson is most practical. Apply it to your life today.

YOUR NEXT ASSIGNMENT:

1. Read (not in chronological order purposely) Psalm 8:4-5; 68:17; 103:20; 104:4; Genesis 16:1-13; 21:17-19; 22:11-16; 31:11-13; Exodus 3:2-4; Jude 9; I Thessalonians 4:16; Colossians 1:16; Hebrews 1:4-14; 12:12; Matthew 25:31; 28:2-4; 22:30; Luke 20:35-36; Ephesians 3:10-11; 6:12; I Peter 1:10-12; 3:22; II Peter 2:10-11; Acts 5:19-20; 8:26; 27:23-25; Revelation 1:1; 1:20.

2. The subject of our next study will be "Angels." Read only the few Scriptures assigned.

3. Review your notes on the Holy Spirit and mark your Bible.

Lesson 13
"Holy Angels"

(Where lines are provided, look up the Scripture and write in the Scripture or its main truth.)

I. INTRODUCTION

The study of Angels reveals two hosts of spirit beings, namely: Holy Angels and Fallen Angels, referred to as demons. This study will deal with the "Holy Angels." The next lesson will cover the "Fallen Angels."

The fact of the existence of Angels can be found through the entire Word of God. Over 273 times in Scripture we find Angels carrying out the will and sovereign purpose of God.

The Hebrew and Greek translate the word "angel" as "messenger, ambassador, minister." The term "angel" is not a personal name, but a title describing the office. The word "angel" is always used in the masculine gender, though sex, in the human sense, is never ascribed to angels.

II. BASIC SCRIPTURES

Psalm 8:4-5; 68:17; 103:20; 104:4; Genesis 16:1-13; 21:17-19; 22:11-16; 31:11-13; Exodus 3:2-4; Jude 9; I Thessalonians 4:16; Colossians 1:16; Hebrews 1:4-14; 12:12; Matthew 25:31; 28:2-4; 22:30; Luke 20:35-36; Ephesians 3:10-11; 6:12; I Peter 1:10-12; 3:22; Acts 5:19-20; 8:26; 27:23-25; Revelation 1:1; 1:20; II Peter 2:10-11.

III. THE NUCLEUS OF THIS TRUTH

Angels constitute a created host, created by the Lord God. They were not brought into being by reproduction but were direct creations of God. They are immortal, infinite spirit beings. The hosts of Angels will remain the same numerically throughout their eternal existence, since they do not procreate. They are the servants and messengers of God. Angels are real. They are a holy subject. The Bible declares what they have done, are doing and shall do in the future. They are presently "sent forth to minister for them who shall be heirs of salvation" (Hebrews 1:14). This means that all Christians have two great gifts from God, the Father and God, the son:

- first, the Holy Spirit indwelling us.
- second, the Angels ministering for us.

The fact of the Holy Spirit indwelling us and the vast hosts of angels ministering for us should give encouragement to the weakest believer.

IV. THE GREAT TRUTH: "HOLY ANGELS"

A. THE CREATION OF ANGELS

1. Angels Were The First and Highest Created Beings.

a. They were present at creation of the earth (Job 38:4-7).

Write in verse 7: _____

_____

_____

The term "sons of God" in verse 7 are angels.

    b. This is affirmed in Colossians 1:16-17. Look up and underline in your Bible.

2. Their Own Creation Is Affirmed.

    a. In the great Psalm of praise to God for His creation, Psalm 148, you will notice "angels" and "hosts" mentioned before the "sun, moon, stars," etc.

    Write in Psalm 148:2: _____

_____

    Underline verse 5.

B. THE FORM AND NATURE OF ANGELS.

1. Angels are Spirits.

    a. This is confirmed in Hebrews 1:7: _____

_____

_____ (See Psalm 104:4).

    Also in Hebrews 1:14: _____

_____

_____

2. Angels Have Power To Become Visible.

    a. Angels have bodies of some kind and perform bodily acts, but not like our bodies. They appeared in the semblance of human form (Luke 1:28-29).

    Write in John 20:12: _____

_____

_____

    b. In Genesis 19:1-3 the angels were visible and Lot prepared food and they ate.

3. Angels Are Manifested In the Form of Man.

    a. Masculine pronouns are always used in referring to them (Matthew 28:2-6)

    b. Sex, in the human sense, is never ascribed to angels.

    Write in Matthew 22:30: _____

_____

_____

4. Angels Will Never Die.

    a. They never cease to exist. Angels will not grow old and pass away (Luke 20:35-36).

    b. The number, therefore, will never decrease—nor increase.

5. Angels Are Innumerable.

    a. Write in Hebrews 12:22: _____

_____

_____

    b. Look up and underline the following Scriptures:

        Daniel 7:10; Luke 2:13; Matthew 26:53.

    All of these Scriptures convey a sense of immensity beyond all human computation.

6. Angels Dwell In "The Heavenlies."

   a. Write in Revelation 5:11: _____

   _____

   _____

   b. Refer to Revelation 7:11; Psalm 103:19-21 and underline.

7. Angels Are Subject To God.

   a. See Psalm 103:20: _____

   _____

   b. Refer to Genesis 19:13 and underline Psalm 91:11.

8. Angels Possess Power and Might.

   a. Angels are not omnipotent, all powerful, but they do possess the power God has given them. One of the examples of power is recorded in II Kings 19:35: _____

   _____

   _____

   _____

   b. Look up Acts 5:19; 12:5-11; 12:23.

C. THE CLASSIFICATION OF ANGELS.

1. Scriptures Reveal Various Ranks and Functions of Angels.

   a. The Cherubim (Plural of Cherub).

   The first appearance of the Cherubim is in the Garden of Eden, where God had placed them to guard the way of the "Tree of Life" from fallen Adam (Genesis 3:24).

   On the Ark of the Covenant, golden replicas of the Cherubim were placed on each end of the Mercy Seat in the Holy of Holies where God dwelt with His people (Exodus 25:18-22; Psalm 80:1; Exodus 26:1; I Kings 6:23-25).

   The Mercy Seat, in its use, was a type of God's throne. Its divine holiness was guarded by the Cherubim.

   b. The Seraphim.

   This is a plural word appearing only once in Scripture. In Isaiah's vision, he saw the Seraphim—meaning "burners," surrounding the throne of God. Read Isaiah 6:1-8 and write in verse 6: _____

   _____

   _____

   These angels are expressive of that holiness which demands cleansing before serving.

2. Three Angels Are Named.

   a. Michael, the Archangel, is the head or the prince of angels. His name means "who is like unto God." He is the messenger of law and judgment.

   His name is mentioned five times in Scripture.

   In Daniel 10:13 Michael is called "one of the chief princes." Two other Scriptures in Daniel refer to Michael (Daniel 10:21; 12:1).

   Michael opposed Satan concerning the body of Moses (Jude 9). It is Michael who leads the angelic army in heaven against "that old serpent, called the Devil," and his angels (Revelation 12:7).

The voice of "the archangel" in I Thessalonians 4:16 will be the voice of Michael. There is only one archangel (the Scriptures do not speak of plural "archangels").

   b. Gabriel means "man of God" or "hero of God." He is named four times in Scripture. Gabriel was given important messages from God to be delivered to Daniel, Zacharias and Mary, the mother of Jesus.

- Underline Daniel 8:16.

- Gabriel delivered to Daniel a revelation of the vision of the "seventy weeks." Gabriel explained to Daniel the meaning of the vision. Turn to Daniel 9:20-27. Underline verses 21 and 23.

- God sent the message to Daniel by Gabriel; therefore, what is usually called "the seventy weeks of Daniel" should be "the seventy weeks of God."

- Gabriel delivered the message to Zacharias announcing the birth of John, the forerunner of Jesus. Write in Luke 1:19: _____

- Gabriel announced the birth of the Saviour to the virgin, Mary. Read Luke 1:26-35 and write in verse 26: _____

   c. Lucifer (the third named angel will be studied in the next lesson).

D. THE MINISTRY OF THE HOLY ANGELS.

   1. They Praise and Adore The Lord.

     a. Write in Hebrews 1:6: _____

     b. Read and underline Isaiah 6:3; Revelation 5:11-12.

   2. They Reveal God's Will To Man.

     a. Underline Luke 1:11-13 and Acts 1:9-11.

     b. Write in Hebrews 2:2: _____

   3. They Are Ministering To the Saints of God.

     a. Write in Hebrews 1:14: _____

     b. Underline I Kings 19:5-7; Acts 10:3-7.

   4.   They Encourage the Child of God.

     a. Underline Acts 27:23-24.

     b. Read Acts 12:5-15 and write in verse 7: _____

    c. Write in Acts 5:19-20: _____

_____

_____

5. They Are Celestial Spectators.

    a. Write in Luke 12:8-9: _____

_____

_____

_____

    b. Underline I Corinthians 4:9.

6. They Rejoice When One Is Saved.

    Write in Luke 15:10: _____

_____

_____

7. They Care For the Wellbeing of Believers.

    a. Underline Psalm 34:7 and Psalm 91:11.

    b. Underline Daniel 6:22.

    c. Write in Matthew 18:10: _____

_____

_____

8. They Convey and Confirm the Word.

    a. Write in Galatians 3:19: _____

_____

    b. Underline Hebrews 2:2.

(We could not mention all the ministeries of angels because of space.).

E. ANGELS AND THE EARTHLY MINISTRY OF JESUS.

    (Because of space limitations we shall list only the events.)

    1. His Life Was Seen of Angels (I Timothy 3:16).

    2. Angels Desired to Understand Secret of So Great Salvation (I Peter 1:10-12).

    3. Gabriel Announced His Birth (Luke 1:31-33).

    4. An Angel Assured Joseph of God's Purpose (Matthew 1:18-25).

    5. Angels Announce His Birth (Luke 2:10-11 and Hebrews 1:6).

    6. Angels Attended Christ In Temptation (Matthew 4:1-11).

    7. Angels Attended Christ In Gethsemane (Luke 22:39-44).

    8. No Angel Ministered at the Crucifixion (Jesus had to bear the full penalty and agony for our sin. He could have no help. He must drink the cup alone).

    9. Angels Announced the Resurrection of Christ (Matthew 28:5-7).

    10. Angels Attended His Ascension (Acts 1:10-11).

F. ANGELS AND THE ENDTIME.

    1. Angels Shall Exalt the Lamb of God (Revelation 5:11-12).

2. Angels Shall Accompany Christ At His Coming (Matthew 25:31; II Thessalonians 1:7).

3. Seven Angels In Presence of God (Revelation 8:2).

4. The Seven Angels Are Given Trumpets of Judgment (Revelation 8 and 9).

5. The Seven Angels With The Vials of God's Wrath (Revelation 15:5-8).

6. Michael and His Angels Fight The Devil and His Angels (Revelation 12:7-12).

7. The Angel and The Everlasting Gospel (Revelation 14:6-7).

8. An Angel Announces the Fall of Babylon (Revelation 14:8).

9. An Angel Announces Doom of Followers of the Antichrist (Revelation 14:9-11).

10. The Vision of Armageddon (Revelation 14:14-20).

11. The Holy Angels Shall Worship God (Revelation 7:11-12).

G. "THE ANGEL OF THE LORD"—THE PRE-INCARNATE CHRIST.

1. **There is a Being of majesty spoken of as "the Angel of Lord"—distinct from other angelic beings.** This "Angel of the Lord" is the Pre-Incarnate Christ—called a "Theophany." "Theophany" means "God—to appear."

Jesus, the Incarnate Christ of the New Testament, is seen throughout Scripture in types, figures and as the "Angel of the Lord" (Jehovah).

2. **Many Scriptures Mention "The Angel of The Lord" (Jehovah).**

   a. He appeared to Hagar (Genesis 16:7-14).

   b. He appeared to Abraham and is called Lord six times (Genesis 18).

   c. He appeared to Abraham (Genesis 22:11-18).

   d. He appeared to Jacob at Peniel (Genesis 32:24-32).

   e. He appeared to Moses in the burning bush (Exodus 3:2-6).

   f. He appeared to Joshua (Joshua 5:13-15).

   g. He appeared to Gideon (Judges 6:11-23).

   h. Compare Exodus 17:2-7 and 23:20-21 with I Corinthians 10:9 and 10:4.

(These are only a few of the Scriptures indicating the "Angel of Jehovah.")

V. WHAT THIS BIBLE TRUTH TEACHES US TODAY.

There are many in our day who deny the existence of angels—as did the Sadducees in the time of Christ. There might be some who deify the office of angels, as did the Essenes.

The ministry of guidance and intercession and strength in our hearts (all who belong to Christ) was never assigned to angels. The Holy Spirit abides in us and Jesus is the only mediator between God and man.

Angels minister to all the heirs of salvation. Jesus could have called 12 legions (72,000) of angels (Matthew 26:53). Angels work for us and with us. The Holy Spirit works in us.

Remember Hebrews 1:14 when in doubt concerning angels.

YOUR NEXT ASSIGNMENT:

1. The Scripture will cover "Fallen Angels," the Devil and his angels. The Scriptures are listed in the order of our study.

   Read Isaiah 14:12-15; Ezekiel 28:15-17; Luke 10:18; Genesis 3:1-19; Job 1:6-12; I Samuel 18:10; I Chronicles 21:1; II Chronicles 11:15; Deuteronomy 18:10-12; I John 3:12; Jude 6-9; Matthew 2:13-16; 4:1-11; 5:1-13; 16:23; Luke 22:3; Ephesians 2:2; 6:12; Acts 5:3,16; I Thessalonians 2:18; II Timothy 3:1-9; 4:3-4; I Timothy 4:1; Matthew 25:41; II Thessalonians 2:9; II Peter 2:4; Revelation 12:7-12; 16:13-16; 19:20; 20:1-3; 20:7-10.

2. Review your notes on this lesson.

3. Mark your Bible where new truths are learned.

Lesson 14
"Satan and His Angels" — Part I

GREAT
TRUTHS
OF THE
BIBLE

(Where lines are provided, look up the Scripture and write in the Scripture or its main truth.)

I. INTRODUCTION

When we study a subject such as Satan and his angels, also called demons, we must realize that Satan's best and most unique work is to convince people that he does not exist. Satan will do all he can to keep the author from writing this lesson. Observe for yourself the ways and the number of times your attention is drawn from this study.

Satan does exist as the leader of the fallen angels. Jesus spoke of "the devil and his angels," identifying them together. The Bible records for us the names, titles, origin, works, power and the limitation of Satan and his cohorts. In the very beginning of the history of man, we see Satan in defiance of God and in harrassment of man; but we know that in the end Satan shall be utterly and forever destroyed.

II. BASIC SCRIPTURES:

Isaiah 14:12-15; Ezekiel 28:15-17; Luke 10:18; Genesis 3:1-19; Job 1:6-12; I Samuel 18:10; I Chronicles 21:1; II Chronicles 11:15; Deuteronomy 18:10-12; I John 3:12; Jude 6-9; Matthew 2:13-16; 4:1-11; 5:1-13; 16:23; Luke 22:3; Ephesians 2:2; 6:12; Acts 5:3, 16; I Thessalonians 2:18; II Timothy 3:1-9; 4:3-4; I Timothy 4:1; Matthew 25:41; II Thessalonians 2:9; II Peter 2:4; Revelation 12:3-12; 16:13-16; 19:20; 20:1-3; 20:7-10.

III. THE NUCLEUS OF THIS TRUTH

The subject of Satan and the fallen angels appears prominently in Scripture. The Scriptures reveal Satan and his angels as a personal, corruptive and evil force in the affairs of man.

Satan and the fallen angels should be studied as one subject because they were one in their rejection of God. If Satan had never become Satan, there would have been no fallen angels (demons).

This sinister force is revealed to us progressively in Scripture, becoming more numerous and more defined as the prophecies of Christ are given—and as He appears as the Incarnate Christ. The battle between Christ and Satan started back in Genesis 3:15 and continues to this day.

To know the truth will make us free. We must be aware of all the truths of God. *Next to knowing the Lord Jesus and His saving grace,* we must know the truth *concerning Satan.* He is like "a roaring lion, seeking whom he may devour" (I Peter 5:8).

The Christian's warfare is three fold: the *world,* the *flesh* and the *devil.*

IV. THE GREAT TRUTH: *"SATAN AND HIS ANGELS"* PART I
A. THE ORIGIN OF SATAN.

1. Satan Was A Created Being.

a. Satan was created as the greatest of all the angelic hosts

(Ezekiel 28:15). He was given the heavenly title, "Lucifer, son of the morning" which is symbolic of his estate in heaven (Isaiah 14:12).

b. Through Isaiah, God addressed him by his heavenly title, "Lucifer." Through Ezekiel, God addressed him by the earthly title, "King of Tyrus," symbolizing the lowest depth of moral depravity. These titles express the highest of all creative power and the lowest depth of pomp and pride as that of Tyre.

c. In Ezekiel 28:12-15, God goes beyond the King of Tyre to speak to Satan. God indirectly addressed Satan in Genesis 3:14-15 and in Matthew 16:23. Also, in Isaiah 14:12. No person could possibly be referred to in either Isaiah or Ezekiel.

d. So, Satan was "Lucifer, son of the morning." Lucifer means "day star, light bearer" (Isaiah 14:12). He was "full of wisdom and perfect in beauty" and he had "been in Eden the garden of God" and was told "thou art the anointed cherub that covereth" (Ezekiel 28:12-15).

2. Satan's Unfallen State.

a. The state of Lucifer, before his fall, is described in Ezekiel 28:12-15. Underline verse 12 in your Bible.

Write in Ezekiel 28:15: _You were blameless in your ways from the day you were created till wickedness was found in you—_

b. He was the "cherub that covereth" indicating he was overlooking the heavenly throne of God.

He was "perfect in thy ways from the day that thou was created (till—." In that little work "till," God opens the subject of iniquity, sin, rebellion and pride.

c. God created all angels, including Lucifer. He made Lucifer superior in every way—in wisdom, beauty, in authority, anointed, perfect.

Therefore, *God did create the angel, Lucifer*, but through the sin of pride, *Lucifer became Satan*.

B. THE SIN AND FALL OF SATAN.

1. What Changed Lucifer into the Devil?

a. Lucifer, "the anointed cherub," became Satan by introducing the original sin into the universe: *pride*.

b. In Isaiah 14:13-14, the sin is given in detail. Notice the words, "I will," in the two verses:
—"I will ascend into heaven—"
—"I will exalt my throne above the stars of God—"
—"I will sit upon the mount of the congregation—"
—"I will ascend above the heights of the clouds—"
—"I will be like the most High."

c. Lucifer became Satan by choosing *his own will* above the will of God.

When Lucifer said, "I will," sin began.

Question: Where did sin originate?

Answer: In heaven, in the heart of Lucifer.

2. The Fall of Satan.

a. God determined the sentence. Whether angel or man, the creature is created to be God-centered. Lucifer was capable of wrong when he became self-centered.

b. The sentence of God was, "thou has sinned: therefore I will cast thee as profane out of the mountain of God: I will destroy thee, O covering cherub—" (Ezekiel 28:16). "How art thou fallen from heaven, O Lucifer, son of the morning! how art thou cut down to the ground—" (Isaiah 14:12).

c. We are a part of that fall when we say, "I will" and not "God's will."

d. Jesus said, "I beheld Satan fall from heaven" (Luke 10:18).

C. THE NAMES AND TITLES OF SATAN.

1. Satan, meaning "Adversary."
See I Chronicles 21:1 and I Peter 5:8.

2. Devil, the "Slanderer."
Write in Revelation 12:9: _The great dragon was hurled down, the ancient serpent called the devil, or Satan who leads the whole world astray._

3. Beelzebub, the "Prince of Demons."
Underline Matthew 12:24 in your Bible.

4. Belial, the "Low One."
In the margin of your Bible, write in the word "Satan" by II Corinthians 6:15.

5. That Old Serpent.
Look up Genesis 3:15 and Revelation 12:9.

6. God of this World.
Underline II Corinthians 4:4 in your Bible.

7. Prince of this World.
Write in John 12:31: _Now this is the time for judgement on this world, now the Prince of the world be driven out._

8. Prince of the Power of the Air.
Write in Ephesians 2:2: _in which you used to live when you followed the ways of this world and the ruler of the Kingdom of the Air_

9. Dragon.
See Revelation 20:2 and underline the name.

10. Angel of Light.
Write in II Corinthians 11:14: _____

_____

11. Accuser of the Brethren.
Refer to Revelation 12:10.

12. Father of Lies.
Underline John 8:44 in your Bible.

(There are more names for Satan than have been listed. His character is revealed in the names and titles given to him.)

D. THE SPHERE OF SATAN'S ACTIVITY.

1. He Has Access to the Throne of God.

a. Write in Job 1:6: _____
_____Satan was present before the Lord again (Job 2:1).

b. He still has access to the throne of God. In the last part of Revelation 12:10 a loud voice said, "for the accuser of our brethren is cast down, who accused them day and night."

2. He Has Access to the Earth.

a. "The Lord said unto Satan, 'Whence comest thou?' Then Satan answered the Lord and said, 'From going to and fro in the earth, and from walking up and down in it' " (Job 1:7; 2:2).

b. Satan appeared in the garden of Eden in the form of a serpent. Satan's unholy ambition was to strike back at God by defeating God's eternal purpose in man.

Satan deceived Eve, and Adam followed in the fatal choice. Sin entered the heart of man. This is known as "the fall of man" (Genesis 3:1-19).

God spoke of His plan of redemption (Genesis 3:15). This is the first direct prophecy of Jesus, the Seed of woman.

c. Another example of Satan's access to the earth is found in I Chronicles 21:1, "And Satan stood up against Israel, and provoked David to number Israel."

d. Satan has access as prince of the power of the air (Ephesians 2:2). He rules the darkness of this world and wickedness in high places (Ephesians 6:12).

E. WHAT SATAN DOES.

1. Satan Tempts People to Sin.

a. From Genesis 3:15 until Matthew 4, Satan's goal was to thwart the plan of God. In Matthew 4 Satan came face to face with Jesus. Satan had his chance to test or tempt the Master (Matthew 4:1-11).

The two were not strangers. They had known each other since the creation of Lucifer (angels were created—Jesus was the Creator).

Jesus defeated Satan in the three testings and the devil left Him (verse 11).

b. Satan entered Judas Iscariot (Luke 22:3).

c. Read about Ananias and Sapphira (Acts 5:1-11). Write in verse 3: _____

_____

2. Satan Deceives the World.

a. "The god of this world hath blinded the minds of them—" (II Corinthians 4:4). He blinds the mind.

b. Satan removes the Word from hearts (Matthew 13:19).

c. Satan traps men—"the snare of the devil" (II Timothy 2:26), "the wiles of the devil" (Ephesians 6:11), and "the devil . . . seeking whom he may devour" (I Peter 5:8).

3. Satan Hinders the Work of God.

a. He opposed Paul's ministry. Write in I Thessalonians 2:18: _____

_____

b. Satan uses Godly actions to his advantage if allowed. Write in II Corinthians 2:11: _____

_____

_____

c. Satan sifts the servants of God.

Write in Luke 22:31: _____

_____

_____

d. Satan sows tares among the people of God.
   Write in Matthew 13:38, 39: _____

_____

_____

e. Satan can constantly cause problems for the servant of the Lord.
   Write in Paul's testimony in II Corinthians 12:7: _____

_____

_____

F. SATAN'S LIMITATIONS.

1. Satan is Not Omnipotent (all powerful).

a. Satan is limited in power by God. He does have power, but he is not all powerful. In Job 1 and 2, the great revelation is not the power of Satan, but the *limitation* of his power. Satan cannot force people to sin. He can tempt, coerce, entice, but he has no power to force transgression.

b. Read Job 2:6. God limits Satan's power. Underline Job 1:22.

2. Satan is Not Omniscient (all knowing).

a. Satan is wise, but not as wise as God; he is not all knowing. He knows the ones to attack, hurt and afflict.

b. Write in I Peter 5:8: _____

_____

Read Luke 22:31 and read the words of Jesus to Simon Peter concerning Satan.

3. Satan is Not Omnipresent (everywhere present).

a. Satan cannot be in more than one place at a time. When he was with Jesus, he was nowhere else. When he left Jesus, it is recorded (Matthew 4:11).

b. Since Satan cannot be everywhere, he has his agents, demons, dispatched at his pleasure. He does have a kingdom of his own. Jesus spoke of that Satanic kingdom (Matthew 12:26).

V. WHAT THIS BIBLE TRUTH TEACHES US TODAY.

Now that we know the origin of Satan—his names, where he works and how he works—the only weapon to defeat him is the Word of God. Jesus used the Word (Matthew 4). Paul instructs us concerning the enemy and how to overcome him in our lives (Ephesians 6:12-17).

Satan is free on earth only in the permissive will of God. He cannot go beyond God's permission—but we must carry out our responsibilities as Christians. We should not give Satan a chance (Ephesians 4:27). We should always accept God's way of escape when tempted (I Corinthians 10:13).

Our Lord is Omnipotent, Omniscient and Omnipresent. He is always with us (I Peter 5:7). Also, I John 4:4.

YOUR NEXT ASSIGNMENT:

1. Read the Scriptures assigned in Lesson 14—plus Matthew 10:8; Luke 9:1-49; 10:17-20; Mark 16:17-18; Acts 8:7; 16:16-18; 19:12-17; Mark 1:23-28; Matthew 8:28-31; I John 2:16-18.

2. This lesson has primarily dealt with Satan, the Devil. Review your notes on this subject.

3. Mark your Bible where new truths are learned.

Lesson 15
"Satan and His Angels"—Part II

(Where lines are provided, look up the Scripture and write in the Scripture or its main truth.)

I. INTRODUCTION

We have studied the "Holy Angels" in Lesson 13 and "Satan" in Lesson 14. Now, we come to a more thorough study of "Satan and His Angels"—the fallen angels.

This lesson shall deal with all of us—where we are, what we have felt in the past, what we face each day because Satan is always trying to entrap us. The person who knows Christ has sufficient strength to overcome Satan because "greater is He that is in you, than he that is in the world" (I John 4:4). This does not eliminate the temptation which is ever present, appealing to the carnal nature.

The person who does not know Christ as Lord and Savior is constantly seeking the things of this world. "All that is in the world, the lust of the flesh, the lust of the eyes, and the pride of life, is not of the Father, but is of the world" (I John 2:16). They are open to the power of Satan and his emissaries.

II. BASIC SCRIPTURES:

All the Scriptures assigned in Lesson 14 plus Matthew 10:8; Luke 9:1-49; 10:17-20; Mark 16:17-18; Acts 8:7; 16:16-18; 19:12-17; Mark 1:23-28; Matthew 8:28-31; I John 2:16-18.

III. THE NUCLEUS OF THIS TRUTH

The fallen angels are the servants of Satan, the old Devil. The word "devil" is best translated *"demon."* There is only one Devil and he is the leader of his army of demons. Demon (devil) possession does take place in our day (I Timothy 4:1). The only solution to such a malady is Jesus Christ. The demons know Him and recognize His authority (Matthew 8:28-32).

The fallen angels serve the Devil, and they are unclean, seductive, evil spirits called demons.

IV. THE GREAT TRUTH: *"SATAN AND HIS ANGELS"* PART II

A. THE FALL OF ANGELS

1. There Are Two Classes of Fallen Angels.

    a. The fallen and chained angels (II Peter 2:4; Jude 6).

        (1).These are the angels who sinned. God did not spare them but cast them down to "Tartarus" (pit of darkness) where they are reserved unto judgment. They are bound in chains.

        Write in II Peter 2:4: _____

_____

Write in Jude 6: _____

_____

_____

(2). Some scholars assert that the sin of this group of fallen angels refers back to Genesis 6:4. They contend that the "sons of God" were "fallen angels." This intrusion into the human sphere produced a race of giants by "the daughters of men."

(3). There is great difficulty in accepting that view. Angels were created a complete and perfect order. They were not created with the ability of reproduction (Matthew 22:30). To be capable of changing their nature (one order to another order of created beings at will) has no support in the Scriptures.

The reference in Genesis 6:2-6 has to do with the breakdown of the separation of the godly line of Seth by intermarriage with the godless line of Cain.

The context of Genesis 6:2-6 states that God "saw the wickedness of *man*—and it repented (sorry at heart) the Lord that He had made *man on the earth* and it grieved Him at His heart."

(4). The argument that angels appeared in human form in the Old Testament does not change the meaning of this subject. The angels appearing in human form were always *holy angels*. They were sent and given form by His sovereign power—for His sovereign purpose. God made their presence visible and understandable to man.

(5). Whichever view one might take does not change the message of God. It is obvious that Satan attempted to corrupt the race so that the Messiah could not come to redeem man. God salvaged a remnant and a godly line was preserved (Genesis 6:7-8).

(6). All the theories and arguments make little difference to the fact; some fallen angels, according to II Peter 2:4 and Jude 6, are already reserved awaiting judgment that shall come upon all evil demons, fallen angels.

b. The fallen and free angels (Ephesians 6:12).

(1). These are the fallen angels who are free to do the work of the Devil. The Devil is their leader. This group fell with the group which was cast into the "pit of darkness." All of them were cast out of heaven with Lucifer, the leader who became Satan.

(2). When the work of Satan and his angels is mentioned, remember that he is the "prince of this world" (Ephesians 6:12, John 12:31).

B. THE POWER OF THE FALLEN AND FREE ANGELS.

1. **Their Names Denote Their Work.**

a. The fallen and free angels are called "demons," meaning "knowing" or "to know." The word in the King James Version is erroneously rendered "devils." There is only one Devil but there is a great multitude of demons (Matthew 7:22).

b. "Satan" is a Hebrew word meaning "adversary." "Devil" is a Greek word meaning "accuser" and is not used in the Old Testament.

c. They are also known as:
—"familiar spirits" (Leviticus 19:31; 20:6).
—"unclean spirits" (Mark 1:23-27).
—"evil spirits" (Luke 7:21).
—"seducing spirits" (I Timothy 4:1).
—"foul spirits" (Mark 9:25).

2. Their Activities Denote Their Power.

a. The demons increase the power of Satan against the church (all Christians). Satan is the "prince of the power of the air" (Ephesians 2:2).

b. The demons increase the power of Satan to control principalities, powers; and they are the rulers of darkness. Their abode is in the heavenly (high) places (Ephesians 6:12).

c. They possess the bodies of individuals. Read the entire story of one possessed by demons (Mark 5:1-9). Notice the power—"no man could bind him even with chains." A person possessed by demons has superhuman power.

d. They possess people and cause physical maladies (Matthew 9:32; 12:22; Mark 9:25-29).

e. They possess people to lust, murder and lie (John 8:44).

f. The demons always speak through the mouths of those they possess (Mark 5:6-12).

Write in Mark 5:9: _____

_____

_____

g. They are the force behind idolatry (Acts 16:16). In this passage, the "spirit of divination" is actually "the spirit of Python," an idol.

h. All of the terms used in Scripture concerning the work of demons are too lengthy to be covered in this lesson. Some of the terms are becoming popular again in our day:
- *Sorcery* (Acts 8:9-11).
- *Witchcraft* (Galatians 5:20).
- *Necromancy* (Isaiah 8:19; Deuteronomy 18:10-12).
- *Astrologers* (Daniel 1:20; 2:2; 4:7).
- *Divination* (Ezekiel 13:6-7; Acts 16:16).
- *Magician* (Daniel 1:20; Exodus 7:11,22).

The word in Galatians 5:20 ("witchcraft" in the authorized version) is the Greek word "pharmakeia." The use of "magic potions" (not to heal) to obtain a "high" or to alter minds is more prevalent than ever. The same word "pharmakeia" means "sorcery." We would call them today "fortune-tellers," abuse of the mind with drugs, people who claim to have magical powers.

The word "necromancy" means "one who converses with the dead." Deuteronomy 18:9-12 should be read here.

These terms and others are in headlines in our time. Even television programs with a "diviner" talking with the dead relatives of viewers.

All of this is demonic and the work of Satan. Do not underestimate the power of fallen and free angels.

C. THE KINGDOM OF SATAN VERSUS CHRIST.

1. Satan Has a Kingdom.

    a. Jesus spoke of the kindom of Satan.

        Write in Matthew 12:26: _____

    b. Paul referred to "the rulers of darkness" when he spoke of the power of Satan.

        Write in Ephesians 6:12: _____

        _____

2. The Subjects of the Kingdom of Satan.

    a. The demons (fallen angels) are his subjects. Jesus mentions them in Matthew 25:41. Underline in your Bible.

    b. The unregenerated (unsaved) human beings. In Matthew 13:38 Jesus said, "the tares are the children of the wicked one."

        Jesus was very specific in the matter. Underline John 8:44 in your Bible. This verse speaks of the fatherhood of Satan (the Devil). In contrast, John 1:12 speaks of the fatherhood of God.

3. Satan and His Demons Are Terrified of Christ.

    a. Satan and his forces are in control of this present world appearing as an "angel of light" (II Corinthians 11:14).

    b. The grand news is—*Satan was judged at the Cross.* Looking toward the cross, Jesus declared doom for Satan.

        Write in John 12:31: _____

        _____

        Underline John 12:32-33. This passage tells how Jesus was to die.

    c. "The demons believe and tremble" (James 2:19).

4. Demons Recognize Christ as the Son of God and as Their Future Judge.

    a. Write in Matthew 8:29: _____

        _____

        _____

    b. Write in Mark 1:24: _____

        _____

        _____

    c. Demons knew Jesus. Write in Mark 3:11: _____

        _____

        _____

        Underline Mark 3:22 in your Bible.

    d. The demons knew Christ because they had known Him in eternity past. They had been in His presence until their fall. Even though these Scriptures seem to indicate to us that the demons were meeting Christ for the first time, they were in fact *declaring His divine authority*.

D. THE DOOM OF FALLEN ANGELS—DEMONS.

1. They Shall Be Judged.

a. The fallen angels, demons, shall be judged. Scripture indicates that they shall be judged in "the great day." This "great day" is the day of the Lord (Isaiah 2:9-22). Refer to Jude 6.

b. The judgment takes place because the "saints," the "saved ones," shall judge the angels with Christ.

Write in I Corinthians 6:3: _____

2. **Satan is Judged.**

a. Satan shall be judged and cast into the "lake of fire" (Revelation 20:10). The leader doomed.

b. The fallen angels, even those held in chains, are "reserved unto judgment" (Refer to the last part of II Peter 2:4).

(Note: This shall be covered in more detail in lessons on the "endtime" and "judgments" near the end of this study.)

V. WHAT THIS BIBLE TRUTH TEACHES US TODAY.

Demonology is a reality today. Yes, it existed in the days of the Old Testament but it still exists in the form of witchcraft, fortune-tellers, astologers, drug abuse, lust, idols and a thousand more names.

The material published on these subjects is big business. The best way to avoid entrapment is to avoid the appearance of these things—books, psychic movies, games, fortune-tellers, occult groups, astrology and the like. Satan works through these demonic devices.

Unbelievers in Christ are open to these influences. The Christian should have spiritual discernment in reference to these things. The babe in Christ, the weakest of believers, can have the provisions made by Christ Jesus. A few of the Scriptures you should remember are: I Peter 5:8; I John 5:18; Ephesians 6:10-17; 2:2-7.

When encountering these demonic objects, the only effective way to deal with the encounter is by using the name of Jesus Christ (James 2:19; Matthew 8:29).

YOUR NEXT ASSIGNMENT:

1. Read Genesis 1:26-31; 2:7-25; 3:1-20; John 3:6; I Thessalonians 5:23; I Corinthians 15:22-53; Philippians 3:21; Romans 5:12-21; 8:7-8; Hebrews 9:27; II Peter 1:4.

2. This lesson has dealt with a subject that is prevalent in our day and shall become more so in the last days. Satan and demons are realities we must deal with in and out of the church. Review your notes on this lesson.

3. Mark your Bible where new truths are learned.

Lesson 16
"Man, His Creation And Fall"

(Where lines are provided, look up the Scripture and write in the Scripture or its main truth.)

I. INTRODUCTION

The entire Word of God has been inspired, written and preserved just for man. It is God's message to man. It contains all of the doctrines (teachings) of God. Every truth of Scripture is related to man; therefore, it is necessary to consider what the Bible says about man.

In the scientific world, this study would be called Anthropology. The word comes from the Greek work "anthropos" meaning "man." Anthropology is "the science of man's origin." The only true source of study about the origin of man is the Bible. Therein we find the source of the creation of man, his fall and God's wonderful provision of redemption.

This subject has become a battleground in schools and even in some theological circles. Our purpose is not to argue the point. There is only one source of truth which is factual and accurate in every respect, and it is the Bible. Set aside preconceived ideas on this subject. Then, open your heart and soul to what God has to say in His Word. The Holy Spirit will teach you "all truth" as you study.

II. BASIC SCRIPTURES:

Genesis 1:26-31; 2:7-25; 3:1-20; John 3:6; I Thessalonians 5:23; I Corinthians 15:22-53; Philippians 3:21; Romans 5:12-21; 8:7-8; Hebrews 9:27; II Peter 1:4.

(There are so many Scriptures on this subject. Time nor space would allow study of all of them. Look in your concordance under "man" for more references.)

III. THE NUCLEUS OF THIS TRUTH

Jesus said, "And fear not them which kill the *body,* but are not able to kill the *soul*—the very hairs of your head are all numbered—ye are of more value than many sparrows" (Matthew 10:28, 30, 31). Jesus placed emphasis on man, his value, his body and soul, and on God's awareness of man to the smallest detail. Jesus was "made *flesh*" (John 1:14); "and was made in the likeness of *men*; and being found in fashion as a *man*" (Philippians 2:7-8). Jesus never went through any phase of evolving into a man—rather, quite the opposite. He descended, came down, to become a man. To evolve means "development, growth, advance." Since Jesus is our supreme example in all things, we must begin with Him. He taught men as men who had a body, a mind, an intellect. Jesus was the Creator (Colossians 1:16). He created all things "after his kind." You will never find in Scripture a record of animal becoming man. David said, "I am fearfully and wonderfully made" (Psalm 139:14).

IV. THE GREAT TRUTH: *"MAN, HIS CREATION AND FALL"*

A. THE CREATION OF MAN.

1. Man is the Crowning Work of God in Creation.

a. Man was created by a direct act of God.

To "create" means to make something out of nothing. The *general* account of the creation of man is stated in Genesis 1:26-27.

b. God the Father, God the Son and God the Holy Spirit created man. Notice the times "us" and "our" are used in Genesis 1:26. The Trinity in unity.

c. The Trinity is One. "So God created man in His (singular) own image, in the image of God created He (singular) him; male and female created He (singular) them" (Genesis 1:27).

d. The *general* account of the creation of man in Genesis 1:26-27 is a double trilogy. In verse 26 the Trinity is mentioned three times. "Let *us* make man in *our* image, after *our* likeness . . ."

In verse 27 the word "create" is used three times.

e. The *particular* account of the creation of man is given in Genesis 2:7, 21-23. This is not another creation in Chapter 2, only a more particular and detailed account of how God made man and woman. Underline in your Bible Genesis 2:21-23.

Write in Genesis 2:7: *The LORD God formes the man from the dust of the groun And breathed into his nostrils the breath of life And the man became a living being*

2. The Original Image of Man.

a. In Genesis 1:26 man was made in the image and likeness of God. What does that imply?

—"image" is the representation—*the moral capacity."*
—"likeness" is "the character—*the spiritual resemblance."*

b. God has always had a form in which He manifests Himself. Yet the Bible says God is Spirit (John 4:24); God is invisible (Colossians 1:15).

(1). Then how does God manifest Himself?

God was made manifest in His Old Testament appearances known as "theophanies." These were the pre-incarnate appearances of God the Son (Isaiah 6:1).

(2). God manifested Himself especially in Jesus Christ in the flesh (incarnate). In this form man saw God (John 1:14). Write in the last sentence of John 14:9: "He that hath _____ *You may ask for anything in My name & I will do it*

Underline in your Bible Philippians 2:6-7.

c. Adam, then, *was* made in the form and image of Christ. Christ was *not* made in the image or form of Adam. (This is a vital truth.)
Write in Romans 5:14: *Nevertheless death reives*

94

From the time of Adam to the time of Moses even over those who did not sin by breaking a command, as did Adam, who was a pattern of one to come.

(Note the last phrase of that verse: Adam "is the figure of Him that was to come.")

3. The Threefold Nature of Man.

a. Man was created with a threefold nature. He was created a trinity, composed of *body, soul* and *spirit*. Therefore, man was made in the image of God and God is a Trinity.

Write in I Thessalonians 5:23: *May God Himself the God of Peace Sanctify you through & through. May your whole spirit, Soul and Body be kept blameless at the Coming of the Lord Jesus Christ*

Write in Hebrews 4:12: *For the word of God sharper than any double edged sword, it penetrates even to dividing Soul and Spirit Joints and Marrow, it judges the thoughts & attitudes of the heart.*

b. The Body. "The Lord God formed man of the dust of the ground" (Genesis 2:7). This was the formation of the body, the external, visible part of man. The body is the seat of the five senses—sight, smell, hearing, taste and touch.

The body is the means of "world-consciousness."

c. The Soul. ". . . and (God) breathed into his nostrils the breath of life; and man became a living soul" (Genesis 2:7). The soul is the seat of emotion, memory, affection, conscience and reason (Genesis 41:10; Mark 14:34).

Read and underline in your Bible Psalm 42:1-6.

The soul is the means of "self-consciousness."

The "heart" in Scripture is used almost synonymously with "soul" (Hebrews 10:22).

A thought of interest to most people is simply this fact: "God breathed into his nostrils the breath of life and man became a living soul." Now notice—the transfusion of the "breath of God" (Spirit) into the "formed man" (Body) produced a "soul." The union of the body and spirit caused man to become a living soul.

d. The Spirit. "the breath (spirit) of life" (Genesis 2:7). The spirit of man is the difference between man and all creatures (Hebrews 12:9). The spirit of man is that part of man which *knows.*

Write in I Corinthians 2:11: *For who Among men knows the thoughts of a man except the mans spirit within him, In the same way no one knows the thoughts of God except the spirit of God.*

The spirit is the deepest part of man. Within the spirit of man are the faculties of faith, hope, worship, prayer, adoration and reverence.

The spirit is the means of "God-consciousness."

B. MAN'S CONDITION BEFORE THE FALL.

1. Man Could Think—He Had Knowledge.

a. Adam was made a man with reasoning powers. He had an intellect—he could think. He was not an infant. He was an adult and he gave names to all the animals that came from the hand of God.

95

Write in Genesis 2:20: _So the Man gave names to All the livestock, the birds of the Air and all the beasts of the field._

b. Man was made with the ability to speak, to express what his mind conceived.

2. The Responsibilities Placed on Man.

a. He was to "be fruitful and multiply"—"replenish the earth and subdue it"—"have dominion over the fish, fowl and every living thing that moveth on the earth" (Genesis 1:28).

Eve was named by Adam. He named her after they fell. Her name means "mother of all living" and indicates Adam's faith in God and God's promises (Genesis 3:20).

Genesis 2:21-23 records how God made a "help meet" for Adam. God made Eve without the help of a woman, as He had made Adam without either man or woman. In Genesis 3:15 He predicts Christ, made without the help of man. (You and I were made *only* by man and woman.) So, Adam and Eve had the responsibility of reproduction.

b. He was to be obedient to God. God placed one restriction upon Adam and Eve—only one. That is found in Genesis 2:17: _but you must not eat from the tree of knowledge of good & evil for when you eat of it you will surely Die_

The test was the test of obedience. The tree was not an "apple tree" but the tree "of the *knowledge* of good and evil."

c. Man was to keep the garden (Genesis 2:15). The employment was one of joy, not one of toil. There were no thorns and thistles, no cursed ground until *after* the fall (Genesis 3:17-18). In Genesis 1:29 and Genesis 2:16 the Lord told them they could eat of the herbs and fruits—in other words, green vegetables and fruit. They were vegetarians in the beginning. (Note: In Genesis 9:3, after the flood, Noah was told he could eat meat.)

The word "keep" in Genesis 2:15 also has the meaning of "guard" or "garrison." So, they were to "dress and to keep the garden." Needless to say, in the fall they lost the garden.

C. THE FALL OF MAN.

1. The One Requirement of God.

a. We have already seen that God placed one restriction upon Adam and Eve (Genesis 2:17). The first and natural question asked by most people is—"Why did God allow them to be tempted by Satan?" God made man (and angels) with a "free will" or "free choice." We are not puppets on a string.

b. God allowed the testing (even though He knew the outcome in His foreknowledge) of man to try him. Adam was created in innocence. Innocence is "void of sin" because it has never faced testing.

Righteousness is innocence that has been tested and has been victorious in the testing. Adam was to be *obedient*. His innocence was being tried and he failed the test.

2. Sin Entered by One Man—Adam.

a. Paul states the fact. Write in Romans 5:12: _____

Theofore just as sin entered the world through one man, sin And death through Sin And in this way Death Came to All men becouse All Sinned

b. Satan, in the form of a serpent, was the source of temptation (Genesis 3:1-6). Satan worked through Eve:

- by casting doubt on God's Word (Genesis 3:1).
- the first lie (Genesis 3:4).
- appealed to her pride (Genesis 3:5).

c. The fall is recorded in Genesis 3:6.

d. The results of the fall were *immediate* . In Genesis 3:7 man became self-conscious; in verse 10, shameful and fearful; in verse 17, condemned to live on cursed ground in sorrow and, verse 18, among thorns and thistles; and in verse 19, to sweat and labor.

In Genesis 3:7 their need for covering their nakedness was brought about by their disobedience.

In Genesis 3:8 we see separation: man hiding, God seeking. They knew good without the power to do it and they knew evil without the power to avoid it.

The sin was disobedience—read again Genesis 3:17.

3. The Fall of All Flesh.

a. Sin is in the bloodstream of humanity, placed there by one man, Adam.

Write in I Corinthians 15:22: *For As in Adam All die so in Christ All will be Made Alive, But each in his own turn*

b. All of us are born in Adam's nature.
Write in Romans 5:12: _____

Underline in your Bible Romans 3:23. Also, Romans 3:10 and Romans 3:19.

c. The sin nature is a part of us.
Write in Psalm 51:5: *Surely I was sinful at birth, Sinful from the time my mother Conceived me.*

d. We are dead spiritually unless the Second Adam (Jesus Christ) has been invited into our lives.
Write in Ephesians 2:1: *As For You, you were dead in your transgressions and Sins in which you used to live when you followed the ways of this world*

D. THE GRACE OF GOD.

1. How God Provided for All Mankind.

a. In Genesis 3:15 God promised a "Seed of woman." That Seed was Christ. At the point of departure by man, God supplied the need. Read Galatians 4:4.

b. In sin, Adam had faith in the promised Seed of Genesis 3:15 when he named his wife Eve "the mother of all living" (Genesis 3:20).

c. Jesus, the Redeemer, was made flesh and took our sins upon Himself at the cross. He was the Second or Last Adam (I Corinthians 15:45, 47).

2. Man Must Accept God's Gift to Escape the Penalty of Sin.

   a. When we accept Christ, we are new creatures in Christ (II Corinthians 5:17; John 3:16).

   b. We are saved by accepting Jesus (II Timothy 1:9).

   c. We have eternal life by accepting Him (John 5:24).

(Space limits us at this point. However, there will be a lesson on Salvation. We could not leave this lesson without mentioning the way of salvation.)

V. WHAT THIS BIBLE TRUTH TEACHES US TODAY

All of us, regardless of pedigree, are born in sin. We are sinners by nature. All of us stem from Adam. Sin is a part of the inherited nature. The only antidote for the poison of sin is faith in Jesus Christ. Most people think they are "good," and probably they are, but the question is not one of being good or bad. The question is: since "all have sinned," have they accepted God's plan of grace? Have you?

YOUR NEXT ASSIGNMENT:

1. Read Isaiah 14:12-15; Ezekiel 28:11-19; II Samuel 24:17; Psalm 51:5; Romans 3:23; 4:5; 5:12; 7:7; Galatians 5:19-21; Ephesians 2:2; 5:6; II Thessalonians 1:7-9; 2:4, 8, 12; Hebrews 12:6; Revelation 20:12, 14.

2. Review your notes on "Man, His Creation and Fall."

3. Mark your Bible where new truths are learned.

Lesson 17
"Sin"

GREAT
TRUTHS
OF THE
BIBLE

(Where lines are provided, look up the Scripture and write in the Scripture or its main truth.)

I. INTRODUCTION

The origin of sin was covered in Lesson 14. In that study we learned that sin originated in the heart and mind of an angel, Lucifer, son of the morning. The sin was pride—a desire to be above God. The sin brought God's judgment. "Thou hast sinned: therefore I will cast thee as profane out of the mountain of God. I will destroy thee, O covering cherub" (Ezekiel 28:16). The account of Lucifer and his fall is given in Ezekiel 28:15-17 and Isaiah 14:12-15. Jesus declared, "I beheld Satan fall from heaven" (Luke 10:18).

There was no sin before Lucifer. He became the Devil, Satan. This great deceiver used the form of a serpent to tempt the first human beings on earth. Sin entered the human race through deception.

There is a need to understand the mind of God in reference to sin. This can only be found in the Scriptures. We live in a permissive society. It is no longer popular to use the words "sin, lost, eternally doomed, depraved" because these terms are too strong for "good people." In the church, the Bible class, the private study of God's Word, we can never change the terminology of God to fit the so-called moral standards of society. Therefore, this will not be a popular study but a needed study in our time. The truth of God always helps, even though it may hurt.

II. BASIC SCRIPTURES:

Isaiah 14:12-15; Ezekiel 28:11-19; II Samuel 24:17; Psalm 51:5; Romans 3:23; 4:5; 5:12; 7:7; Galatians 5:19-21; Ephesians 2:2; 5:6; II Thessalonians 1:7-9; 2:4, 8, 12; Hebrews 12:6; Revelation 20:12, 14.

III. THE NUCLEUS OF THIS TRUTH

Most, if not all, people recognize the conflict between conscience and conduct. Man has a natural tendency to go astray, to think and act in a debasing way. There is the endless struggle to do good but evil is always present to distort, to lead astray. The conflict is real within the heart and soul.

Why the conflict between conscience and conduct? Something happened to the nature of man. It happened in the "fall of man" in Genesis 3. Since then, sin has been inherited. To inherit means "to receive from progenitors." We are born with a sin nature. If you doubt this, then answer the question: "Do you have to teach a child to do wrong?" Quite the opposite—you have to teach the child to do right.

Were this not true, the sacrifice for sin, paid by Christ on the cross, was unnecessary. Jesus came and died to impart a "new nature" to all who will believe.

People who do not understand the nature of sin are offended when someone speaks of them as sinners. Their defense is usually something like—"I'm a good person, pay my debts, attend church occasionally, good to my family and friends, good moral person—" and on and on they go. The question is not "Goodness." The question is, "have you been washed in the blood of the Lamb?" He gives a new nature, making all who come to Him realize that there is no goodness in man. He becomes the source of spiritual awareness and the good things done are done for Him and His glory.

This lesson is not about the "goodness" of "good people" but rather on "sin of all humanity."

IV. THE GREAT TRUTH: *"SIN"*

A. THE FACT OF SIN

1. The Origin of Sin.

   a. Sin originated with Satan (Isaiah 14:12-14).

   b. Sin entered the world through Adam.
   Write in Romans 5:12: _____
   _____

2. Sin is Universal.

   a. Sin was then, and is now, universal—Jesus alone excepted.
   Write in Romans 3:23: _____
   _____
   _____

   Also Galatians 3:22: _____
   _____

   b. Even nature proclaims the fact of sin.
   Write in Romans 8:22: _____
   _____

B. THE TRUE NATURE OF SIN.

1. The Seven Sides of Sin.

   a. Sin is *"transgression"* which is overstepping the law, the divine boundary. There was sin before the law, but no transgression (Joshua 7:11, 15). Underline the verses in your Bible. Refer to I John 3:4.

   b. Sin is *"iniquity"* which is an act inherently *wrong*—wrong morality (Colossians 3:5-9).
   Write in Mark 7:20: _____
   _____

   Underline the words of Jesus in Mark 7:21-23 in your Bible.

   c. Sin is *"disobedience"* which is rebellion against authority.
   Write in Ephesians 5:6: _____
   _____
   _____

   d. Sin is *"missing the mark"* which is a failure to meet the divine standard of God.
   Write in Romans 3:23: _____
   _____

   e. Sin is *"trespassing"* which is placing self-will into the sphere of divine authority, intruding on the will of God (Ephesians 2:1).
   Write in Matthew 6:14: _____
   _____

f. Sin is *"ungodliness."* The Scriptures are self-explanatory.
Write in Romans 4:5: _____

_____

_____

Also Romans 5:6: _____

_____

g. Sin is *"unbelief."* Write in Mark 9:24: _____

_____

_____

Other references (I John 5:10; Romans 3:3).
Write in Matthew 13:58: _____

_____

2. **What Sin Does To People.**

a. Sin causes a *distorted* view of spiritual things. Underline John 9:39. Write in Romans 7:19: _____

_____

b. Sin *corrupts* the soul. Underline in your Bible Romans 1:21-22.
Write in Romans 1:32: _____

_____

_____

c. Sin *blinds*. Write in Ephesians 4:18: _____

_____

_____

d. Sin *hardens the conscience*. Write in Ephesians 4:19: ___

_____

_____

We have listed only a few of the effects of sin. There are many others. List those that come to your mind.

C. THE EXTENT OF SIN.

1. **All Unrighteousness is Sin.**

a. A good definition of sin is simply, "all unrighteousness is sin," says God's Word.
Write in I John 5:17: _____

_____

b. There are none righteous (Psalm 14:1-3).
Write in Romans 3:10: _____

_____

2. **The Two Classes of Sin.**

a. The *open* sins—the sins committed openly, publicly, such as profanity, lying, theft, etc.
Write in Psalm 90:8: _____

_____

b. The *secret* sins—thought of in the secret chambers of the heart, such as envy, jealousy, lust, pride, hatred. The same verse (Psalm 90:8) reveals the secret sins openly in "the light of Thy countenance."

Write in Jeremiah 17:9: _____

_____

_____

3. **The Three Forms in which Sin Appears.**

a. Jesus presents the order of sin (Mark 7:21-23).

Write in Mark 7:21: _____

_____

b. The three forms of sin in that Scripture are:
- in human nature - "out of the heart";
- in the human mind - "evil thoughts";
- in human action - "adulteries, fornications, murders, thefts, etc."

c. In Mark 7:21-22, Jesus mentions 13 sins of the human heart. Jesus was talking to His disciples about the heart of man. The entire context should be read (Mark 7:14-23).

Write in Mark 7:23: _____

_____

4. **The Totality of Sin.**

a. All of man is sinful—his body, soul and spirit. Underline Romans 3:11-12 in your Bible. Also, Galatians 3:22.

b. All of us were born with a sin nature.

Write in Psalm 51:5: _____

_____

c. The sinful nature is like poison.

Write in Psalm 58:3-4: _____

_____

_____

D. THE WAGES OF SIN (THE PENALTY).

1. **The Wages of Sin is Something We Earn.**

a. The term "wages" means we work for an end result. In this life, for a paycheck, for fame, for worldly goods.

b. "The wages of sin is death"—(Romans 6:23). "Death" in Scripture never means "Annihilation." The meaning is "eternal death" (II Thessalonians 1:8-9).

c. "Destruction" (Matthew 7:13).

d. "Everlasting punishment" (Matthew 25:46).

e. "Condemned." Write in John 3:18: _____

_____

_____

2. **The Results of Sin by the Christian.**

a. God chastens His own. Write in Hebrews 12:6: _____

_____

_____

Eternal punishment is for the unbeliever. God deals with His own as a Father. A natural father only chastens his own children.

    b. The Christian should judge himself.

       Write in I Corinthians 11:31-32: _____

       _____

       _____

    c. Confession of sin is necessary for cleansing.

       Write in I John 1:9: _____

       _____

       _____

    Memorize the verse. It is the Christian's bar of soap.

E. THE ONLY REMEDY FOR SIN.

1. The Gospel of Jesus Christ.

    a. "For I am not ashamed of the Gospel of Christ; for it is the power of God unto salvation to everyone that believeth" (Romans 1:16).

    b. He, Jesus, paid the penalty for all sin. Underline I John 2:2 in your Bible.

2. Believe on the Lord Jesus Christ.

    a. Recall to your memory John 3:16. Have you believed?

    b. "The gift of God is eternal life through Jesus Christ, our Lord" (Romans 6:23b).

    (There will be a complete lesson on Salvation. Only a brief outline is given here in case one may accept Christ.)

V. WHAT THIS TRUTH TEACHES US TODAY

The crowning sin of all sins is to refuse the free gift of salvation through faith in Jesus Christ as Lord and Saviour. People are not lost because of sin, but because they will not surrender their hearts and lives to Christ.

There is a difference between "sin" and "sins." *Sin* is that tendency or disposition to sin inherited from Adam. *Sins* are the specific acts of sin that one commits as a result of the sin nature.

Jesus came to provide an atonement for *sin*, not for *sins*. He came to change the hearts of all who would accept Him. He gives to everyone who accepts Him a new nature—a nature to turn from the old life to a new life. Paul said, "Therefore if any man be in Christ, he is a new creation: old things are passed away; behold, all things are become new" (II Corinthians 5:17).

Paul states in a few verses the difference between the two Adams— "The first man Adam was made a living soul; the last Adam (Jesus) was made a quickening spirit" (I Corinthians 15:45). "The first man is of the earth, earthly: the second man is the Lord from heaven" (I Corinthians 15:47). Underline verse 48 in your Bible.

"For as in Adam all die, even so in Christ shall all be made alive" (I Corinthians 15:22).

We are not sinners because we sin—

We sin because we are sinners.

"Believe on the Lord Jesus Christ, and thou shalt be saved" (Acts 16:31).

YOUR NEXT ASSIGNMENT:

1. Read Genesis 3:15; 12:1-3; Matthew 1:21; John 3:3-8; 3:14-17;

Romans 5:8-9; 10:9; I Corinthians 1:18; II Corinthians 6:2; Ephesians 1;13; 2:5-8; I Thessalonians 5:9; II Thessalonians 2:13; Hebrews 2:14-15; 5:9; 9:28; I Peter 1:5-12; 4:13.

2. Review your notes on "Sin." Recall to your mind the Scriptures and truths that helped you.

3. Mark your Bible when the lesson indicates a passage to be underlined. Write in the margin of your Bible.

Lesson 18 "Salvation"

(Where lines are provided, look up the Scripture and write in the Scripture or its main truth.)

I. INTRODUCTION

Have you ever wondered why so many people are faithful to the work of the Lord week after week and even year after year? Most of the dear people who are faithful do so because they have been saved, and they want others to be won to Christ. Granted, a lot of "religious activity" has nothing to do with reaching people. In so many instances the group or person interested in winning someone to Christ is never known. That is the way most "soul winners" would prefer it to be in the first place.

Salvation of lost souls is the reason Jesus died, the reason He established the church, the reason He gave to the church His gifts of "apostles, prophets, evangelists, pastors and teachers" (Ephesians 4:11). These gifts were given to the church for the winning of the lost, then for growth of the new person in Christ and "for the maturing (perfecting) of the saints (saved ones) for the work of the ministry, for the edifying of the body of Christ" (Ephesians 4:12).

Salvation may be gained by one way, and one way only. The way is God's way and is the subject of this study.

II. BASIC SCRIPTURES:

Genesis 3:15; 12:1-3; Matthew 1:21; John 3:3-8; 3:14-17; Romans 1:16; 5:8-9; 10:9; I Corinthians 1:18; II Corinthians 6:2; Ephesians 1:13; 2:5-8; I Thessalonians 5:9; II Thessalonians 2:13; Hebrews 2:14-15; 5:9; 9:28; I Peter 1:5-12; 4:13.

III. THE NUCLEUS OF THIS TRUTH

Salvation is the work of God by which He saves man from the eternal doom of sin. In salvation He gives to man the riches of His grace which means eternal life now and forever. Salvation is the work of God and not a work of man for God.

Salvation is "the new birth." Jesus said to Nicodemus, "Ye must be born again" (John 3:3-7). The new birth is a spiritual birth and is as much a birth as the natural birth. The only way to become a Christian is to be "born again."

The meaning of salvation in the Hebrew and Greek implies the ideas of deliverance, safety, preservation, healing and soundness. Until a person receives Christ as Saviour, that person is lost and has no assurance of deliverance, safety, etc. Good works will never bring salvation to a soul. Being a good person is not salvation. The Bible declares that we are not saved by works. First is salvation—followed by works (Ephesians 2:10).

IV. THE GREAT TRUTH: "SALVATION"

A. SALVATION—THE EXTERNAL PURPOSE OF GOD.

1. **Salvation Was Conceived in the Mind of God.**

    a. The plan of salvation was in the mind of God before the foundation of the world.

Write in Ephesians 1:4: _____

_____

_____

b. Salvation was a result of God's foreknowledge. The plan of salvation was not an afterthought of God. He foreknew (being omniscient) the need for a plan of redemption.

Write in I Peter 1:20: _____

_____

_____

Also Titus 1:2: _____

_____

2. Salvation—The Grace of God.

a. Salvation is not a result of anything we might do, but a result of God's grace.

The word "grace" means: God's
                 Riches
                 At
                 Christ's
                 Expense.

Write in II Timothy 1:9: _____

_____

_____

Write in Titus 2:11: _____

_____

b. Salvation is offered because of God's love toward us.

Write in Romans 5:8: _____

_____

_____

Underline I John 4:9 in your Bible.

B. SALVATION BEFORE AND AFTER THE CROSS.

1. Salvation Before the Cross.

a. God dealt with sin before the cross by atonement. Atonement means "to cover" (Leviticus 16).

b. The Levitical offerings "covered" the sins until, and in anticipation of the cross, but did not "take away" those sins (Hebrews 9:15).

Write in Romans 3:25: _____

_____

Note the words "remission of sins that are past." The word "remission" means "to pass over."

c. The Levitical offering of sacrifice was offered in anticipation of the supreme Sacrifice, Jesus Christ. God had promised a Lamb (Genesis 3:15; 22:8), and had forgiven sin on the basis of His promise.

d. Paul, in his address to the "men of Athens" on Mars' Hill, said, "God winked at the times of ignorance" (Acts 17:30). The word should be "overlooked."

2. Salvation After the Cross.

a. The divine method of dealing with sin since Christ died is based upon ONE OFFERING—the offering of Christ upon the cross (Hebrews 10:12, 14).

b. In His death, Christ did not "cover" sin, but took away (washed clean) the sin. "Behold the Lamb of God, which taketh away the sin of the world" (John 1:29).

Write in Colossians 2;14: _____

_____

_____

C. THE PRICE PAID FOR SALVATION.

1. God's Son, Jesus Christ, Had to Die to Provide Salvation.

a. By the death, burial and resurrection of Christ, He provided a way of salvation for humanity.

Write in Romans 8:11: _____

_____

_____

b. "For God so loved the world, that He gave His only begotten Son, that whosoever believeth in Him should not perish, but have everlasting life" (John 3:16).

God gave—Christ died—His blood shed—the price of salvation proves God's love for us.

2. Jesus Suffered For the Sins of the World.

a. He suffered "that He might bring us to God."

Write in I Peter 3:18: _____

_____

_____

b. His blood was shed for the remission of sin. The word "remission" means "forgiveness." Jesus spoke of this when He instituted the Lord's Supper.

Write in Matthew 26:28: _____

_____

_____

D. SALVATION FROM THE PENALTY OF SIN.

1. Christ Saves From the Guilt and Penalty of Sin.

a. This speaks of past sins. When one accepts Christ, the guilt is removed. The penalty for past sins has been cared for because Christ became sin for all who will believe.

Write in II Corinthians 5:21: _____

_____

_____

b. The past life is forgiven. Read Ephesians 4:31 and write in Ephesians 4:32: _____

_____

_____

2. Christ Will Save All Who Will Come to Him.

a. He always keeps His promises. He is not willing that any should perish.

Write in II Peter 3:9: _____

_____

_____

   b. Notice in II Peter 3:9 that the final decision is left to the individual. God never forces, even though it is His will that none should perish. The action on the part of the individual is found in the last phrase of verse 9, "that all should come to repentance."

E. SALVATION FROM THE POWER OF SIN.

   1. **Christ Ever Lives to Make Intercession For Us.**

      a. Since the Christian *has been* saved from the guilt and penalty of sin, the Lord Jesus provides the Christian with a day by day salvation from the power and dominion of sin.
      Write in Romans 6:14: _____

      _____

      Also Hebrews 9:25: _____

      _____

      _____

      b. This truth speaks of the present tense. Even though a person is saved, Christians still have the disposition to sin.
      Write in I John 2:1: _____

      _____

      _____

   2. **The Christian Can Live a Victorious Life.**

      a. Even though a person accepts God's plan of salvation, there remains the two natures within the heart and soul. There is the old Adamic nature and the divine Spiritual nature received through the new birth. These two natures are constantly striving for control. Paul declares this conflict in his own soul (Romans 7:15-25).

      b. The strife in every Christian can be settled. Paul was victorious.
      Write in Romans 8:1: _____

      _____

      Underline Romans 8:2-3 in your Bible.

      c. The Holy Spirit will settle the strife in the believer's heart (Romans 8:14-16).
      Underline Romans 8:26-27 in your Bible.
      Write in I John 5:20: _____

      _____

      _____

F. SALVATION FROM THE PRESENCE OF SIN.

   1. **Jesus Shall Return to Take the Redeemed From the Presence of Sin.**

      a. This speaks of the future tense. The child of God has been saved from the *penalty of sin (past)*; is being saved from the *power of sin (present)*; and shall be saved from the *presence of sin (future)*.

108

Write in Hebrews 9:28: _____

_____

_____

b. Peter spoke of the future inheritance.
   Write in I Peter 1:4-5: _____

_____

_____

2. **God Sees Christians as They Shall Be.**

   a. We do not expect to be the sons of God—*we are! All* who have accepted Christ are the sons of God *NOW*. Underline I John 3:1 in your Bible.

   b. We know He shall make the difference when He comes for His own. One of the precious verses you should memorize is I John 3:2. Write in the verse _____

_____

_____

_____

G. SALVATION IS THE FREE GIFT OF GOD.

   1. **How Can a Person be Saved?**

      a. Salvation is a *gift* of God to all who will believe.
         Write in Ephesians 2:8-9: _____

_____

_____

_____

      b. Since salvation is a gift of God and His grace is provided, what must a person do?
         Admit and confess that he is a sinner (Romans 3:23).

      c. A person out of Christ earns spiritual death.
         Write in Romans 6:23: _____

_____

_____

         Wages are what we work for every day. The "wages of sin is death"—that is the bad part. It is man's decision.

      d. "But the gift of God is eternal life through Jesus Christ our Lord." That is the grand and glorious gift of God. The choice is left up to the individual.

   2. **How Can a Person Live the Christian Life?**

      a. The power to live the Christian life is given to all who believe.

         Write in John 1:12: _____

_____

_____

      b. Confess every sin and be forgiven.
         Write in I John 1:9: _____

_____

This is not a license to sin. It is God's way to keep us clean. To say we have no sin, is a sin and the truth is not in us (I John 1:8).

V. WHAT THIS BIBLE TRUTH TEACHES US TODAY

Salvation is a free gift of a Holy God to a sinful world. It is obtained only by believing on the Son of God and receiving Him into your heart. It is an act of *faith*. One cannot work his way into Christ, nor can a person buy salvation. It is a personal decision. No one else can save a person. Church membership is not salvation but should be a natural result of salvation.

The "gospel of Christ is the power of God unto salvation to everyone that believeth" (Romans 1:16). It is the "good news" of Jesus paying the price for sin on the cross—and that is the power of God. For God to create, He breathed. He spoke and it was done. To save man from sin and torment, He had to give His blood (John 3:16; Acts 20:28).

Salvation changes the heart, the mind, every part of a person. We become "new creatures (actually "new creations") in Christ Jesus" (II Corinthians 5:17).

We need not worry about being good enough to be saved, because a person never reaches that degree of excellence. If one did, one would have no need of salvation. "All have sinned" is all-inclusive.

Once we belong to Christ we learn to lean on Him. He is with us every moment of every day. Paul says, "Being confident of this very thing, that He which hath begun a good work in you will perform it until the day of Jesus Christ" (Philippians 1:6).

YOUR NEXT ASSIGNMENT:

1. Read Matthew 3:1-2; 4:17; Mark 6:12; Luke 13:5; 24:47; Acts 2:38; 11:18; 20:21; 26:20; Romans 2:4; II Corinthians 7:10; II Timothy 2:24-25; Revelation 2:5, 16, 21; 3:3, 19.

2. Review your notes on Salvation.

3. Mark your Bible where new truths are learned.

GREAT TRUTHS OF THE BIBLE

Lesson 19
"Repentance"

(Where lines are provided, look up the Scripture and write in the Scripture or its main truth.)

I. INTRODUCTION

The truth in this lesson is one seldom mentioned. Repentance is not a popular subject. Repentance is absolutely necessary and is indispensable to salvation. Wherever this subject is taught, it brings forth fruit. Faith in Christ is the goal of teaching and preaching—but that teaching and preaching must stress repentance. Jesus stated that repentance was a necessity for salvation (Luke 13:3).

Webster defines repentance as "to turn from sin and dedicate oneself to the amendment of one's life; to feel regret or contrition." This is partially correct. The noun in Greek is "metanoia" meaning "change of mind." The corresponding verb means "change one's mind." Repentance in the Biblical sense means "to turn, change one's life, change one's direction." The basic meaning you should remember is "to turn in respect to sin."

II. BASIC SCRIPTURES

Matthew 3;1-2; 4:17; Mark 6:12; Luke 13:5; 24:47; Acts 2:38; 11:18; 20:21; 26:20; Romans 2:4; II Corinthians 7:10; II Timothy 2:24-25; Revelation 2:5, 16, 21; 3:3, 19.

III. THE NUCLEUS OF THIS TRUTH

Repentance and faith are the two necessities for conversion. Repentance is turning from self, faith is turning to God; repentance looks within, faith looks above; repentance sees our turmoil, faith sees our Saviour.

Repentance is a threefold action:
- in the *understanding*—knowledge of sin;
- in the *feelings*—pain and grief;
- in the *will*—a change of mind (metanoia) and a turning around. It is a realization of self, the despair of guilt, a renouncing of self.

Paul says the same thing in one brief Scripture, "O wretched man that I am! who shall deliver me from the body of this death?" (Romans 7:24).

"The Lord is not wlling that any should perish" (II Peter 3:9). The condition God has set forth is that a person must believe (receive) His son, Jesus Christ. *Now remember this*—Salvation consists of:
- *Regeneration*—the divine side; God regenerates.
- *Repentance and faith*—man's side; conversion.

Conversion, meaning repentance and faith, is the condition for regeneration (being born again). If you grasp this truth, this lesson will not return void. Repentance is an important truth of God's Word.

IV. THE GREAT TRUTH: *"REPENTANCE"*

A. THE REPENTANCE OF GOD.

1. The Repentance of God is Not the Same as That of Man.

    a. The word "repent" in the *Old Testament* means "to feel sorry, comforted." In order to portray the nature of God in terms we can understand, it is necessary to describe Him in terms of a human personality. The Bible states, "God is not a man, that He should lie; neither the son of man, that He should repent" (Numbers 23:19).

b. The writers in the Old Testament used the word "repent" in the sense of "metanoia" meaning "change of mind." This is seen from a study of all the references in the Old Testamen.

2. **God's Repentance is Based on Conditional and Unconditional Covenants He Has Made With Man.**

a. There would seem to be a contradiction in Scripture. The Bible says in some places that God never repents. In other portions of Scripture we find He does repent.

b. The statements (as we shall see) are *not* a contradiction. The Bible is never contradictory. Whether God repents or not is based on the response of people.

3. **God Does Repent—Based on *His* Conditions.**

a. God "repented that He had made man" (Genesis 6:6). The repentance of God in this passage is based upon the conditional warning in Genesis 6:3.

Write in Genesis 6:3: _____

_____

_____

The warning went unheeded and man did not change. In fact, man became more wicked (Genesis 6:5).

Because of man's failure to change, God repented. He was "*sorry* at heart," that "He had made man and it *grieved* Him at His heart" (Genesis 6:6).

b. God's repentance signifies a change of relations and circumstances. A good example of this is found in Jeremiah 18:5-13.

In this passage you read of God's repentance—"if that nation turn from their evil, I will repent of the evil I thought to do unto them" (Jeremiah 18:8).

Write in Jeremiah 18:10: _____

_____

_____

c. God repented toward Nineveh because they *turned* from evil after Jonah had preached as God had instructed (Jonah 3:2, 9, 10). Underline verses 9 and 10 in your Bible.

d. From these few examples, you see that God repents only when the people meet His conditions. He "turns" from judgment if the people change. He also "turns" to judgment if people do not obey His Word.

4. **God Does Not Repent—Based on Unconditional Covenants.**

a. When God makes an unconditional covenant, He never repents—He never "changes." It stands forever (I Samuel 15:29).

b. God made an unconditional covenant with Abraham (Genesis 12:1-3). That covenant shall stand forever.

Write in the first phrase of Psalm 110:4: _____

_____

c. The covenant God made with David is unconditional (II Samuel 7:12-16).

Write in verse 16: _____

_____

_____

The covenant is immutable (Psalm 89:27-36). The entire Psalm is a confirmation of the Davidic Covenant. Underline verses 27, 34 and 36.

d. God declared Christ to be a Priest after the order of Melchizedek and He will not repent (Psalm 110:4). Underline Hebrews 7:21.

B. THE REPENTANCE OF MAN.

1. The Meaning of Repentance for Man.

a. In the New Testament there are three Greek words for repentance.

(1) The verb "metamelomai" means "regret, being annoyed with the results of sin, remorse." This is the word used by Judas Iscariot (Matthew 27:3). Notice the words, "when he saw that he was condemned, repented himself." The word carries no thought of change of mind. Judas was filled with remorse. This is not a saving repentance.

(2) The usual verb is "metanoeo" meaning to "change one's mind."

(3) The corresponding noun is "metanoia" meaning "change of mind in respect to sin."

b. The meaning of repentance is "a change, an act of the will, with respect to sin that leads to a change in conduct. It is changing one's direction toward God."

2. John the Baptist Preached Repentance.

a. Isaiah had prophesied the mission of John the Baptist in Isaiah 40:3-5. He fulfilled the prophecy in announcing the Messiah (John 1:19-23).

b. Write in Matthew 3:2: _____

_____

Underline Matthew 3:8, 11 in your Bible.

3. Jesus Preached Repentance.

a. Jesus began His public ministry by preaching repentance. Write in Matthew 4:17: _____

_____

_____

b. He called sinners to repentance. Write in Matthew 9:13: _____

_____

_____

c. Jesus used Jonah to teach repentance. Write in Matthew 12:41: _____

_____

_____

4. Repentance Was Preached by the Apostles.

    a. Peter preached repentance. Underline Acts 2:38.

       Write in Acts 3:19: _____

_____

_____

    b. Peter, John and Philip preached repentance in Samaria. Underline Acts 8:22 in your Bible.

    c. Paul preached repentance to the Athenians on Mars' Hill.

       Write in Acts 17:30: _____

_____

_____

    d. When Paul preached to the Ephesians, he gave that great verse on repentance. You should memorize, underline and write in Acts 20:21: _____

_____

_____

       Notice that repentance is toward God; faith is toward our Lord Jesus Christ.

       It takes both, repentance and faith, to be saved.

    e. Paul's teaching concerning Israel and her future is applicable to us.

       Write in Romans 11:29: _____

_____

_____

    f. Paul spoke concerning "Godly sorrow" in II Corinthians 7:9-10. He said, "Godly sorrow worketh repentance to salvation (never to be regretted)." Mere sorrow is not repentance. The sorrow felt because of what sin is in relation to God is "Godly sorrow." Many people sin, face the terrible sentence of a court, face shame and disgrace, and they are sorry for what they face. They show no "Godly sorrow."

    g. In all of the Scriptures studied, the great theme has been "turning from sin to the Lord Jesus as Saviour." A change in thinking about sin, a "repentance toward God and faith toward our Lord Jesus Christ."

C. THE EVIDENCE OF REPENTANCE.

1. A Perfect Illustration of Repentance.

    a. The parable of the prodigal son is our Lord's teaching of real repentance (Luke 15:11-32).

    b. Read the parable and underline verses 17, 18 and 21 in your Bible.

2. Repentance is Evidenced in Three Ways (in this parable).

    a. Intellectually—a change of mind—"he came to himself."

    b. Emotionally—a change of heart—"I have sinned."

    c. Volitionally—a change of will—"I will go to my father."

3. The Evidence of Repentance Seen in Other Men.

a. Thomas repented of his unbelief with his confession, "My Lord and my God" (John 20:24-29). Underline John 20:25 and 27 in your Bible.

b. Paul repented on the road to Damascus (Acts 9:1-18). Underline Acts 9:3 and 5.

Write in verse 6: _____

_____

_____

c. The Philippian jailer "believed in God with all his house" (Acts 16:34) after Paul and Silas answered his plea for help. The entire account is in Acts 16:25-34. Underline verses 30 and 31 in your Bible.

D. INCENTIVES TO REPENTANCE.

1. The Consequences of Sin.

a. Sin leads to destruction. "The wages of sin is death" (Romans 6:23). There is only one way to avoid eternal destruction.

b. Jesus said, "Except ye repent, ye shall all likewise perish" (Luke 13:3).

2. The Goodness of God.

a. His goodness is revealed in daily blessings. Paul said in Romans 2:4, "Or despisest thou the riches of *His goodness* and forbearance and long-suffering; not knowing that *the goodness of God* leadeth thee to repentance?" Every day He gives us tokens of His goodness.

b. His goodness is revealed in His mercy and long-suffering. Why does He contend with sinful people? The answer is in II Peter 3:9. Underline the Scripture in your Bible.

c. The one supreme revelation of God's love for the lost and His goodness toward mankind is in the gift of His Son (John 3:16). In the cross we see the goodness of God; that alone should break the hearts of men and cause them to repent.

V. WHAT THIS BIBLE TRUTH TEACHES US TODAY.

To be converted is to be "turned around." When a person is converted, he turns from something, and he turns to something. One turns from sin and then turns to Christ. The turning from sin is called repentance; the turning to Christ is called faith. So, these are the two steps in conversion: repentance and faith. Paul states so clearly this fact in Acts 20:21, "repentance toward God, and faith in the Lord Jesus Christ."

- So, *to be saved* is *to be converted.*
- *Conversion* requires *repentance* and *faith.*
- This is *man's part* in *his own conversion.*

Once man, of his own free will, confesses his sin and turns to God through faith in Jesus Christ, he has done man's part (Romans 10:9-10).

Then God does the saving, the regenerating. He gives the new life in Christ.

To become a Christian does not require a knowledge of the Bible—that comes after one is saved.

To win a person to Christ does not require a great knowledge of the Bible—only a few verses of Scripture and where to find them. the following is one simple plan:

Romans 3:23—"All have sinned—"

Romans 6:23—"The wages of sin—"

II Thessalonians 1:9—"Destruction from presence of Lord" (what spiritual death is for unsaved).

John 3:16—"God so loved . . ." (the gospel in one verse).

John 1:12—"As many as received Him . . ." (the power, strength to live the Christian life).

YOUR NEXT ASSIGNMENT:

1. Read Deuteronomy 32:20; Habakkuk 2:4; Matthew 6:20; 8:26; 14:31; 17:20; Luke 7:9; 17:5; 18:8; Acts 3:16; 11:24; 20:21; Romans 1:17; 3:28; 10:17; I Corinthians 12:8-9; 15:14; II Corinthians 1:24; 5:7; Galatians 2:20; 3:11; Ephesians 2:8-9; 4:5; Philippians 1:25; Colossians 1:23; 2:5; I Timothy 1:5; 3:13; 4:1; Hebrews Chapter 11; 12:2; James 2:14-18; I Peter 1:7; II Peter 1:1; Jude 20; Revelation 14:12.

2. Review your notes on Repentance. The next lesson will be "Faith." These two lessons go together because they are man's part in salvation.

3. Mark your Bible where new truths are learned.

Lesson 20
"Faith"

(Where lines are provided, look up the Scripture and write in the Scripture or its main truth.)

I. INTRODUCTION

In the last lesson we learned about the first step in conversion—repentance. Repentance is turning away from sin, an act of the will. Paul says, "repentance toward God" (Acts 20:21). We now turn to the second step in conversion—faith. In Acts 20:21 Paul completes the statement, "and faith toward the Lord Jesus Christ." Without faith in the Lord Jesus, repentance turns to remorse and the result seems fruitless. It is faith in the Lord Jesus Christ that saves, "For by grace are ye saved through *faith*" (Ephesians 2:8). Faith takes hold of the repentant heart and leads the person to God, the God of forgiveness. Conversion itself is two-fold: turning from the old life and turning to the Lord Jesus Christ. The "turning from" is repentance. The "turning to" is faith (I Thessalonians 1:9). Repentance looks within—faith looks heavenward; repentance sees our wretchedness—faith sees our Saviour.

II. BASIC SCRIPTURES:

Deuteronomy 32:20; Habakkuk 2:4; Matthew 6:20; 8:26; 14:31; 17:20; Luke 7:9; 17:5; 18:8; Acts 3:16; 11:24; 20:21; Romans 1:17; 3:28; 10:17; I Corinthians 12:8-9; 15:14; II Corinthians 1:24; 5:7; Galatians 2:20; 3:11; Ephesians 2:8-9; 4:5; Philippians 1:25; Colossians 1:23; 2:5; I Timothy 1:5; 3:13; 4:1; Hebrews Chapter 11; 12:2; James 2:14-18; I Peter 1:7; II Peter 1:1; Jude 20; Revelation 14:12.

III. THE NUCLEUS OF THIS TRUTH

Conviction of sin comes from a degree of knowledge of God. There is a threefold nature of man—the body, soul and spirit. Because of the sin nature of man, the spiritual part of man is dormant until he opens his heart to the Lord Jesus. That dormant spirit causes a person to "hear" the message of God's love. Conviction begins through the power of the Holy Spirit.

To have faith one must be informed of the saving power in accepting Jesus as Lord. It is impossible to have faith apart from some verse, or passage from the Word of God. Paul said, "Faith cometh by hearing, and hearing by the Word of God" (Romans 10:17). Actually, a person realizes faith and the power of faith by knowing the source of faith.

One must receive (believe) Jesus Christ by faith. Receiving Him means trusting Him for salvation.

The nucleus stated simply is "faith comes by hearing the Word of God," causing a person to receive (believe) Christ as Lord and Savior. Trust, total trust, in Jesus and His power to save is placing total faith in Him for eternal salvation. To increase one's faith, just study the Word of God.

IV. THE GREAT TRUTH: *"FAITH"*

A. THE OBJECT OF FAITH.

1. **Saving Faith is Faith in a Divine Person.**

   a. "Faith toward our Lord Jesus Christ" is the famous statement of Paul in Acts 20:21. Faith in any other thing or person or organization is not saving faith. Faith must be placed in Jesus Christ.

   b. Faith is not an intellectual assent. It is faith in the Redeemer which effects a transformation in the life of the believer in Christ.

   Look up John 11:25: _____

   _____

   _____

2. **Faith is Absolutely Essential to Salvation.**

   a. "I am not ashamed of the Gospel of Christ: for it is the power of God unto salvation to everyone that believeth . . ." (Romans 1:16).

   b. Paul made the declaration of the power of God in the Gospel. Then, in Romans 1:17, Paul states, "For therein"—meaning the Gospel of verse 16.

   Write in Romans 1:17: _____

   _____

   _____

   c. Write in Romans 3:22: _____

   _____

   _____

   The object of faith is Jesus Christ!

B. THE MEANING OF FAITH.

   1. **The Bible Gives the Definition.**

      a. Through the centuries Bible scholars have given many theories to the meaning of faith. The Bible gives the best meaning of faith, the only "definition" of faith.

      b. That statement of faith is found in Hebrews 11:1: _____

      _____

      _____

      c. The meaning of the Scripture is that one with faith has the spiritual insight to rely on God and His Word even though there is no evidence in sight. This is explained in II Corinthians 4:18: _____

      _____

      _____

   2. **Faith is Taking God at His Word.**

      a. In prayer life, faith is the "confidence that we have in Him, that if we ask anything according to His will, He heareth us" (I John 5:14).

      Write in I John 5:15: _____

      _____

      _____

      b. Faith pleases God. Without faith it is impossible to please Him.

118

Write in Hebrews 11:6: _____

_____

This verse is the *condition of prayer*.

C. FAITH IS THE GIFT OF THE TRINITY.

1. **Faith is a Gift of the Father.**
   Write in Romans 12:3: _____

   _____

   _____

   _____

2. **Faith is a Gift of God the Son.**
   Write in Hebrews 12:2: _____

   _____

   _____

3. **Faith is a Gift of God the Holy Spirit.**
   Write in Galatians 5:22: _____

   _____

   _____

D. THE DEGREES OF FAITH.

1. **The Measure of Faith.**

   a. *"Little faith."* Jesus used the statement when He stilled the waves because of the fear of the disciples (Matthew 8:26).
      He used the statement when Peter walked on the water and became afraid, and doubted.
      Write in Matthew 14:31: _____

      _____

      _____

   b. *"Weak faith."* Paul taught the church to receive the "weak in the faith." The church should not argue over questions of personal liberty when the things are not forbidden in Scripture. Read the context in Romans 14:1-6 and write in Romans 14:1: _____

      _____

      _____

   c. *"Vain faith."* Faith in the truth of the resurrection of Christ is essential.
      Write in I Corinthians 15:17: _____

      _____

      _____

      Underline I Corinthians 15:14 in your Bible.

   d. *"Dead faith."* James placed emphasis on a living faith. Real faith produces works. Works will never produce faith. James illustrated this truth by using Abraham and Rahab of the Old Testament (James 2:21-26).
      Write in James 2:20: _____

      _____

      _____

119

Underline James 2:17 in your Bible.

e. The "measure of faith" mentioned in Romans 12;3 is given for service. It was not given in order to make some spiritually superior to others in the Body of Christ. Thus far, we have seen the lesser degrees of faith—the "little, weak, vain, dead." There are lessons for us in each one mentioned. We can place ourselves in one or more of the "faiths" mentioned thus far.

Now, we turn to victorious types of faith.

2. **The Proportion of Faith.**

a. *"Great faith."* Jesus found a "great faith" in the Roman officer (centurion). The officer had faith that Jesus could heal his servant who was sick and about to die (Luke 7:1-8).

Write in Luke 7:9: _____

_____

_____

b. *"Full of faith."* The twelve apostles told the multitude to select seven men to care for the needs of the people. Among the seven selected was Stephen. In Acts 6:5 you read, "and they chose Stephen, a man full of faith." The phrase is used again.

Write in Acts 6:8: _____

_____

c. *"Rich in faith."* "God hath chosen the poor of this world rich in faith, and heirs of the kingdom which He hath promised to them that love Him" (James 2:5).

d. *"Living faith."* Paul stated the famous words concerning his life in Christ.

Write in Galatians 2:20: _____

_____

_____

e. "Steadfast in the faith." Peter gave us the sweet verse, "Casting all your care upon Him: for He careth for you" (I Peter 5:7). Then, he warns us about the devil, seeking to devour us (I Peter 5:8).

Now, write in I Peter 5:9: _____

_____

_____

Paul mentioned "steadfastness of faith" (Colossians 2:5).

f. *"Precious faith."* Peter described faith in Jesus Christ as "precious."

Write in II Peter 1:1: _____

_____

_____

Faith is the foundation of the Christian life. Read II Peter 1:5-7 and underline the attributes to be added to faith.

g. *"Holy faith."* Jude gave us only 25 verses of Scripture. All of them are to help us in the faith.

Write in Jude 20: _____

_____

E. THE CHRISTIAN LIFE IS A LIFE OF FAITH.

1. **The Life of Faith is a Life of Total Trust.**

   a. Faith is knowing that "all things work together for good to them that love God" (Romans 8:28).

   b. The Christian walks by faith.
      Write in II Corinthians 5:7: _____

      _____

      _____

   c. The Christian life is a life of victory.
      Write in I John 5:4: _____

      _____

      _____

   d. The Christian does good works.
      Write in Titus 3:8: _____

      _____

      _____

      _____

   e. The Christian lives by faith.
      Write in Galatians 2:11: _____

      _____

      _____

2. **Faith Should be the Impelling Force in Life.**

   a. By faith, the Christian acts upon the Word of God when there is no evidence in sight that the action is correct.

   b. In Hebrews 11 we have the "Hall of Faith." The faith of the Old Testament saints inspires us and teaches us:
      - By faith Abel (verse 4)
      - By faith Enoch (verse 5)
      - By faith Noah (verse 7)
      - By faith Abraham (verses 8-19)
      - By faith Sarah (verse 11)
      - Write in verse 13: _____

        _____

        _____

      - By faith Isaac (verses 17-19)
      - By faith Jacob (verses 20-21)
      - By faith Joseph (verse 22)
      - By faith Moses (verses 23-29)
      - By faith Joshua and Israel (verse 30)
      - By faith Rahab (verse 31)
      - The unnumbered heroes of faith (verses 32-40)

   c. All of these had faith. Some might ask, "In what?" In the promises of God in Genesis 3:15 and 12:7. The promise of Jesus Christ. These Old Testament saints had faith as they

121

looked toward the Cross. Our faith is looking back to the Cross. The Old Testament saints teach us the real meaning of Hebrews 11:1, "Faith is the substance of things *hoped for*, the evidence of things not seen." The "substance" is the assurance that God will be faithful to His promises. The "evidence" is ample testimony of God in the direction of their lives.

V. WHAT THIS BIBLE TRUTH TEACHES US TODAY.

Faith is one threefold action:

- in *understanding*—being convinced of redemption;
- in the *feelings*—resting in His saving love;
- in the *will*—devotion to the personal Saviour.

Faith is not the working up of the feelings, no tormenting of self, no dependence upon a person—except Jesus Christ—no covering up guilt; but it is a personal relationship with Christ. Faith experiences the present; *Christ here* and *now*! The "substance" and "evidence" are in the Word of God; therefore, we believe. "Whom having not seen, ye love; in whom, though now ye see Him not, yet believing, ye rejoice with joy unspeakable and full of glory: receiving the end of your faith, even the salvation of your souls" (I Peter 1:8-9).

YOUR NEXT ASSIGNMENT:

1. Read John 3:1-21; Romans 8:7-8; 10:9-10; Ephesians 2:1-18; 4:24; 5:26; Colossians 1:27; Titus 3:5; II Corinthians 5:17; I Peter 1:23-25; II Peter 1:4; I John 5:10-12.

2. Review your notes on Faith.

3. Mark your Bible where new truths are learned.

Lesson 21
"Regeneration" (The New Birth)

(Where lines are provided, look up the Scripture and write in the Scripture or its main truth.)

I. INTRODUCTION

In most Bible studies, conversion and regeneration are considered as being the same experience. Often in teaching and preaching they are used as being reciprocal terms. The two events are closely related; yet, there is a marked doctrinal difference between them.

In all of God's dealings with mankind, there is a divine side and a human side. This can be seen in the giving of the Scriptures. In II Peter 1:21 we read, "For the prophecy came not in old times by the will of man: but holy men of God spake as they were moved by the Holy Ghost." The human side of the revelation of Scripture is seen in the phrase, "holy men of God spake." The divine side of the revelation is in the phrase, "as they were moved by the Holy Ghost."

There was a human side and a divine side to Jesus Christ. He was both God and man. "In the beginning was the Word (Jesus), and the Word (Jesus) was with God, and the Word (Jesus) was God"(John 1:1). That was the divine side of our Lord. "The Word (Jesus) was made flesh and dwelt among us . . ." (John 1:14). That was the human side of Jesus.

There is a human side and a divine side to the experience of salvation. The human side we call *conversion*. The divine side we call *regeneration*.

The distinction between the two terms will be taught in this lesson. However, the thrust of our study shall be on the divine side of salvation—regeneration.

II. BASIC SCRIPTURES:

John 3:1-21; Romans 8:7-8; 10:9-10; Ephesians 2:1-18; 4:24; 5:26; Colossians 1:27; Titus 3:5; II Corinthians 5:17; I Peter 1:23-25; II Peter 1:4; I John 5:10-12.

III. THE NUCLEUS OF THIS TRUTH

Regeneration, from Latin and Greek, means "rebirth." Regeneration is the work of God in the heart of "as many as receive Him (Jesus), to them gave He the power to become the sons of God, even to them that believe on His name: *which were born*, not of blood, nor of the will of the flesh, nor of the will of man, but *of God*" (John 1:12-13).

To receive the "new birth," a person must be "converted," must repent of sin and place faith in the Lord Jesus Christ. Man must believe and receive Jesus by faith. "By grace are ye saved"; but how? "Through faith" (Ephesians 2:8).

Then, instantly God does the divine work in the heart. It is regeneration—the "new birth."

The term "born again" has been highly visible in the last few years. It is not a new term in the English language. Jesus used the term. He made it popular when He was ministering in this world.

IV. THE GREAT TRUTH: *"REGENERATION"*

A. THE MEANING OF REGENERATION.

1. Regeneration is a Rebirth.

    a. It is a new birth—a second birth. It is being "born again." It is an act of God in the heart.

       Write in John 1:13: _____

       _____

       _____

    b. Jesus told Nicodemus about the new birth.

       Write in John 3:3: _____

       _____

       _____

2. Regeneration is by the Mercy of God.

    a. Regeneration is of God, and man cannot perform any works that will save himself.

       Write in Titus 3:5: _____

       _____

       _____

    b. This is the only time "regeneration" is used in the Bible in reference to man. (It is found one other time in Matthew 19:28 and refers to earthly renewal.)

    c. The love of God and the kindness of God was abundantly given through Jesus Christ.

       Write in Titus 3:4: _____

       _____

       and Titus 3:6: _____

       _____

3. The New Birth is An Instantaneous Experience.

    a. The experience of salvation may be a lone experience leading up to it, and the realization of it may not be immediate. The experience of the "new birth" is instantaneous the moment the Holy Spirit comes into the heart.

       Write in John 3:6: _____

       _____

    b. The natural birth is a long process. The actual time of the natural birth is instantaneous. The baby is born, breathes its first breath, cries its first sound.

       So, with the Spiritual birth. When one goes through the pain of sin in this life—sees himself lost and without God—realizes the need to turn from sin, and turn to God through faith—then, he is "born again."

B. THE NECESSITY OF THE NEW BIRTH.

1. A Necessity Declared by the Lord Jesus Christ.

    a. Jesus declared to Nicodemus three times the necessity of the new birth. Nicodemus was a Pharisee and a "ruler of the Jews" (John 3:1). He was a member of the Sanhedrin. He

124

was a religious man, highly cultured and educated. He was destitute of the grace of God. He was lost. Jesus said to him, "ye *must* be born again" (John 3:7).

2. **A Necessity Because of the Sinful Nature of Man.**

   a. Man has a human nature. Man is born in sin.
      Write in Psalm 51:5: _____

      _____

      Write in Ephesians 2:3: _____

      _____

      _____

   b. The new birth is a necessity because of the universal depravity of human nature.
      Write in Romans 3:23: _____

      _____

C. The Nature of Regeneration.

   1. **Regeneration, the New Birth, is a Cleansing Work.**

      a. The new birth is of "water and Spirit."
         Write in John 3:5: _____

         _____

         _____

      b. What is the meaning of "born of water"? In the Scripture, water stands for the Word of God.
         Write in I Peter 1:23: _____

         _____

         Write in John 15:3: _____

         _____

         Read again Titus 3:5. Notice the words, "according to His mercy He saved us, by the washing of regeneration . . . "
         Write in Ephesians 5:26: _____

         _____

         _____

   2. **Regeneration is the Gift and Work of God.**

      a. The new birth is the gift of God.
         Write in Ephesians 2:8 _____

         _____

         _____

      b. It is God's work in the repentant heart.
         Write in Ephesians 2:4-5: _____

         _____

         _____

         _____

         Underline Ephesians 2:1. Also, underline in your Bible Ephesians 2:6-7.

   3. **Regeneration is a New Creation of God.**

      a. The new birth is not reformation—it is a new creation.

Write in II Corinthians 5:17: _____

_____

_____

b. The new creation is seen in Ephesians 1:10: _____

_____

_____

D. REGENERATION IS THE WORK OF THE TRINITY.

1. God the Father Effected the New Birth.

    a. "Which were born, not of blood, nor of the will of the flesh, nor of the will of man, but of God" (John 1:13).

    b. Write in I John 3:1: _____

_____

_____

2. Jesus Gave His Life to Redeem Mankind.

    a. Jesus told Nicodemus, "As Moses lifted up the serpent in the wilderness, even so must the Son of man be lifted up: that whosoever believeth in Him should not perish, but have eternal life" (John 3:14, 15). Then, follows the Gospel in a nutshell (John 3:16).

    Write in John 3:17: _____

_____

_____

    b. Read John 12:23-31 and write in John 12:32-33: _____

_____

_____

_____

    The death Jesus referred to was crucifixion.

3. The Holy Spirit is Active in Regeneration.

    a. The Holy Spirit is the One who convicts of sin and presents the glory of Jesus the Son. He is the One who dwells in all believers (John 16:7-15).

    b. The Holy Spirit cleanses and renews and quickens (makes alive) (Titus 3:5; Ephesians 2:1).

    c. Jesus used the illustration of the wind to explain the work of the Spirit to Nicodemus.

    Write in John 3:8: _____

_____

_____

_____

    Therefore, the work of God the Father, Jesus the Son, and the Holy Spirit effected the new birth which is Regeneration. It is all the work of the Trinity—not the work or works of man. All man can do is repent and place faith in the Lord Jesus Christ. The plan of eternal life is offered but man must accept and receive that plan as his gift from God.

E. THE EVIDENCES OF REGENERATION.

1. The Marks of Regeneration.

a. One who is Regenerated has the witness *in himself*.
   Write in I John 5:10: _____

   _____

   _____

   Underline Romans 8:16 in your Bible.

b. One who is Regenerated *abides in Christ*.
   Write in I John 3:24: _____

   _____

   _____

c. One who is Regenerated *loves the brethren*.
   Write in I John 3:14: _____

   _____

   _____

d. One who is Regenerated *overcomes the world*.
   Write in I John 5:4-5: _____

   _____

   _____

   _____

e. One who is Regenerated *is led by the Holy Spirit*.
   Write in Romans 8:14: _____

   _____

   _____

2. **Regeneration is a Lifechanging Experience.**

   a. Because a person realizes the need for a new life in Christ, confesses sin, turns from the old life to Christ, and accepts Him by faith, God does the Regenerating work in the heart. This changes a person's nature, thoughts and actions. Underline II Peter 1:4 in your Bible.

   b. The new birth places one among "the fellowship of the saints, and of the household of God" (Ephesians 2:19).

   c. One receives a new life in Christ Jesus.
      Write in I John 5:12: _____

      _____

      _____

   d. One becomes a new creation in Christ. Underline II Corinthians 5:17 in your Bible.

   e. One receives a new mind in Christ.
      Write in Philippians 2:5: _____

      _____

   f. One receives "the blessed hope" of being with the Lord when absent from the body.
      Write in II Corinthians 5:8: _____

      _____

      _____

   Underline II Corinthians 5:6-7 in your Bible.

V. WHAT THIS BIBLE TRUTH TEACHES US TODAY

The sinner (unredeemed) receives the pardon of his guilt on the ground of the priestly sacrifice of Christ on the cross. In this he is renewed (Titus 3:5), transformed (I Corinthians 6:11), made alive (Ephesians 2:5), and born of God (I John 5:1). Regeneration is the real entrance into His redemption (Titus 3:5).

Jesus was God who "took upon Himself the likeness of man" that He might impart His life to all who accept Him—which is a mystery—"which is Christ in you, the hope of glory" (Colossians 1:27). Only by Regeneration do we become "new" men (Colossians 3:10), and members of His Body.

Regeneration is the divine side of man's salvation. Conversion is twofold: repentance and faith. Conversion is the human side of man's salvation.

The new birth is a necessity to inherit eternal life. Reformation, good intentions will not save. Only faith in the blood of Jesus, our Lord.

Regeneration, the new birth, is so easy to understand. A child can comprehend and accept it, while a learned Nicodemus will ask foolish questions. The amazing thing is the answers Jesus gave—not so much the questions asked (John 3).

Do you have the marks of Regeneration in your life?

YOUR NEXT ASSIGNMENT:

1. Read Acts 13:37-39; Romans 3:20, 24, 26; 4:1-8; 4:24-25; 5:1-13; 8:33; I Corinthians 6:11; Galatians 2:16-17; 3:8, 11, 24; Ephesians 4:6; Titus 3:7; Hebrews 11:7; James 2:21-32.

2. Review your notes on Regeneration.

3. Mark your Bible where new truths are learned.

Lesson 22
"Justification"

(Where lines are provided, look up the Scripture and write in the Scripture or its main truth.)

I. INTRODUCTION

The doctrine of justification runs through the Word of God. It is found in Genesis 15:6 in God's dealings with Abraham. It is in the New Testament that we find the teaching of this truth in all its fullness. Paul uniquely interprets the teaching of justification in the book of Romans. At one time in history, this teaching was almost covered over by false teachings. Religion became a system of forms, rituals and ceremonies. It was the rediscovery of the doctrine of justification by faith that brought about the Protestant Reformation. Martin Luther, while ascending the flight of 28 marble steps (which traditionally came from Pilate's Palace and which Jesus was supposed to have ascended, and were brought to Rome by the Empress Helena, mother of Constantine) ceased the climb as he shouted the declaration, "the just shall live by faith," with new meaning, and it changed him. This was the beginning of the Reformation. Martin Luther had found the real meaning of Romans 1:17 and Galations 3:11 (quoted from Habakkuk 2:4).

II. BASIC SCRIPTURES:

Acts 13:37-39; Romans 3:20, 24, 26; 4:1-8; 4:24-25; 5:1-13; 8:33; I Corinthians 6:11; Galatians 2:16-17; 3:8, 11, 24; Ephesians 4:6; Titus 3:7; Hebrews 11:7; James 2:21-32.

III. THE NUCLEUS OF THIS TRUTH

Regeneration is the change in the inner man through faith in Christ, while justification is a legal term which pictures the believer's new status before God. Justification is grounded on the fact of man's sin being laid on Christ (Isaiah 53:6). Jesus bears the sin of all who accept Him. He is our substitute (I Peter 2:24). As the sinful nature in man was caused by the *fall*, one single event (Genesis 3), so man, in the same manner, must be raised from the *fall* by the Lord Jesus Christ through one supreme event, the Cross (Romans 5:18-19).

Who is it that justifies? Paul answers in Romans 8:33, "It is God that justifieth." No one can justify himself. Jesus told the Pharisees, "Ye are they which justify yourselves before men; but God knoweth your hearts: for that which is highly esteemed among men is abomination in the sight of God" (Luke 16:15).

No one can justify himself before God outside of faith in Christ.

IV. THE GREAT TRUTH: *"JUSTIFICATION"*

A. THE MEANING OF JUSTIFICATION.

    1. **Justification Originates in the Grace of God.**

        a. To justify does not mean to make one righteous. God, in His grace, justifies freely.

        Write in Romans 3:24: _____

b. By the grace of God, His love was shed abundantly through Jesus Christ our Saviour (Titus 3:4-7).

Write in Titus 3:7: _____

_____

2. **Justification is the Act of God Whereby the Guilty Sinner is Declared Just by Faith in Christ.**

a. The justified believer is declared righteous; God does not make him righteous. It is the judicial act of God. The believer's sins were put to Christ's account and He paid the price in full. Underline Romans 8:1 and 8:31-32.

Write in Romans 8:33: _____

_____

_____

b. God declares that a Christian is righteous in Christ Jesus— not a pardoned criminal. God sees the Christian *as though he had never sinned*.

Write in Acts 13:38-39: _____

_____

_____

_____

This is one of the great Scriptures on justification. Underline it in your Bible.

3. **Justification is Based on the Completed Work of Christ.**

a. The redemptive work of Christ consists of more than His atoning death on the cross. It includes His resurrection as well.

Write in Romans 4:25: _____

_____

b. Justification, therefore, is the act of God which declares Christians not only *pardoned* but also *just*. "He was delivered for our offences (sins)"—in other words, He died for our sins. "And raised again for our justification."

The redemptive work (redeem means "to deliver by paying a price") of Jesus Christ on the cross paid the penalty of sin for the sinner. It is through the resurrection of Christ that the sinner is declared justified. Thereafter, he stands in the sight of God *not as a pardoned sinner* but as a *justified saint*, and is *in Christ* before God as though he had never committed one single sin.

c. The believer is justified by first, His blood, and second, His resurrection.

Write in Romans 5:9: _____

_____

B. AN OLD TESTAMENT EXAMPLE OF JUSTIFICATION.

1. **Paul's Inspired Teaching of Justification.**

a. Paul describes in the first three chapters of Romans three sinners representing all the world who is guilty before God. First, the barbarian uncivilized pagan (Romans 1:18-23). Second, the self-righteous Gentile (Romans 2:1-3, 14).

Third, the Jew of Paul's day (Romans 2:17).

Paul charges all three are under the judgment of God, "For all have sinned and come short of the glory of God" (Romans 3:23).

b. Paul concluded that salvation is all of grace and grace alone.

Write in Romans 3:28: _____

_____

2. **The Familiar Illustration of Abraham.**

a. Paul selected the illustration of Abraham in Genesis 15 because they were all familiar with Abraham. This is found in Romans 4. Notice in verse 1, Paul calls Abraham "our father as pertaining to the flesh."

b. Paul is illustrating in Romans 4 *justification by faith without the works of the law*.

Read Genesis 15:1-6 and underline verses 4 and 6 in your Bible.

Write in Romans 4:3: _____

_____

_____

c. God had told Abraham He would do the impossible. He would give to Abraham and Sarah a son in their old age—past the age of childbearing. Abraham simply believed (had faith) "and it was counted unto him for righteousness." He only had God's Word—nothing else. That was enough for Abraham.

d. Read and underline Romans 4:13. The promise to Abraham *was not through the law*—but through *faith*. Abraham was not justified through the law, for the law came 430 years afterward.

Write in Galatians 3:17: _____

_____

_____

Which covenant is referred to in verse 17? The answer is in the next verse—Galatians 3:18: _____

_____

_____

e. Abraham was not saved through religion or ceremony: you read in Romans 4:11-12 that Abraham was counted righteous before he received the seal of circumcision. Underline Romans 4:12.

So, neither the law nor works had anything to do with the justification of Abraham. Underline Romans 4:20-24. (We have discussed verse 25.)

3. **God Has Not Changed.**

a. Salvation is still all grace and is appropriated by faith in God through Jesus Christ our Lord. We need no more evidence or signs. The Bible contains the Word and contains the entire message of justification.

b. Man is not justified by deeds.

Write in Galatians 3:11: _____

_____

Write in Romans 4:5: _____

_____

   c. Abraham is in the "Hall of Faith" in Hebrews 11. Read Hebrews 11:8-19. Underline the words "by faith" in this portion of Scripture. Underline verse 13.

C. THE METHOD OF JUSTIFICATION.

1. Man is Justified by Faith Alone.

   a. Paul states that justification is not by works of the law, but by faith in Christ.

Write in Romans 3:28: _____

_____

   b. Faith in Christ alone justifies.

Write in Romans 3:26: _____

_____

_____

2. James Declares That a Man is Justified by Works.

   a. Does this present a conflict? No! Paul and James are not in conflict, because both wrote under the inspiration of the Holy Spirit. The difficulty lies in our understanding—rather than in the Word of God. Paul states, "Being justified freely by His grace though the redemption which is in Christ Jesus" (Romans 3:24). Read again Romans 3:28.

   b. James states, "Ye see then how that by works a man is justified, and not by faith only" (James 2:24).

This is not a conflict. Paul and James are not at odds in their theology. When one reads the context of James 2:21-26, there is revealed the fact that Abraham's works made his faith perfect. The works were a result of faith (verse 22). The same is presented concerning Rahab (verse 25).

   c. "Faith without works is dead," James states (James 2:26). This is true—just as a tree without fruit is useless. What is the explanation to this question between Paul and James?

James says, "*Show me* and I will show *thee*" (James 2:18).

Jesus said, "By their fruits shall *ye* know them" (Matthew 7:20).

Paul tells us how a sinner *is justified in God's sight* by faith, apart from works. James speaks of the ones already justified by faith and how these people *may be justified in the sight of men*. So, the two great writers are simply saying:

     —before God, "Justified by faith"
     —before men, "Justified by works"

3. God Looks Upon the Heart.

   a. God does not need to see our works to know that a person believes. He looks upon the heart while men look at the outward appearance (I Samuel 16:7).

   b. But no one will know a person is saved *until they see evidence* in his life and works. Works are the evidence of faith. God sees the faith—man sees the works and will never believe a person is saved until they see a change in action and attitude.

   c. To underscore this truth, James uses Abraham as an illustration—just as Paul did. Paul selected Genesis 15 which states that Abraham "believed God and it was counted unto him for righteousness."

James selected Genesis 22 to illustrate how a man is justified by works (see James 2:21). It is an entirely different incident in the life of Abraham which James uses. Abraham offered his son Isaac as an evidence of his faith in God. This was many years *after* Abraham had been justified by faith in the sight of God. God demonstrated before all the world the faith that justified Abraham. God knew Abraham's faith— but men needed to see that faith. Read James 2:23-24.

4. **Faith Which Works by Love.**

   a. Paul states, "For in Jesus Christ neither circumcision availeth anything, nor uncircumcision; but *faith which worketh by love*" (Galatians 5:6).

   b. The world looks for a real demonstration of faith which works in love. Not simply running to a meeting, a service, a religious organization, and then, fighting and arguing among Christians as if to destoy one another.

      The world needs love, kindness, gentleness, a smile in face of discouragement, a word of faith, a helping hand. All done in *love* because we have been "*justified*."

V. WHAT THIS BIBLE TRUTH TEACHES US TODAY

In justification the sinner stands before God as the accused and is declared free (Romans 8:33). The sinner is forgiven. In forgiveness he stands before God as a debtor and receives his discharge (Ephesians 1:7; 4:32).

We are "justified freely by His grace through the redemption that is in Christ Jesus" (Romans 3:24). God sees us *in Christ* and it is *just as if we had never sinned*. Praise God!

Does your life demonstrate the faith you confess? We should never be satisfied with justification in *His sight*, but strive for our faith to be demonstrated before the world so they might see our justification.

YOUR NEXT ASSIGNMENT:

1. Read Joshua 3:5; 7:13; I Samuel 16:5; Jeremiah 1:5; John 10:36; 17:17-19; Acts 20:32; 26:18; Romans 15:16; I Corinthians 1:2, 30; 6:11; Ephesians 5:26; I Thessalonians 5:23; II Thessalonians 2:13; I Timothy 4:5; II Timothy 2:21; Hebrews 2:11; 10:10, 14; 13:12; I Peter 3:15; Jude 1.

2. Review your notes on Justification.

3. Mark your Bible where new truths are learned.

Lesson 23
"Sanctification"

(Where lines are provided, look up the Scripture and write in the Scripture or its main truth.)

I. INTRODUCTION

The truth, the doctrine, the teaching of sanctification has been neglected in most circles of Bible study. Because some use different terms, or interpret the subject differently, many have cast aside the study of sanctification. (The same can be said about the second coming of Christ.) Sanctification is one of the great truths of God's Word, and we should learn what the Bible says about the subject. Since the Holy Spirit is our teacher—and He never divides, never confuses—then we must seek His guidance in understanding the Word. Persons who have been born again will be driven to the Bible, over and over again, if there is any question in their hearts. (Before we enter the study, I must say that the differences in the study of sanctification can usually be found in the terminology. Regardless of the terminology, a "sanctified" person, one who is "holy," "set apart," will never become intolerant or critical of another Christian. Christians can differ in love, the first fruit named in the "fruit of the Spirit" (Galatians 5:22-23). If this study drives you to the Bible, it will have done its work).

II. BASIC SCRIPTURES:

Joshua 3:5; 7:13;I Samuel 16:5; Jeremiah 1:5; John 10:36; 17:17-19; Acts 20:32; 26:18; Romans 15:16; I Corinthians 1:2, 30; 6:11; Ephesians 5:26; I Thessalonians 5:23; II Thessalonians 2:13; I Timothy 4:5; II Timothy 2:21; Hebrews 2:11; 10:10, 14; 13:12; I Peter 3:15; Jude 1.

III. THE NUCLEUS OF THIS TRUTH

Sanctification begins with the experience of the new birth, continues with a process of growth and development, and is consummated in a glorious transformation of soul and body into the image of the Son of God (I John 3:2; Romans 8:29).

IV. THE GREAT TRUTH: *"SANCTIFICATION"*

A. THE MEANING OF SANCTIFICATION.

1. **There Have Been Two False Teachings.**

   a. The Antinomian View. The term "antinomian" means "against law" and teaches that the forgiveness found in Christ makes it legitimate for a Christian to do things which the Bible forbids. In other words, one can live as one pleases. The more one sins, the more chance there is for divine grace to work. Paul touches on this false view in his teaching: "What shall we say then? Shall we continue in sin, that grace may abound? God forbid" (Romans 6:1-2). This is a perverted view of the truth.

   b. The Perfectionist View. This theory teaches that a person can become perfectly free from sin in this life. This is called sinless perfection. There is no foundation in Scripture for this belief. No one, except Jesus, ever claimed to be without sin. Paul never made such a claim. Paul stated quite the opposite in describing the two natures (Romans 7:15-25). The Bible definitely declares that no one is without sin.

Write in I John 1:8: _____

_____

Dr. A. J. Gordon once said, "If the doctrine of sinless perfection is a heresy, the doctrine of contentment with sinful imperfection is a greater heresy. It is not edifying to see a worldly Christian throw stones at a Christian perfectionist." Either extreme is dangerous and not Scriptural.

2. **The Biblical Meaning of Sanctification.**

   a. Sanctification means "to be set apart" or "separation." To sanctify always means to be set apart for a purpose—the purpose of God.

   b. There are two words in the original from which our English word "sanctification" comes. One is in the Old Testament Hebrew, "qadash"—and one in the New Testament Greek, "hagios." These two words are the root words for a number of words in English. For example, the Hebrew word is translated as:

   —"saint, sanctify, holy, consecrate, hallow, dedicate."

   The Greek word is translated as:

   —"saint, sanctification, holiness, consecration, dedication."

   (Now you see the reason for some misunderstanding.)

   c. The Old Testament uses the term, generally speaking, to describe *things*.

   The New Testament uses the term to denote *persons*.

   Throughout Scripture, both persons and things are spoken of as "holy"—"set apart" for a divine purpose.

B. GOD SANCTIFIES BELIEVERS FOREVER FOR HIMSELF.

1. **The Three Steps in Sanctification.**

   a. *The believer's experience* (past).

   Write in I Corinthians 6:11: _____

   _____

   _____

   We are sanctified the moment we believe. The Scripture above declares that we are sanctified before we are justified—ruling out a second or third work of grace. Underline I Corinthians 1:2 and notice the same placement of the two words.

   Write in II Thessalonians 2:13: _____

   _____

   _____

   Underline I Peter 1:2. Sanctification is first in all of the above Scriptures. God places us in the position of being "set apart" to Him and He never wants us to make ourselves "set apart" from others to show a false, sanctimonious attitude.

   So, in the experience of salvation, God "sanctified" us at that moment.

   Write in I Thessalonians 4:3-4: _____

_____

_____

b. *The believer's present state of growth.*

A person is sanctified when saved. God does that work in us. Justification is what Christ has already done for us on the Cross. Sanctification is what He is doing *now* in us. (Sanctification is a past experience at the time of our new birth—and a present progressive work in us now.)

The believer is to grow in grace. Sanctification is "being set apart" each day for Christ. It is a growth process of Bible study, prayer, yielding, cleansing, seeking to become more like Christ. This growth continues throughout life.

Write in the words of Jesus from John 17:19: _____

_____

_____

Underline John 17:14 and 16.

Write in Colossians 1:10: _____

_____

_____

Write in Hebrews 2:11 _____

_____

_____

c. *The ultimate sanctification of believers (future).*

Finally, we will be completely perfected in Him. This is the goal of our salvation—the ultimate purpose of our redemption. When we meet the Lord—then, we shall be like Him—sinless. Paul speaks of the church (saved ones) when he says, "That He might present it to Himself a glorious church, not having spot, or wrinkle, or any such thing; but that it should be holy and without blemish" (Ephesians 5:27).

The bride will be totally sanctified and ready for the wedding.

Write in I Thessalonians 5:23-24: _____

_____

_____

Sanctification has to do not only with oursoul and spirit but also with our bodies. Since these bodies will not become completely, fully and actually redeemed until Jesus comes, our sanctification cannot be complete until our bodies are perfectly redeemed.

Write in Philippians 3:20: _____

_____

_____

Underline I Thessalonians 3:12-13 in your Bible.

Write in I John 3:2: _____

_____

_____

C. THE SOURCE OF SANCTIFICATION.

1. **It is *Not* of Man.**

   a. Sanctification has to do not only with our soul and spirit but also with our bodies. Since these bodies will not become completely, fully and actually redeemed until Jesus comes, our sanctification cannot be complete until our bodies are perfectly redeemed.

   b. The old nature cannot be eradicated by an experience which renders a person sinless in this life. If sanctification does mean "sinless perfection," why do we not find it in Scripture? Jesus was sanctified—yet sinless (John 10:36)—*the only one*. Carnal Christians are sanctified—but this does not do away with the sinful nature (I Corinthians 3:1-3).

2. **Sanctification is of God.**

   a. God sanctifies.
   Write in Jude 1: _____
   _____
   _____

   b. We are to sanctify the Lord God in our hearts.
   Write in I Peter 3:15: _____
   _____
   _____

3. **Sanctification is of Christ.**

   a. The acceptance of Christ as Lord is essential to being "set apart" for God. Jesus died for our sanctification.
   Write in Hebrews 10:10: _____
   _____

   b. The work of Jesus was perfect and everlasting.
   Write in Hebrews 10:14: _____
   _____

   Read again I Corinthians 6:11.

4. **Sanctification is of the Holy Spirit.**

   a. The Holy Spirit convicts and is active *in* us and is the active cause of sanctification.
   Write in Thessalonian 2:13 _____
   _____

   b. Paul speaks of sanctification by the Holy Spirit in reference to the Gentiles.
   Write in Romans 15:16: _____
   _____
   _____

   Read I Peter 1:2 again.

5. **Sanctification is by the Word of God.**

   a. Jesus declared the fact of sanctification by the Word.
   Write in John 17:17: _____
   _____

   b. Paul preached sanctification by the Word.
   Write in Ephesians 5:26: _____

D. THE EVIDENCE OF SANCTIFICATION.

1. **The Saints are to Serve.**

   a. Jesus said in John 17:19, "And for their sakes I sanctify myself, that they also might be sanctified through the faith." What did Jesus mean by "I sanctify myself"? He was perfect, holy, sinless. The answer is in John 17:18: _____

   _____

   Jesus is speaking of service in this world. He is speaking of service with power to carry out the assignment He gave to them. He "set Himself apart" in the form of humanity for us. He was holy, He was God, He was made flesh "for our sakes."

   b. The "saved ones" (called "saints") are to serve even in adversity.
   Write in I Peter 1:6: _____

   _____

   _____

   Underline verse 7 in your Bible.

2. **The Saints are to Manifest the Fruit of the Spirit.**

   a. The fruit (notice, singular) of the Spirit should be evident in the believer's life.
   Write in Galatians 5:22-23: _____

   _____

   _____

   b. The good works should please the Lord Jesus.
   Underline Hebrews 13:21 in your Bible.

3. **The Saints are to be Obedient to the Word of God.**

   a. The Christian is cleansed by the Word.
   Write in John 15:3: _____

   _____

   b. Study of the Word is a delight.
   Write in Psalm 1:2: _____

   _____

4. **The Saints are to be Separate from Sin and Submissive to God.**

   a. The "saved ones" are to resist the devil.
   Write in James 4:7: _____

   _____

   b. Christians are to stay close to the Lord and humble in His sight.
   Write in James 4:8 and 10: _____

   _____

   _____

   c. Christians are to be "holy"—"set apart" in conversation. Underline I Peter 1:15. We are to be holy because He is holy (I Peter 1:16).

V. WHAT THIS BIBLE TRUTH TEACHES US TODAY

Sanctification is presented in three tenses. The past, present and future. Every born again believer *has already been* sanctified (set apart, dedicated, consecrated, separated), and that sanctification is once and for all. We are *now being* sanctified through the Spirit and the Word. We *shall be* ultimately, wholly, completely sanctified when we meet the Lord Jesus Christ.

Every Christian still has two natures—the old Adamic, carnal nature and the new spiritual nature (I Corinthians 3:1-3).The growth of the spiritual comes through a daily dedication, a daily cleansing (I John 1:9), a daily study of the Word, a constant prayer in the heart. We grow in sanctification—we can never grow to the point of total sanctification in this life. Every believer is a "saint," a person "set apart" to God.

"Wherefore Jesus also, that He might sanctify the people with His own blood, suffered without the gate" (Hebrews 13:12).

YOUR NEXT ASSIGNMENT:

1. Read Psalm 49:8; 111:9; Luke 2:38; 21:28; Romans 3:24; 5:1-21; 8:23; Galatians 1:4; Chapters 3 and 4; Ephesians 1:2; Colossians 1:9-23; Hebrews 9 and 10; Titus 2:14; I Peter 1:18-19; Revelation 5:9.

2. Review and understand sanctification. Search the Scriptures for answers to any questions.

3. Mark your Bible where new truths are learned.

Lesson 24
"Redemption"

GREAT TRUTHS OF THE BIBLE

(Where lines are provided, look up the Scripture and write in the Scripture or its main truth.)

I. INTRODUCTION

The truths of REDEMPTION and ATONEMENT are two of the cardinal doctrines of the Christian faith. This lesson shall deal with redemption. The next lesson will deal with the atonement. Both of these truths are the result of the finished work of Christ on the cross.

Redemption and the atonement are the basis for regeneration, justification, sanctification, reconciliation, and all the doctrines of grace. Therefore, we are on holy ground in this lesson and the next lesson.

Redemption is the great plan of God and it covers the work of God in Christ. The Bible is filled with redemption. The *theme* of all Scripture is Jesus Christ but the *message* of the Bible is redemption.

II. BASIC SCRIPTURES:

Psalm 49:8; 111:9; Luke 2:38; 21:28; Romans 3:24; 5:1-21; 8:33; Galatians 1:4; Chapters 3 and 4; Ephesians 1:2; Colossians 1:9-23; Hebrews 9 and 10; Titus 2:14; I Peter 1:18-19; Revelation 5:9.

III. THE NUCLEUS OF THIS TRUTH

Redemption is of God through the Person of His Son, Jesus Christ, our Lord. Every great truth of Scripture is dependent on the "blood of Christ." Redemption is based on the blood of Christ (Hebrews 9:12). The blood of Christ is to the Bible what the blood is to our bodies (life). The death of Christ is the ransom, or redemption, paid to the demands of God for the sin of the world.

IV. THE GREAT TRUTH: *"REDEMPTION"*

A. THE MEANING OF REDEMPTION.

    1. Redemption in the Old Testament.

        a. The first promise of a Redeemer is found in Genesis 3:15. God made the promise. There would be One who would defeat Satan.

        Write in Genesis 3:15: _____

        _____

        _____

        b. The lineage of the promised Redeemer did not just happen. The Godly line included Abel, Seth, Noah, Shem, Abraham, Isaac, Jacob, Judah, David on to Christ—Immanuel. He was the promised Redeemer.

        c. Leviticus 25 gives the law of the "goel," or kinsman-redeemer. "Goel" is the Hebrew word for kinsman-redeemer. Additional Old Testament passages on the "goel" are found in Numbers 35 and Deuteronomy 19 and 25.

        d. There were three requirements of the kinsman-redeemer.

(1) He must be *willing* to redeem (Leviticus 25:25).

(2) He must be a kinsman, have the *right* to redeem (Leviticus 25:48-49).

(3) He must have the means, the *power* to redeem (Leviticus 25:52).

e. The story of Ruth and Boaz (Ruth 2, 3, 4) is a perfect illustration of the kinsman-redeemer. Boaz is a picture of the Kinsman-Redeemer promised back in Genesis 3:15.

2. The Meaning is Pictured in the Old Testament.

a. We see that redemption was the promise of God.

b. It was written in the law by the Lord God.

c. It was put to practical use in the life of Israel.

d. Then, it must have a message, or lesson, for us. You find that in Romans 15:4: _____

_____

_____

3. The Meaning of Redemption in the Old Testament.

a. There are three Hebrew words meaning similar truths. Simply, "redemption" or "redeem" means—

—"to set free, to let go." Write in Deuteronomy 21:8:

_____

_____

—"out of bondage." Write in Exodus 14:30: _____

_____

_____

—"to ransom, recover." Write in Exodus 6:6: _____

_____

_____

b. From these Old Testament truths we can see the heart of God. Redemption in the Old Testament means "to set free, ransom, rescue, recover, out of."

c. One thing is missing thus far. "Blood" has not been mentioned. Purposely it has been kept separate. The word "division" in Exodus 8:23 is from the Hebrew, meaning "redemption." The "division" between Israel and others was brought about by blood. The sprinkled blood of a spotless lamb was the price of redemption (Exodus 12:12-13). Underline the two verses in your Bible.

Do you see the picture now?

d. Redemption was the payment of a price in order that a slave, widow or even the nation Israel be set free. The payment was made by one who was able and willing to pay the ransom price—as did Boaz in the book of Ruth. When blood was required, a spotless lamb was offered as in Exodus 12. This is the meaning in the Old Testament.

4. The Meaning of Redemption in the New Testament.

a. All that we have studied thus far has pointed to the true Redeemer, Christ (I Corinthians 10:11).

b. In the New Testament, redemption means
    —"the price paid," "to release by paying a ransom," "to

142

deliver by paying a price." Write in Titus 2:14: _____

_____

—"redemption is through the blood of Christ."
Write in Ephesians 1:7: _____

_____

—"to buy out of the market place" which adds the
thought of removal from sale as well as the purchase
price. Write in Galatians 3:13: _____

_____

_____

_____

c. The sum of the Old and New Testament meaning of
redemption is, "to deliver by paying a price" by a near
kinsman.
The price was paid by Christ on the cross and fulfilled the
Old Testament prophecies of redemption.

B. THE PERSON OF REDEMPTION

1. The Requirements of the Kinsman-Redeemer.

a. Earlier in this lesson we studied the requirements of the
kinsman-redeemer in the Old Testament. They were real
shadows of the Supreme Kinsman-Redeemer in the New
Testament—Jesus Christ.
(1) He must be *willing* to redeem. Jesus was willing to "pay
the price." He was made flesh to redeem all who accept
Him.
Write in Galatians 4:4, 5: _____

_____

_____

Underline Philippians 2:6-7 and write in verse 8: _____

_____

(2) He must be a Kinsman—have the *right* to redeem.
Christ as our Kinsman-Redeemer has the right.
Write in Hebrews 2:11: _____

_____

_____

(3) He must have the power—the *means* to redeem. Jesus
had the power, the means to redeem.
Write in John 10:11: _____

_____

_____

Also John 10:18: _____

_____

_____

b. Christ has met every requirement to be our Redeemer. He
has paid the price on the cross. All who believe are redeemed.

C. THE PRICE OF REDEMPTION

1. The Precious Blood of Christ.

a. The price of our redemption was high. It required the incorruptible blood of our Lord Jesus Christ.

Write in I Peter 1:18-19: _____

_____

_____

_____

b. The blood of Christ is indestructible because it is still working. His blood was innocent blood (Matthew 27:4). Even today people are redeemed by the sinless blood of Christ. It will never lose its power.

2. Life is in the Blood.

a. "The life of the flesh is in the blood . . . " (Leviticus 17:11). Without blood in our arteries and veins we could not live. It must be human blood—"after our kind."

b. The blood of human beings are all one blood.

Write in Acts 17:26: _____

_____

_____

The Bible classifies humanity into nations, tribes, tongues and peoples. Never does the Scripture state that we are divided into many races. By our natural birth there is only one human race and this race is distributed among peoples, nations tribes and tongues. We belong to the same fallen race of Adam "for there is no difference." The only two races recognized in Scripture by the Lord God are the *fallen* race of Adam and the *redeemed* race of the Lord Jesus. We are all of one blood, regardless of origin or geographical location.

c. The blood of Christ places believers in the redeemed race.

Write in Hebrews 10:22: _____

Underline Hebrews 10:14 in your Bible.

d. Christ has purchased the church, "the called out ones," with His own blood.

Write in Acts 20:28: _____

_____

_____

D. THE COMPLETION OF REDEMPTION.

1. A Possession to be Redeemed.

a. Christ died for all—He paid the full price for the world. Only those who receive Him share in the redemption by His blood (I Peter 1:18).

b. The Scripture indicates a future redemption. Paul says in Ephesians 1:13, "In whom ye also trusted, *after* ye heard the word of truth, the Gospel of your salvation; in whom also after ye believed, ye were sealed with that Holy Spirit of promise."

Now, write in Ephesians 1:14: _____

_____

_____

Notice one word in verse 14, "until." Until what? Paul gives the answer.

There is yet a possession to be redeemed.

c. *Creation* is yet to be redeemed.

Write in Romans 8:21: _____

_____

_____

Adam lost the inheritance of the earth as God had made it, and it passed into the possession of Satan. Christ has paid the purchase price for creation but its redemption is yet in the future.

Underline Romans 8:19-20 and 22.

2. **The Redemption of the Body.**

a. The soul of the believer has been redeemed but not his body. The resurrection body is hard for us to comprehend. The transfiguration of Christ gives us only an idea of that body—also His resurrected body gives us another glance of what we shall be like when redemption is complete. Paul tells us vividly.

Write in Romans 8:23: _____

_____

_____

b. Redemption is not complete until these vile bodies are changed.

Write in Philippians 3:21: _____

_____

_____

c. Read in detail I Corinthians 15:35-50. Underline verses 38, 39, 42-45, 49, 50.

d. Once redeemed by the blood of Christ, we are sealed until "the day of redemption."

Write in Ephesians 4:30: _____

_____

_____

E. THE BLESSINGS OF REDEMPTION.

1. **The Present Blessings in Christ.**

a. "We are not our own." We belong to Him (I Corinthians 6:19-20).

b. "We have—forgiveness of sins" (Ephesians 1:7).

c. "He cleanses us" (I John 1:9).

d. "He keeps us" (Philippians 4:7).

e. "God gives us power (the Holy Spirit) and love and a sound mind" (II Timothy 1:7).

f. "God has not given us the spirit of fear" (II Timothy 1:7).

(There are hundreds of blessings for the redeemed. Space does not permit more. This is the positive side in this life. Think of the things we have been redeemed from—for example: Galatians 4:5; 3:13; Titus 2:14).

2. **"Lift up Your Heads—Your Redemption Draweth Nigh" (Luke 21:28).**

a. The Lord Jesus said these words in His Olivet Discourse. He was talking about His return.

b. Full and complete redemption will be at the return of our Lord Jesus Christ (I Corinthians 15:52).

c. The redeemed of all ages groan with us awaiting that glorious day of complete redemption.

V. WHAT THIS BIBLE TRUTH TEACHES US TODAY

Being a Christian, a redeemed person, places a responsibility and an obligation to always glorify the Father because we have been bought with a price. The price paid for our redemption was the shed blood of Jesus Christ—the only thing and the only Person who could redeem sinful man. We must be willing to proclaim His Word, tell of His saving grace, live a life to portray the life of a redeemed person. "Lift up your heads . . . your redemption draweth nigh" (Luke 21:28). "Looking for that blessed hope, and glorious appearing of the great God and our Saviour, Jesus Christ" (Titus 1:13). He could appear at any time. Is He your "blessed hope"—your Lord and Saviour?

YOUR NEXT ASSIGNMENT:

1. Read Genesis 3:15-21; Exodus 12; Leviticus 16 and 17; Romans 3 and 5; II Corinthians 5:21; I Timothy 2:5; Hebrews 9 and 10; I Peter 1:13-19; 2:23.

2. Review your notes on Redemption.

3. Mark your Bible where new truths have been learned.

GREAT TRUTHS OF THE BIBLE

Lesson 25 "Atonement"

(Where lines are provided, look up the Scripture and write in the Scripture or its main truth.)

I. INTRODUCTION

There is a mystery about the atonement that makes it impossible for our finite minds to comprehend the fullness of this truth. Yet, it is the foundation and basis for all the other doctrines surrounding the salvation of all who will accept Christ. The blood of Jesus Christ is clearly the price paid for the atonement. It is a pivotal doctrine of the Bible. The word occurs many times in the Old Testament but is found only once in the King James Version of the New Testament. The Revised Standard Version does not use the word in the New Testament. The fact of the atonement can be found in the Gospels and in the writings of Paul, Peter and John.

In theology, atonement is a word which covers the entire sacrificial work of Christ. In the Old Testament, atonement is the English word used to translate the Hebrew "kaphar," which means "to cover, to make a covering."

Before we proceed with the study of atonement, it is imperative that a few words be understood. We have studied some of these words before, but we shall set them off in a group so you will recall the meaning of each word as we study this lesson on atonement.

- *Reconciliation*–"the restoration of man to fellowship with God."
- *Propitiation*–"the satisfaction of the just demands of God's holiness for the punishment of sin."
- *Redemption*–"a ransom, the price paid to free a slave—to be bought—to deliver by paying a price."
- *Justification*–"to declare one righteous (to justify does not make one righteous). God declares a person just on the basis of acceptance of the shed blood of Christ."
- *Substitution*–"the death of Christ was substitutionary, in our place, because He tasted death for every man."
- *Sacrifice*–"One who gives what is necessary to bring God and man together; Christ was sacrificed for us."
- *Type or Shadow*–"a person or incident which carries a prophetic significance beyond itself. Old Testament types are pictures of the New Testament fulfillment, such as the sacrificial system of the Old Testament was a type of the ultimate sacrifice, the atonement of Christ on the cross."

II. BASIC SCRIPTURES:

Genesis 3:15-21; Exodus 12; Leviticus 16 and 17; Romans 3 and 5; II Corinthians 5:21; I Timothy 2:5; Hebrews 9 and 10; I Peter 1:13-19; 2:23.

III. THE NUCLEUS OF THIS TRUTH

Atonement is the reconciling work of Christ; which, through the sacrifice of Himself on behalf of sinful men, made possible man's forgiveness in that it (His substitutionary death) satisfied the just and holy demands of God. It is Christ paying the price to make man "at-one" with God. Atonement is "at-one-ment" with God.

IV. THE GREAT TRUTH: *"ATONEMENT"*

A. OLD TESTAMENT SACRIFICES WERE SHADOWS OF THE ATONEMENT OF CHRIST.

1. The Promise of the Atonement.

a. The cross was not an afterthought of God. It was the working out of an eternal plan and purpose of God. It was the fulfillment of a promise of God. The cross spoke of "the Lamb slain from the foundation of the world" (Revelation 13:8).

b. The promise of the atonement is found in Genesis 3:15. The promise is found in God's pronouncement of the curse upon the serpent.
Write in Genesis 3:15: _____

_____

_____

c. This was a prophecy of a conflict which would culminate in the victory of the cross. Satan was to be defeated by the "seed of woman." That Seed was and is Jesus Christ.

2. Shadows of the Atonement.

a. When God made coats of skin to cover the nakedness of sinful man, He foreshadowed the atonement (Genesis 3:21).

b. The sacrifice of the Passover lamb and the sprinkling of the blood on the doorposts of the homes pointed to the Cross of Calvary. Jesus shed His blood and became our Passover (I Corinthians 5:7).

c. In the system of the Old Testament sacrifices, established by the Lord God, the atonement was pictured. For all those years, God kept before the people one great "object lesson." The shedding of the blood of animal sacrifices reminded the people of the fact that without blood there could be no atonement for their sins. There was one day in the year set apart as the "day of atonement" (Leviticus 16:29-30). Read Leviticus 16 and you will find *the* great chapter in the Old Testament on the atonement. In the chapter, atonement is mentioned 16 times and you should underline these in your Bible.

d. The blood of the animal sacrifices only "covered" the sins of Israel in anticipation of the cross. The Old Testament sacrifices were merely an "offering," a divinely appointed temporary means to "atone"—"to cover"—the sins of the people.
Write in Hebrews 10:4: _____

_____

Read Hebrews 9:1-10 to know the meaning of the tabernacle.

All of the Old Testament sacrifices were "shadows"—"pictures"—pointing to Christ and they were fulfilled in Him.

B. THE PERSON OF THE ATONEMENT.

1. The Central Figure of the Atonement.

148

a. In the Old Testament the high priest was the central figure. It was he who offered the sacrifice and sprinkled the blood of atonement on the mercy seat, in the holy of holies, in the tabernacle.

b. In the New Testament, Jesus Christ is the great High Priest. He not only offered the sacrifice to make atonement for sin, He was Himself the sacrifice. The blood of Christ is clearly the price involved in the atonement. Underline Hebrews 9:11.

Write in Hebrews 9:12: _____

_____

_____

Underline Hebrews 9:26 in your Bible. Notice the fact that Jesus, in His atoning work, did not just cover sin, He "put away sin."

2. He Must Be Without Sin.

a. In the Old Testament, the high priest washed himself in water and put on clean garments (Leviticus 16:4, 24) on the day of atonement. He had to be clean to minister. The sacrifices that were brought had to be without blemish (Leviticus 4:3).

b. This was a shadow of Christ, our sacrifice—without spot or blemish. He was sinless.

Write in Hebrews 4:15: _____

_____

_____

To atone for our sins, Jesus had to be without sin.

3. He Had to Be Divine.

a. The atonement is based on the deity of Christ. Jesus claimed deity for Himself.

Write in John 10:17: _____

_____

Underline John 10:18, 28, 30.

b. His character and His image prove Him to be divine.

Write in Colossians 1:15: _____

_____

4. He Had To Identify With Mankind.

a. Jesus was made flesh and lived among men without sin. He was made God-Man (John 1:14).

b. To be a merciful High Priest and to make reconciliation, He had to identify with man.

Write in Hebrews 2:17: _____

_____

_____

_____

C. THE PLAN OF THE ATONEMENT.

1. The Atonement Removed the Sins of the Old Testament Saints.

a. The Day of Atonement only "covered" the sins of the Old

149

Testament saints. The atoning work of Christ removed the sins "that are past."

Write in Romans 3:25: _____

_____

_____

    b. The sacrifice of Christ established the new covenant and redeemed the transgressions that were under the old covenant.

       Write in Hebrews 9:15: _____

_____

_____

2. The Atonement Was the Divine Plan of God.

    a. The incarnation of Jesus was for the purpose of the atonement.

       Write in Romans 5:8: _____

_____

    b. The atonement was necessary to make God and man "at-one" with each other. The love of God provided the Redeemer to take our sins and not "cover" them, but "remove" them. "Remission" means "to send off or away." The atonement, the shed blood of Christ, was for the remission of sins (Matthew 26:28).

       Write in Psalm 103:12: _____

_____

_____

D. THE PURPOSE OF THE ATONEMENT.

    1. The Atonement is the Pivotal Doctrine of Scripture and Encompasses the Total Work of Christ on the Cross.

       a. Atonement includes "reconciliation" (see introduction).

         Write in Romans 5:10: _____

_____

_____

         Underline II Corinthians 5:19 in your bible.

       b. Atonement includes "propitiation" (see introduction).

         Write in I John 2:2: _____

_____

       c. Atonement includes "redemption" (see introduction).

         Write in Colossians 1:14: _____

_____

         Underline I Corinthians 1:30 in your Bible.

       d. Atonement includes "justification" (see introduction).

         Write in Romans 3:28: _____

_____

       e. Atonement includes "substitution" (see introduction).

         Write in I Peter 2:24: _____

_____

_____

Write in II Corinthians 5:21: _____

_____

    f.   Atonement includes "sacrifice" (see introduction).
        Write in I Corinthians 5:7: _____

_____

        Write in Hebrews 10:12: _____

_____

2. The Scope of the Atonement is Unlimited.

    a. The death of Christ was for all the sins of the world.
        Write in Matthew 20:28: _____

_____

    b. God sent His Son to save the world.
        Write in John 3:17: _____

_____

    c. The gift of God is eternal life.
        Write in Romans 6:23: _____

_____

E. THE POWER OF THE ATONEMENT.

    1. Christ's Atonement Conquered Sin.

      a. Only one atonement was necessary.
          Write in Hebrews 9:28: _____

_____

      b. Jesus came to save from sin.
          Write in Matthew 1:21: _____

_____

    2. The Atonement Cleanses.

      a. The blood of Christ clenses.
          Write in I John 1:7: _____

_____

      b. The atonement transforms a life. Underline Romans 12:2 in
          your Bible.

V. WHAT THIS BIBLE TRUTH TEACHES US TODAY

The atonement places several obligations upon all Christians.
We should hate sin. It was our sin that nailed Jesus to the cross. He shed His blood so that we might become "new creatures in Christ." His death on the cross was the price He had to pay for our salvation.

We should love the Lord with all our being. If He loved us enough to leave His place in heaven, was made flesh in our likeness, offered Himself on the cross and died that we might live, then, we should love Him enough to live for Him and even die for Him if necessary.

We should tell the world the message of our Lord. He is our Saviour. He is our peace, our hope, our joy, our love, our light, our intercessor, our rest, our assurance of eternal life.

Are you "at-one" (atone) with Christ?

YOUR NEXT ASSIGNMENT:

1.   Read Zechariah 4:7; John 1:14-17; Acts 4:33; 11:23; 14:3; Romans 3:21-26; 4:4-5; 4:24-25; 5:2, 20; II Corinthians 12:9; Ephesians 2:1-9; Titus 3:5-7; James 4:6; II Peter 3:18.

       151

2. Review your notes on Atonement.

3. Mark your Bible where new truths are learned.

Lesson 26
"Grace"

(Where lines are provided, look up the Scripture and write in the Scripture or its main truth.)

I. INTRODUCTION

The teaching of grace is seldom approached in most Bible studies. It has become an accepted fact that the pupils know what grace means and do not need it explained. To overlook the importance of this subject is to overlook the true character of God.

The words "grace" and "gracious" can be found almost 200 times in Scripture. The word comes from the Greek word "charis" and the Greeks admired the word. It refers to that heartfelt attraction to someone. The Greeks often used the word to express generosity, without thought of a reward or favor from the other person. The Christians exalted the word to mean "a gift" and that came to mean the "gift of salvation"—"the kindness and love of God in forgiving us and saving us."

In our day it is said that a person has "charisma," meaning "one with an attractive, appealing personality—a magnetism."

II. BASIC SCRIPTURES

Zechariah 4:7; John 1:14-17; Acts 4:33; 11:23; 14:3; Romans 3:21-26; 4:4-5; 4:24-25; 5:2, 20; II Corinthians 12:9; Ephesians 2:1-9; Titus 3:5-7; James 4:6; II Peter 3:18.

III. THE NUCLEUS OF THIS TRUTH

Probably the best known meaning of this important Biblical term is "unmerited favor" or "divine favor"—a favor freely bestowed upon those totally unable to return the favor. Grace is God's free action in behalf of those who are without merit. Grace demonstrates the goodness of God toward those who deserve His wrath. On the basis of the substitutionary death of Christ, God's grace provides a way for God to offer the free gift of eternal life to a guilty sinner. We deserved punishment. God's grace removes the punishment and grants to us the salvation we did not deserve. It is truly "unmerited favor."

IV. THE GREAT TRUTH: *"GRACE"*

A. THE SCRIPTURAL MEANING OF GRACE.

1. Gracious Words of our Lord.

    a. The significance of grace is spoken by the Lord Jesus as He opened the Book and read the words of the prophet. In the synagogue in Nazareth Jesus was known as "Joseph's son." When He spoke, "they wondered at the *gracious words* which proceeded out of His mouth" (Luke 4:22).

    b. The Lord is gracious to all who have tasted His Word. Write in I Peter 2:2-3: _____

_____

_____

2. **The Biblical Definition of Grace.**

   a. Most scholars accept Titus 3:4-5 as the Scriptural definition of grace. There are other Scriptures which are very meaningful but let us accept this one as a basis for the definition.
   Write in Titus 3:4-5: _____

   _____

   _____

   _____

   b. Grace expresses God's love toward those who are unlovely. God's great mercy and love even when we were dead in sin is grace.
   Write in Ephesians 2:4-5: _____

   _____

   _____

   c. Grace precedes mercy. It is an expression of God's love. Paul used the order in most of his epistles. "Grace, mercy, and peace from God our Father and Jesus Christ our Lord" (I Timothy 1:2 and II Timothy 1:2).

B. THE CHANNELS OF GRACE.

   1. **Grace Comes to Us From God the Father.**

      a. Grace characterizes the nature of God.
      Write in I Peter 5:10: _____

      Write in James 4:6: _____

      _____

      _____

      b. Grace is an attribute of God.
      Write in II Timothy 1:9: _____

      _____

   2. **Grace Comes To Us From Christ Jesus.**

      a. The Son of God came "full of grace and truth."
      Write in John 1:14: _____

      _____

      b. John gave testimony of grace by Jesus Christ.
      Write in John 1:17: _____

      _____

   3. **The Spirit of Grace Comes From the Holy Spirit.**

      a. The promise of the Spirit of grace was given in Zechariah 12:10. Underline in your Bible.

      b. The Scriptural definition of grace was given in Titus 3:4-5. Now read verses 6 and 7. We are "renewed by the Holy Spirit which is shed on us abundantly through Jesus Christ, our Saviour, that being justified by His grace." This is an all inclusive statement of God the Father, the Holy Spirit, Jesus Christ and grace. Underline Titus 3:6-7 in your Bible.

C. THE GRACE OF GOD PROVIDES SALVATION.

   1. **Grace is the Love and Mercy of God in Action.**

a. God showed mercy in love by the death of His Son on the cross.

Write in John 3:16: _____

_____

_____

b. An acrostic will cause you to remember the truth of God's grace:

G od's
R iches
A t
C hrist's
E xpense.

All believers have God's riches because Christ has paid the price in full.

2. We Are Justified By His Grace.

a. In order for men to be justified and have peace with God, He deals with them in grace (Titus 3:7).

Write in Romans 3:24: _____

_____

_____

b. The forgiveness of sins is according to His grace.

Write in Ephesians 1:7: _____

_____

_____

Underline Ephesians 1:8 in your Bible.

3. We Are Saved by Grace.

a. God's kindness toward us is grace.

Write in Ephesians 2:7: _____

_____

_____

Underline Ephesians 2:4-5 in your Bible.

b. The great passage on grace and faith is Ephesians 2:8-9.

Write in the passage: _____

_____

_____

_____

Now, try to memorize those two verses.

4. The Grace of God is Sufficient.

a. A "thorn in the flesh, the messenger of Satan" kept Paul from being exalted above measure (II Corinthians 12:7-8).

b. The Lord's answer is a dynamic statement for every Christian.

Write in II Corinthians 12:9: _____

_____

_____

_____

D. THE MANIFESTATION OF THE GRACE OF GOD.

1. Grace is Abundant.

   a. The Lord is able to make us strong in our weakness.
   Write in I Timothy 1:14: _____

   _____

   b. Grace produces patience. In I Peter 2:19-20 you read, "For this is thankworthy (margin "grace") if a man for conscience toward God endure grief, suffering wrongfully."

2. Grace Imputes Righteousness.

   a. By God's grace, the righteousness of God is put to the account of anyone who accepts Christ.
   Write in Romans 4:4-5: _____

   _____

   _____

   b. Through Jesus Christ we have access to His grace.
   Write in Romans 5:2: _____

   _____

   _____

3. Grace Produces A New Nature.

   a. When we are saved we become new persons.
   Write in Ephesians 2:10: _____

   _____

   _____

   b. We become renewed in our mind.
   Write in Ephesians 4:24: _____

   _____

4. Grace Gives Instruction.

   a. A Christian can learn spiritual things. The grace that saves also teaches spiritual truths.
   Write in Titus 2:11-12: _____

   _____

   _____

   b. We are to speak with grace.
   Write in Ephesians 4:29: _____

   _____

   _____

E. THE AGE OF GRACE.

1. There Was Grace Before the Incarnation of Christ.

   a. The first reference of grace in Scripture is in Genesis 6:8. "Noah found grace in the eyes of the Lord."

   b. Moses found grace in the sight of the Lord (Exodus 33:12).
   Write in Exodus 33:17: _____

   _____

   _____

   c. On through the Book there are references to the grace of God.

156

2. **The Difference Between the Old Age and the New Age.**

   a. "The difference between the two ages is not a matter of no grace and some grace, but rather that today grace reigns" (Scofield Reference).

   Write in Romans 5:21: _____

   _____

   _____

   b. Under the old covenant the sheep died for the shepherd. Under the new covenant the Shepherd died for the sheep (John 10:14).

   c. Paul speaks of "the dispensation of the grace of God" (Ephesians 3:2). He speaks of deliverance from the old principle of works to the principle of grace.

   Write in Romans 6:14: _____

   _____

   d. The ministry to the Gentiles (all people who were not Israelites) was all of grace.

   Write in Ephesians 3:8: _____

   _____

   _____

F. GRACE AND CHRISTIAN GROWTH.

   1. **Salvation is by Grace—Then Growth.**

      a. Salvation is an act of grace (Acts 15:11). We cannot grow into a relationship of grace with God; works will not produce grace. Grace is a gift of God as a result of our faith in His Son.

      b. Once we have experienced salvation by grace, we should begin to grow in grace.

      Write in II Peter 3:18: _____

      _____

      _____

   2. **Grace is the Basis of Christian Growth.**

      a. The marks of grace should be apparent in the Christian life. The marks of grace come from a study of the Word which should dwell *in* us richly and in all wisdom.

      Write in Colossians 3:16: _____

      _____

      _____

      b. Grace changes our speech.
      Write in Ephesians 4:29: _____

      _____

      _____

      Write in Colossians 4:6: _____

      _____

      _____

      c. Grace causes us to pray boldly. Underline Hebrews 4:16 in your Bible.

d. Grace changes our attitude toward giving to the Lord's work. Giving is a grace.

Write in II Corinthians 8:7: _____

_____

_____

Underline II Corinthians 9:7-8 in your Bible.

e. Grace gives comfort and hope and strength for every need. Underline II Thessalonians 2:16-17 in your Bible.

V. WHAT THIS BIBLE TRUTH TEACHES US TODAY

Grace is of God. We cannot produce grace, nor can we work to earn grace. When we accept Jesus Christ, Paul says, "For by *grace* are ye saved through faith; and that not of yourselves, it is the gift of God . . . not of works" (Ephesians 2:8-9). Grace is what God does in our heart—faith is our part. Salvation is an act of grace. As we grow in grace, we should have less of our own ego and pride. We should "humble ourselves in the sight of the Lord, and He shall lift you up." Grace becomes a reality and force in life. We should realize that as Christians, we have all of "**G**od's **R**iches **A**t **C**hrist's **E**xpense." Grace is God's favor toward us—it is His love toward us. We deserve nothing. He gives forgiveness, salvation and eternal life to all who will accept Jesus Christ as Saviour. In "the ages to come, He might show the exceeding riches of His grace in His kindness toward us through Christ Jesus" (Ephesians 2:7). The last verse of the Bible says, "The grace of our Lord Jesus Christ be with you all. Amen." (Revelation 22:21).

YOUR NEXT ASSIGNMENT:

1. Read Exodus 20:1-26; 21:1 to 24:11; 24:12 to 31:18; Matthew 5 through 7; John 1:17; Acts 15:1-31; Romans 3:21-31; 7:4; 10:3-10; Galatians 2:19; 3:13-25; 5:16-18; I Timothy 1:9-10.

2. Review your notes on Grace.

3. Mark your Bible where new truths are learned.

Lesson 27
"Law and Grace"

(Where lines are provided, look up the Scripture and write in the Scripture or its main truth.)

I. INTRODUCTION

This subject is clearly taught in the Scriptures, yet it is one of the most debated and abused subjects in the circle of the Christian faith. Some argue that sin should abound so that grace can more abound. This is usually argued because people do not know Scripture. Then, there are those who live under "legalism," which is another word for "their interpretation" of the law.

Both groups are in error. The Bible clearly teaches us about the age in which we live—the age of grace—the age of the church. When God's Word speaks there is no room for argument.

In the last lesson the subject of *"grace"* was covered. In this lesson we shall consider both, *"law and grace."* What is the difference? How does the subject affect us in the church age? Why was the law given? What was the purpose of the Law? The Scriptures give the answers.

II. BASIC SCRIPTURES

Exodus 19:3-12; 20:1-26; 21:1 to 24:11; 24:12 to 31:18; Matthew 5 through 7; John 1:17; Acts 15:1-31; Romans 3:21-31; 7:4; 10:3-10; Galatians 2:19-20; 3:13-25; 5:16-18; I Timothy 1:9-10.

III. THE NUCLEUS OF THIS TRUTH

The purpose of the law was never to save. The law was a "schoolmaster to bring us to Christ" (Galatians 3:24). The law revealed man's sinfulness and inadequacy. The law provided a perfect standard by which man could measure himself morally and spiritually. In the law we see the perfection of God and the imperfection of man. The word "schoolmaster" ("paidagogos" the Greek word for "a child leader") refers to the slaves in whose charge the children were committed. It was their responsibility to see that the children were taken to school to the teacher (the "didaskalos"). Paul uses the same imagery of the "schoolmaster," (paidagogos), "a child leader," to deliver us to the Master Teacher, Jesus Christ, that we might be saved. After we have been delivered to the Teacher there is no longer any need for the "paidagogos"—the "child leader." Paul states, "But after that faith is come, we are no longer under a schoolmaster" (Galatians 3:25).

IV. THE GREAT TRUTH: *"LAW AND GRACE"*

A. THE PURPOSE OF THE LAW

   1. **"By the Law is the Knowledge of Sin."**

      a. The law was given that men might know what sin is, "for by the law is the knowledge of sin" (Romans 3:20).

      b. Paul said, "I had not known sin, but by the law."
         Write in Romans 7:7: _____

         _____

         _____

2. **The Law Declares the World Guilty Before God.**

   a. The law was given to "stop mouths."

   Write in Romans 3:19: _____

   _____

   _____

   _____

   b. God's law condemns man. David reveals this in Psalm
   14:2-3. Underline in your Bible.

   Write in Romans 3:10: _____

   _____

3. **The Law Was Given to Show the Real Nature of Sin.**

   a. Paul gives his own personal testimony of the effect of the
   law in his life (Romans 7:7-14). When Paul was converted
   there came a new revelation about the law.

   He was "alive without the law once: but when the commandment (law) came, sin revived, and I died" (Romans
   7:9).

   b. The law was from God, and holy.

   Write in Romans 7:12: _____

   _____

   c. Sin is exceedingly sinful when measured by the standard of
   the law.

   Write in Romans 7:13: _____

   _____

   _____

   _____

   _____

B. WHY THEN THE LAW?

1. **"Wherefore Then Serveth the Law?"**

   a. A literal translation of the question in Galatians 3:19 would
   simply be, "Why then the law?"

   b. The law was "added because of transgressions." Added to
   what? The verb "added" indicates that the law was added to
   something, and Paul gives the answer to the question
   because of what he has said in the first part of Galatians 3.

   c. In Galatians 3:6-8 Paul states that all of us—Old Testament
   saints as well as New Testament saints—are saved by grace
   and not by the law, even as Abraham believed God and it
   was accounted to him for righteousness.

   Write in Galatians 3:7 and 8: _____

   _____

2. **The Abrahamic Covenant and Promises of God Were First.**

   a. The law was added to the Abrahamic Covenant. Paul said
   that the covenant and promise made to Abraham antedated
   the law by 430 years. God gave to Abraham and to his
   descendants a way of salvation 430 years before the law was
   given.

Write in Galatians 3:17: _____

_____

_____

b. God made a promise and He kept it.

Write in Galatians 3:18: _____

_____

c. The law was "*added*" to the covenant and promises of God—"*until*." Underline the two words in Galatians 3:19.

d. "Until the Seed should come." The Seed is Christ—a descendant of Abraham.

Write in Galatians 3:16: _____

_____

_____

_____

Underline this verse in your Bible.

e. "No man is justified by the law in the sight of God." Paul states this fact in Galatians 3:11. To substantuate the fact, he quotes Habakkuk 2:4, "The just shall live by faith." Underline Galatians 3:11 in your Bible.

3. **Why Did God Give the Law?**

a. The law was given that we might see how sinful sin is. The law is a plumbline that we might see how uneven our lives are without Christ. The plumbline will not make one straight, but prove one crooked. Underline Amos 7:7-8 and Isaiah 28:17.

So, the law was added because of transgressions that we might see how sinful we are.

b. Second, Paul says that the law was given in order that, being found sinners by the standard of the law, all of us might be saved through faith in Jesus Christ who is the Seed of Abraham. The law implanted in the heart of man his sense of sin and his need for a Saviour. The law could not save (Galatians 3:21). The law reveals our sinfulness, our lostness.

c. In the law we are led to find forgiveness in Jesus Christ. Without a sense of lostness, we would never seek forgiveness nor would we know the true meaning of Christ as Saviour.

C. THE LORD JESUS WAS BORN UNDER THE LAW.

1. **Jesus, Born Under the Law, Rendered Complete Obedience to the Law.**

a. He was born under the law.

Write in Galatians 4:4: _____

_____

b. He was circumcised and presented to the Lord God in the Jewish temple. A sacrifice of turtledoves was offered "according to the law of the Lord" (Luke 2:21-24).

2. **Jesus Came to Fulfill the Law—Not to Destroy the Law (Matthew 5:17).**

a. He lived in perfect obedience to the law (Matthew 3:17; 17:5; Luke 2:39).

161

b. He confirmed the promises made to the fathers under the law (Romans 15:8).

c. He fulfilled all the types of the law by His life and sacrificial death (Hebrews 9:11-26). Read all the passage.

d. He redeemed man from the curse of the law that the blessings of the Abrahamic Covenant might come on all who believe.

Write in Galatians 3:13-14: _____

_____

_____

_____

_____

e. He is the mediator of the New Covenant by His blood (Hebrews 8:6-13).

D. BEFORE AND AFTER THE LAW.

1. Before the Law.

a. Before the law was given there was no transgression. One cannot transgress something that does not exist. The word "transgression" comes from two words—"trans" and "gresso"—and means "to go beyond." The Scripture is clear on this point.

Write in Romans 4:15: _____

_____

_____

b. The question in every mind at this point is, "Was there no sin before the law?" Yes—and just as wicked and terrible as after the law was given. Man did not realize the gravity of his sin and God gave the law to reveal the sinfulness of sin. The sin which had always been *morally* wrong now became *legally* wrong.

c. The law revealed sin to be a transgression against God and to convince the sinner of his need for salvation. Paul says, "For until the law sin *was* in the world; but sin is not imputed ("charged to someone—blamed on someone") where there is no law" (Romans 5:13).

Sin was in the world before the law. The only specific penalty pronounced on sin generally was death, given when God said to Adam, "the day that thou eatest thereof thou shalt surely die." There was no law for specific sins such as murder, theft, adultery, etc. Only the penalty of death was pronounced.

2. After the Law.

a. The law came from God with detailed instructions and specific penalties. The law gave the sins the nature of transgression which they had never had before God gave the law.

The law did not produce sin, nor was the law itself sin. It was given to show the exceeding sinfulness of sin.

b. The law showed the true nature of sin. "Moreover, the law entered, that the offence might abound" (Romans 5:20).

c. The law stirred sin within the human heart.

Write in Romans 7:5: _____

_____

_____

Notice the word "motions." Paul says the law put sin in motion. Before the law, the same sins were committed but they were undisturbed by a law to punish and reveal them. The law stirred up the sin, and guilt was felt because blame could be placed. A good example—parents can forbid a child to go into the attic. Until then, the attic had never been of interest to the child but now, the parents have stirred up a curiosity, a desire to know why one can't go into the attic. The parents have put "in motion" something which the child had never thought about before. The demand was not wrong but it stirred up a temptation. Now, read again Romans 7:5. It has a new meaning, doesn't it?

d. The law is for sinners, not the saved ones (saints). Paul states very definitely this truth. Read I Timothy 1:5-8 and write in verse 9: _____

_____

3. **Is the Christian Under the Law?**

(This is always a question in Bible study. The answers shall be Scripture only.)

a. Christians are *not* under the law. Look up Romans 6:14 and underline in your Bible.
   - Also, Romans 6:15
   - Also, Galatians 5:18
   - Also, I Corinthians 9:20 (American Standard Bible)

b. The Christian is not under the law as a means of being saved. Underline Romans 3:20. It says, "by the deeds of the law shall no flesh be justified in His sight."

Read again Romans 6:14 and Galatians 3:12.

Underline Romans 8:3-4 in your Bible.

Read Acts 15:1-11.

c. The Christian has been delivered from the law.

Underline Romans 10:4.

Read in detail II Corinthians 3:6-18.

The Answer: No, the Christian is not under the law!

V. WHAT THIS BIBLE TRUTH TEACHES US TODAY

The contrasts which the Bible gives of law and grace will stay in our hearts as truth for each day:
- The law prohibits—grace invites and gives.
- The law condemns the sinner—grace redeems the sinner.
- The law says "do"—grace says, "it is done."
- The law curses—grace blesses.
- The law condemns the best man—grace saves the worst man.
- The law reveals sin—grace atones for sin.
- The law was given by Moses—Grace and truth came by Jesus Christ.
- The law demands obedience—grace gives power to obey.
- The law was written on stone—grace is written in the heart.
- The law was done away in Christ—grace abides forever.
- The law says, "the soul that sinneth, it shall die"—grace says, "believe and live."

163

YOUR NEXT ASSIGNMENT:

1. Read Romans 3:21-28; 4:1-7; 8:3-4; 10:1-10; I Corinthians 1:29; II Corinthians 5:21; Philippians 3:7-9; James 2:23. (There will be many more Scripture passages used—but please read these before the study of the lesson.)

2. Review your notes on Law and Grace.

3. Mark your Bible where new truths are learned.

Lesson 28
"Righteousness"

(Where lines are provided, look up the Scripture and write in the Scripture or its main truth.)

I. INTRODUCTION

Righteousness is a gift of God through Jesus Christ. Man is far from being righteous. The Scriptures declare the sinfulness of man and the righteousness of God.

Accordingly, the term "righteousness" is applied to man's condition to designate the state of all who have responded in faith to the redeeming work of God through Christ. Having responded to the plan of salvation, man is accepted and approved of God.

The teaching of the "goodness" of man only points out the sinfulness of the human heart. Scripture says, "There is none righteous, no, not one" (Romans 3:10).

Righteousness and justification are inseparable in Scripture by the fact that the same word is used for both. Justification is through the redemptive work of Christ. It is by faith, not works and is the judicial act of God whereby He can justly declare *righteous* one who believes in Jesus Christ. The two truths are vital to our understanding of the Christian life.

II. BASIC SCRIPTURES

Romans 3:21-28; 4:1-7; 8:3-4; 10:1-10; I Corinthians 1:29; II Corinthians 5:21; Philippians 3:7-9; James 2:23.

III. THE NUCLEUS OF THIS TRUTH

By the act of the grace of God, the righteousness of God, is *credited, given, put to the account* (all mean "impute") of a believing sinner. Righteousness requires that which is right in character. God never requires anything which is not right—never instructs us to do wrong (Hebrews 1:8-9). The righteousness of God can be obtained only by accepting Jesus Christ as Saviour and Lord.

IV. THE GREAT TRUTH: *"RIGHTEOUSNESS"*

A. GOD IS RIGHTEOUS

1. **God Loves Righteousness and Hates Sin.**

   a. God cannot and will not accept unrighteousness.
      Write in Deuteronomy 25:16: _____

      _____

      _____

   b. The wrath of God is revealed against unrighteousness.
      Write in Romans 1:18: _____

      _____

      _____

2. **Righteousness and Unrighteousness Can Never Blend Together.**

a. Fellowship between the two is impossible.
   Write in II Corinthians 6:14: _____

   _____

   _____

b. God judges unrighteousness. It is against His nature.
   Underline Romans 3:5-6 in your Bible.

3. The Nature of God is Righteousness.

a. God is the source of righteousness.
   Write in Romans 1:17: _____

   _____

   _____

   (Marginal - "a righteousness of which God is the source.")

b. God's righteousness is all He demands.
   Write in Romans 3:21: _____

   _____

   (We shall speak of the "manifestation" later.)

B. THE UNRIGHTEOUSNESS OF MAN

1. The Bible Declares the Sin of Man.

a. With the revelation in Scripture that God is supremely righteous, there is also the revelation that "all our righteousnesses are as filthy rags."
   Write in Isaiah 64:6: _____

   _____

   _____

b. "There is none righteous, no, not one." In Romans 3:9-18 Paul declares the sinful state of the human race. This passage is a picture of the real nature of fallen man.
   Wirte in Romans 3:10-11: _____

   _____

   _____

   _____

2. The Heart of Man is Wicked.

a. The heart of man is exceedingly wicked. Satan has tried every scheme to propagate the lie that the heart of man is "naturally good." The Bible says just the opposite.
   Write in Jeremiah 17:9: _____

   _____

   _____

b. The carnal (fleshly) mind is against God. Read Romans 8:5-8 and write in verses 7 and 8: _____

   _____

   _____

   _____

   _____

3. **Self Righteousness Cannot Produce Salvation.**

   a. There has always been a futile effort on the part of man to "be good"—to work out (as though under law) a character which God might approve. Paul gives a perfect example of this in his own life in Philippians 3:4-8.

   Write in verse 8: _____

   _____

   _____

   _____

   _____

   b. People are still "going about to establish their own righteousness." In other words, people "go about"—stay busy—rush from one "good" thing to another—in order to appear (establish) their own righteousness. They try to make up by *doing* what they lack in *being*. One of the great verses on self righteousness is found in Romans 10:3.

   Write in the verse, Romans 10:3: _____

   _____

   _____

   _____

   _____

   c. "The wrath of man worketh not the righteousness of God" (James 1:20).

C. THE BASIS FOR RIGHTEOUSNESS

1. **The Righteousness of God is in Christ Jesus.**

   a. We are *not* righteous. All the righteousness that God requires and approves is found in His Son, Christ Jesus. He met every requirement and He manifested (became visible) the righteousness of God (Romans 3:21).

   Write in Romans 3:22: _____

   _____

   _____

   b. Jesus Christ is "made unto us righteousness."
   Write in I Corinthians 1:30: _____

   _____

   _____

2. **Righteousness is a Gift of God.**

   a. Just as by one man sin entered into the world (the first Adam), so in Jesus Christ (the Second Adam) comes the free gift of righteousness.

   Write in Romans 5:17: _____

   _____

   _____

   Underline Romans 5:12 and 15 in your Bible.

   b. Christ is the righteousness of God to all who will believe.
   Write in Romans 10:4: _____

   _____

167

Also, write in Romans 10:9: _____

_____

_____

_____

3. Jesus Was Made Sin that we Might be Made Righteous.

a. Underline II Corinthians 5:14-15. Jesus, who knew no sin, was made sin for us (Jesus took our sins upon Himself).
Write in II Corinthians 5:21: _____

_____

_____

_____

b. Jesus became the sin offering for the whole world. When one accepts Christ, God looks upon that one as having died with Christ.
Write in Romans 6:6: _____

_____

_____

_____

c. Jesus died for us; He tasted death for every one.
Write in Hebrews 2:9: _____

_____

_____

4. The Righteousness of God is Given to All Believers.

a. A believer in Christ becomes a part of the Body of Christ.
Write in I Corinthians 12:13: _____

_____

_____

b. God sees a believer through His Son, Jesus Christ, and is justified in forgiving sin. Christ met the just demands of a righteous God by His shed blood. Jesus became the "propitiation"—the "mercy seat"—the satisfaction which God required. Propitiation is satisfying the righteousness of God and making it possible for Him to forgive.
Write in Romans 3:25: _____

_____

_____

c. Jesus is the righteous advocate for believers.
Write in I John 2:1: _____

_____

_____

Also, I John 2:2: _____

_____

_____

d. Christ is the righteousness of God; therefore, those who are saved are made the righteousness of God, which is not

168

increased by works nor decreased by faults (II Corinthians 5:21).

    e. Works cannot produce righteousness—only faith in Jesus Christ.

       Write in Romans 4:5: _____

       _____

       _____

       Underline Romans 4:6 in your Bible.

5. Christians Are Made the Righteousness of God *in Christ*.

    a. The believer is complete in Christ. Paul uses the term "in Christ" throughout his writings.

       Write in Colossians 2:9-10: _____

       _____

       _____

       _____

    b. In Ephesians and Philippians, underline the following verses, all stating that the believer is "in Christ":

Ephesians 1:1	Ephesians 5:8
" 1:3	" 6:10
" 1:4	Philippians 1:1
" 2:6	" 1:13
" 2:10	" 1:14
" 2:13	" 2:5
" 2:21	" 3:3
" 2:22	" 3:14
" 3:6	" 4:1
" 4:15	

    c. The believer's righteousness, we see from Scripture, is not *something* but *Someone*.

D. RIGHTEOUSNESS IS BY FAITH IN CHRIST

1. Righteousness of God is by Faith in Christ.

    a. Faith in Christ removes self righteousness.

       Write in Philippians 3:9: _____

       _____

       _____

    b. The Gospel contains the power of God unto salvation, and the righteousness of God.

       Write in Romans 1:16-17: _____

       _____

    c. Read and underline Romans 3:22 in your Bible.

2. Abraham Was a Good Example.

    a. "Abraham believed God and it was counted (imputed) unto him for righteousness" (Romans 4:3).

    b. The faith of Abraham was strong. Underline Romans 4:13, 16, 19, 20.

E. THE RIGHTEOUSNESS OF GOD SHOULD BE EVIDENT
IN THE CHRISTIAN LIFE.

1. **The Spiritual Things Should Come First.**

   a. The old battle of the flesh and the Spirit is usually the most
   evident.
   Write in Romans 8:5: _____

   _____

   _____

   b. The Spiritual should not be a "show" for the world to see,
   but a way of life which attracts people to Jesus Christ.
   Write in Romans 8:10: _____

   _____

   _____

2. **The Holy Spirit Produces the Fruit and Walk of the Spirit.**

   a. The fruit of the Spirit is a part of the Christian character, a
   manifestation of the graces in Galatians 5:22-23: _____

   _____

   _____

   _____

   b. Our walk should be in the Spirit.
   Write in Galatians 5:25-26: _____

   _____

   _____

3. **The Righteous Life is the Result of Salvation.**

   a. By God's grace the Christian can live righteously because
   he nas been made righteous by accepting Christ.
   Write in I John 3:7: _____

   _____

   _____

   b. We are to seek first things *first*.
   Write in Matthew 6:33: _____

   _____

   _____

   Memorize this verse and let it be a part of your everyday life.

V. WHAT THIS BIBLE TRUTH TEACHES US TODAY

When Christ died on the cross, it was the greatest evidence of the
righteousness of God. The sins "that are past" had been passed over
and God had "winked at" or "overlooked" them, but at the cross God
paid the full price. Only the atoning death of His Son, our Saviour and
Lord Jesus Christ, could justify the past, present and future of a
righteous and supreme Creator of the world.

All the *past* could be "winked at" before the death of Christ because
God foreknew of the cross (Romans 3:25).

All *future* forgiveness is righteous only by looking back at the cross
(Romans 3:26).

All *present* unrighteousness is made righteous by His cleansing (I John 1:9).

The past, present and future meet at the cross (Romans 5:8). The righteousness of God is revealed in the Gospel of Jesus Christ (Romans 1:17).

Therefore, none of us are righteous. Righteousness is of God. *If* we have accepted His Son, then He sees in us "the righteousness of God in Christ."

YOUR NEXT ASSIGNMENT:

1. Read John 6:37; 10:27-28; 14:27; 16:33; 19:30; 20:19-31; Romans 1:7; 5:1; 8:31-39; 16:20; I Corinthians 1:3; II Corinthians 6:10; Galatians 5:22-23; Ephesians 2:12-17; Philippians 1:6; 4:7; Colossians 1:20; 2:2, 13; 3:4; I Thessalonians 1:5; 5:23; II Timothy 1:12; Titus 2:13; Hebrews 2:18; 3:6, 14; 6:11; 7:25; 10:22; 12:24; 13:5; I Peter 1:4, 5, 23; II Peter 1:4; 3:14; The Book of I John; Jude 24, 25.

2. Review your notes on Righteousness.

3. Mark your Bible where new truths are learned.

Lesson 29
"Assurance and Peace"

(Where lines are provided, look up the Scripture and write in the Scripture or its main truth.)

I. INTRODUCTION

Assurance is a gift of God through faith in Jesus Christ. The world would call this gift peace of mind, meaning all is well for the future. Psychology would define it as a personality free of all frustration. The Bible sets forth this gift of assurance as a certainty, a knowledge, an assurance concerning one's personal relationship to God. For the believer, assurance is your rightful possession and God wants you to possess it as your gift from Him.

Assurance is an inner consciousness and confidence that a right relationship exists between you and God. Assurance is a subjective experience. Many who believe in the "security of the believer" do not have the assurance of salvation. It is not honoring to Him to doubt and have a lack of assurance. Salvation is not temporary or conditional (I John 5:12-13). Isaiah says, "And the work of righteousness shall be *peace*; and the effect of righteousness quietness and *assurance* forever" (Isaiah 32:17).

A simple illustration might help at this point. An expert driver of a race car invites you to ride with him in a test of the car. You are afraid, but you have enough faith to finally get into the car. Whatever security the car offered was yours as well as his. You tremble at every turn, while he has the understanding, knowledge and experience to enjoy the ride. He had assurance—you did not; yet both had the same security. Now, do you understand?

Assurance is absolutely necessary to have peace of mind and soul. This is true in all areas of life. You have assurance of love from family or friends; and you have peace concerning that area of life. You have some degree of assurance about your ability to work; and you have peace. You might have the assurance of good health (after you see your doctor), so you leave the doctor's office with a sense of peace.

God wants you to be happy in Christ, to enjoy your salvation. He cares for you and gives assurance and peace to you.

This lesson, therefore, covers both assurance and peace. There can be no peace without assurance.

II. BASIC SCRIPTURES

John 6:37; 10:27-28; 14:27; 16:33; 19:30; 20:19-31; Romans 1:7; 5:1; 8:31-39; 16:20; I Corinthians 1:3; II Corinthians 6:10; Galatians 5:22-23; Ephesians 2:12-17; Philippians 1:6; 4:7; Colossians 1:20; 2:2, 13; 3:4; I Thessalonians 1:5; 5:23; II Timothy 1:12; Titus 2:13; Hebrews 2:18; 3:6, 14; 6:11; 7:25; 10:22; 12:24; 13:5; I Peter 1:4, 5, 23; II Peter 1:4; 3:14; The Book of I John; Jude 24, 25.

III. THE NUCLEUS OF THIS TRUTH

The Bible is filled with admonitions for every believer to have full assurance and peace of mind and soul. The gifts of assurance and peace are from God, and given to every believer who will only accept them from a loving Father. Can we know that we are the children of God? Yes. Paul says, "Being *confident* of this very thing, that He which hath begun a good work in you *will perform it until* the day of Jesus Christ" (Philippians 1:6). Can we know a peace down deep in our soul? Yes. "And the peace of God, which *passeth all understanding*, shall keep (guard) your hearts and minds through Christ Jesus" (Philippians 4:7).

Assurance is necessary for peace of mind. In a world yearning for peace, there must be individual peace to exist. This individual peace can last only if it is based upon faith in the Lord Jesus Christ. Among the truths of the Bible, none is more personal and more satisfying than the assurance of faith and the peace of God.

IV. THE GREAT TRUTH: *"ASSURANCE AND PEACE"*

A. ASSURANCE COMES FROM GOD

1. The Testimony of the Word of God Gives Assurance.

a. The promises of God are just as valid today as in the days of the Old Testament. The unconditional promises of God do not depend on human resources.

One of the great proclamations of assurance is Romans 8:28: _____

_____

_____

b. In God's eternal purpose, through the Gospel of Christ, He assures every believer of His love. One of the great peaks of Scriptural truth is found in Romans 8:31-39.

Write in Romans 8:31-32: _____

_____

_____

_____

_____

c. Underline Romans 8:33-34. Write in verse 35: _____

_____

_____

Write in Romans 8:37: _____

_____

_____

Write in Romans 8:38-39 and try to memorize these verses:

_____

_____

_____

_____

2. Taking God at His Word Gives Assurance.

a. It is not necessary to doubt the promises of God. Simply taking God at His Word gives assurance.

Memorize and write in II Timothy 1:12: _____

_____

b. The Bible declares many times that the believer is "in Christ."

Write in Colossians 2:6: _____

_____

Underline Colossians 2:7 in your Bible.

Write in Colossians 2:10: _____

_____

Write in Colossians 3:2-3: _____

_____

_____

Paul states the fact of the believer being "in Christ" throughout his writings.

3. **The Power of God is Sufficient to Give Assurance.**

a. God wants to assure you that you are His child through faith in Jesus Christ.

"But as many as received Him, to them gave He power (authority—the right) to become the sons of God, even to them that believe on His name: which were born, not of blood, nor of the will of the flesh, nor of the will of man, but of God" (John 1:12-13).

b. The Christian is kept by the power of God. Underline I Peter 1:3-4 in your Bible and write in I Peter 1:5: _____

_____

_____

_____

B. THE WORK OF CHRIST GIVES ASSURANCE

1. **The Finished Work of Jesus Gives Blessed Assurance.**

a. When Jesus died on the cross, He paid the total price to save all who will surrender their lives to Him.

Write in John 19:30: _____

_____

b. In the Lord's Prayer (not the model prayer in Matthew 6:9-13) in John 17, Jesus speaks seven times of believers as given to Him by the Father (John 17:2, 6 twice, 9, 11, 12, 24).

c. Jesus finished the redemptive work He was sent to accomplish. Underline Hebrews 10:10 and 12 in your Bible.

Write in Hebrews 10:14: _____

_____

2. **The Intercession of Christ as Our High Priest Gives Assurance.**

a. The believer has access to God the Father because Jesus is our High Priest—interceding for His own. Underline in your Bible Hebrews 10:19-22; 7:26-27.

Write in Hebrews 7:25: _____

_____

_____

b. Most of Christianity prays to God "in the name of Jesus Christ." Why do most prayers close with those words?
Write in I Timothy 2:5: _____

3. **Jesus, as Our Present Advocate in Heaven, Gives Assurance.**

   a. The never failing ministry of Jesus is His advocacy (an attorney—one who defends) in behalf of believers. Christians are not perfect and Satan glories in being able to "accuse the brethren before God day and night" (Revelation 12:10). But Jesus is there in Heaven for us.
   Write in Hebrews 9:24: _____
   _____
   _____

   b. The present work of Jesus gives Christians indisputable evidence for assurance. Jesus is always faithful in defending His own when confession of sin is made in prayer.
   Write in I John 1:9: _____
   _____
   _____

   Write in I John 2:1: _____
   _____
   _____

   Underline the two verses (above) in your Bible.

C. THE WORK OF THE HOLY SPIRIT GIVES ASSURANCE

   1. **The Holy Spirit makes the Word Powerful.**

      a. Words are more than words when the Holy Spirit implants them in the heart.
      Write in I Thessalonians 1:5: _____
      _____
      _____

      b. Notice I Peter 1:22 and write in I Peter 1:23: _____
      _____

   2. **The Holy Spirit Indwells Christians.**

      a. Assurance belongs to the Christian because the Holy Spirit constantly abides in the heart of the believer.
      Write in I Corinthians 3:16: _____
      _____
      _____

      b. The Christian is not his own, but belongs to Christ.
      Underline I Corinthians 6:19 and write in verse 20: _____
      _____
      _____

      c. Christians are sealed by the Holy Spirit.
      Underline Ephesians 4:30 in your Bible.
      All of these verses, and hundreds more, give the "blessed assurance that Jesus is mine."

D. THE PEACE THAT PASSETH ALL UNDERSTANDING

  1. **Peace With God.**

    a. When a person accepts Christ, that person enters into the work of Christ by faith.
Write in Romans 5:1: _____

_____

    b. Jesus is our peace.
Write in Ephesians 2:14: _____

_____

    and underline verses 15 through 17. Notice the word "peace."

  2. **Peace of God.**

    a. This is inward peace.
Write in Philippians 4:7: _____

_____

    b. Inward peace comes as a result of committing all anxieties to God through prayer. Underline Philippians 4:6 in your Bible.

    c. Jesus gave His peace to His own.
Write in John 14:27: _____

_____

  3. **Peace From God.**

    a. The great invocations of the epistles speak of "peace from God." Paul used the term in Romans 1:7: _____

_____

    Also in I Corinthians 1:3: _____

_____

    Underline II Corinthians 1:2: Galatians 1:3; Ephesians 1:2; Philippians 1:2; I Thessalonians 1:1; II Thessalonians 1:2; I Timothy 1:2; II Timothy 1:2; Titus 1:4; Philemon 3. All of these salutations by Paul speak of "peace from God."

    b. John used the phrase in II John 3.

    c. All of these greetings using "peace from God" mean the peace of God in our daily lives. In each one of the phrases it is said in the same sense as "grace and mercy." The meaning is that the "peace from God" would surround, keep, bless each child of God.

V. WHAT THIS BIBLE TRUTH TEACHES US TODAY

The absence of assurance in the Christian life brings about doubt, frustration, which means an absence of peace. We have tried to point you to enough Scripture to give peace and assurance. Now, if there is still a question concerning assurance, read the little book of I John. Therein you will find the word "know" some 38 times. This epistle is the "book of assurance." This should be the first book of the Bible recommended to new Christians.

Assurance can be yours if you are saved. Satan will cause you to doubt your salvation each day. The only way to defeat Satan is to believe and stay in the Word of God and pray without ceasing.

Peace was given to us by God the Father and our Lord Jesus Christ. Jesus said, "My peace I give unto you" (John 14:27). Do we accept His Word? Assurance of our relationship with Jesus Christ gives to us "the peace of God, which passeth all understanding" (Philippians 4:7). The only way to be at peace and have assurance is to

- stay in the Word—study it.
- pray without ceasing.
- stay in fellowship with the saints. This is usually found in a good Bible based church. You need to assemble with the household of God.

YOUR NEXT ASSIGNMENT:

1. Read Leviticus 4:1-4, 12; 16:21-22; Psalm 22:1-26; Isaiah 53:4-12; Matthew 20:28; Luke 22:37; Romans 4:25; 5:6-8; II Corinthians 5:14-21; Galatians 1:4; 3:13; Hebrews 9:12, 22, 26, 28; I Peter 2:21-25.

2. Review your notes on Assurance and Peace.

3. Mark your Bible where new truths are learned.

Lesson 30
"Substitution"

GREAT TRUTHS OF THE BIBLE

(Where lines are provided, look up the Scripture and write in the Scripture or its main truth.)

I. INTRODUCTION

The subject of this lesson is often mentioned by teachers and preachers but seldom is taught or explained. Those of us in the ministry often refer to the substitutionary death of Christ as His vicarious atonement. The words "vicarious" and "substitution" mean the same thing. Webster defines "substitution" as "a person that takes the place of another." He defines "vicarious" as "a substitutionary sacrifice suffered by one person as a substitute for another." So you see the two words are synonymous. Seldom is this fact ever mentioned to a class or congregation. After the sin of Adam and Eve, God could not do away with the penalty He had spoken to them: "In the day that thou eatest thereof thou shalt surely die" (Genesis 2:16-17). God had spoken and He could not break His Word. It became necessary that the penalty, if it was not to fall on Adam and Eve, should fall on someone who could and would take their place. The substitute that God provided was *Himself* in the person of Jesus Christ. Jesus was none other than God manifest in the flesh. "Great is the mystery of Godliness: God was manifest in the flesh (Jesus), justified in the Spirit, seen of angels, preached unto the nations, believed on in the world, received up into glory" (I Timothy 3:16). Substitution is based upon representation—a representative being one appointed to act in the place of another.

Substitution is one of the Bible's basic doctrines, yet the words "substitution" and "vicarious" are not found in the Bible. The Scriptures reveal the fact that the death of Christ was vicarious, meaning that He suffered in the place of the sinner. He was a substitute—one to take the penalty of sin to satisfy a Holy God. The death of Christ, a substitute on the cross, was the redemptive price paid to the demands of God for sin, freeing the sinner from condemnation once he accepts Christ as Saviour.

II. BASIC SCRIPTURES

Leviticus 4:1-4; 16:21-22; Psalm 22:1-26; Isaiah 53:4-12; Matthew 20:28; Luke 22:37; Romans 4:25; 5:6-8; II Corinthians 5:14-21; Galatians 1:4; 3:13; Hebrews 9:12, 22, 26, 28; I Peter 2:21-25.

III. THE NUCLEUS OF THIS TRUTH

Jesus has already taken upon Himself the divine judgments against the sinner to the complete satisfaction of God. There is but one thing left for the sinner to do. He must make a choice. The choice being to accept the Substitute, Jesus, as Saviour; or remain in his sinful condition and receive eternal punishment.

It is important to note that the word *"for,"* meaning "instead of" or "in place of," is used in every passage where mention is made of the death of Christ as a ransom. An example: "Who gave himself a ransom *for* all, to be testified in due time" (I Timothy 2:6).

Jesus in His death was actually the substitute dying in the place of sinful man. The substitution of Jesus provided a just way for God to care for the penalty of sin. His substitutionary work is the heart of the Gospel.

IV. THE GREAT TRUTH: *"SUBSTITUTION"*

A. SUBSTITUTION IN THE OLD TESTAMSNT

1. Substitution Was Provided by God the Father.

a. Man failed the test of obedience in the Garden of Eden. The Lord God made coats of skins to cover Adam and Eve. A shadow of Christ—the animal was the substitute to cover the sin. The divinely provided garment made the *first* sinners fit for the presence of God.

Write in Genesis 3:21: _____

_____

b. The Substitute, Jesus, was promised by the Lord God.

Write in Genesis 3:15: _____

_____

_____

2. The Old Testament Foreshadows the Substitutionary Work of Christ.

a. The sacrifice for sin was always by the shedding of blood. The sinner identified himself with the sin and his offering by placing his hand on the head of the sacrifice. Leviticus 4 gives the Word of God for a sin offering. The sin offering was a compulsory (non-sweet savor) offering. Underline in your Bible Leviticus 4:3, 4, 12, 13, 15, 21, 22, 24, 26, 27, 29, 31, 33.

b. The sin offering of Leviticus 4 cared for:
- the sins of ignorance (verses 1, 2)
- the sins of priests (verses 3-12)
- the sins of the congregation (verses 13-21)
- the sins of the ruler (verses 22-26)
- the sins of the common people (verses 27-35)

All of these sin offerings required a substitute and the shedding of blood to cover sin.

c. The sin offering is preeminently a type, a picture, a shadow of Jesus Christ carrying the believer's sin in the place of the sinner who has accepted the substitutionary work of Christ. The sin offerings were substitutionary—looking toward the supreme offering of God's Son once and for all.

d. The sin offering points to the death of Christ as the Substitute for sinners as declared by Old Testament writers. The fact of the prophecy of Christ and how He was born, lived and died confirms the pictures of Jesus and His substitutionary work as described in Leviticus and the Pentateuch.

e. The Old Testament concept of substitution can be seen in Isaiah 53. This is probably the clearest picture of Christ as the Substitute for sin to be found in the Bible:
- "He hath borne our griefs and carried our sorrows" (Isaiah 53:4).
- "He was wounded *for* (in place of) our transgressions" (Isaiah 53:5).
- "He was bruised *for* (in place of) our iniquities (sins)" (Isaiah 53:5).
- "The chastisement *for* (in place of) our peace was upon Him and with His stripes we *are* healed" (Isaiah 53:5).

- "The Lord (God) laid on Him (Jesus) the iniquity of us all" (Isaiah 53:6).
- "He is brought as a lamb to the slaughter . . . He openeth not His mouth" (Isaiah 53:7). (Recall the sin offering?)
- "He was made an offering *for* (in place of our) sin" (Isaiah 53:10). God's grace caused Him to offer His only Son as an offering for sin.

f. Psalm 22 foreshadows the substitutionary work of Jesus on the cross. The Shepherd gave His life *for* (in place of) the sheep.

g. A type of the substitutionary work of Christ is found in Genesis 22:2-13.

   Isaac was a type of Christ, obedient unto death just as Jesus, the only begotten Son (Genesis 22:9).

   Christ is seen in the ram offered as a substitute for Isaac—note "in the stead of his son" (Genesis 22:13).

   The faith of Abraham is seen in his belief that God would provide a substitute (Genesis 22:8).

   Write in the verse, Genesis 22:8: _____

   _____

   _____

   Underline in your Bible the words, "God will provide Himself."

B. THE FACT OF SUBSTITUTION

1. **Christ is Our Substitute.**

   a. The Bible declares "all under sin." Underline Galatians 3:22 and write in Romans 3:23: _____

   _____

   b. But Christ died *for* (in place of) our sins.
   Write in I Peter 3:18: _____

   _____

   _____

   c. He was made sin *for* (in place of) us.
   Write in II Corinthians 5:21: _____

   _____

   _____

2. **Jesus Came Voluntarily to Die *for* (in place of) Sinners.**

   a. He gave His life *for* (in place of) many.
   Write in Matthew 20:28: _____

   _____

   _____

   b. Jesus paid the ransom *for* (in place of) all.
   Write in I Timothy 2:6: _____

   _____

   c. Jesus gave Himself *for* (in place of) us to redeem us.
   Write in Titus 2:14: _____

   _____

3. **Jesus Died as a True Substitute *for* (in place of) Sinners.**

   a. He gave His life *for* the sheep.
      Write in John 10:11: _____

      _____

   b. He died *for* the ungodly.
      Write in Romans 5:6: _____

      _____

      Also, Romans 5:8: _____

      _____

   c. Christ suffered *for* us.
      Write in I Peter 2:21: _____

      _____

      Also, write in I Peter 2:24: _____

      _____

      _____

      _____

4. **Jesus Was Made a Curse *for* Us.**

   a. Jesus has borne the curse of the law.
      Write in Galatians 3:13: _____

      _____

   b. The believer is redeemed from the law by Jesus.
      Underline Galatians 4:4-7 in your Bible.

C. SUBSTITUTION IS CHRIST BEARING THE SINS OF ALL BELIEVERS

1. **The Significance of Christ's Ministry as Substitute.**

   a. Jesus paid the price to redeem sinful men.
      Write in I Corinthians 6:20: _____

      _____

      Underline I Corinthians 7:23.

   b. God sent His Son because of sin.
      Write in I John 4:10: _____

      _____

      _____

   c. God gave eternal life in His Son. Underline I John 5:11-12 in your Bible.
      Write in I John 4:14: _____

      _____

   d. "He died *for* our sins."
      Write in I Corinthians 15:3: _____

      _____

      _____

e. "He gave Himself *for* us." Underline Galatians 2:20 in your Bible.

2. **Jesus Was Made Flesh to Die on the Cross.**

   a. Jesus humbled Himself in the flesh and became obedient unto death. Underline Philippians 2:5-8 in your Bible. Also, John 1:14.

   b. Jesus prayed for all who believed.
      Write in John 17:2: _____

      _____

      Underlind John 17:23. (John 17 is the prayer of our Lord.)

   c. Jesus taught His Substitution when He instituted the Lord's Supper.
      Write in Matthew 26:28: _____

      _____

      _____

      Notice that Jesus said, "This is my blood—which is shed *for* (in place of) many . . . "

   d. Jesus had to become flesh, thus He was the God-Man, to become our Substitute.

D. ERRORS REGARDING SUBSTITUTION

1. **How Could God Lay the Sins of the Guilty on an Innocent Victim?**

   a. This is one of the questions asked by those who would like to prove God unholy and unloving. The question has no merit because the Bible is always correct. The Bible says that "God was in Christ reconciling the world unto Himself" (II Corinthians 5:19).

   b. The question has no merit because Jesus willingly became the Substitute for sinners. He was in obedience to His Father's will (John 13:1, 20; Hebrews 10:7).

2. **Guilt is Non-transferable! (Another error.)**

   a. Guilt is present because sin has been committed. Sin is against God and His will has been violated. God forgives on the basis of His justice. In Christ the guilt is transferable because He died *for* (in place of) the sinner.

   b. Such a transfer of guilt is not unjust because Christ came voluntarily to die for sinners (John 10:10, 18).

3. **How Can Christ be a Substitute of the Sinner?**

   a. Another confusing question which must be thought through. Here, we must guard against Universalism, which believes that all people will be saved eventually.
      The Answer is easy if you understand the question.

   b. *The Answer*! Christ is the Substitute for the believer. He cannot be a Substitute for the unbeliever *until* He is accepted as such by the unbeliever.

V. **WHAT THIS BIBLE TRUTH TEACHES US TODAY**

Jesus tasted death for every man. He died in our place—the Substitute. We know from Scripture that Jesus died on the cross and because He died, we live. Because He bore the penalty of sin, we need not bear it. By dying as our Substitute, He answered the demands of God's justice and God's wrath against sin. Dying in our place, as our Substitute, He expressed God's infinite love for us. Through His death he has reconciled us to God (II Corinthians 5:18-19). The summary of Substitution, the vicarious atonement of Christ, is I Peter 3:18, "Christ also hath once suffered for sins, the just *for* (in place of) the unjust, that He might bring us to God."

YOUR NEXT ASSIGNMENT:

1. Read Romans 5:1-11; 11:15; I Corinthians 7:11; II Corinthians 5:14-21; Ephesians 2:16; Colossians 1:20-22; Hebrews 2:17.

2. Review your notes on Substitution.

3. Mark your Bible where new truths are learned.

Lesson 31
"Reconciliation"

(Where lines are provided, look up the Scripture and write in the Scripture or its main truth.)

I. INTRODUCTION

In the Old Testament the word "reconciliation" is used to refer to the divinely appointed "covering" of sin by the blood of the sacrifice. In these Old Testament passages, the Authorized Version renders the Hebrew word "kaphar" "to make reconciliation" while the other translations render the same word "to make atonement." There is no word in the Old Testament properly translated to mean "reconcile." The word is found in the Authorized Version (King James) in Leviticus 6:30; 8:15; 16:20; I Samuel 29:4; Ezekiel 45:15, 17, 20; Daniel 9:24 but always meaning "atonement" or "covering."

Reconciliation is a New Testament doctrine which is one phase of God's gracious work in Christ when He died on the cross. The death of Christ was for the whole world (John 3:16) and provided redemption (I Timothy 2:6), reconciliation (II Corinthians 5:19), and propitiation (I John 2:2) for all who will believe. The atoning death of Christ reveals God's changeless love for sinful man and constitutes an appeal to man to abandon his old life and be reconciled to God.

II. BASIC SCRIPTURES

Romans 5:1-11; 11:15; I Corinthians 7:11; II Corinthians 5:14-21; Ephesians 2:16; Colossians 1:20-22; Hebrews 2:17.

III. THE NUCLEUS OF THIS TRUTH

Reconciliation is another significant part of the New Testament doctrine of salvation. Reconciliation has reference to a change in relationship of man to God. The atonement of Christ on the cross propitiated, or satisfied, the wrath of God and reconciled man to God. The Bible pictures man as the enemy of God in his unredeemed state (Romans 5:10; Ephesians 2:12, 15). In repentance toward God and faith in Jesus, a person is reconciled to God by the death of Christ.

IV. THE GREAT TRUTH: *"RECONCILIATION"*

A. THE MEANING OF RECONCILIATION

1. **Reconciliation on the Human, Worldly Level.**

   a. Webster defines "reconcile" as meaning "to restore to friendship, harmony, or communion; to settle differences; to cause to submit to; to accept."

   b. Among individuals, reconciliation usually means compromise. Two offended parties are brought back into agreement by each one "giving in" to try to meet each other half way. One can see this in home life where a separation takes place. To be reconciled, each partner has to compromise in order to have a new relationship (I Corinthians 7:11).

2. **Reconciliation on the Spiritual Level.**

   a. Spiritually, reconciliation speaks of sinful man out of fellowship with God—being transformed and brought into a right relationship with God by the atoning work of Christ on the cross. The fellowship of man, broken and lost in Adam, is restored in Christ. This is graphically stated by Paul in Romans 5:10.

Write in Romans 5:10: _____

_____

_____

   b. Reconciliation is a part of the saving work in God in Christ. When a person accepts Christ, his soul is saved and he is restored to fellowship with God. This is man's part in his own salvation and is called "conversion." The change in his relationship to God is called "reconciliation." The new walk with Christ gives real joy in Christ Jesus. The "old man" has taken a step to meet God.

Write in Romans 5:11: _____

_____

_____

   (If your Bible says "atonement" at the close of verse 11, it should read "reconciliation." Refer to any new King James or other versions for clarification.)

   c. "Reconciliation" means to cause, or effect a thorough change in man, thereby restoring to fellowship with God through faith in Christ.

B. THE WORK OF GOD INVOLVES TWO DISTINCT RE-CONCILIATIONS

   1. **The Relationship Between God and the World Was Changed.**

      a. Dr. C. I. Scofield says, "The death of Christ did not change God for He had always loved the world; nor was the world changed, for it continued in rebellion against God. But by the death of Christ the relationship between God and the world *was* changed. The barrier caused by sin was taken away, enabling God to show mercy where judgment was deserved."

      b. "This reconciliation was the work of God alone, in which man had no part." This is clearly stated in II Corinthians 5:19. (Write in this passage.) _____

_____

_____

_____

   2. **God Fashioned A Reconciliation in the Sinner.**

      a. This reconciliation, based upon "the blood of the cross," was wrought (formed, fashioned) by the Father, whereby the sinner becomes changed in his rebellious attitude toward God. He is then ready to receive the reconciliation already accomplished at the cross. Paul expresses this in plain and simple words.

Write in Colossians 1:21-22: _____

_____

_____

186

_____

_____

b. "It pleased the Father that in Him (Christ) should all fullness dwell" (Colossians 1:19). The Father fashioned reconciliation only upon the work of Christ—to reconcile *all* things unto Himself (God).

Write in Colossians 1:20: _____

_____

_____

_____

C. RECONCILIATION IS A PART OF THE FINISHED WORK OF CHRIST ON THE CROSS.

1. The Finished Work of Christ Provided *Redemption* for the World.

a. The death of Christ was a work for the whole world (John 3:16). Again we read, "But we see Jesus, who was made a little lower than the angels for the suffering of death, crowned with glory and honor, that *He, by the grace of God, should taste death for every man*" (Hebrews 2:9).

b. The death of Christ provided redemption; He paid the price of redemption by His shed blood.

Write in Romans 3:24: _____

_____

_____

(We have studied this in Lesson 24, but must include a summary here to realize its relationship to reconciliation.)

2. The Finished Work of Christ Provided *Reconciliation* for the World.

a. The object of reconciliation is man. Those who "sometimes were far off are made nigh by the blood of Christ" (Ephesians 2:13).

b. The means of reconciliation is by the death of Christ on the cross (Romans 5:10).

c. The scope of reconciliation is the whole world (Colossians 1:20).

3. The Finished Work of Christ Provided *Propitiation* for the World.

a. "Propitiation" is a Scriptural word which is seldom explained. The word means "satisfaction" in the sense that the death of Christ "satisfied" the just demands of God's holy judgment of sin. It sounds like a difficult truth, but the Scriptures are very clear if one remembers that the word means "the satisfaction of God."

b. A major truth to remember is that *man is reconciled, God is propitiated*. Scripture never states that God is reconciled.

c. Christ was sent by the Father to be the "propitiation" for sin.

Write in I John 4:10: _____

_____

_____

d. This "propitiation" includes the "sins of the whole world." Write in I John 2:2: _____

_____

e. Christ is the "propitiation through faith in His blood." Write in Romans 3:25: _____

_____

_____

_____

f. The place of propitiation in the Old Testament was the mercy seat, the lid of the ark of the covenant in the Tabernacle. The mercy seat was sprinkled with sacrificial blood on the Day of Atonement, and this became the place where God met man. The broken law was covered by innocent blood changing a judgment seat into a mercy seat until the time when Christ would die as the one complete and everlasting satisfaction for sin.

Underline Hebrews 9:5 and write in Hebrews 9:12: _____

_____

_____

g. The justice of God had to be *satisfied* for Him to forgive sin. God is *propitiated*—satisfied. Man is *reconciled* to God.

4. **The Three Truths Express the Finished Work of Christ.**

a. The three primary truths covered in this part of this lesson express the finished work of Christ in the salvation of the lost.

b. Sinful man is *redeemed*—bought with the precious blood of Christ.

The person is *reconciled* to God—brought about by the death of Christ on the cross.

God is *propitiated*—God is fully satisfied with the death of His Son "whom God has set forth to be a propitiation through *faith in His blood*."

(The lesson is reconciliation but the truth of "propitiation" had to be covered in order to comprehend the full meaning of reconciliation.)

D. THE MINISTRY OF RECONCILIATION

1. **The Assignment Has Been Given to Christians.**

a. The assignment God has given to all the saints (saved ones) is the "ministry of reconciliation"—the joyful experience of reconciling an estranged soul to the Lord Jesus Christ.

Write in II Corinthians 5:18: _____

_____

_____

b. Paul tells what the ministry of reconciliation is in the next verse: "to wit (namely) that God was in Christ reconciling the world to Himself, not imputing (counting) their trespasses unto (against) them, and (He) hath committed (or placed in us) the word of reconciliation" (II Corinthians 5:19).

2. **"We Are Ambassadors for Christ."**

a. Now that the believer has been reconciled to God through

faith in the Lord Jesus Christ, he immediately becomes an ambassador for Christ. An ambassador is a "resident representative, an authorized messenger" of another.

Write in II Corinthians 5:20: _____

_____

_____

_____

    b. The believer is to pray for reconciliation on the part of another. The word "beg" in II Corinthians 5:20 could read "pray."

V. WHAT THIS BIBLE TRUTH TEACHES US TODAY

The character of God's ministry today is simply that all of us who are Christians are ambassadors for Christ. Our obligation is to tell the lost to "be ye reconciled to God." God uses human instrumentality to win the unsaved. The Scripture includes all Christians—"Now, then, *we are* ambassadors for Christ . . ." It does not mean that ambassadors are "honorary"; it means a present active duty for every Christian.

To witness to a person is a joy, a blessing. You should tell how you were "once alienated and enemies in your mind by wicked works, yet now has He reconciled in the body of His flesh through death, to present you holy (set apart) and unblamable and unreprovable in His sight, if we continue in the faith grounded and settled . . ." (Colossians 1:21-23).

In reconciliation the lost person is restored to the position God intended. Reconciliation is unlimited—it is for all who will believe.

This is another "Great Truth" of the Bible.

YOUR NEXT ASSIGNMENT:

1. Read Genesis 48:4; Exodus 2:10; Esther 2:7; Psalm 91:1-11; Romans 8:14-17, 23; 9:4-5; II Corinthians 6:18; Galatians 3:25-26; 4:1-7; Ephesians 1:3-14; Hebrews 2:10-11; 12:23; I John 3:1-2; Revelation 21:7.

2. Review your notes on Reconciliation.

3. Mark your Bible where new truths are learned.

Lesson 32 "Adoption"

(Where lines are provided, look up the Scripture and write in the Scripture or its main truth.)

I. INTRODUCTION

We do not belong to the family of God by natural birth. There is a separation, an alienation between man and God caused by sin. That sin began in the Garden of Eden, and the repercussion of that sin is felt and experienced by all mankind. In the foreknowledge of God, He provided a way of salvation in Christ. When we are born the second time we are *adopted*—one of the great truths of Scripture. The Bible says, "He came unto His own, and His own received Him not. But as many as received Him, to them gave He power (the privilege, the prerogative) to become the *sons* of God, even to them that believe on His name" (John 1:11-12). The *adoption* is based upon the free will of man. "As many as" indicates a choice—some accept Christ and some do not and will not. When one accepts Christ as Saviour, he is born the second time. God accepts the very wicked as He accepts the "very good" (if there be such a person). By exercising the free will of man and choosing Christ, that person is "born again" and becomes "the chosen in Christ" (Ephesians 1:3-4). Therefore, *adoption* is based upon one accepting Christ and receiving the "power, the privilege, the prerogative to become a son of God."

II. BASIC SCRIPTURES

Genesis 48:4; Exodus 2:10; Esther 2:7; Psalm 91:1-11; Romans 8:14-17, 23; 9:4-5; II Corinthians 6:18; Galatians 3:25-26; 4:1-7; Ephesians 1:3-14; Hebrews 2:10-11; 12:23; I John 3:1-2; Revelation 21:7.

III. THE NUCLEUS OF THIS TRUTH

Adoption in our day is quite different from the adoption taught in Scripture. On the human level a child is adopted because of the couple's desire to have children. When the prospective parent or parents have a choice, a child may be selected because he or she has a perfect body, facial beauty or other qualities. Other children are adopted because of a deformity or because they are retarded mentally or physically. Once adopted, the child belongs to the parents just as though they were the natural parents. They give the child their name, care for and plan for the future of the child. However, they can never give the child the genetic qualities, the hereditary characteristics which they possess.

Spiritual adoption is quite different. When persons receive Christ they become "new creatures in Christ Jesus"—they have a new nature, a divine nature. Christians receive spiritual qualities and a spiritual disposition because of their faith in Christ. Adoption is of God whereby one who accepts Christ is placed in the position of a grown son (Galatians 4:1-5).

The question naturally comes to mind—"if a believer is a son of God by regeneration into the family of God, how can the same person then be adopted?" God only adopts those who have been born again, just as people desiring to adopt can only adopt a child which has been born.

After the birth, the child is placed in a home as a son or daughter.

Dr. Ian Thomas once said, *"Regeneration is son making–adoption is son placing."*

IV. THE GREAT TRUTH: *"ADOPTION"*

A. ADOPTION IN THE OLD TESTAMENT.

1. Moses Was Adopted.

The Pharoah of Egypt had given orders to the midwives to destroy all the new born males among the Hebrews (Exodus 1:16). The midwives did not obey the Pharoah; therefore, he charged all the people to destroy the male babies by casting them into the Nile River.

Under such orders, Jochebed, the mother of Moses, placed the baby Moses in an ark and placed the ark in the River Nile. Pharoah's daughter saw the ark, opened it and saw the beautiful baby. God worked in a mysterious way. The babe was nursed by his own mother. Jochebed brought the baby to the daughter of Pharoah and "he became her son" and she named him Moses (Exodus 2:2-10).

2. Genubath, the Son of Hadad, Was Adopted.

This little known character was the son of Hadad, who was an adversary to Solomon. Genubath was born in Egypt to Hadad and the sister-in-law of the Pharoah. The story is found in I Kings 11:14-20.

Write in verse 20 of that Scripture passage: _____

_____

_____

_____

3. Esther Was Adopted.

Esther was adopted by Mordecai, the Jew who was from the line of Benjamin. Esther was the daughter of Abihail, the uncle of Mordecai. The beautiful story of this adoption is in Esther 2. Read the first 7 verses of Esther 2 and write in verse 7: _____

_____

Here we see that Mordecai took Esther as his own daughter—but let's turn the thought around. Mordecai was in Esther's life by adoption.

(There are other suggestions or thoughts of adoption in the Old Testament. Examples: Genesis 48:4-5; Genesis 16:1-3.)

B. THE NEW TESTAMENT MEANING OF ADOPTION.

1. Paul's Use of the Word "Adoption."

a. The Greek word translated "adoption" is made up of "thesia," "placing," and "huios," "son." When put together the word "huiothesia" means "placing a son."

The word is peculiar to Paul who uses it several times in the New Testament.

b. When Paul used the word, he took it from a vast background of Roman law. In Roman law, adoption implied a ceremony of conveyance of one to the family desiring to adopt. The parents who adopted a child were given the legal power over the adopted child—the same responsibilities and privileges as if the child had been born to them. The child, in his new family, enjoyed the same rights and privileges as if he had been born into the family.

c. Paul wrote that a child differed little from a servant or slave (Galatians 4:1). Upon a day selected by the father, at about the age of 12, the child was declared of age and granted privileges and freedom. They were no longer under tutors and governors (Galatians 4:2).

2. The Known Used to Teach the Unknown.

a. Paul used the background of "bondage under the elements of the world" (that is, tied to a great number of ceremonies and rituals) to declare the blessed truth of a new era, a new age (Galatians 4:3).

b. The blessed truth Paul spoke of was the time appointed by the Father—the time when He would put an end to legal ceremonies and bondage and no longer deal with us as children, but as sons.

Write in Galatians 4:4: _____

_____

_____

c. Paul took the customs of the day and taught a spiritual truth. "When the fulness of time was come, God . . . ." The father selected the time and all under bondage (servants) were redeemed from under the law. Why did God send forth His Son?

Write in Galatians 4:5: _____

_____

_____

C. THE BELIEVER IS MADE A SON AND HEIR IN ADOPTION.

1. A Sure Sign of Adoption is the Leading of the Spirit.

a. "As many as"—those words again indicating the free will of man (Romans 8:14).

Write in Romans 8:14: _____

_____

_____

b. It is the character of all believers to be led by the Holy Spirit of God. Therefore, "they are the sons of God."

c. Believers "have not received the spirit of bondage again to fear," such as Paul in Acts 9:6, or the Philippian jailer in Acts 16:30. All believers can recall the bondage of sin before becoming Christians. Paul says, "this fear is over" for believers.

2. The Spirit of Adoption

a. God gives the Spirit of adoption which works in the children of God a childlike love toward the Father. The Spirit of adoption gives to believers a delight in Him and a dependence upon Him as a Father.

Write in Romans 8:15: _____

_____

_____

b. The word "cry" in verse 15 means "pray." The adoption makes possible a remarkable and intimate relationship with

193

God whereby we can pray to Him as "Abba, Father." "Abba" is the Aramaic word of endearment for "Father" and can be translated "daddy" (which would be sacreligious to most of us). Why both terms, "Abba, Father" in verse 15? Because Christ used the endearing term in Mark 14:36 and we have received the Spirit of the Son (Galatians 4:6).

3. **The Holy Spirit Confirms Sonship.**

   a. The Holy Spirit seals (Ephesians 1:13), and the adoption is sealed—the believer is in the family of God through faith.

   b. Believers in Christ have the Holy Spirit witnessing with their spirit speaking peace and comfort and assurance that "we are the children of God."

      Write in Romans 8:16: _____

      _____

   The Spirit in the heart cannot contradict the Spirit of the Word of God.

4. **The Inheritance of the Christian.**

   a. The believer is an heir of God and joint-heir with Christ (Romans 8:17). All that God has is ours and the honor and happiness of an heir lies in the value and worth of the inheritance.

      "The Lord is the portion of mine inheritance" (Psalm 16:5).

   b. Jesus Christ is heir of all things (Hebrews 1:2). All believers are joint-heirs with Jesus Christ and shall inherit all things (Revelation 21:7). All who have become Christians and are His brethren in the world and even suffer for Him—shall someday partake of His glory (John 17:24).

      All of the riches of His creation are ours now. We accept them with little gratitude—life, health, beauty of a sunset or sunrise, and planting of a seed to grow for food. These things and a thousand more God does and they are ours.

      As sons we join with Christ in the ultimate and final inheritance (Revelation 11:15; 21:3).

D. THE INCOMPARABLE PRIVILEGES OF ADOPTION.

   1. **The Gift of Sonship.**

      a. When one accepts Christ there is an adoption in redemption which entitles the believer to the privileges of a son (Galatians 4:5, 7).

      b. In Christ the gift of sonship is bestowed upon us when we are adopted into the family of God. The adoption is something God does for us. He elevates us from "a slave" into the glorious privileges of sonship. The Son came to redeem us (Galatians 4:4).

   2. **The Leading of the Holy Spirit.**

      a. The adopted one is led by the Holy Spirit (Romans 8:14, 16).

      b. The Holy Spirit gives victory over the old life (Romans 8:2-4; Galatians 5:16-18). The adopted ones are God led because the Holy Spirit is *in* them and they have a new nature.

   3. **The Liberty of Adoption.**

      a. As we have seen, adoption frees us from tutors and governors and rituals and the law (Galatians 4:7).

    b. This liberty is not given in order that we might do as we please. Liberty is given *from* sin *to* freedom in Christ (Romans 8:5-9). Underline verses 5 and 6 in your Bible.

4. The Supernatural Care of God, the Holy Spirit.

    a. The Holy Spirit is present within the Christian to assist in moments of moral, physical or emotional weakness. The approach to God is often speechless—one cannot find the words to pray. God has provided for such a moment (Romans 8:26).

    b. The person does not speak—the Holy Spirit "makes the intercession for the saints according to the will of God" (Romans 8:27).

5. The Privilege of Having God as Father.

    a. He becomes the Father to only those who accept His Son, and then they are called "sons of God."
    Write in John 1:12: _____

    _____

    _____

    b. He provided a way for all to become "sons" and "heirs" with Him through His Son (Galatians 4:7).

6. Adoption is the Father's Good Pleasure.

    a. The date of our adoption was in the dateless past. God chose us "before the foundation of the world."
    Write in Ephesians 1:4: _____

    _____

    _____

    b. He adopted us (all who believe) "to the praise and glory of His grace."
    Write in Ephesians 1:5: _____

    _____

    _____

    _____

    Underline Ephesians 1:6.

V. WHAT THIS BIBLE TRUTH TEACHES US TODAY

Today's world is one of frustration, sin and little regard for the things of God. Yet God knows you, personally. If you have accepted Jesus Christ, you are the "chosen in Him before the foundation of the world." He allows you the "free will" to choose His Son. He does not force. When you accept Christ, you are adopted as a son into the family of God. By adoption we are made His sons. First, birth (regeneration), then adoption.

The full manifestation of adoption is yet future. The complete revelation of the believer's sonship awaits the resurrection, change and translation of the saints which is known as "the redemption of the body" (Romans 8:23; Ephesians 1:14; I John 3:2).

If you are adopted—saved—you have a happy present and a glorious future in Christ Jesus. One who belongs to His family should not bring shame or sorrow on the family, but stay in close fellowship with the saints, with our Lord and His Word.

(Do not be concerned about some of the words of Scripture in this

195

lesson. We shall cover "Free will and Election and Predestination and Foreknowledge" in the next two lessons.)

YOUR NEXT ASSIGNMENT:

1. Read John 1:12, 13; 3:16; 5:40; 6:37; 15:16, 19; Acts 9:15; Romans 8:28-34; 9:11-21; 10:13; 11:5-6; Ephesians 1:4, 5, 11; 2:3; I Thessalonians 1:4-5; II Thessalonians 2:13; II Timothy 1:9; I Peter 1:2, 19, 20; Revelation 22:17.

2. Review your notes on Adoption.

3. Mark your Bible where new truths are learned.

Lesson 33 "Election and Free Will"

GREAT TRUTHS OF THE BIBLE

(Where lines are provided, look up the Scripture and write in the Scripture or its main truth.)

I. INTRODUCTION

The truths, or doctrines, of "*election* and *free will*" are taught in Scripture. As we have studied in previous lessons, in salvation there is the divine side—the Godward side, often called "election, the chosen, the elect or the called ones." Also in salvation there is the human side, called in Scripture "the will of man; whosoever; as many as; receives; chooses." These two truths are called "election" and "free will." Election and free will are two of the four themes which should be studied together. Therefore, this lesson shall cover two truths, and the next lesson shall cover "foreknowledge" and "predestination." If some of the four themes should be found in every lesson, don't be surprised. It is difficult to teach them totally isolated as one subject.

As you study these two lessons, ask the Holy Spirit to reveal to you the truths of God in reference to these four subjects. There is so much confusion concerning them and little factual information written for the lay person.

II. BASIC SCRIPTURES

John 1:12, 13; 3:16; 5:40; 6:37; 15:16, 19; Acts 9:15; Romans 8:28-34; 9:11-21; 10:13; 11:5-6; Ephesians 1:4, 5, 11; 2:3; I Thessalonians 1:4-5; II Thessalonians 2:13; II Timothy 1:9; I Peter 1:2, 19, 20; Revelation 22:17.

III. THE NUCLEUS OF THESE TRUTHS

The nucleus of both of these truths was simply stated by the great scholar Henry Ward Beecher. He said, "The elect are the whosoever wills and the non-elect are the whosoever won'ts."

Paul describes three groups of people and these are the three groups in the world today: "But we preach Christ crucified, unto the Jews a stumblingblock, and unto the Greeks foolishness; but unto them which are called, both Jews and Greeks, Christ the power of God, and the wisdom of God" (I Corinthians 1:23-24). The Jews trusted in religion and ritual. To them, the cross was a stumblingblock. The Greeks (the Gentiles) trusted in philosophy and human wisdom. To them, the cross was foolishness. "The called" was a group out of both Jews and Greeks who were *chosen* not because of any merit on their part. To them, the cross was the power of God unto salvation. "The called," "the elected," heard God's call and responded. In the last group we have "election" and "free will."

IV. THE GREAT TRUTHS: *"ELECTION AND FREE WILL"*

A. ELECTION IN THE OLD TESTAMENT

1. God Chose, Elected, Israel (Corporate Election).

a.   The world had become corrupt and God had destroyed it
     with a flood. After the flood, man again turned from God
     and wickedness was repeated. God's divine plan of redemp-
     tion could not be defeated. God selected one man to become
     the father of a new nation, a peculiar people. The Lord told
     Abraham, "I will make thee a great nation."

     Write in Genesis 12:2: _____

     _____

     Underline verse 3 in your Bible.

b.   The Lord confirmed the Abrahamic Covenant in Genesis
     15:1-21; 17:4-8; 22:15-24; 26:1-5; 28:10-15.

c.   In the election of a nation, God made sure that the covenant
     with that nation was repeated.

2. **God Chose Israel for His Sovereign Purpose.**

a.   Israel was chosen, elected, to witness and illustrate to the
     world the blessedness of serving the one true God
     (Deuteronomy 33:26-29).

b.   To receive, preserve and transmit the Scriptures
     (Deuteronomy 4:5-8). Read and underline in your Bible.

     Write in Romans 3:1-2: _____

     _____

     _____

     This confirms the Old Testament Scripture.

c.   To produce the Lord Jesus Christ, a Jew, of the seed of
     Abraham and of the tribe of Judah (Genesis 3:15; Isaiah
     7:14; 9:6).

3. **God Elects, Chooses, Individuals.**

a.   Abraham is the great example of divine election in the Old
     Testament. He was a pagan in a strange land, the Ur of the
     Chaldees. He was no better than the rest of his family, yet
     God chose him.

     Write in Genesis 12:1: _____

     _____

     _____

     That was God's part—the *choosing, electing*.

     Write in Hebrews 11:8: _____

     _____

     _____

     That was Abraham's part—*obeying* God.

b.   Isaac is another example of divine election.

     Write in Genesis 17:19: _____

     _____

     _____

c.   Jacob was chosen, elected by God. There was nothing in
     Jacob's life to commend him to God for any special favor.
     He was a schemer, he lied to his father, conspired with his
     mother—and on we could go. Yet, God chose Jacob. God
     changed his name to "Israel."

     Write in Genesis 32:28: _____

_____

_____

Israel had twelve sons; thus the twelve tribes of Israel.
Now, turn to Romans 9:8-12. Read the Scripture and write
in verse 11: _____

_____

_____

B. ELECTION IN THE NEW TESTAMENT.

1. **Election is Sure to All Who Believe.**

a. Before we get too far, and too mixed up, the one great fact
about this age of Grace is *Election is Certain to Every
Believer by the Fact that He Believes*.
Write in I Thessalonians 1:4: _____

_____

b. God chooses the foolish things of the world.
Write in I Corinthians 1:26: _____

_____

Underline verse 27 in your Bible.

2. **Election Was Before the Foundation of the World.**

a. God, in Christ, provided a way for all who accept Him to be
chosen—elected.
Write in Ephesians 1:4: _____

_____

_____

b. Write in the words of Jesus in John 15:16: _____

_____

_____

_____

3. **Paul and the Apostles Were Elected.**

a. Paul's conversion was not by accident.
Write in Acts 9:15: _____

_____

_____

b. All the Apostles are included in Acts 10:41. Underline the
verse in your Bible.

c. Ananias confirmed the election (choosing) of Paul.
Write in Acts 22:14: _____

_____

_____

4. **The Saved Are Elected - The Church, The Bride of Christ.**

a. Write in II Thessalonians 2:13: _____

_____

_____

Refer back to I Thessalonians 1:4.

b. Write in II Timothy 2:10: _____

_____

_____

c. Underline Titus 1:1 in your Bible.

5. The Scattered Saints Were Elected.

a. The body of Christ is scattered all over the world. They are still the elected, the chosen, because they have believed in Jesus Christ. Underline I Peter 1:1 and write in 1:2: _____

_____

_____

b. Write in Romans 11:5: _____

_____

_____

Election is certain and sure to all who freely exercise their free will in accepting Christ. God, in Christ, does the electing and *that is God's responsibility*. Man must realize his need of a Saviour—repent and accept Jesus on his own volition. *That is man's responsibility*. Now we shall study "free will" of man.

C. THE FREE WILL OF MAN.

1. Man Must Choose for Himself.

a. We are to believe in God's elective purpose and also believe that He has given us the "will" to choose. A person must accept God's plan of salvation—that is why Christ died. The one verse that sets forth God's plan is so simple that you probably know it from memory.
Write in John 3:16: _____

_____

_____

b. Jesus said, "*Come* unto me, all ye that labor and are heavy laden, and I will give you rest" (Matthew 8:28). That invitation "come" is found 642 times in Scripture. The word requires a response.

2. *"Whosoever"* Follows Jesus—Denies Self.

a. The word "whosoever" is all inclusive. It includes *all* who will accept Christ—Jew or Gentile, rich or poor, the good and bad.
Write in Romans 8:34: _____

_____

Underline Mark 8:35 and 38 in your Bible.

3. God Calls—The Individual Must Answer.

a. Jesus states these two truths in one verse of Scripture. "All that the Father giveth me shall come to me." The Father, through the Person of the Holy Spirit, woos, draws, convicts. That is God's work. There is more to the same verse—"And him that cometh to me I will in no wise cast out" (John 6:37). The person must respond of his own "free will."

b. A good example of what Jesus said in the verse above can be found in Abraham. He was a pagan in a strange land. God chose him, elected him, and that was God's part.

Now, write in Hebrews 11:8: _____

_____

_____

Notice the two words "called" and "obeyed."

4. How Does One Know if He is Elected?

a. Simply by obeying the Word of God. Remember earlier in this lesson you learned that *Election is Certain to Every Believer by the Fact that He Believes*. The New Testament message is *"Come."* The great commission of Jesus is, "Go, Preach, Teach, Baptize" (Matthew 28:19-20).

b. God has elected all who will accept His Son.
Write in Romans 10:13: _____

_____

c. Believe, accept Christ. That is man's part.
Write in Acts 16:31: _____

_____

5. How Many Are Elected—Chosen?

a. That seems like a foolish question, but the Bible gives the answer many times.
Write in John 1:12: _____

_____

_____

b. Write in the words of Jesus in John 17:2: _____

_____

_____

Seven times Jesus speaks of Christians as having been given to Him by the Father—John 17:2, 6 (twice), 9, 11, 12, 24. Jesus Christ is God's gift to the world; believers are the Father's gift to Jesus Christ.

c. Write in Acts 13:48: _____

_____

_____

(The word "ordained" should be "elected.")

d. Write in Romans 8:14: _____

_____

_____

Do you find the answer? The answer is *"as many as."* That involves believing, receiving, accepting, repenting, praying.

6. The Last Invitation in the Bible.

a. Jesus, the Root and offspring of David, said, "And the Spirit (Holy Spirit) and the bride (the Church) say, *Come*. And let him that heareth say, *Come*. And let him that is athirst *come*. And *whosoever will* let him take of the water of life freely" (Revelation 22:16-17).

b. Write in the words of Jesus in Matthew 7:13-14: _____

201

V. WHAT THIS BIBLE TRUTH TEACHES US TODAY

During this great and glorious age of the grace of God, the age of the church, the Gospel is to all and for all who will believe. The Gospel is to be preached to all the world, said Jesus. Some might say, "How do I know I am one of the elected ones?" The answer is simple. Become one of the "whosoever wills" and you will be "elected." The reason Jesus came into the world was to save all who will accept Him. "For God sent not His Son into the world to condemn the world, but that the world through Him might be saved" (John 3:17). Yes, God knows who will and who will not come to Christ. Whatever your decision, it does not shock God (as we shall see in the next lesson).

This lesson presents an open Gospel to all the people everywhere. Dr. J. Vernon McGee, former Pastor of the Church of the Open Door in Los Angeles, tells a story that sums up this lesson. A young lad was being questioned by some deacons about his salvation experience. The deacons asked, "How did you get saved?" The lad answered, "God did His part and I did my part." The men then asked, "What was God's part and your part?" The young boy said, "God's part was saving and my part was sinning. I ran from Him as fast as I could, but He took out after me till He ran me down." That is God and that is human nature. Ever since Adam hid from God in the garden, man has been hiding—God has been seeking.

If you are not a Christian, "*come*" to Jesus. He will save you. You will be in the "elect" of God.

YOUR NEXT ASSIGNMENT:

1. Read John 1:12, 13; 3:14-17; Romans 8:14-39; 9:11-21; 10:1-17; 11:5-6; I Corinthians 2:7; Ephesians 1:3-11; I Thessalonians 1:2-5; II Timothy 1:9; I Peter 1:1-21.

2. Review your notes on Election and Free Will.

3. Mark your Bible where new truths are learned.

Lesson 34
"Foreknowledge and Predestination"

(Where lines are provided, look up the Scripture and write in the Scripture or its main truth.)

I. INTRODUCTION

We come to two teachings of the Word of God which is a continuation of the last lesson. To fully comprehend the mind of God in "foreknowledge and predestination" is infinitely impossible. We can learn what His Word says about these truths and accept them without question. Our lives are enmeshed in a plan, a purpose in which God is sovereign. The great mysteries of God we do not fully comprehend; but they are God's plan, His mysteries, and we accept what He reveals to us (Deuteronomy 29:29).

There is no room for theological argument in subjects such as these. Arguments have often taken God's Word and placed it to one side in order for a man to make a point. The amazing thing is, God knew all along that such things would happen in the lives of the guilty ones, and He was not—and is not—shocked. This lesson is for the layperson. "Theological scholarship" is not the intention of the author. We shall take the "light" God has given in the Bible and that will be sufficient to bless us because we are a part of the foreknowledge and predestination of the Lord God.

II. BASIC SCRIPTURES

John 1:12, 13; 3:14-17; Romans 8:14-39; 9:11-21; 11:5-6; I Corinthians 2:7; Ephesians 1:3-11; I Thessalonians 1:2-5; II Timothy 1:9; I Peter 1:1-21.

III. THE NUCLEUS OF THESE TRUTHS

In the letter to the Ephesians, Paul uses three words which will help us understand God's foreknowledge and predestination.

First, the word "chosen" refers to God's election of all who accept Christ, and it refers back to the "eternal past." "According as He (God) hath *chosen* us in Him before the foundation of the world" (Ephesians 1:4).

Second, "predestination" refers to the inheritance of all who believe, and refers to the "eternal future." "In whom also we have obtained an inheritance, being *predestinated* according to the purpose of Him who worketh all things after the counsel of His own will" (Ephesians 1:11).

Third, "foreordination" refers to our works in Christ Jesus and speaks of the "living present." "For we are His workmanship, created in Christ Jesus unto good works, which God hath *before ordained* that we should walk in them" (Ephesians 2:10).

The third truth links the believer with the first two truths and shows God's will and man's will in the process of salvation. All Scripture, including prophecy, is based on God's foreknowledge, but it does not predetermine human conduct. God's foreknowledge of what people will do does not compel people to do those things. God foreknew that Adam would fall and that Judas would betray Jesus. His foreknowledge of what they would do did not force them to do what they did. What they did, they chose to do and God held them responsible.

It is clear that God's choice or predestination of individuals is based on His foreknowledge of what they would do when the Gospel was offered to them. It is not a compulsory choice and does not conflict with the free will of man (last lesson).

Now, we shall take this apart and have a better understanding of foreknowledge and predestination.

IV. THE GREAT TRUTHS: *"FOREKNOWLEDGE AND PREDESTINATION"*

A. THE DIVINE ORDER OF GOD

1. The Words to be Understood.

a. We may discuss who is right or wrong in reference to how God works. The only blueprint we have to work with is His Holy Word. Therefore, from His Word we learn this order of events:

- "foreknowledge" as seen in I Peter 1:2.
- "election" as seen in I Peter 1:2 and Romans 11:5-6 and is totally a work of grace.
- "predestination" as seen in Romans 8:29-30.

b. The comments on this subject by Dr. C. I. Scofield, in the Scofield King James Bible, set forth the truth in brief form:

"The divine order is foreknowledge, election and predestination. That foreknowledge determines election or choice is clear from I Peter 1:2, and predestination is the bringing to pass of the election. Election looks back to foreknowledge: predestination forward to the destiny."

2. The Free Moral Agency of Man.

a. We are morally responsible. Freedom of choice belongs to moral accountability. There is also a sovereignty of God above history and mankind. These two things, the sovereignty of God and the free moral agency of man, are things we cannot reconcile. They are of God.

b. We can only observe those two things. Charles Haddon Spurgeon once said of those two lines, "I cannot make them meet, but you cannot make them cross."

The foundational fact in life and in history is that God is, God rules, God is sovereign. His foreknowledge, election and predestination are only parts of His sovereign will.

B. THE FOREKNOWLEDGE OF GOD

1. God is Omniscient.

a. The word means "all knowledge," "all knowing." God is perfect in knowledge. He knows everything (Job 37:16).

b. God knows everything about the world and nature. He made them (Isaiah 40:12, 15, 28; Matthew 10:29).

Write in Psalm 147:5: _____

_____

_____

c. God knows everything about man.
   Write in Matthew 10:30: _____

   _____

   Write in Psalm 94:11: _____

   _____

   Underline Hebrews 4:13 in your Bible.

d. God knows all about the past, present and future. With God there is only the eternal now. He knows all things.
   Write in Acts 15:18: _____

   _____

2. The Sovereignty of God.

a. God has absolute power, authority and control. God must be omniscient and know all things or cease to be a sovereign God. The Psalmist, David, wrote about God's omniscience in Psalm 139:16: _____

   _____

b. God is eternal. He is a timeless being. We live in the past, present and future. God existed before there was time and matter. He knows all things and from an eternal position knew every detail which would ever come to pass in the history of mankind. Underline Isaiah 46:9-10 in your Bible.

3. God's Foreknowledge and Man's Free Will.

a. Perfection of foreknowledge (know before) belongs to God, and He has a clear complete knowledge of all events before they occur. Since God knows everything from the beginning, He knew from the beginning who would exercise free will and choose His plan of redemption. He also foreknew all who would exercise free will and refuse His plan of redemption. There should be no objection to the "election" of those who believe and not electing those whom He knew would not believe.

b. Peter wrote in his first epistle to the scattered believers concerning this blessed truth.
   Write in I Peter 1:2: _____

   _____

   Note: "*elect* according to the *foreknowledge* of God."

c. The details of salvation were planned "before the foundation of the world."
   Write in Ephesians 1:4: _____

   _____

d. The invitation of God to "come" to Him through Jesus Christ is to all people. Yet, God knows, in advance, that all will not come. Underline Isaiah 55:1 and write in Isaiah 55:6: _____

   _____

   Jesus said, "*Come* unto me, *all* ye that labor and are heavy laden, and I will give you rest" (Matthew 11:28).

e. Paul taught the people of Thessalonica great truths of the

205

Bible. He was there less than a month. The "babes in Christ" learned the fact of their "election"

Write in I Thessalonians 1:4: _____

_____

The context shows that their "election" was of God because they believed on the Lord Jesus Christ.

f. Foreknowledge is an attribute of God. Since He knows all things, foreknowledge belongs to Him. We predict, guess and wonder—God knows all.

C. PREDESTINATION.

1. Predestination is Found Throughout the Bible.

a. Defining the word, "pre" means "before" and "destined" means "destiny." Predestination means "to determine beforehand" the eternal destiny of individuals and events.

b. The working out of the purpose of God is mentioned many times in Scripture. "The Lamb slain from the foundation of the world" (Revelation 13:8).

"The precious blood of Christ, as of a lamb without blemish and without spot: who verily was foreordained before the foundation of the world, but was manifest (made visible) in these last times for you" (I Peter 1:19-20).

The working out a plan of redemption was "foreordained" by God in His Son. The purpose of God was predetermined.

c. God gave to Abraham and Sarah a son, Isaac, in old age. They doubted but God predetermined the "seed" of Abraham and He brought it to pass (Genesis 15:2-5; 21:1-3).

d. God directed and purposed all history toward one moment in time.

Write in Galatians 4:4: _____

_____

_____

"In the fulness of time." "The Word (Jesus) was made flesh and dwelt among us . . . " (John 1:14).

e. The climax of the plan of God can be seen in the cross and the resurrection. All had been prophesied (Psalm 16; Psalm 22; Isaiah 53) and had come to pass as God had predetermined (Matthew 27 and John 19).

These are only a few examples of predestination in the Scriptures. God predetermines and He is never surprised. He knows beforehand all that man will do.

2. The Sovereign Purpose of God.

a. Predestination in Scripture is not difficult to understand. Write in the most famous verse on this subject:

Romans 8:29: _____

_____

_____

b. Notice, first "He foreknew." His "foreknowledge" concerns the "chosen, elected"—those "whosoever wills." We are elected to be His because we have accepted His plan of redemption in Christ, and that is exercising our "free will." God knew all who would accept Christ.

   c. "Whom He did foreknow . . . ."

       "He also did predestinate." To what?

         "to be conformed to the image of His son"

                         (Romans 8:29).

       Predestination deals with our spiritual growth and development of character. It means that we are to be more like Jesus as we mature and in the end to be perfected "for we shall be like Him" (I John 3:2). *God sees the "elected, chosen" ones* (because we have accepted Christ) *as we shall be!*

   d. We are predestinated to become more like Jesus. This is often a painful process. All the experiences of life for the Christian are God's way of carrying out His plan, to make us like His Son.

       Underline Ephesians 1:3-4 in your Bible.

       Write in Ephesians 1:5: _____

       _____

       Notice verse 4, "that we should be holy and without blame before Him in love." That is predestination. The next verse says, "having predestinated us . . . ."

   e. How do we become "conformed to the image of His Son?" Paul says, "it is God which worketh in us both to will and to do His good pleasure" (Philippians 2:13).

3. "Predestinated According to His Purpose"

   a. Write in Ephesians 1:11: _____

       _____

       _____

   b. We are "to be the praise of His glory, who first trusted in Christ" (Ephesians 1:12).

   c. The Holy Spirit seals our acceptance of Jesus and He (the Holy Spirit) "is the earnest (guarantee) of our inheritance until the redemption of the purchased possession, unto the praise of His glory" (Ephesians 1:13-14).

   d. Write in Philippians 3:21: _____

       _____

       _____

       That is *glorification*. (We have studied election and justification.) Underline Romans 8:30 in your Bible.

V. WHAT THIS BIBLE TRUTH TEACHES US TODAY

Predestination from a spiritual standpoint means that Christians are "to be conformed to the image of Christ." This takes in sanctification (Lesson 23), of which Christ is the supreme example. Christ is the express image of the Father and Christians are to be conformed to the image of His Son. We cannot conform ourselves to Christ. By giving ourselves to Christ, God gives us to Jesus (John 17:3, 6, 9, 11, 20, 21, 24); and in giving us to Him, He predestinated us to be conformed to His image. *God sees us as we shall be!* He looks back to Genesis 1:26-27.

Yes, "we shall be like Him; for we shall see Him as He is" (I John 3:2).

YOUR NEXT ASSIGNMENT:

  1. Read Genesis 1:26-27; 2:7, 21-23; 3:1-21; Matthew 4:1-11; Romans 5:12, 17; 7:7-24; 8:33-39; I Corinthians 15:22, 45-50; I Thessalonians 5:23; Hebrews 4:12; 9:26; I John 2:16.

2. Review your notes on Foreknowledge and Predestination.
3. Mark your Bible where new truths are learned.

Lesson 35
"The Two Adams"

GREAT
TRUTHS
OF THE
BIBLE

(Where lines are provided, look up the Scripture and write in the Scripture or its main truth.)

I. INTRODUCTION

The first Adam, the head of the human race, was made in God's image with a personality, intellect, emotions and will, so that there could be communion and fellowship between God and man. God created all things for His good pleasure (Revelation 4:11; Philippians 2:13). Scripture reveals that Adam was deluded—beguiled—into choosing his own way. In choosing to disobey God, Adam became self-centered instead of God-centered; dead to God, who is the source of all life—dead in trespasses and sins. In this fallen state Adam "begat a son in his own likeness, after his (fallen) image" (Genesis 5:2). Thus Adam brought forth a sinful, self-centered, ungodly race born dead in trespasses and sins.

God has been seeking man ever since the fall of Adam. His great plan of redemption called for "the seed of woman"—Jesus Christ—to crush the head of Satan. At the set time, "God sent forth His Son, born of a woman" (Galatians 4:4). In Christ, the image of God is back in its pure sinless form. Jesus became the "last Adam" to provide a plan of redemption for fallen man. Our natural birth made us members of the fallen Adamic race. The transition from the old sinful race to the Godly race is called the "new birth."

By the first Adam sin entered.

By the last Adam "shall many be made righteous."

II. BASIC SCRIPTURES

Genesis 1:26-27; 2:7, 21-23; 3:1-21; Matthew 4:1-11; Romans 5:12, 17; 7:7-24; 8:33-39; I Corinthians 15:22, 45-50; I Thessalonians 5:23; Hebrews 4:12; 9:26; I John 2:16.

III. THE NUCLEUS OF THIS TRUTH

A child always has the nature of his father and mother. Man, who is born of Adam, has the nature of Adam which is sinful. The "father" of Adam's sinful nature is Satan. Therefore, the nature of our father, Adam, is the same as the nature of Satan which means that our nature is the same as Adam's—a sinful nature. Jesus made clear the Satanic nature in John 8:44, "Ye are of your father the devil, and the lusts of your father ye will do. He was a murderer from the beginning, and abode not in the truth, because there is no truth in him. When he speaketh a lie, he speaketh of his own; for he is a liar, and the father of it." Jesus was speaking of Satan. But Jesus was talking to the Pharisees—you might say. Yes, He was, but His words were not limited to the Pharisees as is made plain in I John 3:8-10.

If Satan is the father of the unsaved by the natural birth—we must experience a supernatural birth in order to have God as our Father. The entire world is divided into two divisions:

- those who remain the children of the first Adam

- those who have *become* the children of God by accepting the second Adam—Jesus Christ.

Which division are you in today?

IV. THE GREAT TRUTH: "*THE TWO ADAMS*"

A. THE FIRST ADAM

1. Adam Was Made in the Image of God.

    a. The first man, Adam, was created in the "image" and "likeness" of God. These two words express man's condition as he came from the hand of God in the record of creation. The word "image" means "a resemblance." The word "likeness" means "a model." Underline Genesis 1:26 in your Bible (note the Trinity in verse 26—"us" and "our").

    Write in Genesis 1:27: _____

_____

_____

    b. Since God is a Spirit, one God consisting of three Persons—Father, Son and Holy Spirit—the "image of God" implies that man "resembled" God when he was created as a body, soul and spirit. Adam was created a trinity in unity (three in one). (Genesis 1:26-27 gives the *fact* of man's creation. The account in Genesis 2:7 gives the *manner* of man's creation.)

2. Adam Was Body, Soul and Spirit.

    a. The trinity of man is expressed in the record of creation:

    "The Lord God *formed* man of the dust of the ground (his body), and *breathed* into his nostrils the breath of life (his spirit); and man became a living soul (the soul of man)" (Genesis 2:7).

    b. The *body* related Adam to the physical creation. He could see, smell, taste, touch and hear. He had the five senses of a normal human body.

    c. The *soul* related Adam to others. The soul is the seat of emotion, reason, affection, memory and conscience of good and evil. The soul is a part of man closely related to the spirit of man.

    Write in Hebrews 4:12a: _____

_____

_____

    You can see that only the Word of God, the Sword of the Spirit can divide the soul and spirit of man.

    d. The *spirit* related Adam to the spiritual—the very breath of God made him a living soul.

    Write in Genesis 2:7: _____

_____

_____

    The first Adam was a spiritual being. He was related to the world by his body—to others by his soul and to God by his spirit.

- the body represents world consciousness
- the soul represents self consciousness
- the spirit represents God consciousness

3. The First Adam's Companion.

a. Eve was "made" from man (Genesis 2:21-23). She was fashioned from Adam's side to show that their relation, as man and wife, was to be as "one flesh." God ordained marriage immediately (Genesis 2:23-24). They were to be the counterpart of each other.

b. In this respect Adam and Eve are a picture, a type, of the Last Adam and His Eve—the church, His bride (Ephesians 5:25-32).

4. **The Fall of Man - The First Adam.**

a. When Adam and Eve sinned, the image of God was destroyed. God had said, "the day thou eatest thereof thou shalt surely die" (Genesis 2:17). The restriction was given to Adam. The only limit God placed on Adam was his partaking "of the tree of knowledge of good and evil."

b. Satan tempted Eve and she saw that the "tree was good for food .. pleasant to the eyes .. made one wise .. she gave also to her husband and he did eat" (Genesis 3:6).

c. The Lord God sought them and covered their nakedness with coats of skins (Genesis 3:8-11,21).

d. The plan of redemption—the promise of a redeemer—was given to Adam and Eve.
Write in Genesis 3:15: _____

_____

_____

(Refer to "Through The Bible In One Year" Vol. 1, page 6 for more details.)

e. Adam, the federal head of humanity, chose to sin and in so doing, "he begat sons and daughters in his own likeness and after his (fallen) image" (Genesis 5:3-4).

B. THE FALLEN RACE

1. **Sin Became Universal—Involves All Humanity.**

a. Our natural birth made us members of the fallen, sinful, Adamic race.
Write in Romans 5:12: _____

_____

b. "All have sinned and come short of the glory of God" (Romans 3:23).

c. We were conceived in sin—by parents with the same sin nature as Adam (Psalm 51:5).

2. **Man is Still a Trinity.**

a. Man is born a body, soul and spirit.
Write in I Thessalonians 5:23: _____

_____

Read again Hebrews 4:12.

b. Then, how can the "natural" man—one who is born in sin—spiritually dead, be restored into the "image of God"?
An illustration from the Old Testament shines a bright light on this subject.

After the completion of the tabernacle, it remained empty of the presence of God until the "Spirit of God" descended and took up His abode in the "most holy place." So, a man

211

might be a body, soul and spirit, but his spiritual nature will remain dormant until the Holy Spirit enters and takes possession of that spiritual part of his nature. God only entered the "most holy place" after a sacrifice was offered and blood was shed (Exodus 40).

3. **How Can Man Be Reconciled to God?**

    The total story is revealed in two Scriptures (Genesis 3:15; John 3:16). The promise of a Redeemer to defeat Satan and the promise of eternal life to all who will believe in the Redeemer, Jesus Christ.

C. THE SECOND ADAM - THE LAST ADAM

1. **Jesus Christ, the Last Adam, Restored the Image of God in Man.**

    a. God is still carrying out His purpose of making man in His image. Although His original purpose is the same, He is not using the first Adam to bring it to pass. All is now centered in the Last Adam, the Lord Jesus Christ. Jesus was the first since Adam to bear the lost image of God.

        Write in Colossians 1:15: _____

        _____

        Write in Hebrews 1:3: _____

        _____

        _____

    b. God was the only One who could restore His image in man. Underline II Corinthians 4:4, 6 in your Bible.

        Write in II Corinthians 3:18: _____

        _____

        _____

2. **The Victory Over Sin and Death.**

    a. Jesus was tempted in the wilderness by Satan. The three temptations were the same as the first Adam had encountered and failed. Read Matthew 4:1-11. Underline verses 3, 6, and 9.

    b. Victory was in the Word of God. Notice Matthew 4:4, 7, and 10.

    c. All of the temptations we face can be summed up in the temptation of Eve and the three temptations of Jesus. They are named in I John 2:16:

        ● "the lust of the flesh" - desire to indulge

        ● "the lust of the eyes" - desire to possess

        ● "the pride of life" - desire to impress

    d. Jesus was "tempted in all points like as we are, yet without sin" (Hebrews 4:15).

    e. Jesus became the "sin bearer" who died to restore us to the image of God (I Peter 2:24).

    f. Jesus died for our sins, was buried and was raised on the third day. Underline I Corinthians 15:3-4 in your Bible.

3. **The Last Adam Provides Eternal Life.**

    a. Since the promise of the "Seed of woman" in Genesis 3:15, the Word of God has revealed again and again the sin of mankind and the prophecy of a Saviour—the Messiah. The

212

Lord Jesus came "in the fullness of time"—born of a virgin—taking upon Himself the form of humanity and became our Redeemer, Saviour, Lord (Galatians 4:4; Philippians 2:6-8).

b. To Restore the image of God in man required a new creation. Just as God reached down and breathed into the nostrils of the first Adam—once again the new life, the new creation, the restoration of God's image can only come by the breath, the Spirit of God, entering into the unregenerated. Then, and only then, can man become a new creation.

Write in II Corinthians 5:17: _____

_____

_____

c. He, Jesus, has made us partakers of His Divine nature (II Peter 1:3-4). Underline in your Bible.

D. THE TWO ADAMS—A CONTRAST

Romans 5:12-21

The First Adam **Head of the Original Creation**	The Last Adam—Christ **Head of the New Creation**
• by one man sin entered (*verse 12*)	
• through the offense of (*verse 15*) one many die	• the grace of God and gift by grace, Jesus Christ
• judgment by one to (*verse 16*) condemnation	• the free gift—unto justification
• by one man's offense (*verse 17*) death reigned	• grace and righteousness shall reign in Jesus Christ
• by offense of one, (*verse 18*) judgment	• by righteousness of one, justification of life
• by one man dis- (*verse 19*) obedience many were made sinners	• by obedience of one, shall many be made righteous
• sin hath reigned unto (*verse 21*) death	• grace reigns unto eternal life by Jesus Christ

I Corinthians 15:21, 22, 45-55

• by man came death (*verse 21*)	• by Man came the resurrection of the dead
• in Adam all die (*verse 22*)	• in Christ shall be made alive
• first Adam a living soul (*verse 45*)	• last Adam, a life giving spirit
• the first (Adam) was (*verse 46*) natural	• afterward that which is spiritual (Christ)
• the first man earthy (*verse 47*)	• the second man is Lord from Heaven
• such are they also that (*verse 48*) are earthy	• such are they also that are heavenly
• as we have borne image (*verse 49*) of the earthy	• we shall also bear the image of the heavenly
• this corruptible—this (*verse 52-53*) mortal (body)	• must put on incorruption and immortality
• the sting of death is sin (*verse 54-55*)	• death is swallowed up in victory

213

V. WHAT THIS BIBLE TRUTH TEACHES US TODAY

The secret to a happy life is to know and claim Romans 8:28-29. "But that was in the last lesson," you say. Yes, but it is the summation of this lesson and pinpoints the truth for practical Christian living. In I Corinthians 15:49, Paul gives the great promise: "As we have borne the *image* of the earthy (Adam) we shall also bear the *image* of the heavenly (Christ)."

"For we know that all things work together for good to them that love God, to them who are the called according to His purpose. For whom He did foreknow, He also did predestinate to be conformed to the *image* of His Son" (Romans 8:28-29). The "good" for which God is working all things together is to restore His original purpose of making us in His image. If we belong to Christ, we shall be able to rest in Him regardless of the attacks of Satan. We can stand like Job, and say, "Though He slay me, yet will I trust Him" (Job 13:15).

All of us were born with the nature of the first Adam. By accepting Christ as Saviour, we become "new creations in Christ Jesus" and take on the nature of the Second Adam, Christ. "We know that when He shall appear, we shall be like Him; for we shall see Him as He is" (I John 3:2).

YOUR NEXT ASSIGNMENT:

1. Read Romans 7:7-25; 8:5-14; I Corinthians 2:9-15; Galatians 2:20; 4:19; 5:16; 6:14; Ephesians 2:10; 4:17-32; Colossians 3:3, 4, 10; Hebrews 12:1.

2. Review your notes on The Two Adams.

3. Mark your Bible where new truths are learned.

Lesson 36
"The Two Natures"

(Where lines are provided, look up the Scripture and write in the Scripture or its main truth.)

I. INTRODUCTION

A person who is unregenerahed, unsaved, has only one nature. Only a person who has been regenerated, born again, saved, has two natures—the natural fleshly nature and the new nature given when one is "born of the Spirit." Paul says, "The flesh lusteth against the Spirit, and the Spirit against the flesh; and these are contrary the one to the other, so that ye cannot do the things that ye would" (Galatians 5:17).

Because of a lack of knowledge of the two natures, many new believers find themselves on a spiritual mountaintop only to discover in a short time that the old fleshly desires and thoughts are not dead. The old nature is still present and the young believer is often deceived by Satan to doubt the experience of salvation. Satan works hard and fast at this point and tries to make the newborn babe in Christ believe that he was never converted in the first place. If the new convert knows that the battle really begins when he accepts Christ, he will then be prepared for the Satanic attack. Jesus said, "That which is born of the flesh is flesh; and that which is born of the Spirit (the Holy Spirit) is spirit" (John 3:6). Here Jesus describes the two natures of every believer—the "flesh" and the "spirit." These two natures are described by Paul as the "natural man" and the "spiritual man." In every believer there are the "fleshly" and the "spiritual" natures. Jesus declared the fact in the above Scripture (John 3:6).

II. BASIC SCRIPTURES

Romans 7:7-25; 8:5-14; I Corinthians 2:9-15; Galatians 2:20; 4:19; 5:16; 6:14; Ephesians 2:10; 4:17-32; Colossians 3:3, 4, 10.

III. THE NUCLEUS OF THIS TRUTH

Since every child of God has two natures, he must understand that the old nature can never be eradicated while he lives in the flesh. Therefore, we have the constant battle between the old and new natures. The healthy new birth starts out with a strong love and devotion to the Lord Jesus, but then comes the depressing realization that there remains within that old nature. It pulls one back to the world, to self centeredness, to sin. This experience of the reigning power of the old nature should be the beginning of Spiritual growth. It should make the "babe" in Christ look to Jesus, not only as Saviour, but as Lord of life. "For me to live is Christ" (Philippians 1:21). The believer will come to know the Lord Jesus as his Life when he realizes from experience that the old nature is still within and the battle is constant. As the believer grows in the Lord, Jesus becomes his Life. This growth will not come by rushing from one meeting to another or staying busy doing "good things," but will come about by rushing to the Word of God, joining a strong Bible class and attending a strong Bible centered church. Give the new nature the food it needs to grow and mature in the Lord.

IV. THE GREAT TRUTH: *"THE TWO NATURES"*

A. THE NATURAL MAN

1. **The Characteristics of the Natural Man.**

    a. The natural man is the fleshly, carnal, unregenerated man. He has the nature of Adam which all of us possess at birth. We are born to sinful parents. Every person born since Adam possesses the Adamic nature. We were born "dead in trespasses and sins" (Ephesians 2:1).

    b. He is thoroughly corrupt before God. He produces the works of the flesh.
    Write in Galatians 5:19: _____

    _____

    _____

    Underline Galatians 5:20-21 in your Bible.

    c. He is "by nature the children of wrath."
    Write in Ephesians 2:3: _____

    _____

    _____

2. **Scriptural Names Given the Old Nature (Natural Man).**

    a. *The flesh*. "That which is born of the flesh is flesh" (John 3:6a). Jesus spoke the words. When we speak of "the flesh," we do not mean the body made of tissue and the various elements of the body. "The flesh" means the old carnal nature.
    Write in Romans 8:8: _____

    _____

    b. *The carnal mind*. "Because the carnal mind is enmity against God; for it is not subject to the law of God, neither, indeed, can be" (Romans 8:7).

    c. *The natural man*. The natural man cannot perceive or understand or comprehend the truths of God. The old nature—the unregenerated mind—cannot grasp the things of God.
    Write in I Corinthians 2:14: _____

    _____

    _____

    d. *The sensual man*. The old nature thrives on the lust of the flesh. The flesh must be satisfied.
    Write in Jude 19: _____

    _____

    Write in James 3:15: _____

    _____

    _____

    Notice again Ephesians 2:3.

    e. *The blindness of heart*. "Having the understanding darkened, being alienated from the life of God through the ignorance that is in them, because of the blindness of their heart" (Ephesians 4:18).
    Jesus presented the logical order of sin:
    - "Out of the heart of men" - *man's nature*
    - "evil thoughts" - *man's mind*

- "adulteries, fornications, murders—" - *man's action*
Underline this order in Mark 7:21-22 in your Bible.
Write in Mark 7:23: _____

_____

f. *The old man*.
Write in Ephesians 4:22: _____

_____

_____

_____

Underline Colossians 3:9 in your Bible.

g. *The outward man*. "Though our outward man perish, yet the inward man is renewed day by day" (II Corinthians 4:16).

h. *Sinners*. "There is none righteous, no, not one" (Romans 3:10).
Write in Romans 3:23: _____

_____

3. The End Result of the Natural Man.

a. Spiritual death is the end result of all who do not accept Jesus Christ as Lord.
Write in Romans 5:12: _____

_____

_____

"For to be carnally minded is death . . ." (Romans 8:6).

b. What is Spiritual death? Paul gives the answer in II Thessalonians 1:7-9. Underline verses 7 and 8 in your Bible.
Write in II Thessalonians 1:9: _____

_____

_____

That is Spiritual death. Memorize the verse.

B. THE SPIRITUAL MAN

1. The Characteristics of the Spiritual Man.

a. The new birth imparts a new nature. Jesus said, "That which is born of the Spirit is Spirit" (John 3:6).

b. With a new nature, born of the Holy Spirit, the new believer learns "*Not I–but Christ* liveth in me; and the life which I now live in the flesh I live by the faith of the Son of God, who loved me and gave Himself for me" (Galatians 2:20).

c. The new birth means that Christ is in the heart of all who accept Him.
Write in Colossians 1:27: _____

_____

_____

d. The fruit of a Christian is called "the fruit of the Spirit." Christian character is produced by the Holy Spirit and not by self effort.
Write in Galatians 5:22-23: _____

_____

_____

_____

_____

Underline Galatians 5:24-25 in your Bible.

e. The Christian is "clean through the Word" and abides in Christ.

Write in John 15:3-4: _____

_____

_____

_____

f. The believer is a new creation. "Therefore if any man be in Christ, he is a new creation: old things are passed away; behold, all things are become new" (II Corinthians 5:17).

g. The "divine nature" is given to the Spiritual man. "According to His divine power hath *given unto us all things that pertain unto life and Godliness* through the knowledge of Him that has called us to glory and virtue; whereby *are given unto us exceeding great and precious promises*: that by these *ye might be partakers of the divine nature*, having escaped the corruption that is in the world through lust" (II Peter 1:3-4).

2. **Scriptural Names Given the New Nature (Spiritual Man).**

a. *Christian*. The name indicates that a believer belongs to Christ, and is called a "Christ-ian."

Write in the last sentence of Acts 11:26: _____

_____

Write in I Peter 4:16: _____

_____

_____

b. *The new man*.

Write in Ephesians 4:24: _____

_____

_____

Underline Colossians 3:10 in your Bible.

c. *The inward man*. " . . . the inward man is renewed day by day" (II Corinthians 4:16).

d. *Saints*.

Write in Ephesians 2:19: _____

_____

_____

Write in Romans 8:27: _____

_____

_____

Understand thoroughly these two verses of Scripture.

e. *Priests*. "Ye also, as living stones, are built up a spiritual house, an holy priesthood, to offer up spiritual sacrifices, acceptable to God by Jesus Christ" (I Peter 2:5).

Underline Revelation 1:6 and 5:10 in your Bible.

Write in I Peter 2:9: _____

_____

_____

_____

    f. *Ambassadors*. Underline II Corinthians 5:20 in your Bible.

    g. *Children of God*. "The Spirit Himself beareth witness with our spirit, that we are the children of God" (Romans 8:16). This is also mentioned in verses 17 and 21 and means "one born," "a child."

    h. *Heirs of God–Joint-heirs with Christ*. Underline Romans 8:17 in your Bible.

    i. *The temple of God*.

    Write in I Corinthians 3:16: _____

_____

_____

Underline the next verse (17) in your Bible.

3. **The End Result of the Spiritual Man.**

    a. The new man, the regenerated person looks forward to the coming of the Lord. He will be among all of the redeemed, called the church. The church, the bride of Christ (John 3:29; Ephesians 5:23-29) shall be called to meet Christ "in the air, and so shall we ever be with the Lord." Read I Thessalonians 4:13-18.

    b. Those who have died (physically6 in Christ shall be raised first—resurrected to be with Jesus and all of the redeemed (I Thessalonians 4:16).

    Underline I Corinthians 15:23, 51-53 in your Bible.

    c. Victory in Christ is the end result of the believer.

    Write in I Corinthians 15:57: _____

_____

_____

V. WHAT THIS BIBLE TRUTH TEACHES US TODAY

All believers have two natures—the old Adamic nature and the nature born of the Spirit of God. Paul illustrates the battle of these two natures in the life of all Christians. In Romans 7:15-25, Paul speaks of the strife in his own soul between the flesh and the Spirit. The old nature is not dead. No provision should be made for the flesh (Romans 13:14). The old nature should be starved out by he Word of God.

The Christian must *accept the fact* that the old nature is always present. The Bible says to mortify the flesh—put it to death (Colossians 3:5). The great lesson is this—the old life has become a new life in Christ: "we should walk in the newness of life" (Romans 6:4). The new life is to be nourished by the cleansing Word of God, which washes and makes clean (John 15:3; 17:17; Ephesians 5:26). The new life in Christ means that one has become a new creation but is born as a babe in Christ. Give the Lord time enough in your life to grow from "the milk of the Word" (I Peter 2:2) to "strong meat" (Hebrews 5:12, 14). Spiritual food will starve the old nature. When you do sin, confess it only to God through Christ. Use the Christian's "bar of soap" several times each day. That "bar of soap" is found in I John 1:9. Memorize the verse. When you sin, confess and *forget it*. The verse not only says, "If we confess our sins He will forgive," but it also says, "He will cleanse us from all unrighteousness."

Let the Holy Spirit guide and direct your life. He will guide you into all truth (John 16:13).

YOUR NEXT ASSIGNMENT:

1. Read Matthew 6:3-15; 7:7-11; 18:19; Mark 9:23; Luke 11:9; John 17; Acts 7:59-60; Romans 8:26; Ephesians 3:20; Philippians 4:19; Colossians 4:2; I Thessalonians 5:17; Hebrews 10:19-22; James 4:2-3; Revelation 22:20.

2. Review your notes on The Two Natures.

3. Mark your Bible where new truths are learned.

Lesson 37 "Prayer"

GREAT TRUTHS OF THE BIBLE

(Where lines are provided, look up the Scripture and write in the Scripture or its main truth.)

I. INTRODUCTION

Prayer is one of the highest functions and most important privileges of the Christian life. Prayer is the immediate desire of the heart of a new life in Christ to talk with, commune with the Father. The Holy Spirit indwells the believer and plants the "spirit of prayer" in the heart. Prayer is mostly thought of as *asking* and *receiving*. Prayer is that and much more. Prayer is manifesting the Christian life in communion with God through His Son and our Saviour. Prayer is dependence upon God—not self. It is an expression of the heart of devotion and thanksgiving for God's love and care. Words are not the important part of prayer; the *spirit* of prayer is what God sees and understands. To pray is as much a part of the Christian life as breathing is to the natural life. To pray is to grow; to pray is a privilege. More is accomplished by prayer than has ever been accomplished by all the "religious activities" in the world.

II. BASIC SCRIPTURES

Matthew 6:3-15; 7:7-11; 18:19; Mark 9:23; Luke 11:9; John 17; Acts 7:59-60; Romans 8:26; Ephesians 3:20; Philippians 4:19; Colossians 4:2; I Thessalonians 5:17; Hebrews 10:19-22; James 4:2-3; Revelation 22:20.

III. THE NUCLEUS OF THIS TRUTH

Saying prayers and praying are two different things. A self righteous Pharisee excelled in saying prayers. A regenerated soul can enjoy the privilege of prayer. The spirit of prayer is the spirit of a new creature in Christ Jesus. The language of prayer is the utterance of the new life—the regenerated life. A child by natural birth may ask for a great many foolish things, but he could not ask if he had not *life*. The ability and the desire to ask are proofs of *life*. When Saul (Paul) of Tarsus passed from his old life into his new life, the Lord said of him, "Behold, he prayeth" (Acts 9:11). As a "Pharisee of the Pharisees" Paul had undoubtedly "said long prayers"; but when he saw Jesus and heard His voice, it was then that Paul surrendered and said, "Lord what wilt thou have me to do?" (Acts 9:6).

The disciples of Jesus did not ask Him to teach them to preach. They asked Jesus for one great thing: "Lord, teach us to pray" (Luke 11:1). The gift of prayer is for all who love the Lord God. Jesus said, "Man ought always to pray, and not to faint" (Luke 18:1). One does not need a special call to have a ministry of prayer. The greatest power committed to every believer is the power of prayer.

IV. THE GREAT TRUTH: *"PRAYER"*

A. THE PATTERN OF PRAYER

1. The Lord's Rules Concerning Prayer.

    a. The Lord gave some general rules concerning prayer before He gave to the disciples the "Model Prayer." These *"nega-*

tive" teachings on prayer are found in Matthew 6:5-8.

b. "Thou shalt not be like the hypocrites" (Matthew 6:5). Jesus teaches that a hypocrite's prayer is in public, and they love to be seen and heard of men. They stand so all can see them.

Underline Matthew 6:5 in your Bible.

c. Jesus taught against the "long prayers" of the hypocrites. Write in Matthew 23:14: _____

_____

_____

d. Jesus warned about "vain repetitions."

Write in Matthew 6:7: _____

_____

_____

There is room at this point for all of us to review our prayer life. Think of the phrases or words used over and over again. Take out the vain repetitions, and the prayer would be half as long. Look at verse 7 again—"they think they shall be heard for their much speaking."

e. The prayers of Jesus and of Paul teach us how to pray. Both prayed for long periods of time, but you will not find long prayers recorded by either one. The longest prayer of Jesus is John 17 and it would require about three minutes to read. They prayed in private. Jesus told us to pray privately.

Write in Matthew 6:6: _____

_____

_____

2. The Elements of Prayer.

a. "After this manner pray ye" (Matthew 6:9).

The prayer Jesus gave to the disciples is the Model Prayer—not to be vainly repeated—but a Model Prayer to teach the real structure and "positive" meaning of prayer. Jesus said, "After this manner, therefore, pray ye." Let the prayer be a pattern for all praying. In a prayer of about thirty seconds, Jesus taught the scope of our needs in spirit, soul and body.

b. The *three elements* of prayer are found in the Model Prayer:

- **Godward** - "Our Father which art in heaven, Hallowed by Thy name. Thy kingdom come. Thy will be done in earth, as it is in heaven" (Matthew 6:9-10).

This *Godward* element of prayer is called *Communion*.

- **Inward** - "Give us this day our daily bread" (Matthew 6:11).

This *Inward* element of prayer is called *Petition*.

> ● **Outward** - "Forgive us our debts, as we forgive our debtors" (Matthew 6:12).

> This *Outward* element of prayer is called *Intercession*.

   c. A summary for remembrance is set forth:

> ● Communion - Godward Attention

> ● Petition - Inward Attention

> ● Intercession - Outward Attention

3. The Three Elements of Prayer Explained.

   a. Communion is that part of prayer which removes every hindrance between God and ourselves. It is an act of worship and adoration. It is an attitude of thanksgiving and submission. Communion with God does something *to us*.

   b. Petition is that part of prayer in which we can ask anything according to His will and He will give it to us—*if* the first element of communion has been observed. In petition we have something done *for us*.

   c. Intercession is that part of prayer which causes us to lose the element of self and become concerned about others. In intercession we have something done *through us*.

Write in John 15:7: _____

_____

_____

   d. The three elements of prayer are taken from the Model Prayer in Matthew 6:9-13—a part of the Sermon on the Mount delivered by the Master. Mark these elements of prayer in your Bible.

B. THE POWER OF PRAYER

1. The Unlimited Power of Believing Prayer.

   a. "Ask, seek, knock." The Father has all power and He knows our needs. The Bible definitely teaches that we, His children, must "ask, seek, knock" when we pray. Just as a natural father will give good gifts to his own children, so God the Father gives to His own who ask Him.

Write in Matthew 7:7: _____

_____

_____

Write in Matthew 7:11: _____

_____

_____

   b. "Ask in faith, nothing wavering." Faith is essential to the unlimited power of prayer. The Bible teaches this fact again and again.

Write in James 1:6: _____

_____

_____

Write in James 1:7: _____

_____

c. Jesus taught the necessity of faith in prayer. Underline Mark 11:23 in your Bible.
Write in Mark 11:24: _____

_____

Write in Mark 9:23: _____

_____

_____

2. The Abundant Grace of God in Christ.

a. The power of prayer is based upon asking "in the name of Jesus."
Write in John 14:13-14 _____

_____

_____

b. The "chosen," or the saved ones, are to ask the Father in the name of Jesus
Write in John 15:16: _____

_____

_____

c. We pray, usually closing our prayer with the words, "In Jesus' name we pray." Why? Jesus told us to pray in His name. You have seen that in the passages studied. Now, underline John 16:23-24 in your Bible.

d. God supplies our needs by Christ Jesus.
Write in Philippians 4:19: _____

_____

_____

e. Assurance comes through answered prayer. Read I John 5:12-13.
Write in I John 5:14: _____

_____

_____

Underline the next verse, verse 15.

3. Prayer is What One Claims in the Name of Jesus.

a. God has given to all of us the ability to speak, to work, to become skilled. These are gracious gifts of God, but the circle of influence is limited.

b. However, when it comes to prayer, we can enter the outlets of God's power through Jesus Christ. We can pray and our prayers become omnipotent (all powerful) simply by praying in the name of Jesus, according to His will. Prayer can remove mountains (Matthew 17:20). Prayer, in Jesus' name, is all powerful. (We are not omnipotent, the prayers are.)

c. Our prayers can reach around the world, right now. Prayers of the saints are omnipresent (everywhere present). We can pray for God's will for a person in China, Africa, Israel or any place in the world. If the prayer is in the name of Jesus, the prayer is not limited by miles. (Again, the prayer is not omnipresent, but the prayer is.) Underline Ephesians 3:20 in your Bible.

C. HINDRANCES TO PRAYER

1. The Hindrances Are Caused by Man, not God.

a. We lack confidence.
   Write in Hebrews 11:6: _____

   _____

   _____

b. We pray amiss.
   Write in James 4:3: _____

   _____

c. We are not persistent. "Pray without ceasing" (I Thessalonians 5:17). "Continue in prayer, and watch with thanksgiving" (Colossians 4:2).

d. Sin hinders prayer.
   Write in Psalm 66:18: _____

   _____

   _____

2. God Expects Us to Answer Some of Our Own Prayers.

a. God does not answer prayers when He expects us to answer them for ourselves. All of us have heard people pray for God to save the lost. The same person has probably met or worked with many lost people every day, and has never said a word about their relationship to Christ. Our faith is a reasonable faith. God always uses human instrumentality.

b. Faith and works go together. Practical Christianity is advised in James 2:14-16. Pious prayers for the poor are a farce if one is in a position to help and refuses to do so. God expects us to act as well as pray.

D. OUR ACCESS TO GOD THROUGH CHRIST

1. We Can Enter the Presence of God Through Jesus Christ.

a. Underline Hebrews 10:19-22 in your Bible.

b. When we ask according to His will and *two* have agreed, Jesus says that the Father will answer. Underline Matthew 18:19 in your Bible.

2. The Holy Spirit Makes Intercession for Us.

a. Read and underline Romans 8:26 in your Bible.

b. Underline Jude 20, 21 in your Bible.

3. The High Priestly Prayer of Jesus Assures Us.

a. The "Lord's Prayer" is recorded in John 17. Read the entire chapter and notice that His prayer assures Christians of our being in Him and in the Father. We have access to God because we believe in His Son.

V. WHAT THIS BIBLE TRUTH TEACHES US TODAY

Prayer is discovering God's will—not trying to change His mind. Prayer is coming to God in absolute faith that what we need will be given to us in answer to our prayers. The Bible definitely teaches that our prayers should be according to His will (I John 5:14-15).

God always answers prayer. The prayers of faith, the believing prayer for the glory of God, is always answered. The prayer for something that is not good for us is answered with a ''no.'' The prayer for something or someone is often delayed until God knows that by answering the prayer it will work for good.

So, the three answers to prayer are:

- *Yes*, your prayer is in the will of God.

- *No*, to answer your prayer would do you no good.

- *Wait*, God knows what is best and at what point we can accept His positive answer.

Some find a conflict with Matthew 6:8. If the Father knows what we have need of, why should we pray and ask God? Because God is God, He knows all things before we even think of them. He is still our Father and He wants us to ask Him, pray to Him. Read Matthew 7:7-8 again.

Communion with God opens the way for *Petition*, which opens our concern for others, which is *Intercession*.

Prayer should be as much an attitude as an outward act. The person who communes with God in silence almost constantly is the one who has discovered the secret of prayer. (We shall touch on prayer again in the lessons on the church.)

YOUR NEXT ASSIGNMENT:

1. Read Romans 12; 13; 14:1-8; I Corinthians 6:19-20; Hebrews 13:1-17; James 1:1-25; 4:1-17; I Peter 2:1-20.

2. Review your notes on Prayer.

3. Mark your Bible where new truths are learned.

Lesson 38
"The Christian Life"

(Where lines are provided, look up the Scripture and write in the Scripture or its main truth.)

I. INTRODUCTION

The Christian life begins with the initial experience in which we pass "from death unto life." From that point, Christianity is a life to be lived, a continuous development of the new life in Christ. In this lesson we shall deal with the Christian life in terms of its beginnings, its continuance, the Scriptural commands and how to maintain and develop the Christian life. The Scriptures dealing with discipline and discipleship are rarely studied in detail. Misunderstanding at this point could cause a person to be just the opposite of what the Scriptures teach.

For instance, the Christian life is *not* isolation from the world—retreating to a solitary place. The Christian life is not legalistic, composed of a great number of things "you don't do"—a "holier than thou" attitude. The Christian life *is* getting out into the world and showing the world the standards of the Christian life. It is life at its best, a life of joy which should be shared. By example in our conduct, act and deed, others should be able to see Christ. The life of a Christian has only one code of ethics—the Word of God. Being a Christian means "Christ in you."

II. BASIC SCRIPTURES

Romans 12; 13; 14:1-8; I Corinthians 6:19-20; Hebrews 13:1-17; James 1:1-25; 4:1-17; I Peter 2:1-20.

III. THE NUCLEUS OF THIS TRUTH

A Christian is separated or set apart for God. According to the Scriptures, Christians are "called to be saints" (Romans 1:7; I Corinthians 1:2). The word "saint" means all who are regenerated, saved, set apart for God. The separation, or setting apart, takes place at the time of conversion. God sets the person apart for Himself.

Christianity is not something to accept intellectually, but something that changes the heart. It has a powerful effect upon morality, character and conduct. It is a positive dedication of every phase of life to Christ. It is a voluntary committal of the whole person to God.

IV. THE GREAT TRUTH: *"THE CHRISTIAN LIFE"*

A. THE BEGINNING OF THE CHRISTIAN LIFE

1. **A Living Devotion to Christ.**

   a. The Christian life begins by turning from the old life and trusting in Jesus Christ as Saviour and Lord. It is a decision made by the free will of man which is called "repentance" (Matthew 9:13; Luke 13:3-5).

   b. The Christian life begins with "regeneration" or a new birth. This is God's doing, once repentance takes place (John 1:12).

   ("Repentance" and "Regeneration" are Lessons 28 and 29.)

227

c. The Christian life is a *turning from* the old life and a *turning to* a new life in Christ. The Christian life is the outward manifestation to the inward work of grace. By faith, one receives Jesus Christ and God does the altering of the heart; one becomes a living devotion to Christ.

2. **The New Life Cannot be Hid.**

   a. When a person accepts Christ, the first desire and the first natural act is to tell others, to confess the new birth before men.

   Write in the words of Jesus in Matthew 10:32: _____

   _____

   _____

   b. The saved person is to confess Christ with the mouth. This is as natural as a baby crying for the first time. Confession does not save, but saving faith will lead to confession. It is not a silent faith.

   Write in Romans 10:9: _____

   _____

   _____

   c. The heart believes—the mouth confesses.

   Write in Romans 10:10: _____

   _____

   d. The believer is not to be ashamed.

   Write in Romans 10:11: _____

   _____

   Many people stop short of an open confession.

   e. A verbal statement or intellectual assent does not meet the standard of Christ or Paul. One cannot be "a living devotion to Christ" and hide his faith. The Christian life should show; it should be evident in every aspect of life.

B. THE CONTINUATION OF THE CHRISTIAN LIFE

   1. **Jesus Christ is the Standard for the Christian Life.**

      a. Union with Christ affects conduct.
      Write in Philippians 1:27: _____

      _____

      _____

      _____

      b. The standard is Christ. The Christian should think like Him.
      Write in Philippians 2:5: _____

      _____

      c. The Christian should walk like Him.
      Write in I John 2:6: _____

      _____

      _____

      Underline I Peter 2:21 in your Bible.

   2. **The Christian Life Should Become a Standard.**

228

a. The Christian is a pattern.
   Write in Titus 2:7: _____

   _____

b. The Christian is a light. Jesus spoke the words, "Ye are the light of the world" (Matthew 5:14).
   Write in Matthew 5:16: _____

   _____

   _____

   Underline John 8:12 and Ephesians 5:8 in your Bible.

c. The Christian is the salt of the earth.
   Write in Matthew 5:13: _____

   _____

   _____

d. The Christian is new, is different from the world.
   Write in II Corinthians 5:17: _____

   _____

   _____

e. The Christian is patient in trials and testing.
   Write in James 1:3: _____

   _____

   _____

f. The Christian is victorious. Underline I John 5:4 and write in I John 5:5: _____

   _____

   _____

g. The Christian rejoices in the Lord.
   Write in Philippians 4:4: _____

   _____

C. THE CHRISTIAN LIFE MEANS FULL DEDICATION TO CHRIST

1. The Christian is to be Transformed.

a. Romans 12:2 gives no choice. It is a statement of fact. "And be not conformed to this world, but be ye transformed by the renewing of your mind, that ye may prove what is that good, and acceptable, and perfect, will of God."

b. The transformation comes easy to those who present themselves as a sacrifice (meaning "that which is utterly devoted to Christ") to God.
   Write in Romans 12:1: _____

   _____

   _____

3. The Christian is to be Separated, Different.

a. The Christian is to be separated *from* the things of the world—and separated *to* God.
   Write in II Corinthians 6:17: _____

   _____

b. Separation from evil means separation in desire, motive and act. Separation does not mean isolation from the world, but from conformity to the world. Jesus set forth this truth in His intercessory prayer for believers. Underline John 17:14 and write in verse 15: _____

_____

_____

Underline John 17:16-18 in your Bible.

c. The Christian must not love the things of the world.
Write in I John 2:15: _____

_____

_____

d. The extent of separation is given in I John 2:16, "For all that is in the world—
- the lust of the flesh
- the lust of the eyes
- the pride of life

is not of the Father, but is of the world."

Every temptation for the Christian can be placed under one of these categories. Jesus was tempted in the wilderness in the same three ways (Matthew 4:1-11).

e. The believer is to "have **no** fellowship with the unfruitful works of darkness" (**Ephesians** 5:11).

f. The believer is to "keep himself unspotted from the world" (James 1:27).

D. THE GOAL OF THE CHRISTIAN LIFE

1. **Christlikeness in Character.**

   a. The purpose of separation and devotion to God is to make the believer more like Christ. The believer has been saved and set apart "to establish your hearts unblamable in holiness before God" (I Thessalonians 3:13).

   b. Christian character is produced by the Holy Spirit. The fruit of the Spirit is the possession and manifestation of the graces mentioned in Galatians 5:22-23.
   Write in Galatians 5:22-23: _____

   _____

   _____

   _____

   c. This in no way means sinless perfection in this life; and yet, Jesus has set His standard and perfection as our goal (Matthew 5:48).

2. **Christlikeness in Service.**

   a. The Christian is to bear fruit. The purpose of discipleship is to be a branch which bears fruit because the branch is attached to the Vine.
   Read John 15:1-4 and write in verse 5: _____

   _____

   _____

b. The believer is to serve for the glory of Christ, with His Spirit. Christlikeness in service is one of the most difficult attributes for the average Christian today. Remember that Jesus said, ''As My Father hath sent Me, even so send I you'' (John 20:21).

c. The Christian is told what to do in the Lord's great commission (Matthew 28:19-20). The service includes ''Go ye''—''teach''—''baptize''—''teach all things.''

Then, the promise, ''I am with you always, even to the end of the age.''

E. MAINTAINING THE CHRISTIAN LIFE

1. By Bible Study and Prayer.

a. The development of the Christian is largely the work of the Holy Spirit. There are important things for the Christian to perform in order that the Holy Spirit may do His work. God has placed in the hands of all believers certain means to keep the Christian vital and growing. The Word of God provides the food for proper growth.

Write in Colossians 1:10: _____

_____

_____

b. God's Word nurtures the Christian life. Without it, one becomes weak, fruitless and often useless in the work of the Lord. In the parable of the sower, our Lord warned of distractions, ''And the cares of this world, and the deceitfulness of riches, and the lust of other things entering in, choke the Word, and it becometh unfruitful'' (Mark 4:19).

Jesus knew the importance of the Word of God and He prayed for His own (Christians) to be sanctified, set apart, made holy by the Word.

Write in John 17:17: _____

_____

c. Prayer is as vital to the spiritual life as breathing is to the natural body. It is through prayer that the spiritual life is kept healthy and clean. Prayer is talking to God. Prayer is adoration, confession, thanksgiving, petition and intercession. Prayer is communion with God through Jesus Christ. He is the Father listening to His children.

Write in James 5:16: _____

_____

Underline I Thessalonians 5:17 and Philippians 4:6 in your Bible.

2. By Worship.

a. Worship with the people of God is imperative to maintain the Christian life. Church should be a place of worship, teaching and fellowship. The local church plays a vital role in the development of Christians.

b. Christ loved the church and established the church upon Himself, the Rock (Matthew 16:18).

c. The church is to assemble—to meet, for worship.

Write in Hebrews 10:25: _____

_____
_____
_____

3. By Serving.

    a. Opportunities for service in the work of the Lord are available to every Christian. The Hold Spirit has given to every Christian a gift, or gifts, to use in the service of the Lord. He, the Holy Spirit, qualifies us for the office He has given us. There is really no excuse to be given for not serving.

    b. Write in Colossians 3:23-24: _____

_____
_____
_____

V. WHAT THIS BIBLE TRUTH TEACHES US TODAY

The Christian life is "Christ in you" (Colossians 1:27). When Christ is in a life, the "reasonable service" (Romans 12:1)(more literally, "logical ministry") is presented as a living sacrifice. A sacrifice is that which is totally devoted to God. The Holy Spirit renews the mind, making it possible for the believer to test, or prove, that good and acceptable and perfect will of God.

The Christian life is a positive walk of fellowship with God and His people. The pleasures of sin are replaced with the things of God. With Christ as Lord, the Holy Spirit indwelling the believer and God as Father, the things of this earth grow very dim. The Christian life becomes a positive, joyful walk with the Lord. It is not a negative creed filled with legalism. Jesus said, "If the Son, therefore, shall make you free, ye shall be free indeed" (John 8:36).

YOUR NEXT ASSIGNMENT:

1. Read Genesis 8:20; 26:15; Exodus 19:6; 28:1;Hebrews 4:14-16; 5:1; 7:11-28; 8:1-5; 9:7-28; 10:1-25; 13:9-14; I Peter 2:1-10.

2. Review your notes on The Christian Life.

3. Mark your Bible where new truths are learned.

Lesson 39
"The Priesthood of the Believer"

(Where lines are provided, look up the Scripture and write in the Scripture or its main truth.)

I. INTRODUCTION

One of the great truths of Scripture is the fact that every believer in the Lord Jesus Christ is a priest. A priest is one who speaks to God for others. A prophet is one who speaks to men for God. In this lesson we shall set forth the Scriptural teaching of the priesthood of the believer.

In the beginning, God stipulated that the husband and father in the home be the family priest. This is illustrated in Genesis 8:20; 26:25; 31:54 and many other places in Scripture. When God gave the law at Mt. Sinai, He gave the People of Israel an opportunity to become a kingdom of priests and a holy nation. The people agreed and said, "All that the Lord hath spoken we will do" (Exodus 19:5-8). Israel failed and violated the law. God removed their opportunity to become a kingdom of priests. Instead, He selected Aaron and his family, appointing the tribe of Levi to minister to Israel. The typical priesthood was constituted by God (Exodus 28:1). This was the order and practice until the day our Lord was crucified. During that crucifixion there came one moment when the veil in the temple was rent in two from the top to the bottom (Matthew 27:50-51). Notice, it was not torn from the bottom to the top, but God rent the veil from the top to the bottom. From that moment there has been no need for a select group of priests. The sacrifice of Jesus, the rent veil, opened the way to the holy of holies directly into the presence of God. From that moment, every believer has become a priest, a part of God's royal priesthood. When a person accepts Christ as Saviour, he becomes a priest; and as a priest, he has the privilege of going directly to the throne of God through Jesus Christ, our High Priest. Praise God! (And this is only the introduction.)

II. BASIC SCRIPTURES

Genesis 8:20; 26:15; Exodus 19:6; 28:1; Hebrews 4:14-16; 5:1; 7:11-28; 8:1-5; 9:7-28; 10:1-25; 13:9-14; I Peter 2:1-10.

III. THE NUCLEUS OF THIS TRUTH

Christians are "priests"—a word indicative of privilege in having access to God in the name of Jesus. This priesthood is based upon faith and acceptance of the High Priest, Jesus Christ—not upon man's goodness nor a church pronouncement. The function of believers, priests, is to "show forth" the praises of God. The old priesthood of offering sacrifices, interceding for the people and, on the Day of Atonement entering before God with a blood sacrifice, was over. Since Jesus paid the price "once and for all," every believer has access to God through Christ to praise Him, to thank Him and to intercede for those in need of prayer. Every believer has the responsibility of the priestly functions of teaching and witnessing.

IV. THE GREAT TRUTH: *"THE PRIESTHOOD OF THE BELIEVER"*

A. THE FOUNDATION OF THE CHRISTIAN PRIESTHOOD

1. The Living Stone.

a. The priesthood of the believer is based upon a "living Stone" who is Jesus Christ.

Write in I Peter 2:4: _____

_____

_____

b. The apostle, Peter, had good cause to use the term "living Stone." He had been the one to express his confession of faith in Jesus Christ. Turn to Matthew 16:13-16 and read the context.

Write in Matthew 16:16: _____

_____

_____

c. Jesus responded to Peter's confession, "Thou art Peter, and upon this Rock (Christ) I will build My church, and the gates of hell shall not prevail against it" (Matthew 16:18).

d. The foundation of the church of God and practical Christianity are found in the conversation between Jesus and Peter. In writing his epistle, Peter alludes to that Rock, Jesus, as the living Stone.

2. The Living God.

a. In Peter's confession he said, "Thou art the Christ, the Son of the living God." The foundation of the Christian priesthood is solid—built on the *living God* and the living *Stone*.

b. The living God made the foundation sound and sure. He (the Lord God) said He would lay the foundation.

Write in Isaiah 28:16: _____

_____

_____

c. The same statement is quoted by Peter (I Peter 2:6). God has laid the foundation and that foundation is Jesus Christ, the living Stone.

3. The Living Stones.

a. The life of Christ, the Son of the living God, flows from Him to all who believe and receive Him.

Write in I Peter 2:5: _____

_____

_____

b. All believers are built upon the living Stone, Christ, and are *living stones* and are partakers of His risen, victorious life.

c. He is a living Stone—Christians are living stones.
He is a precious Stone—Christians are precious stones.
He is a rejected Stone—Christians are rejected stones, and are identified with Him in every respect.

d. The solid foundation of the Christian priesthood is sure—

the living God; the living Stone, the living stones. A life flows from God—through a living channel, Christ—to all believers.

e. Paul speaks of the Stone.

Write in I Corinthians 10:4: _____

_____

_____

Also, write in Ephesians 2:20: _____

_____

_____

B. THE STRUCTURE OF THE CHRISTIAN PRIESTHOOD

1. All Believers Are a Part of the Holy Priesthood.

a. Christians are not only "living stones," but a part of the "spiritual house, a *holy priesthood*."

Write in I Peter 2:5: _____

_____

_____

You have written this verse before. The emphasis now is upon "the holy priesthood."

b. The priesthood of the Christian is a birthright. When one is born again, one becomes a priest with the rights and privileges of that office—just as every descendant of Aaron was born to the priesthood. Underline Hebrews 5:1 and 4 in your Bible.

c. The main privilege of a priest is access to God. Under the old covenant, the high priest could enter the "holy of holies" only once each year with the blood of sacrifice.

Write in Hebrews 9:7: _____

_____

_____

(For the new Bible student, the "holy of holies" was the most holy place in the tabernacle which God gave to Israel. The Scriptural account is in Exodus 25 through 40. That was a picture of the life and work of Christ for us. Notice Hebrews 9:8-10 and underline in your Bible.)

2. To Become a Priest, There Must be a High Priest.

a. Peter used the term "a holy priesthoot" because he knew the Old Testament and had been with our Lord. The priesthood of the believer is based upon Jesus as the Great High Priest.

Write in Hebrews 9:11: _____

_____

_____

_____

b. There was the requirement of One qualified to be the High Priest. Jesus was the only One.

Write in Hebrews 4:14: _____

_____

_____

c. The priests required a sacrifice and the shedding of blood. In the Old Testament, Aaron and the priests offered the blood of animals to cover the sins of themselves and the people. Jesus did away with that ritual when He shed His own blood once and for all for the sin of the world.

Also, Hebrews 9:14: _____

_____

_____

_____

Underline Hebrews 9:15, 22.

3. Because of Jesus, the High Priest, Believers Have Access to the Throne of God.

    a. Jesus is in glory for us.

       Write in Hebrews 9:24: _____

_____

_____

    b. Jesus put away sin by His own sacrifice on the cross (Hebrews 9:26).

    c. Believers have the right and privilege to enter boldly into the presence of God.

       Write in Hebrews 10:19 and 20: _____

_____

_____

_____

_____

    d. Jesus is the High Priest over the house of God (Hebrews 10:21).

    e. Christians, as priests, can have assurance as they approach God.

       Write in Hebrews 10:22: _____

_____

_____

    f. This privilege of priesthood is not earned. It cannot be bought. It is a gift at birth—the new birth. It is the Christian's birthright. Claim it, accept it, never doubt Him.

4. The Nature and Character of a Priest.

    a. Peter says, "a holy priesthood, to offer up spiritual sacrifices, acceptable to God by Jesus Christ" (I Peter 2:5).

    b. The nature of the believer should be "praise" to God. This should not be an occasional thing which takes place only when all is going well, but in times of distress as well.

    c. The character of the believer priest should be indicated by the inward nature. The entire meaning of Peter's statement "to offer up sacrifices" can be found in Scripture.

    d. The believer priest is to praise God _continually_. The _fruit of his lips_ is praise and thanks.

       Write in Hebrews 13:15: _____

_____

C. THE SUPERSTRUCTURE OF THE CHRISTIAN PRIEST-HOOD

1. The Christian Priest is a Member of a Chosen Generation.

a. The first thought is—"Isn't Peter talking about Israel?" If you read I Peter 1 and 2:1-3, you have the answer.

b. In I Peter 1:9, Peter says, "But ye are a chosen generation." This means believers—an elect people. Here we refer you back to Lesson 33 on "Election and Free Will."

2. The Believer Priest is in the *Royal* Priesthood.

a. Peter says in I Peter 2:9, "But ye are a chosen generation, a *royal priesthood*, a holy nation, a peculiar people; that ye should show forth the praises of Him who hath called you out of darkness into His marvelous light."

b. As "holy priests," believers draw nigh to God and present the sacrifice of praise. As "royal priests," believers *go forth* in every aspect of life to "*show forth*" the virtues and graces and the moral features of Jesus Christ. Every part of the life of a believer priest should show loveliness of the High Priest, Jesus Christ.

c. The apostle does not say, "ye ought to be royal priests." He says, "*ye are* a royal priesthood."

The Christian is called to be an expression of a royal Leader—Jesus Christ.

d. The term "holy nation" actually means in the Greek, "people." Believers are a "holy people."

e. "A peculiar people" simply means a "valuable people"—not because of what one might be or might own, but because he has accepted Christ and has become the possession of God.

V. WHAT THIS BIBLE TRUTH TEACHES US TODAY

The truth of this lesson can best be set forth by example, an illustration taken from Acts 16:19-34. Paul and Silas have been put in jail at Philippi. At the midnight hour, in jail with wounds on their backs, what do you think they were doing? They were not complaining and pitying themselves. Those two "*living stones*"—two "*holy priests*"—were offering the sacrifice of praise to God. The Scripture says, "And at midnight Paul and Silas prayed, and sang praises unto God; and the prisoners heard them" (Acts 16:25). They were there also as "*royal priests*." How does this virtue show in their action? In the touching words of Paul, "Do thyself no harm, for we are all here" (Acts 16:28).

The voices of the "holy priests" offered the sacrifice of praise and did their work there at the throne of God; and the words of the "royal priests" went directly to the jailer's heart and did their work there. The two "*living stones, holy priests, royal priests*," glorified God; and the jailer and his family were saved.

This is "the priesthood of the believer." If you are a Christian, then "there is one God, and one mediator between God and man—the Man, Christ Jesus" (I Timothy 2:5).

YOUR NEXT ASSIGNMENT:

1. Read Matthew 28:18-20; Mark 4:28; 16:15-16; Hebrews 5:12; 6:1; 10:7-24; 13:1-16; I John 4:17.

2. Review your notes on The Priesthood of the Believer.

3. Mark your Bible where new truths are learned.

Lesson 40 "The Price of Discipleship"

(Where lines are provided, look up the Scripture and write in the Scripture or its main truth.)

I. INTRODUCTION

The Lord Jesus was most explicit and firm when He mentioned discipleship. Matthew, Mark and Luke record His words; we take Luke's account here. "And He said unto them all, If any man will come after me, let him deny himself, and take up his cross daily, and follow me" (Luke 9:23). "And whosoever doth not bear his cross, and come after me, cannot be my disciple" (Luke 14:27). Christians should understand that bearing the cross does not refer to the trials of this life, which some people call "my cross." Some confuse the words "a cross" with "the cross." In self pity, some believers will say, "I must take my cross and bear it for Jesus." This is a wrong attitude. The believer's cross is *the cross of Calvary*. It means dying to self. Because of His cross, there is resurrection life, newness of life. Paul said, "I am crucified with Christ, nevertheless I live; yet not I, but Christ liveth in me . . ." (Galatians 2:20).

Voluntarily, the Christian begins to "glory in the cross of our Lord Jesus Christ" (Galatians 6:14). The cross gives freedom from the old life. It means liberation and joy in Christ even in the midst of some suffering for His sake.

The Lord Jesus never gives us a "cross to bear." He gives us His cross, His life, His ministry to share with the world. If trial and tribulation be a part of that ministry—He gives the strength and power to overcome.

II. BASIC SCRIPTURES

Matthew 28:18-20; Mark 4:28; 16:15-16; Hebrews 5:12; 6:1; 10:7-24; 13:1-16; I John 4:17.

III. THE NUCLEUS OF THIS TRUTH

The principle of discipleship and Christian growth is, "first the blade, then the ear, after that the full corn in the ear" (Mark 4:28). For most believers it takes a long time to grow from the tiny blade up to the "full corn in the ear." The idea of maintaining a measure of Christian respectability by staying busy, attending aimless meetings, doing what seems right, in no way makes real disciples of the Lord Jesus. For the blade to grow requires spiritual food from the Word of God.

There is a vast difference between coming *to* Jesus for salvation and coming *after* Jesus for service. Coming *to* Christ makes one a believer, while coming *after* Christ makes one a disciple. A believer accepts the invitation of the gospel. A disciple is one who obeys the challenge to live a life of dedicated service. Salvation is free. Discipleship involves paying the price of the sacrifice of self.

The word "disciple" means "a learner" or "one who is taught."

IV. THE GREAT TRUTH: *"THE PRICE OF DISCIPLESHIP"*

A. THE PROCESS OF DISCIPLESHIP

1. **The Preacher and Teacher are to Make Disciples out of Saints.**

   a. The book of Hebrews was written to a people who were still "babes in Christ." They were believers, but knew little about discipleship.

   Write in Hebrews 5:12: _____

   _____

   _____

   They were still on milk like a baby. They should have become teachers. Instead they had to be taught again the first principles of the Word of God. This sounds much like the day in which we live.

   b. They were merely believers and should have had the desire to become mature disciples. They were told to grow up—to learn.

   Write in Hebrews 6:1: _____

   _____

   _____

   The word "perfection" means "maturity."

2. **The Lord Jesus Gave Instruction in His Great Commission (Matthew 28:18-20).**

   a. The commission of Christ has *power*. Jesus said, "All power (authority) is given unto me in heaven and in earth" (Matthew 28:18).

   His next words were, "Go ye therefore." The same power is given for service. The "therefore" indicates the power of verse 18, and that power is given to the believer who does what Jesus taught in His last message before He ascended back into glory.

   b. Jesus gave instruction to "teach." The word "teach" in verse 19 means "disciple."

   Write in Matthew 28:19: _____

   _____

   _____

   To make disciples, instruction is necessary. Disciples are believers who are "learners" because they have been taught.

   c. Jesus placed emphasis upon obedience. "Teaching them to observe (obey) all things whatsoever I have commanded you" (Matthew 28:20).

   d. Jesus promised to be with all who carry out His instructions. "Lo, I am with you alway, even unto the end of the world" (Matthew 28:20).

   Underline in your Bible the Lord's Commission (Matthew 28:18-20).

B. THE POSITION OF A DISCIPLE

1. **The Three Pillars of the Christian Faith (Hebrews 10:7-24).**

   a. The Will of God.

   (1) In Hebrews Chapter 10, one can see the inadequacy of

240

the sacrifice under the law. "The law, having a shadow of good things to come—can never with those sacrifices which they offered year by year continually make those who come to it perfect" (Hebrews 10:1). Underline verse 2.

(2) The law was not sufficient to take away sin. In Hebrews 10:4-10, we are taken to the purpose and counsel of the *will of God* before the foundation of the world. It was the *will of God*, from all eternity, that the Son should be manifested "to take away the first that He may establish the second; by which will we are sanctified through the offering of the body of Jesus Christ" (Hebrews 10:9-10).

(3) Jesus came to do "thy will, O God" (verses 7 and 9). Write in Hebrews 10:7: _____

_____

_____

Notice the words, "In the volume of the book it is written of me."

Read Psalm 40:6-8 and underline in your Bible.

b. The Work of Christ

(1) It was the delight of the Lord Jesus to do His Father's will and finish His work. From Bethlehem to the cross of Calvary, His one grand object was to glorify God.

(2) The work of Christ is found in Hebrews 10:10, 12, 14. Write in verse 10: _____

_____

_____

(3) He finished God's plan of redemption, as it was "written in the volume of the book," and is now seated at the right hand of God. The work of Christ was *complete, finished*. His blood was shed *once* for all the world (John 3:16). What a comparison to the priests of the Old Testament. Read Hebrews 10:11 and see that in the Levitical priesthood:
  • every priest
  • standeth daily
  • offering often
  • the same sacrifices
  • which can never take away sins.

(4) Compare the above with verse 12:
  • this man (a Priest)
  • offered *one* sacrifice
  • for sins *forever*
  • sat down on the right hand of God.

(5) Write in Hebrews 10:14: _____

_____

_____

c. The Witness of the Holy Spirit.

(1) This third pillar on which the position of the Christian rests is the witness of the Holy Spirit.

Write in Hebrews 10:15: _____

_____

_____

Read Hebrews 10:16-18.

(2) We now have the solid foundation of the Christian's position. The Trinity has spoken. The *will* of God, the *work* of Christ, the *witness* of the Holy Spirit—all done to give us a sure foundation on which we can base our faith.

2. **The Christian is in Christ.**

   a. The Christian position (his standing) is in Christ, with Christ "who suffered outside the gate" (Hebrews 13:12). Write in Hebrews 13:13: _____

   _____

   b. The Christian is identified with Christ. In I John 4:17 the last phrase states, "because as He is, so *are* we in the world." We are His and He is ours! The position of Christ defines the position of the Christian.

C. THE WORK OF A DISCIPLE

1. **We Are to Praise God Continually.**

   a. The Christian has much to do—sometimes too much. Hebrews 13:15 gives one of the grand things a Christian should do.
   Write in Hebrews 13:15: _____

   _____

   _____

   b. So, we are to praise God continually. Praise is forgotten oftentimes in favor of activity. Praise glorifies God—not man. "Rejoice in the Lord alway: and again I say rejoice" (Philippians 4:4).

   c. What is meant by "the sacrifice of praise"? We are to offer our sacrifice of praise by the hand of our Great High Priest, Jesus Christ. Note the first two words of Hebrews 13:15, "By Him." Jesus presents the sacrifices of praise to the Father.
   Look up the following spiritual sacrifices:
   - Psalm 51:17
   - Psalm 27:6
   - Romans 12:1

   d. "The fruit of our lips giving thanks to His name" (Hebrews 13:15). The "fruit of our lips" is a "sacrifice of praise." What we say (our faithfulness to Christ may cost us something) may require a sacrifice.

2. **We are to do Good and Share.**

   a. The second grand thing a Christian is to do is to be good to others.
   Write in Hebrews 13:16: _____

   _____

   _____

The word "share" is translated "communicate" in some versions of the Bible.

b. It pleases God when a Christian performs the work he is to do in the name of Christ. He is to help those in need. The Christian should actually be a demonstration of the love of Christ.

c. Are these the only two things? They are the most important because the two *are* the great commandment of Jesus in action (Matthew 22:37-39).

3. **The Practical Teachings For a Disciple.**

a. There are practical teachings throughout the Word. The two we just studied will affect every other part of our Christian life. We shall remain in Hebrews 13 and point out the practical teachings for a disciple in this one chapter.

b. As a disciple grows in the Lord, He expects some fruit because of the adequate provision made for both our justification and sanctification. Now, turn to Hebrews 13 and see:
- brotherly love (verse 1)
- hospitality (verse 2)
- sympathy (verse 3)
- personal purity (verse 4)
- contentment (verse 5)
- confidence (verse 6)
- intercession (verse 7)
- stability (verse 9)

(We have studied the remainder of the chapter in other parts of this lesson.)

V. WHAT THIS TRUTH TEACHES US TODAY

A Christian becomes a disciple when he begins to learn, to grow, to become the "full corn of the ear." The twelve were disciples, then apostles (Matthew 10). A disciple is a "learner"—an apostle is "one sent forth." The price of real discipleship is small compared to the price our Lord had to pay for our salvation.

Our position, or our standing, as a disciple was established by the will of God, the work of Christ, and the witness of the Holy Spirit. Just think—the Trinity established our position, our standing. We are "in Christ"—we are called Christians. We are identified with Christ. "As He is, so *are* we in this world." (present tense)

Christians who continue to be "babies" in the faith after 10, 20, 40 years are not learners. The message of this lesson, and of the book of Hebrews, is "let us go on to maturity" (Hebrews 6:1). Become teachable, become learners. Then, you are really disciples of the Lord Jesus.

True discipleship means that we love one another, respect one another. There is so little accomplished by arguing, by speculation, by splitting hairs about the Bible. So much could be done for Christ were that energy spent on teaching, learning, helping, praising, thanking God continually. The *process* of discipleship has been established by the Trinity. The *price* of discipleship is your decision. You can say with Paul, "For me to live is Christ" (Philippians 1:21). "For in Him we live, and move, and have our being . . . ." (Acts 17:28).

YOUR NEXT ASSIGNMENT:

1. Read John 16:33; Romans 5:3; II Corinthians 12:7-9; II Timothy 2:12; 3:12; Hebrews 2:10, 18; 12:6-14; James 5:13-16; I Peter 3:14-15; 4:12-16.

2. Review your notes on The Price of Discipleship.

3. Mark your Bible where new truths are learned.

Lesson 41
"Why Do Christians Suffer?"

(Where lines are provided, look up the Scripture and write in the Scripture or its main truth.)

I. INTRODUCTION

The question, "Why do Christians suffer?" has been asked thousands of times by God's people in every generation. If God is kind and loving to the extent that He gave His only Son to save us, then why do Christians still have to suffer tribulations, trials, persecution, sickness and pain? The Bible gives many reasons for Christians suffering and this will not cease until the Lord Jesus Christ comes to restore all things. There are some lessons God would have us learn which can only be learned through suffering, affliction and pain. Jesus Himself had to suffer for our salvation. "It became Him, for whom are all things, and by whom are all things, in bringing many sons unto glory, to make the captain of their salvation perfect through suffering" (Hebrews 2:10). Jesus said, "In this world ye shall have tribulation" (John 16:33). When God saves us, He begins a work which has as its ultimate goal our being conformed to the image of His Son. God loves us too much *not* to let us suffer for His sake. We learn lessons and receive blessings which could only come through trials and testings.

Christianity has been bathed in the blood of martyrs since the first century. Paul describes his zeal and love for the Lord when he said, "that I may know Him, and the power of His resurrection, and the fellowship of His sufferings, being made conformable unto His death" (Philippians 3:10).

Jesus suffered for us. He died for us. God is the same Father who sent His Son to die for our sins. When one compares his own suffering with the suffering of Christ, he can see the vast difference. We should never complain.

This lesson will tell us why Christians suffer.

II. BASIC SCRIPTURES

John 16:33; Romans 5:3; II Corinthians 12:7-9; II Timothy 2:12; 3:12; Hebrews 2:10, 18; 12:6-14; James 5:13-16; I Peter 3:14-15; 4:12-16.

III. THE NUCLEUS OF THIS TRUTH

Christianity is not an inoculation against suffering, trials and tribulations. In His infinite wisdom, God has placed obstacles in our way, not to hinder or hurt but to test our devotion to Him. He is our Father, and He deals with His own as children. He chastens only those He loves and those who belong to Him. Part of the training—part of the growing pains—include suffering. Scripture is factual at this point; therefore, if you are a Christian, God will chasten you because He loves you (Hebrews 12:6).

IV. THE GREAT TRUTH: *"WHY DO CHRISTIANS SUFFER?"*

A. THE REASONS CHRISTIANS SUFFER

1. **Christians Suffer Because of Willful Ignorance.**

    a. The first reason God's children suffer is because of our own selfishness and willful ignorance. We try to blame God when, in reality, it is our fault.
    Write in I Peter 2:20: _____

    _____

    _____

    Some may say they have faith, yet still walk and live in darkness.
    Write in I John 1:6: _____

    _____

    _____

2. **Christians Suffer When They Stand for Righteousness.**

    a. The second reason God's children suffer is because they take a stand for righteousness and for Christ.
    Write in I Peter 3:14: _____

    _____

    _____

    b. Peter says, "don't be troubled" if you know you are right. Don't be afraid—but be happy. Then the great verse of Scripture is given on witnessing.
    Write in I Peter 3:15: _____

    _____

    _____

    Try to memorize this verse of Scripture.

3. **Christians Suffer Because of Unconfessed Sin.**

    a. The third reason God's children suffer is because of unconfessed sin. If a Christian sins, does he get by with it? No!
    Write in I Corinthians 11:31: _____

    _____

    _____

    b. Self judgment is often the most severe judgment. It is a self condemnation for allowing sin to take control even for a little while. God gives us an opportunity to confess that sin and make it right.
    Underline I Corinthians 11:32 in your Bible.

    c. Memorize and write in I John 1:9: _____

    _____

    _____

    (The important word in that verse is "if.")

4. **Christians Suffer Because of Past Sins.**

    a. The fourth reason a Christian suffers is because of the sins of the past. The first thought you will have is, "When I came to Christ, was not all sin forgiven?" Yes! All sin was forgiven and God does not remember them at all.

    A Christian suffers then because of the *results*, the afteref-

246

fects of sin. From the moment of Paul's conversion, he suffered because of his persecution of God's people before he was saved. Read of Paul's conversion in Acts 9:1-19.

Write in Acts 9:23: _____

_____

_____

b. Our past sins are forgiven but that does not remove the effects of past sins. We could all give testimony of this truth.

An example: A man who was an alcoholic is gloriously saved. He is forgiven and he knows the joy of salvation. But he still has the stomach and the liver which alcohol ruined. He must live with the aftereffects of past sins. Gradually, he becomes a healthy person, but he has to work at it and take care of himself.

We could tell of the effects of past sins on families, children, the home, the church. Space does not permit.

Write in Galatians 6:7: _____

_____

_____

5. **Christians Suffer for the Glory of God.**

a. The fifth reason a Christian suffers is because God ordains the suffering. Take Job for an example. He suffered because Satan made an accusation against Job and God. Read Job 1:1-10.

Write in Job 1:11: _____

_____

Notice that God allowed the testing of Job, beginning at verse 12.

b. God had a divine plan for Paul. He was to take the message of Christ to the Gentiles and also suffer in the name of the Lord. Underline Acts 9:15.

Write in Acts 9:16: _____

_____

6. **Christians Suffer for Their Faith.**

a. The sixth reason some Christians suffer is because of their faith in the Lord Jesus Christ. James endured martyrdom (Acts 12:2). Peter was imprisoned (Acts 12:4), and later martyred (II Peter 1:14; John 21:18-19).

b. Hebrews 11 records two groups of people:

- In Hebrews 11:33-35 there is a group who had, by faith, gained great victories for God.

- In Hebrews 11:35-38 there is a group of martyrs.

How does one explain this paradox? The answer is God's. There are some people whom God permits to suffer; they are ready to glorify Christ as did James, Peter and Paul. Others do not suffer because God knows they could not take it.

7. **Christians Suffer to Learn Discipline.**

a. The seventh reason a Christian suffers is to learn discipline from the hand of God. This is a glorious suffering because it proves that we belong to Him.

Write in Hebrews 12:6: _____

247

The word "chasten" means "child training" or "discipline."

b. God deals with His own as sons—His children. As a father disciplines only his own children, so it is with God the Father. Underline Hebrews 12:7 in your Bible.

B. THE RESULTS OF SUFFERING FOR CHRIST

1. **God Uses the Suffering of His Children to Silence the Enemy.**

   a. The purpose for some suffering is to show forth the faithfulness of God. This stops the mouths of Satan's followers like nothing else in the world.

   b. Job was such a man. Underline Job 1:21 in your Bible.

   The greatest testimonies, prayers, smiles and encouragement will come from the mouths of those who are suffering Christians. They become the prayer warriors and Satan can't defeat them.

2. **God Uses Suffering that We Might Glorify Him.**

   a. Jesus permitted Lazarus to become sick and die. Jesus said, "This sickness is not unto death, but *for the glory of God*, that the Son of God might be glorified thereby" (John 11:4).

   b. Jesus raised Lazarus from the grave and said to Martha, "if thou wouldest believe, thou shouldest see the *glory of God*" (John 11:40). Read John 11:41-44.

3. **God Uses Suffering to Make Us More Like the Lord Jesus Christ.**

   a. God at times uses suffering, testing and trials to accomplish His ultimate purpose for which He has called us. That purpose is found in Romans 8:29, "For whom He did foreknow, He also did predestinate *to be conformed to the image* of His Son . . ."

   b. If that be His purpose for Christians, that means that there must be suffering, pain and sorrow because Christ experienced these things. Paul describes this perfectly.

   Write in Philippians 3:10: _____

   _____

   _____

4. **God Uses Suffering to Teach Us Dependence Upon Him.**

   a. All of us have felt indispensable in our home or business. When the Lord laid us aside with illness, or some other cause, the family and business got along just fine without us. We learn that He is able to guide us through experiences which we thought we could never get through at all. We learn that "God is our refuge and strength, a very present help in trouble" (Psalm 46:1).

   b. He teaches us a precious lesson when we learn that God can undertake for us beyond our comprehension.

   Write in Zechariah 4:6: _____

   _____

5. **God Uses Suffering to Strengthen our Faith.**

   a. By suffering, we mean not only the physical but that which comes from trials, tribulations and concerns. God uses these events to strengthen our faith. Only exercise can give strength. A faith that is not exercised is a faith that will not grow. A faith which is not tried will never be strong. (See Hebrews 12:11) Underline Hebrews 11:1 in your Bible.

    b. One of our most trying experiences is when God causes us to just sit still. "Be still and know that I am God" (Psalm 46:10).

6. God Uses Suffering to Teach Us Patience.

    a. Patience can only be learned by enduring. What leads to patience? Paul says, "knowing that tribulation worketh patience; and patience, experience; and experience, hope: and hope maketh not ashamed" (Romans 5:3-5).

    b. Patience is not a birthright. It is learned through the experience of tribulation and suffering—then "the love of God is shed abroad in our hearts . . ." (Romans 5:5).

7. God Uses Suffering to Make Us Sympathetic.

    a. The great discourse on suffering and tribulation is given by Paul in the first eleven chapters of II Corinthians. Read and underline II Corinthians 1:3-6.

    b. So, we are comforted in our tribulations so that we, in turn, can comfort others in the same difficulty. The people who really sympathize are the ones who talk from personal experience. They usually talk less, but sympathize more.

8. God Uses Suffering to Keep Us Humble.

    a. God exalts the humble—He hates pride. God places enough trials in our path to cause us to destroy "self" and learn humility.

    Write in I Peter 5:6: _____

_____

    b. Paul is a perfect example of humility. The Lord gave him a "thorn in the flesh" so that Paul would not exalt himself. Read II Corinthians 12:7-10.

    There are many more results from tribulation and suffering recorded in Scripture, but these few will teach us how God uses incidents to mold us to be "more like the Master."

C. THE BLESSINGS OF SUFFERING AS CHRISTIANS

1. The True Believer Learns That God Chastens Those He Loves (Hebrews 12:5-8).

2. The Christian Learns the Blessings of Being in Subjection to God (Hebrews 12:9).

3. The Believer Becomes Partaker of His Holiness Through Chastening From God (Hebrews 12:10).

4. The Christian Learns Through Suffering the Peaceable Fruit of Righteousness (Hebrews 12:11).

5. The Christian Learns the Blessings of Assurance (Hebrews 12:8).

6. The Christian Learns Through Tribulation to Grow Up and be Productive (Hebrews 12:12-13).

V. WHAT THIS TRUTH TEACHES US TODAY

What is your reaction to the chastening of the Lord—to the trials and tribulations of life? Hebrews 12:5 says, "Despise not the chastening of the Lord." How does one despise it? Simply by ignoring the fact that God is trying to teach you something—so let Him. Another way you can react to God's discipline is to take on a good dose of self pity. "Why did God let this happen to me?" The Bible says, "Faint not when you are rebuked of Him" (Hebrews 12:5). That suffering, or problem, has come to you as a challenge to trust Him through it all. Then, there are those with a super-pious attitude. They will say, "This is my cross and I'll bear it," when all the time there is rebellion inside their heart and soul. "No chastening for the present seemeth to be joyous, but grievous; nevertheless, afterward it yieldeth the peaceable fruit of righteousness unto them who are exercised by it" (Hebrews 12:11).

Finally, we are to endure chastening—suffering (Hebrews 12:7). The hardest lesson for most of us is to endure anything very long. Do you ever take an inventory of your life when trouble comes? Job said, "When He has tested me, I shall come forth as gold" (Job 23:10). "Draw near to God and He will draw near to you" (James 4:8).

YOUR NEXT ASSIGNMENT:

1. Read Isaiah 66:8; Jeremiah 30:4-7; Ezekiel 20:37; 22:17-22; Zechariah 12:10-11; 13:1; Matthew 25:31-46; John 5:24; 12:31; Romans 8:1-2; 5:9; I Corinthians 3:12-15; 6:3; 9:25-27; 11:31-32; II Corinthians 5:10, 21; I Thessalonians 2:19-20; 4:13-18; II Timothy 4:8; Hebrews 10:17; James 1:12; I Peter 5:2-4; I John 2:1; Jude 6; Revelation 20:10-15.

2. Review your notes on "Why Do Christians Suffer?".

3. Mark your Bible where new truths are learned.

Lesson 42 "The Seven Great Judgments of God"

(Where lines are provided, look up the Scripture and write in the Scripture or its main truth.)

I. INTRODUCTION

There is nothing in Scripture which teaches one general judgment. A great many in the theological world adhere to this theory but it cannot be supported by Scripture. The Bible does teach that God does "judge the world in righteousness, He shall minister judgment to the people in uprightness" (Psalm 9:8). The Father "hath committed all judgment unto the Son: that all men should honor the Son, even as they honor the Father" (John 5:22-23).

There are many judgments in the Scripture. Some are past, many are future. Throughout the Old Testament God judged people and nations. In both the Old and the New Testament there are prophetic statements of judgment. In this lesson we shall look at the seven great judgments—one past, one present and five future.

II. BASIC SCRIPTURES

Isaiah 66:8; Jeremiah 30:4-7; Ezekiel 20:37; 22:17-22; Zechariah 12:10-11; 13:1; Matthew 25:31-46; John 5:24; 12:31; Romans 8:1-2; 5:9; I Corinthians 3:12-15; 6:3; 9:25-27; 11:31-32; II Corinthians 5:10, 21; I Thessalonians 2:19-20; 4:13-18; II Timothy 4:8; Hebrews 10:17; James 1:12; I Peter 5:2-4; I John 2:1; Jude 6; Revelation 20:10-15.

III. THE NUCLEUS OF THIS TRUTH

Since God is just and holy, His judgments are a manifestation of perfect justice. If there is no judgment upon men and nations for sins, then what God has said in His Word is false. God is a God of love—but He is also a God of judgment. All judgments are tempered with mercy. All of his judgments are just. A day of judgment will come to those who reject His plan of redemption through His Son. To those who have accepted Christ, His judgment for sin has redeemed you. To those who have not accepted Christ, the judgments of God are yet future and will vindicate God's justice.

IV. THE GREAT TRUTH: *"THE SEVEN GREAT JUDGMENTS OF GOD"*

A. THE JUDGMENT OF SIN BY JESUS CHRIST ON THE CROSS

1. **This Judgment Was for all Believers.**

   a. The result of this judgment was death for the Lord Jesus Christ and justification for all believers.

   You probably know John 3:16. Now underline John 3:17 and write in John 3:18: _____

251

_____

_____

b. The one who has accepted Christ "has *now* everlasting life and shall not come into judgment, but is passed from death unto life" (John 5:24).

c. Jesus died that the believer could be justified once and for all and not face condemnation.
Write in Romans 8:1: _____

_____

_____

d. Jesus condemned sin in the flesh.
Underline Romans 8:3 in your Bible.

e. Jesus was made sin for us.
Write in II Corinthians 5:21: _____

_____

_____

_____

2. **The Offering of Christ Was Once For All.**

a. The one sacrifice of God's Son was sufficient to sanctify—set apart—make holy—save all who believe (Hebrews 10:10).

b. The sacrifice was everlasting.
Write in Hebrews 10:14: _____

_____

_____

c. Once a sin is confessed, God forgives and remembers it no longer.
Write in Hebrews 10:17: _____

_____

The believer should not doubt God's ability to forgive and forget. The same sin should not be brought before the Lord again and again. If the Bible is true, *and it is*, He remembers the sin or sins no more. Underline Psalm 103:12 in your Bible.

B. THE JUDGMENT OF BELIEVERS

1. **The Christian's Judgment is at the Judgment Seat of Christ.**

a. This judgment is for Christians only. It is *not* a judgment to determine whether we are saved or lost. That has been determined when one accepts Christ.
Write in II Corinthians 5:10: _____

_____

_____

_____

Underline Romans 14:10 in your Bible.

b. The judgment seat of Christ will be a judgment of the believers' works done for the glory of the Lord. Paul describes the works that will abide and the works that shall burn. Note in I Corinthians 3:11-15:

252

- the foundation is Christ (verse 11)
- build with gold, silver, precious stones (verse 12)
- or build with wood, hay, stubble (verse 12)
- every man's work shall be made manifest (verse 13)
- the fire shall test every man's work (verse 13)
- if man's work abide (verse 14)
- he shall receive a *reward* (verse 14)
- if man's work is burned, he shall suffer loss (verse 15)
- *but* he himself shall be saved, yet as by fire (verse 15).

  c. So, the judgment for the Christian is at the judgment seat of Christ (the Bema seat). The judgment has to do with rewards or loss of rewards—not salvation.

  d. This judgment shall take place when the Lord calls the church to meet Him in the air.

Write in I Thessalonians 4:17: _____

_____

_____

2. The Five Crowns of Reward Given at This Judgment.

(We shall only mention them because of space.)

  a. The "Crown of Life" - (Revelation 2:10; James 1:12)
- The martyr's crown or reward.

  b. The "Crown of Glory" - (I Peter 5:4)
- The pastor's and/or teacher's crown or reward.

  c. The "Crown of Rejoicing" - (I Thessalonians 2:19-20)
- The soul-winner's crown or reward.

  d. The "Crown of Righteousness" - (II Timothy 4:8)
- The crown or reward for those who long for the coming of Christ.

  e. The "Incorruptible Crown" - (I Corinthians 9:25-27)
- The crown or reward for victorious living.

(These are incentives for service and they will revolutionize a Christian's life.)

C. THE SELF JUDGMENT OF THE BELIEVER

1. Self Judgment is the Realization of Sin in the Believer's Life.

  a. The Christian recognizes that he has allowed sin in his life. This is often the most severe judgment because a person has difficulty admitting guilt and forgiving himself. "But let a man examine himself" (I Corinthians 11:28).

  b. We are to judge ourselves as Christians.

Write in I Corinthians 11:31: _____

_____

2. Self Judgment Avoids the Chastening of the Lord.

  a. The believer's judgment can take place anytime—at the moment there is the realization of sin which results in confession and forgiveness.

  b. If self judgment is neglected, the Lord chastens but never condemns.

Write in I Corinthians 11:32: _____

_____

c. The secret of self judgment is *confession* of sin. Every believer still has the "old nature" to contend with in his new life and must realize that there will be sin in his life.

Write in I John 1:8: _____

_____

Write in I John 1:9: _____

_____

(The Bible distinguishes three judgments for the believer. One which is *past*—for our sin at Calvary by Jesus. Another which is *present*—self judgment by the believer. Another which is *future*—the judgment seat of Christ for rewards or lack of rewards, and does not judge our salvation. We have studied, briefly, the three. Remember them well.)

D. THE JUDGMENT OF ISRAEL

1. The Judgment of Israel is the Time of Jacob's Trouble.

a. The Jews will be judged by the Lord God after He has regathered them from all nations (Ezekiel 20:34).

b. Israel shall be placed under "the rod" to purge out those who will not accept the Messiah.

Write in Ezekiel 20:37: _____

_____

_____

c. This judgment occurs during the tribulation and is called "the time of Jacob's trouble" (Jeremiah 30:7).

2. The Results of the Judgment on Israel.

a. They shall recognize the pierced Messiah (Zechariah 12:10).

b. They shall mourn because of their rejection of Christ (Zechariah 12:10).

Write in Zechariah 12:10: _____

_____

_____

c. They who pass under the rod (judgment) shall be saved. No one enters the Kingdom of Christ except those who accept Christ. All are saved the same way. Read Jeremiah 30 and 31:1-11.

d. There shall be a nation born in a day (Isaiah 66:8).

Write in Romans 11:26: _____

_____

_____

E. THE JUDGMENT OF THE GENTILE NATIONS

1. The Time of This Judgment.

a. This judgment occurs "when the Son of Man shall come in His glory" (Matthew 25:31).

b. This is at the second coming of Christ after the tribulation.

c. The subjects of this judgment are "all nations"—Gentiles then on the earth (Matthew 25:32). Three classes of people are named:

- "sheep" - the saved Gentiles
- "goats" - the unsaved Gentiles
- "brethren" - the people of Israel

2. The Reason for the Judgment.

a. The basis of this judgment is the treatment of the Jews called "My brethren" (Matthew 25:40).

b. The Gentiles which are "sheep" are on the "right hand" of the Lord. They have been saved during the tribulation (Matthew 25:34).

c. The "goats" are the Gentiles who were not saved during the same period and did not respect nor treat Israel with kindness (Matthew 25:41).

Underline in your Bible Matthew 25:31-33, 40.

F. THE JUDGMENT OF THE FALLEN ANGELS

1. The Judgment Shall Occur When Satan is Judged.

a. The fallen angels are the cohorts of Satan, the devil. His doom is given in Revelation 20:10. This is the final judgment upon Satan as he is cast into the lake of fire. Underline Revelation 20:10 in your Bible This is after he has been bound one thousand years and loosed for a season (Revelation 20:2-3).

b. It is only logical that the "judgment of the great day" is the same time of judgment for the fallen angels.

Write in Jude 6: _____

_____

_____

_____

Underline II Peter 2:4 in your Bible.

2. Christians Will be a Part of That Judgment With Christ.

a. We, who are Christians, shall reign with Christ in judging the world and the fallen angels.

Write in I Corinthians 6:3: _____

_____

_____

b. Jesus declared their doom in Matthew 25:41. Underline in your Bible.

G. THE JUDGMENT OF THE WICKED DEAD

1. This is the Judgment of the Great White Throne.

a. This is the last and most terrible of all God's judgments. It is for the wicked—and those who died without accepting Christ (Revelation 20:11-12).

b. This judgment takes place 1,000 years after the "first resurrection" (Revelation 20:4-5).

c. They are judged according to their works (Revelation 20:12-13).

2. The Book and the Books.

a. The two witnesses against them are the book and the books (Revelation 20:12).

b. The book (singular) is the "book of life."
Write in Revelation 20:15: _____

_____

_____

c. The books (plural) are the books of works.

d. "This is the second death" (Revelation 20:14). This means eternal doom in the lake of fire. The judgment is eternal separation from God (II Thessalonians 1:9).

V. WHAT THIS TRUTH TEACHES US TODAY

The main thrusts of this study have been the great joys and blessings of the Christian life as compared to the doom of eternal damnation because one dies in unbelief. If this lesson has taught you the "rewards" of the Christian life; that you can judge yourself and confess and be forgiven; that Jesus died for you *regardless* of your past sins—then, this lesson will have accomplished its purpose.

The God of judgment is the same God who gave His Son to save you. We do not have the right nor the authority to question His Word. Accept His judgments and you will accept His Son. When you accept His Son, you will accept your "gift" to serve where He places you (I Corinthians 4:5—read now).

YOUR NEXT ASSIGNMENT:

1. Read Genesis 1:28-29; 3:14-19; 9:1-17; 12:1-3; 13:14-17; 15:1-8; 17:1-14; 22:15-24; 26:1-5; 28:10-15; Exodus 19:5-7; 34:10; Deuteronomy 5:1-4; 7:6-11; 30:1-20; II Samuel 7:12-16; Hebrews 8:6-13.

2. Review your notes on The Seven Great Judgments of God.

3. Mark your Bible where new truths are learned.

Lesson 43
"The Eight Great Covenants of God"

(Where lines are provided, look up the Scripture and write in the Scripture or its main truth.)

I. INTRODUCTION

There are certain segments of Scripture which must be understood in order to understand the vast scope of the Word of God. Some of these segments of Scripture are called "covenants." Webster says that a covenant is "an agreement between persons or parties to enter into a formal agreement." There are so many agreements and contracts in Scripture which were binding on the parties involved. For example, when two were married, the marriage became a covenant. Another example is given concerning Jonathan and David: "Then Jonathan and David made a covenant, because he loved him as his own soul" (I Samuel 18:3).

There are eight covenants which God made and they disclose God's purpose for us in the world. All Scripture crystalizes around these eight covenants of God. All Scripture is a development of these covenants.

II. BASIC SCRIPTURES

Genesis 1:28-29; 3:14-19; 9:1-17; 12:1-3; 13:14-17; 15:1-8; 17:1-14; 22:15-24; 26:1-5; 28:10-15; Exodus 19:5-7; 34:10; Deuteronomy 5:1-4; 7:6-11; 30:1-20; II Samuel 7:12-16; Hebrews 8:6-13.

III. THE NUCLEUS OF THIS TRUTH

The nucleus, the life, the heart of this truth lies in the fact that God is a covenant *maker* and a covenant *keeper*. He made the covenants with the people as a whole and not with individuals. He has kept and will keep every covenant He has made.

Another part of the nucleus is the fact that there are two kinds of covenants in Scripture:

- First, there are *unconditional* covenants—meaning that God has said, "I will do."
- Second, there are *conditional* covenants—where God says, "If thou wilt, then I will."

Out of eight great covenants of God which we shall study, six are *unconditional*—that is, they are dependent upon God—and two are conditional: the Edenic covenant and the covenant with Moses. This is an astonishing thing. God makes the covenant and keeps the covenant regardless of what man does, *in all but two*.

IV. THE GREAT TRUTH: *"THE EIGHT GREAT COVENANTS OF GOD"*

A. THE EDENIC COVENANT (GENESIS 1:26-31; 2:16-17)

1. **The Elements of the Covenant.**

   a. God gave to the first man, Adam, the responsibilities of multiplying the human race—subduing the earth and having dominion over all living things. He was not to eat of the tree of knowledge of good and evil (Genesis 1:28-30; 2:16-17).

   b. The plan of God was frustrated by the disobedience of Adam and Eve (Genesis 3:1-13).

2. **The Edenic Covenant Is A Conditional Covenant.**

   a. This is a universal covenant because the entire race is present in Adam—including our generation.

   b. It is conditional in that God made the covenant to depend on the faithfulness of Adam.

B. THE COVENANT WITH ADAM (GENESIS 3:14-19).

1. **The Elements of the Covenant.**

   a. The serpent, the tool of Satan, is cursed (Genesis 3:14).

   b. God placed enmity between the Seed of woman (Jesus) and the seed of the serpent (Satan).
   Write in Genesis 3:15: _____

   _____

   _____

   _____

   c. This is the first direct prophecy of Jesus Christ in Scripture. Here begins the great redemptive plan of God—the promise of a Redeemer.

   d. In this covenant God gave to woman sorrow in childbirth (Genesis 3:16).

   e. In this covenant God placed the man and wife in a proper relationship in the home. God is a God of order. He had already declared them to be "one flesh" (Genesis 2:24). After the relationship was declared (Genesis 3:16), God called "*their* name Adam" (Genesis 5:2).

   f. In this covenant God cursed the earth for the sake of man (Genesis 3:17-18).

   g. In this covenant God gave to man physical labor—"in the sweat of thy face shalt thou eat bread" (Genesis 3:19).

   h . In this covenant God spoke of death of the body—"for dust thou art, and to dust shalt thou return" (Genesis 3:19).

2. **The Adamic Covenant is an Unconditional Covenant.**

   a. God is going to fulfill all the conditions of the Adamic Covenant. It is unconditional and does not depend upon man.

   b. The promise of a Redeemer in Genesis 3:15 was fulfilled in Christ. The Seed of woman was Christ.
   Write in Galatians 4:4: _____

   _____

   c. A picture of God's grace in Jesus Christ can be seen in the "coats of skin" God provided for the nakedness of Adam and Eve" (Genesis 3:21).

   d. To a large extent man continues under the Adamic Covenant:

258

- we are born with the Adamic nature.
- we toil the cursed earth of thorns and thistles.
- women conceive and give birth in pain and sorrow.
- we die physically and return to dust.

    e. Through the sacrifice of Christ, believers are clothed with the righteousness of Christ and possess a spiritual nature.

C. THE COVENANT WITH NOAH (GENESIS 8:20 TO 9:27).

1. The Elements of the Covenant.

    a. God guaranteed the stability of the natural law following the flood (Genesis 8:20-22).

    b. God added meat to man's diet (Genesis 9:2-3).

    c. God placed in this covenant the preciousness of life (Genesis 9:5-6).

    d. God declared that the world would never again be judged by a flood (Genesis 9:11).

    e. God confirmed the covenant with a rainbow in the cloud. This is "God's signature" (Genesis 9:12-16).

    f. This covenant is confirmed to all generations. It is an "everlasting covenant" (Genesis 9:16).

    g. The prophecy of the descendants of Noah's three sons is given (Genesis 9:25-27). Shem was the one through whom the Lord Jesus was to come. All divine revelation was through Semitic men—the Hebrews, the Jews. In Genesis 11:10-30 the generation of Shem leads to Abraham.

    (For study of "Noah and His Sons" see "Through The Bible in One Year, Volume 2, Bible Characters," page 13.)

2. The Covenant With Noah is an Unconditional Covenant.

    a. God will fulfill the covenant in detail. Man has nothing to do with keeping the agreement. God has declared it, and He will do all He has said.

    b. We see the seasons, the day and night, as proof of a covenant keeping God.

    c. The rainbow is visible in all generations to remind us of God's declaration in His covenant with Noah. It is an "everlasting covenant" between God and perpetual generations. The rainbow is a "token" (a sign or symbol) which God places in the clouds to remind Him and us of the covenant He made with Noah (Genesis 9:16-17).

D. THE COVENANT WITH ABRAHAM (GENESIS 12:1-4; 13:14-17; 15:1-7; 17:1-8).

1. The Elements of the Covenant.

    a. In this covenant God promised Abraham a great nation. "I will make of thee a great nation" (Genesis 12:2). This promise refers to Israel, the descendants of Jacob, to whom the everlasting possession of the land is promised (Genesis 17:8).

    Abraham was to be the father of many nations (Genesis 17:5), and this was fulfilled through Ishmael and Esau.

    b. God promised a personal blessing to Abraham and that his name would be great. Abraham was blessed to be a blessing.

    Write in Genesis 12:2: _____.

_____

_____

c. God promised all nations a *blessing* if they blessed and honored Abraham and his seed (Israel)(Genesis 12:3). He also promised a curse to those who cursed Abraham and his seed (Israel)(Genesis 12:3).

d. "In thee shall all the families of the earth be blessed" (Genesis 12:3). This was the great promise of blessing through Abraham's Seed, Jesus Christ (Galatians 3:14-16). Underline John 8:56-58 in your Bible.

2. The Covenant With Abraham is an Unconditional Covenant.

a. The purpose of God in the Abrahamic Covenant was the origin of the nation Israel as a people and as a land.

b. The purpose of God was to provide redemption through Israel in bringing forth the Redeemer, Jesus Christ.

c. In spite of Israel's many failures, God's sovereign purpose as detailed in the Abrahamic Covenant has been and is being fulfilled. This is an unconditional covenant, and God does it regardless of the action of men and nations.
Write in Galatians 3:14: _____

_____

_____

_____

E. THE COVENANT WITH MOSES (EXODUS 20:1 TO 31:18).

1. The Elements of the Covenant.

a. In this covenant God gave to Moses the law which was to govern His relationship to the children of Israel:
  - The *commandments*—governing moral life (Exodus 19-20)
  - the *judgments*—governing social life (Exodus 21-23)
  - the *ordinances*—governing religious life (Exodus 24-31)

b. The basis of the covenant was Israel's deliverance from Egypt (Exodus 19:4), which was the outcome of God's covenant with Abraham (Exodus 19:5).

c. This covenant revealed the holiness of God and the sinfulness of man (Deuteronomy 4; Romans 3:19; 7:13).

d. The law could not save. God had made a covenant with Abraham 430 years before, which was a covenant of promise (Exodus 19:5; Galatians 3:24).

e. The law was the "schoolmaster" which leads to Christ (Galatians 3:24).

2. The Covenant With Moses is a Conditional Covenant.

a. A conditional covenant depends on man obeying the Lord. The basis for this conditional covenant is
Exodus 19:8: _____

_____

_____

260

b. The covenant was broken—again showing sin as exceedingly sinful (Exodus 32). The Lord would bless if the people obeyed. If they did not obey, the Lord would discipline. A good picture of this is in Deuteronomy 28:15-68.

c. What was the relationship of Christ to the law? Jesus was born under the law (Galatians 4:4). He fulfilled, or kept, the law (Matthew 5:17-19). He has borne the curse of the law for us (Galatians 3:13-14).

d. The law was added to the Abrahamic Covenant because of sin—until the *Seed* (Jesus) should come.
Write in Galatians 3:19: _____

_____

_____

Read Galatians 3:16-18.

e. The law condemns—faith saves. Underline Romans 3:20-22 in your Bible.

F. THE COVENANT WITH ISRAEL (PALESTINIAN COVENANT)(DEUTERONOMY 30:1-20).

1. The Elements of the Covenant.

a. The purpose of the covenant was to set forth the conditions regulating possession of the promised land. The covenant was entered into just before they crossed the Jordan River into Canaan. They were in the land of Moab (Deuteronomy 29:1).

b. In the covenant God foresees world-wide dispersion of Israel (Deuteronomy 30:1).

c. He foresees the repentance of Israel (Deuteronomy 30:2).

d. He foresees the regathering of Israel to the land (Deuteronomy 30:3, 5).

e. He foresees the conversion of restored Israel (Deuteronomy 30:6).

f. He foresees judgment upon Israel's oppressors (Deuteronomy 30:7).

g. He foresees the prosperity of Israel (Deuteronomy 30:9).

2. The Covenant With Israel is an Unconditional Covenant.

a. God shall complete the fulfillment of this covenant. It does not depend on the Jew or Gentile—it is *unconditional*.

b. Israel was in Egypt but returned to a part of the land.

c. Because of sin, they were taken by the Assyrians and Babylonians as captives, but a remnant returned to the land.

d. In 70 A.D. Jerusalem was destroyed and again they were scattered, but shall return in safety and blessing (Ezekiel 39:25-29).

G. THE COVENANT WITH DAVID (II SAMUEL 7:4-16).

1. The Elements of the Covenant.

a. God promised David the divine confirmation of the throne of Israel (II Samuel 7:13).

b. God promised the perpetuation of the Davidic rule, and three things are made sure to David:

- "house" - or posterity (verses 11 and 13)

- "throne" - or royal authority (verse 13)
    - "kingdom" - or sphere of rule (verse 13) and all are secured forever (verse 16).

  c. Psalm 89 is a confirmation of the Davidic Covenant.

  d. The prophets spoke of Jesus from the seed of David (Isaiah 11:1; Jeremiah 23:5; Ezekiel 37:25).

2. **The Covenant With David is an Unconditional Covenant.**

  a. It is unconditional because Jesus, the Son of God, the Son of David, shall be the fulfillment of the covenant. He shall set up His kingdom and He shall reign on the throne of David forever (Isaiah 11:1-10; 9:6-7).

  b. The angel Gabriel confirmed this to Mary before the birth of Christ (Luke 1:31-33).

H. THE NEW COVENANT (JEREMIAH 31:31-33; HEBREWS 8:7-13).

1. **The Elements of the Covenant.**

  a. It was established upon the sacrifice of Jesus (Romans 8:2-4).

  b. Israel shall be brought into the New Covenant (Hebrews 8:8; Jeremiah 31:31-33).

  c. It secures the eternal blessedness, under the Abrahamic Covenant, of all who believe (Galatians 3:13-29).

  d. The New Covenant is for Jew and Gentile. God says, "I will make a new covenant with Israel and Judah" (Hebrews 8:8).

2. **The New Covenant is an Unconditional Covenant.**

  a. God has declared unconditionally what He will do for those who trust in Him (John 5:24; 6:37; 10:28).

  b. No responsibility is committed to man except believing in Jesus. It is final and unconditional. God has done and will do every part of this covenant.

V. WHAT THIS TRUTH TEACHES US TODAY

What does all of this mean today? The fact that God has made these covenants indicates their importance.

All of these covenants meet in Christ:

- In the Edenic Covenant, the need of a Redeemer is established.
- In the Adamic Covenant, He is the Seed of woman.
- In the Noahic Covenant, all divine revelation is through the Semitic line of Shem. Christ, after the flesh, descends from Shem.
- In the Abrahamic Covenant, He is the Seed of Abraham.
- In the Mosaic Covenant, He bore the curse of the Mosaic Covenant (the law) for us.
- In the Palestinian Covenant, He lived as a Jew in the land.
- In the Davidic Covenant, He is the greater Son of David. He is the coming King.
- In the New Covenant, He is the foundation and the sacrifice for Jew and Gentile. The New Covenant is sealed by His sacrifice.

Finally, a Biblical covenant is a sovereign pronouncement of God by which He establishes a relationship of responsibility between Himself and a person, all mankind, a nation, a specific family.

YOUR NEXT ASSIGNMENT:

1. Read Matthew 13:11; Romans 11:25; I Corinthians 15:23, 51, 52; Ephesians 1:9-10; 3:1-11; 5:22-33; Colossians 1:26-27; 2:1-2; II Thessalonians 2:1-12; I Timothy 3:16; Revelation 1:20; 17:5-7.

2. Review your notes on the Eight Covenants of God.

3. Mark your Bible where new truths are learned.

Lesson 44
"The Twelve Great Mysteries of God" Part I

(Where lines are provided, look up the Scripture and write in the Scripture or its main truth.)

I. INTRODUCTION

In classical Greek, a "musterion" (translated in the King James Version of the Bible as "mystery"), was primarily that which was known only by the initiated. Some organizations are known as "secret orders," and they make known the secrets, or mysteries, to those who are accepted and initiated. The Greeks used the word in that manner for hundreds of years. In the English language we have made the word mean an "enigma, a puzzle, a story or novel." *In the New Testament, a mystery is that which, being outside the range of natural apprehension, can be made known only by divine revelation, and is made known in a manner and at a time appointed by God.*

II. BASIC SCRIPTURES

Matthew 13:11; Romans 11:25; I Corinthians 15:23, 51, 52; Ephesians 1:9-10; 3:1-11; 5:22-33; Colossians 1:26-27; 2:1-2; II Thessalonians 2:1-12; I Timothy 3:16; Revelation 1:20; 17:5-7.

III. THE NUCLEUS OF THIS TRUTH

A mystery in Scripture is a secret kept in the heart of God until He revealed it to man. It is something that human reason could not discover. It must come from God. Paul said, "But we speak the wisdom of God in a mystery, even the hidden wisdom, which God ordained before the world unto our glory . . . but God hath revealed them unto us by His Spirit: for the Spirit searcheth all things, yea, the deep things of God" (I Corinthians 2:7, 10).

There are twelve *great* mysteries in the Bible. There are many more, of course, but the twelve mysteries in our study are of paramount importance to this age in which we live. One mystery is revealed by Christ, nine by Paul, and two by the Apostle John.

IV. THE GREAT TRUTH: *"THE TWELVE GREAT MYSTERIES OF GOD" Part I*

A. THE MYSTERY OF THE KINGDOM OF HEAVEN

    1. **The Mystery is Stated by Jesus.**

        a. Jesus spoke in parables when He spoke of the Kingdom of Heaven. In Matthew 13 there are seven such parables in that one chapter. The disciples asked, "Why speakest thou unto them in parables?" (Matthew 13:10).

        b. Jesus gave His answer.

Write in Matthew 13:11: _____

_____

_____

   c. Underline Matthew 13:16-17 in your Bible. The Old Testament prophets saw in one vision the rejection and crucifixion as King, and His glory as the Son of David, the Messiah King (Jeremiah 33:15-17).

2. The Mystery Explained.

   a. The Kingdom was announced as "at hand" by John the Baptist (Matthew 3:1-2).

   b. The kingdom was announced as "at hand" by Jesus (Matthew 4:17).

   c. It was announced as "at hand" by the twelve apostles as they were instructed by Jesus (Matthew 10:7).

   d. The kingdom was announced as "at hand" by the seventy (Luke 10:9).

   e. The kingdom was announced and Jesus came. As a King in His Kingdom, He was rejected. He fulfilled the words of the prophets when He came as the "Lamb of God . . . the suffering servant." He entered Jerusalem as "the King of Israel . . . thy King cometh" (John 12:13, 15; Zechariah 9:9).

   f. The *mystery* Jesus talked about in Matthew 10:7 is this: there were to be two comings of Christ—the *first* time, He came as the Lamb of God to take away the sin of the world; the *second* time, He shall come as King and Lord of the universe. *The mystery is the interval between Christ's first coming and His second coming.* The King was rejected and died. *His kingdom during this interval is described in mystery form by parables.* The prophets could not see this interval called the church age. It was never revealed to them (Matthew 13:17). It was revealed from the heart of God as a mystery.

B. THE MYSTERY OF ISRAEL'S PARTIAL BLINDNESS

1. The Mystery Stated by Paul.

   a. Paul identified himself an Israelite (Romans 11:1) and was a part of the remnant who believed in Jesus as the Messiah (Romans 11:5). God did not cast away His people, Israel.

   b. Some accepted the "election" (they received the Messiah like Paul) and the "rest were blinded" (Romans 11:7).

   c. Write in the mystery in Romans 11:25: _____

_____

_____

_____

2. The Mystery Explained.

   a. "Blindness in part is happened to Israel, *until* the fulness of the Gentiles be come in" (Romans 11:25). During this age, blindness in part has happened to Israel, but Israel never ceases to exist as a people.

   b. Israel's "blindness in part" will continue as long as the church is in the world. Through the blindness of Israel, salvation came to the Gentiles (Romans 11:11)—the wild olive tree (the Gentiles) was grafted in to the good olive tree (Romans 11:17, 23, 24). The olive tree is Israel with Abraham as the root.

c. The mystery is this: God has *not* cast away Israel; she is partially blind *"until* the fulness of the Gentiles be come in." God has given the Gentiles a time. That time began in Acts 10:34-48 in the house of Cornelius, and confirmed by the Jerusalem Council (Acts 15:14). The time will continue until the completion of the purpose of God, which is the calling out from among the Gentiles a people for His name. "The fulness of the Gentiles" concludes when the Body of Christ is complete. This is as much a part of the mystery as the partial blindness of Israel. At that time, the blindness of Israel will be over, and she will receive the Deliverer, Jesus, the Messiah (Romans 11:26). The ultimate salvation of Israel was seen by the prophets (Isaiah 35:1, 5; 59:20; Ezekiel 36:24-26; Zechariah 12:10). They did not see the "fulness of the Gentiles"—the church age.

C. THE MYSTERY OF THE TRANSLATION OF THE SAINTS, LIVING AND DEAD.

1. The Mystery Stated by Paul.

a. The mystery *is the calling out of the church and the resurrection of the dead in Christ.*
Write in I Corinthians 15:51-52: _____

_____

_____

_____

b. "Behold, I show you a mystery." What did we say a mystery was? It is a secret in the heart of God that human reason could never have known, but it is revealed to us by God from heaven (Deuteronomy 29:29).

2. The Mystery Explained.

a. This mystery is described in detail in I Thessalonians 4:13-18. The translation of the living saints and the resurrection of the dead in Christ was something human reasoning could never conceive. The mystery was revealed from the heart of God to Paul. We know these mysteries by the revelation of the Word of God.

b. The church is called out to meet Christ. We who are alive will follow those who are "dead in Christ." "So shall we ever be with the Lord" (I Thessalonians 4:15-17). This is called by most evangelicals "the rapture of the church."

c. Write in Philippians 3:21: _____

_____

_____

D. THE MYSTERY OF THE DIVINE WILL OF GOD

1. The Mystery Stated by Paul.

a. Write in Ephesians 1:9-10: _____

_____

_____

    b. Underline Romans 8:21-23 in your Bible.

2. The Mystery Explained.

    a. The mystery is *the restoration of all things in Christ*, to undo all that sin has done and to restore all things in Christ as they were before the fall of man.

    b. When does this happen? "In the dispensation of the fulness of times." This is the time of the "kingdom of heaven" when Christ shall reign as King in His Kingdom for one thousand years. The Old Testament abounds in references to this period (II Samuel 7:8-17; Isaiah 65:18-25; Zechariah 14).

    c. The angel Gabriel told Mary of this Kingdom of Christ (Luke 1:30-33).

E. THE MYSTERY OF THE CHURCH

1. The Mystery Stated by Paul.

    a. The church cannot be found in the Old Testament. It was a mystery.
    Write in Ephesians 3:3: _____

    _____

    b. Underline Ephesians 3:5, 6, 9 in your Bible.

    c. Write in Ephesians 3:10: _____

    _____

    _____

2. The Mystery Explained.

    a. The wall of partition between the Jew and Gentile was broken down to make in Christ one body which is the church (Ephesians 2:14-18).

    b. The revelation of this "mystery" of the church was foretold by Christ but not explained (Matthew 16:18).

    c. The church is the body of Christ with many members in the body (Corinthians 12:12).
    Write in I Corinthians 12:13: _____

    _____

    _____

    d. The church is not Israel (Galatians 3:27-29).

    e. The church is one organic unity. When one suffers, the body suffers, etc. (I Corinthians 12:25-27).

    f. Jesus is the Head of the church (Ephesians 1:22-23).

    g. The church is a holy temple for the habitation of God through the Spirit (Ephesians 2:19-22).
    Write in verse 22: _____

    _____

    _____

F. THE MYSTERY OF THE CHURCH AS THE BRIDE OF CHRIST

1. The Mystery Stated by Paul.

    a. The entire passage must be read first. Read Ephesians 5:23-33.

b. The mystery is found in verse 32: _____

_____

2. **The Mystery Explained.**

   a. In Ephesians 5:30, Paul says, "For we are members of His body, of His flesh, and of His bones." He then takes a Scripture from Genesis 2:24 and quotes it in Ephesians 5:31.

   b. What is Paul saying? He is saying that the Lord caused a deep sleep to fall on Adam. While Adam slept, God took from his side and made a Woman. God brought her to Adam and Adam said, "This is now bone of my bone, flesh of my flesh; she shall be called Woman, because she was taken out of Man" (Genesis 2:23). So, Paul is saying, "this is a great mystery, but I speak concerning Christ and the church" (Ephesians 5:32).

   c. As Eve was taken from the side of Adam, so the church is taken out of the pierced side of our Lord. The church is born out of His blood, His sufferings, His cross.

   d. Christ is the Head of the church and the church is subject to Him (Ephesians 5:23-24).

   e. "Christ loved the church and gave Himself for it" (Ephesians 5:25). That is a *past* labor of love.

   f. "That He might sanctify and cleanse it with the washing of water by the Word" (Ephesians 5:26). That is a *present* work of love.

   g. "That He might present it to Himself a glorious church, not having spot, or wrinkle, or any such thing; but that it should be holy and without blemish" (Ephesians 5:27). That is a *future* reward for His sacrifice.

   h. The first Adam had a bride. The Second Adam has a bride—His church.

   So, the sixth mystery is the mystery of the church as the bride of Christ. The reasoning of man could never have dreamed of such a thing. It was a hidden truth in the heart of God and revealed to the "holy apostles and prophets by the Spirit" (Ephesians 3:5).

   We have covered only six of the twelve mysteries. The next lesson shall be the completion of the mysteries.

V. WHAT THIS TRUTH TEACHES US TODAY

A mystery in Scripture is not an "American mystery." We think of a mystery as "something to solve," a story, a puzzle. In the Bible a mystery is a previously hidden truth revealed from the heart of God. It is something that human reasoning, the human mind, could never conceive. Therefore, when we read the word "mystery" in the Bible, it is a signal for us to stop and investigate what God is revealing in the passage.

(In this lesson we have covered only half of the mysteries that we want to study. The "Mysteries of the Kingdom" was the first and needs more study and thought. We shall cover more on this subject in Lesson 46.)

YOUR NEXT ASSIGNMENT:

1. Read all the Scriptures assigned in Lesson 44. Also, read all of Matthew 13 and all of II Thessalonians (three chapters).

2. Review your notes on the "Great Mysteries of God" studied in this

lesson.

3. Mark your Bible where new truths are learned.

Lesson 45 "The Twelve Great Mysteries of God" Part II

(Where lines are provided, look up the Scripture and write in the Scripture or its main truth.)

I. INTRODUCTION

The mysteries of God are a fascinating study. Because they are called "a mystery," the average person reads on to the next thought. In essence, the mysteries of God teach us some of God's great truths. Remember, "a mystery is that which is outside the range of natural apprehension and can be made known only by divine revelation—made known in a manner and at a time appointed by God." If that definition be true, and it is, why do we not study the mysteries of God more often? Here we must admit that most of us who lead in churches have been guilty. These are truths which all of us can learn together. These two lessons on the subject will not answer all of your questions, but they will get you involved in the study of the mysteries. We are living in the age of the New Testament and these mysteries are written in the Scripture for our learning. The Old Testament prophets never saw these mysteries.

II. BASIC SCRIPTURES

All the Scriptures of Lesson 44 and read all of Matthew 13 and all of II Thessalonians (three chapters).

III. THE NUCLEUS OF THIS TRUTH

The nucleus of the last lesson applies to this lesson. You should remember that one mystery is revealed by Christ, nine by Paul and two by the Apostle John. This lesson shall cover the last six mysteries. (Before you start this lesson, read all of Lesson 44 for continuity in thought and pattern of study.)

IV. THE GREAT TRUTH: *"THE TWELVE GREAT MYSTERIES OF GOD" PART II*

(We begin with the 7th mystery and shall continue the outline starting with "G" and on through "L.")

G. THE MYSTERY OF THE INDWELLING, IN-LIVING CHRIST

1. **The Mystery Stated by Paul.**

   a. In Colossians 1:25-26 Paul says, "Of which (the church) I am made a minister, according to the dispensation of God which is given to me for you, to fulfill the Word of God, even the *mystery* which hath been hidden from ages and from generations, but *now* is made manifest to His saints."

271

b. Then, Paul states the mystery.
Write in Colossians 1:27: _____

_____

_____

c. The mystery, then, is "Christ in you, the hope of glory."

2. The Mystery Explained.

a. It is the union of the divine nature with our nature. It is the new birth. We are a part of Christ as members of His body (I Corinthians 12:12-13).

b. If Christ is in us, we are made *new*, having become a partaker of the divine nature.
Write in II Peter 1:4: _____

_____

_____

_____

c. The new man is Christ "formed" in the believer.
Write in Galatians 2:20: _____

_____

_____

d. Underline II Corinthians 5:17; I John 4:12-13 in your Bible.

e. Notice the number of times Paul uses the term *"in Christ"* in Ephesians. Ephesians 1:1, 3, 4; 2:6, 10, 13; 3:6, 17, 20; 4:6; 6:10.

f. Jesus states the same truth in His prayer. Underline John 17:21, 23.

g. The "hope of glory" is the result of "Christ in you." We have that "blessed hope" of Titus 2:13.
Write in I Peter 3:15: _____

_____

_____

H. THE MYSTERY OF THE DEITY OF CHRIST

1. The Mystery Stated by Paul.

a. In Colossians 2:2 Paul says, "That their hearts might be comforted, being knit together in love and unto all riches of the full assurance of understanding, to the acknowledgement of *the mystery of God, and of the Father*, and *of Christ*."

b. Paul is speaking of the incarnate fulness of the Godhead being in Christ—God the Father, Son and Holy Spirit in Christ when He was in the flesh.

c. Write in Colossians 2:3: _____

_____

_____

d. The mystery is "the mystery of God, and the Father, and of *Christ in whom are hidden all the treasures of wisdom and knowledge*." Christ was the incarnate Trinity.

2. The Mystery Explained.

a. Much Scripture is given to make this mystery very clear. Write in I Corinthians 2:7: _____

_____

_____

b. Write in Colossians 1:15: _____

_____

_____

Underline Colossians 1:16-18 in your Bible.

c. Write in Colossians 1:19: _____

_____

God the Father was in Christ (John 17:21-23).

God the Holy Spirit was His in full measure (John 3:34-35).

d. Write in Colossians 2:9: _____

_____

e. Underline I Corinthians 1:24, 30 in your Bible.

To the believer, all knowledge and all wisdom finds its ultimate meaning in Christ Jesus. No man knows that until it is revealed to him by the Holy Spirit. To think of God the Father, Son and Holy Spirit in the flesh, incarnate in Christ, could never have been conceived by man. It was a mystery in the heart of God.

I. THE MYSTERY OF GODLINESS

1. **The Mystery Stated by Paul.**

   a. Write in I Timothy 3:16: _____

   _____

   _____

   _____

   b. The mystery is *the incarnation by which godliness is restored to man.*

2. **The Mystery Explained.**

   a. The mystery of godliness (God-likeness) can be explained as that process (the six things of I Timothy 3:16) by which man can be born again. Consider the six things of I Timothy 3:16.

   b. "God was manifest in the flesh." This was the incarnation of God in the flesh in His Son.

   Write in John 1:14: _____

   _____

   _____

   c. "Justified in the Spirit." He was raised by the Spirit (Romans 8:11). He was raised for our justification (Romans 4:25).

   d. "Seen of angels." The angels worshipped Him.

   Write in Hebrews 1:6: _____

   _____

   _____

e. "Preached unto the nations (Gentiles)." Underline Acts 13:38, 47, 48 in your Bible.

f. "Believed on in the world." The reception of Christ by the world is best illustrated in Acts where we see the rapid reception in the early days of Christianity:

- Acts 1:14-15 - 120 in upper room
- Acts 2:41 - 3,000 souls added
- Acts 4:4 - 5,000 men plus women and children
- Acts 5:14 - Multitudes added
- Acts 6:7 - Multiplied greatly
- and on we could go. Jesus was believed on in the world.

g. "Received up into glory"—Underline Luke 24:51; Acts 1:9-11.

This "mystery of godliness" is the incarnation of Christ by which godliness can be restored to man. In plain words, it is God's plan of salvation. It is the making of "new creatures in Christ Jesus." It is being born again. This is the "mystery of godliness."

J. THE MYSTERY OF INIQUITY

1. The Mystery Stated by Paul.

a. "For the mystery of iniquity doth already work: only He (the Holy Spirit) who now letteth (hinders) will let (hinder), until He (the Holy Spirit) be taken out of the way. And then shall that Wicked be revealed . . ." (II Thessalonians 2:7, 8a).

b. "Even him, whose coming is after the working of Satan with all power and signs and lying wonders" (II Thessalonians 2:9).

c. Paul has revealed the "mystery of godliness"—God manifest in the flesh, Christ.

In this Scripture, Paul reveals the "mystery of iniquity"—the Antichrist. The "mystery of iniquity" will be Satan manifest in the flesh.

2. The Mystery Explained.

a. The explanation Paul gives is clear and understandable. In II Thessalonians 2:1, Paul refers to the "coming of the Lord and our gathering together unto Him." The context is about the "coming of the Lord."

b. A description of "that day" is given in II Thessalonians 2:3. Notice:

- "that day" (the Day of the Lord)
- "shall not come, except there be a falling away first"—apostasy, false teaching. The act of *professed* Christians who deliberately reject revealed truth of the Word of God (II Timothy 3:1-8).
- "and that *man of sin* be revealed, the *son of perdition*." Only Antichrist could fit this description.

c. The work and description of the Antichrist (II Thessalonians 2:4).

- "who opposeth and exalteth himself above all that is called God, or that is worshipped." He opposes God.
- "so that he (the Antichrist) as God sitteth in the temple of God, showing himself that he is God." He will declare himself God in the rebuilt temple at Jerusalem.

d. Satan, the Antichrist, will have total power when the power that restrains him is removed. Read II Thessalonians 2:6.

e. "Only He (the Holy Spirit) who now letteth (hinders) will let (hinder), until He (the Holy Spirit) be taken out of the way. And *then* shall that Wicked . . ." A simple explanation is all that is needed. The only thing that keeps Satan from having total power now is the presence of the Body of Christ—the believers in the world. Where is the Holy Spirit now? In the hearts of believers, the Body of Christ. We are the ones which must be "taken out of the way" and then, the Holy Spirit's restraining ministry through the Body of Christ will cease.

f. Only "then shall the Wicked be revealed."

The Antichrist is called the "Wicked" (verse 8), the "man of sin" (verse 3), the "son of perdition" (verse 3), "the mystery of iniquity" (verse 7). All of these names in II Thessalonians 2:3-8.

g. A description of the work of Satan is expanded in II Thessalonians 2:9-12.

h. "The mystery of iniquity" is Satan manifest in the flesh. Jesus was God manifest in the flesh.

This takes us back to Genesis 3:15. God said to the serpent (Satan), "I will put enmity between thee and the woman, and between *thy seed* and *her Seed*." The woman's Seed was Christ; the serpent's seed is the Antichrist. The battle is still raging but we know the One who shall be victorious. The end of the "mystery of iniquity," the Antichrist, is found in Revelation 19:20.

K. THE MYSTERY OF THE SEVEN STARS AND SEVEN CANDLESTICKS (LAMPSTANDS)

1. The Mystery Stated Through the Apostle John.

a. Write in Revelation 1:20: _____

_____

_____

_____

b. Two mysteries are named—the "seven stars" and the "seven candlesticks."

2. The Mystery Explained.

a. The total context gives the total answer. The context begins at Revelation 1:9 and continues through verse 20.

b. Jesus is the speaker. (This is the only book in Scripture with four authors named—Revelation 1:1-2.) Notice:
- "God gave to Jesus"
- "Jesus to the angel"
- "to His servant John"—

c. What John writes, he writes from God. He saw seven golden candlesticks (Revelation 1:12-13). In the midst of the seven candlesticks "one like unto the Son of man" (Jesus).

d. Then, John describes Jesus (Revelation 1:13-16). In the right hand of Jesus, John saw "seven stars" (verse 16). What were the seven candlesticks and seven stars?

e. The answer is in Revelation 1:20. "The mystery of the seven stars . . . and the seven golden candlesticks." The seven stars *are* the angels (messengers, pastors) of the seven churches: and the seven candlesticks *are* the seven churches.

So, John wrote what he was inspired to write, and he sent it to the seven churches of Asia (Revelation 1:11). In those seven letters He wrote about all of the churches of all the ages in history.

L. THE MYSTERY OF BABYLON

1. The Mystery Stated Through the Apostle John.

a. Write in Revelation 17:5: _____

_____

_____

_____

b. The mystery is a woman, "the great harlot" of verse 1.

2. The Mystery Explained.

a. The "mystery, Babylon the great, the mother of harlots, etc." is ecclesiastical Babylon (Revelation 17:1-7) and is destroyed by political Babylon (Revelation 17:15-18).

b. The angel states that he will "tell the mystery" to John in Revelation 17:7. From verse 8 and on is the description of the dominion of the Antichrist and the power of ecclesiastical Babylon which is apostate Christendom.

c. Revelation 17 is a description of a system. Revelation 18 is a description of the judgment of God on mercantile Babylon.

V. WHAT THIS TRUTH TEACHES US TODAY

The mysteries of God are given in Scripture for all who have been "initiated" into the saving life of Christ. Jesus answered His disciples in Matthew 13:11, "Because it is given unto you to know the mysteries of the kingdom of Heaven, but to them it is not given." God has revealed these mysteries in His Word for this age. "Eye hath not seen, nor ear heard, neither have entered into the heart of man, the things which God hath prepared for them that love Him. But God *hath revealed them unto us* by His Spirit" (I Corinthians 2:9-10). Now, read I Corinthians 2 in detail. We can know the mysteries of God in this age.

YOUR NEXT ASSIGNMENT:

1. Read Matthew 13; 18:21-35; 20:1-16; 22:2-14; 25:1-13; 25:14-30; I Corinthians 15:24.

2. Review your notes in Lessons 44 and 45 on the Twelve Great Mysteries of God.

3. Mark your Bible where new truths are learned.

Lesson 46
"The Mysteries of the Kingdom of Heaven" (The Twelve Parables of the Kingdom)

(Where lines are provided, look up the Scripture and write in the Scripture or its main truth.)

I. INTRODUCTION

This lesson is written for the layperson and young people and not for theologians. We shall be dealing with "mysteries," but in a form that can be understood.

First, just what is the Kingdom? There is the Kingdom of God and the Kingdom of Heaven. What is the difference?

The *Kingdom of God* is the reign of God over all the universe. It includes time and eternity; it includes heaven and earth. It is spiritual; as the Lord says in Luke 17:20-21, "The Kingdom of God cometh not with observation . . . For behold the Kingdom of God is in the midst of you." (The older King James Version says, "The Kingdom of God is in you." This could not be said to a Christ rejecting Pharisee, although Christ was in their *midst*.) The Kingdom of God is not something you see with the naked eye. Paul states in Romans 14:17, "For the Kingdom of God is not food or drink, but righteousness, and peace, and joy in the Holy Spirit." It is an invisible Kingdom and entered into by the new birth. "Except a man be born again, he cannot see the Kingdom of God" (john 3:3).

The *Kingdom of Heaven* is a New Testament term used only by Matthew, 32 different times. Matthew wrote of Jesus as a King; thus, the Kingdom of Heaven in his writing. The Kingdom of Heaven is limited in time and sphere. The *time* of the Kingdom of Heaven is from the first coming of Christ to the end of His Kingdom. The *sphere* is Christendom. Let us clarify all of this.

The Kingdom of Heaven was announced by John the Baptist as "at hand" (Matthew 3:1-2). The Kingdom of Heaven was announced as "at hand" by Jesus (Matthew 4:17). It was announced by the 12 Apostles (Matthew 10:7). The seventy made the same announcement (Luke 10:9). Jesus came as a King to be over a kingdom, as foretold by the Old Testament prophets. The Kingdom and the King were to be literal, actual, not symbolic. It is described in Isaiah 2:1-4; 9:6-7; 11:1-10; Jeremiah 23:5, 8; Daniel 7:13-14; Zechariah 14:9 and other places. When Christ came, the Jews rejected Him as King. He came as a King (John 1:49; 12:12-16; 18:33, 37; 19:19-22). Jesus died as a King—a King rejected—a King crucified—a King buried and resurrected. The setting up of the Kingdom of Heaven was postponed and the King ascended into glory. He is in Heaven—He is in exile. Between the time of His ascension and His return is this interlude, the time known as a "musterion" that God kept in His heart. Jesus talked about the "mysteries of the Kingdom of Heaven" in parables, for us to understand, and these shall be the bulk of this lesson—the twelve mystery parables of the Kingdom of Heaven.

II. BASIC SCRIPTURES

Matthew 13; 18:21-35; 20:1-16; 22:2-14; 25:1-13; 25:14-30; I Corinthians 15:24.

III. THE NUCLEUS OF THIS TRUTH

In Acts 1:6, the apostles asked Jesus, "Lord, wilt thou at this time restore again the Kingdom to Israel?" His answer is in Acts 1:7. He shall return as King, not as King of the church—He *is* Head of the church. He shall be King over His Kingdom; and we, the church, shall reign with Him (II Timothy 2:12; Revelation 1:6; 5:10). The mysteries of the Kingdom of Heaven, described in the twelve parables, give the earthly aspect, the propagation, the form it takes between the two comings of Christ. If you would know what to look for while the Lord Jesus is absent from the earth, the secrets of these parables will tell you. The Kingdom of Heaven is a world view of how the world responds to the Word of God. It is a mixture of good and bad, of wheat and tares. The Holy Spirit will have to be our teacher in the study of His Word.

IV. THE GREAT TRUTH: *"THE MYSTERIES OF THE KINGDOM OF HEAVEN"*

A. THE PARABLE OF THE SOWER

1. **The Mystery of the Parable (Matthew 13:3-9).**

   a. The fact that Christ spoke in parables is the mystery. A parable is "an earthly story with a heavenly meaning." In this parable, Jesus speaks the parable and then interprets the meaning.

   b. The parable shows the sower, the seed and the soil (Matthew 13:3-9).

2. **The Interpretation of the Parable.**

   a. Jesus interpreted only two of the parables, and this is one of them. His pattern should be applied to all twelve parables.

   b. The interpretation is given in Matthew 13:18-23.

   The seed is the Word of God. The Sower is the Son of Man. The field is the world (verses 37-38). The seed sown brings only a partial response. Some receive the Word momentarily, and then they are gone (verses 20-21). There are those who are taken by worldly affluence (verse 22). But some receive and respond and bear fruit (verse 23).

   c. This parable shows us that the world will never be converted—always there is a partial response. This is the day for seed sowing. The fowls, birds (picture of the devil) take away some of the seed, but we are to continue to sow the seed of the Word of God.

B. THE PARABLE OF THE TARES AND WHEAT

1. **The Mystery of the Parable (Matthew 13:24-30).**

    a. The tares (weeds) are sown among the wheat. Both of them grow until the proper time of harvest.

    b. Who would sow tares with wheat?

2. **The Interpretation of the Parable (Matthew 13:36-43).**

    a. The Sower is the Lord. Satan is the enemy who sows tares among the wheat. The tares are the children of Satan; the wheat is that which the Word produces, the children of the Kingdom. The wheat and the tares are both growing today. The true believers, the Body of Christ, and the children of darkness are growing. The harvest shall come at the end of this age (verse 39).

    b. Underline Matthew 13:37-39 and 43 in your Bible. (Christ only interpreted two of the parables—the first two. The same principles of interpretation should be applied to the remaining parables.)

C. THE PARABLE OF THE MUSTARD SEED

1. **The Mystery of the Parable (Matthew 13:31-32).**

    a. Could a tree come from an herb producing seed? Never! Read Genesis 1:11-12.

    b. The mustard seed, never meant to be anything but a shrub, develops unnaturally into a tree. A tree in the Old Testament represented an earthly kingdom, such as the vision of Nebuchadnezzar, which Daniel interpreted (Daniel 4:20-22).

    c. This unnatural tree could not be the growth of the number of believers—its roots are in the world.

2. **The Interpretation of the Parable.**

    a. In the first parable the fowls that devoured the seed were "that wicked one," Satan and his agents.

    b. The same truth applies in this parable. The devil is active in Christendom (anywhere the Gospel is preached). The outward unsubstantial growth of "religion" is the tree from the mustard seed.

    c. The tree is large and the birds of the air lodge in the branches. Evil is getting into every form of "religion" which has grown into a vast system.

D. THE PARABLE OF THE LEAVEN

1. **The Mystery of the Parable (Matthew 13:33-35).**

    a. Leaven is *not* the gospel, as some say. The word is used 98 times in Scripture and is always used in a bad sense. It was never to come in contact with a sacrifice (Exodus 34:25; Leviticus 2:11; 10:12).

    b. Leaven represents evil. In that sense Christ used the word in Matthew 16:6 and Mark 8:15. Paul knew it meant evil. Read I Corinthians 5:6-8 and Galatians 5:9.

2. **The Interpretation of the Parable.**

    a. Just as the mustard seed, growing into a tree, is a mystery in the Kingdom of Heaven, so is the leaven.

    b. The leaven permeates all through the Kingdom of Heaven. It becomes weak and sometimes sinful. All of it is in the name of Christ.

c. The leaven is "hidden in the meal" (verse 33). The meal is the gospel, which is made out of the wheat seed, which is the Word of God. So, the leaven is hidden in the Word as it is taught or preached.

d. This means that the Kingdom (Christendom) has been and is being infiltrated by a vast amount of leaven. Leaven causes corruption. Jesus used the term to reveal to us that sin would invade a place where the gospel is preached. Underline Matthew 13:33 in your Bible.

E. THE PARABLE OF THE HIDDEN TREASURE

1. The Mystery of the Parable (Matthew 13:44).

a. The mystery is evident in the reading of the parable.

2. The Interpretation of the Parable.

a. The field is the world (verse 38). The hid treasure in the field is Israel.

Write in Exodus 19:5: _____

_____

_____

Underline Psalm 135:4 in your Bible.

b. Israel is hid among the nations of the world. They will be until the realization of Romans 11:26-29 (Underline). The "man" of the parable is the "Deliverer," Jesus Christ.

F. THE PARABLE OF THE PEARL OF GREAT PRICE

1. The Mystery of the Parable (Matthew 13:45-46).

a. Again, the mystery is evident in the reading. Remember that Jesus is revealing these mysteries for the first time. He is the One talking in parables.

2. The Interpretation of the Parable.

a. The "pearl of great price" is the church. The One who purchased the pearl is Jesus Christ. He paid with His blood the full price of redemption (Acts 20:28).

b. Covering the same time period as the mysteries of the Kingdom is the mystery of the church (Ephesians 3:3-10).

c. The Kingdom is *not* the church. The true children of the Kingdom during the fulfillment of these mysteries (baptized by one Spirit into one body) compose the church, the pearl of great price (I Corinthians 12:12-13). The church is *in* the Kingdom of Heaven, but the Kingdom is a term encompassing all Christendom. Every place the Word is preached produces a Kingdom of Heaven condition, but in no place has any section of the world been totally converted. (See V at close of this lesson.)

d. The pearl of great price is something Jesus buys. "You are not your own for you have been bought with a price" (I Corinthians 6:19-20).

G. THE PARABLE OF THE DRAG-NET

1. The Mystery of the Parable (Matthew 13:47-51).

a. The mystery is the net which is like the Kingdom of Heaven. When the net is cast into the sea of humanity, it gathers the good and the bad.

b. There must be a separation. Notice, the net is not the church.

280

2. The Interpretation of the Parable.

a. Jesus says in verses 49 and 50 that the passage refers to "the end of the age." At the end of this age some will be lost and some saved. In the net there is a mixture of good and bad.

b. Jesus said, "the angels shall separate the wicked from the righteous, and shall cast them into the furnace of fire; there shall be wailing and gnashing of teeth" (Matthew 13:49 and 50). This does away with the theory that the whole world is to be saved.

H. THE PARABLE OF THE UNMERCIFUL SERVANT

1. The Mystery of the Parable (Matthew 18:21-35).

a. To teach the extreme importance of forgiveness, the Lord uses an illustration of a king who forgave his servant, who in turn refused to forgive another.

b. The statement of Jesus was to forgive seven times seventy (verse 22).

2. The Interpretation of the Parable.

a. "The Kingdom of Heaven is likened unto . . ." (verse 23). After Jesus told Peter to forgive 490 times, He likened forgiveness to the Kingdom of Heaven (verses 22, 23).

b. We ought to always forgive one another.

c. Write in Matthew 18:35: _____

_____

I. THE PARABLE OF THE VINEYARD LABORERS

1. The Mystery of the Parable (Matthew 20:1-16).

a. Some laborers worked longer than others, but received the same pay. This is a story revealing the mystery of God in dealing with us for the task He has given us.

b. The parable seems unfair, but it teaches a truth of God.

2. The Interpretation of the Parable.

a. God will reward His servants, not on the amount of time you serve, or prominence of position—but on faithfulness to the task He has given. What a lesson we should learn in this parable.

b. Now, you understand the meaning of Matthew 20:16.
Write in Matthew 20:16: _____

_____

_____

(Notice it is also the closing verse of Matthew 19.)

J. THE PARABLE OF THE MARRIAGE FEAST

1. The Mystery of the Parable (Matthew 22:1-14).

a. Who was the king, the son, and what does this mean?

b. What does the marriage feast mean?

2. The Interpretation of the Parable.

a. The King is God the Father. The Son is Jesus. The bidding (invitation) was to the Jewish nation (verse 3).

b. The Jewish nation made light of it and went on their way (verse 5).

c. The destruction of the city has taken place (70 A. D.).

d. The invitation is to everyone. This is always the invitation of our Lord. The wedding garment is the righteousness of Christ (Romans 3:21). The one who was without the wedding garment was speechless (verse 22). The invitation is to you, but you have to come on the King's terms.

K. THE PARABLE OF THE TEN VIRGINS

1. The Mystery of the Parable (Matthew 25:1-13).

a. Who are the ten virgins and what is the meaning of the two groups?

b. What is the meaning of the oil, the wise and foolish?

2. The Interpretation of the Parable.

a. The ten virgins—divided into two groups—are the wise and the foolish. This parable presents the Lord's return as *testing profession*. We cannot determine the true and false professors in this life. It is a picture of possessors of Christ and professors of Christ. Five have a false faith. Five have real faith.

b. The oil is always a symbol of the Holy Spirit.

c. The Kingdom of Heaven here is the sphere of profession just as in Matthew 13. All have lamps, but the foolish virgins took no oil (the Holy Spirit) and Jesus said, "I know you not."

Write in Romans 8:9: _____

_____

d. We can never distinguish between the true and false professors of Christ. This is the same situation as the "wheat and tares." They grow together and the Lord does the dividing.

L. THE PARABLE OF THE TALENTS

1. The Mystery of the Parable (Matthew 25:14-30).

a. What is the meaning of some receiving more than others?

b. Does this apply to us?

2. The Interpretation of the Parable.

a. The Lord is testing the service. All were given some talent and told to use the talents profitably. One buried the talent and the others used theirs.

b. The same commendation is given to the servant with two talents (verse 23) as the one with five talents (verse 21). The Lord is testing faithfulness in service. We lose what we don't use. This is a parable of our stewardship of talent and time to God.

V. WHAT THIS TRUTH TEACHES US TODAY

When the disciples asked Jesus why He spoke in parables, He gave the familiar answer in Matthew 13:11, "Because it is given unto you to know the *mysteries of the Kingdom of Heaven*, but to them it is not given." The parables describe the result of the presence of the gospel in the world during this period between His first and second coming. "Many prophets and righteous men have desired to see those things which you see—and hear those things . . ." (Matthew 13:17). Jesus explains the reasons for the parables. We must be born again to discern what He says in the parables. They are for us.

Briefly, let me set forth the Kingdom:

• A Christian becomes heir to the Kingdom when he is saved.

- We, the true Body of Christ from all over the world, will reign with Christ when He sets up His Kingdom.
- The Kingdom of Heaven shall be literal—a real King, Jesus, in His Kingdom.
- At the end of the Kingdom age, Christ, having put all enemies under His feet, will present "deliver up the Kingdom to God even the Father" (I Corinthians 15:24).
- Then, there will be the Kingdom of God forever and ever.
- The church is not the Kingdom—but is heir of the Kingdom.

These truths in the twelve parables are revealed to us in this era by the Lord Jesus Christ. You shall not comprehend all during one study, but if this causes you to dig into the Word, it shall delight your soul as you learn new truths about the "Mysteries of the Kingdom."

YOUR NEXT ASSIGNMENT:

1. Read Matthew 16:17-19; I Corinthians 10:32; 12:12-13; 15:52; Ephesians 1:22-23; 3:1-12; 5:22-33; Colossians 1:18, 24; Hebrews 12:23.

2. Review your notes on the Mysteries of the Kingdom.

3. Mark your Bible where new truths are learned.

Lesson 47
"The Church — The Body of Christ"

(Where lines are provided, look up the Scripture and write in the Scripture or its main truth.)

I. INTRODUCTION

There are many local churches in the world, but there is ONE TRUE CHURCH. It is called by many names in the Bible. It is called "the body of Christ, the bride of Christ, God's building, God's temple, the flocks of Christ, a peculiar people, a chosen nation, a royal priesthood, a purchased possession, the salt of the earth, the light of the world." There are many other names for the church.

The Bible uses the word "church" in two senses or applications, which *must* be understood.

First, the word "church" is applied to a local assembly of believers— the local church. (The lesson for the next study.) The Bible teaches the *local* church, such as "the church at Corinth, the church at Ephesus, etc." the names were used to identify groups in different places.

Secondly, the word "church" is used to encompass all believers in the Lord Jesus Christ. It is called "one body." "For by one Spirit are we all baptized into one body" (I Corinthians 12:13-14). "There is *one body*, one Spirit . . ." (Ephesians 4:4-6).

This lesson shall focus on the second use of the word—the "one body" of Christ. The next study shall be on the local assembly—the local church.

II. BASIC SCRIPTURES

Matthew 16:17-19; I Corinthians 10:32; 12:12-13; 15:52; Ephesians 1:22-23; 3:1-12; 5:22-33; Colossians 1:18-24; Hebrews 12:23.

III. THE NUCLEUS OF THIS TRUTH

There is "one body of Christ." It is made up of all true believers, regardless of church names and affiliations. It is composed of every race and color with *one* creed. It is composed of the visible and the invisible (don't panic at that statement). The visible can be seen by another visible person. The *invisible* are the dead in Christ. They are a vital part of the "body of Christ." All of the redeemed, living and dead (physically), are visible to Him who is the Head of the church.

IV. THE GREAT TRUTH: *"THE CHURCH–THE BODY OF CHRIST"*

A. THE MEANING OF THE WORD "CHURCH"

1. The Church is an Organism.

a. The church is an organism—a living thing with vital signs of life. The church is not merely an organization. One often hears the expression, "the organized church." That has reference to structure and administration of a local church.

b. The church is made up of people who have been born anew

by accepting Christ as personal Saviour. They become a part of the body of Christ which is alive.

2. The Word "Church."

    a. For three hundred years after Christ, what our Lord created was called the "ecclesia." When Constantine was converted and built those gorgeous temples, the "ecclesia" was changed to "kuriakos" meaning "a lordly house." The same word moved through the languages—"kuriakos, kirkus, kirk (Scottish)" to "church" in English.

    b. In the Bible the word is "ecclesia." The word "church" is a rendition and not a translation.

B. THE NATURE OF THE CHURCH

1. The Church is a "Called Out" Assembly.

    a. The New Testament word for church is "ecclesia" meaning "a called out" assembly. The word is not limited to Christians. Originally it meant to the Greeks, an assembly of people convened for the purpose of deliberating. When used of the Christian Church, the word means an assembly of "called out" people. They have been called out of the world into fellowship with Christ and other Christians.

    b. The children of Israel were a called out company from Egypt but they were not a part of the body of Christ. The word "church" is used to describe them—strictly meaning "a called out" assembly. A better translation would be "congregation." Underline Acts 7:38 in your Bible.

2. The Church is a Divine Institution.

    a. The church is the body of believers in the Lord Jesus. The church was a mystery hidden in the heart of God until He revealed the meaning. Christ is the Head of the church. God exalted Him to that position.

    Write in Ephesians 1:22-23: _____

    _____

    _____

    _____

    b. Christ mentioned the church first in Matthew 16:18. When Jesus made the revelation of the church to Peter and the disciples, the church was still in the future. Jesus said, "Upon this Rock (Christ) *I will* build my church." He did not say, "I will continue to build" but "I will build."

    c. The church took its outward form at Pentecost. The mystery (which we have studied in the last two lessons) was no longer a mystery. Read and underline Ephesians 3:9, 10 in your Bible.

C. THE FOUNDATION OF THE CHURCH

1. The Foundation is Jesus Christ.

    a. Untold hours have been spent by students and teachers discussing Matthew 16:13-18. When Jesus stated to Peter, "Thou art Peter, and upon this rock ("Rock" - margin) I will build my church; and the gates of hell shall not prevail against it," just what did Jesus mean?

    b. We shall let the Scripture speak for itself. Underline I Corinthians 3:9-10 and write in verse 11: _____

_____

_____

2. **Jesus Christ is the Rock.**

   a. In Matthew 16:18 the meaning should be made clear. The name Peter, used here by the Lord, is "PETROS" in Greek, and means a "little rock." Then, the word translated "rock" is "PETRA" in Greek, and means a "large Rock." Therefore, Jesus said, "Thou art a little rock, but upon this big Rock I will build my church."

   b. Scripture speaks loud and clear at this point.

      Write in I Corinthians 10:4: _____

      _____

      _____

      Christ was the Rock in the Old Testament, and He is the Rock upon which the Church is built. He is seen in Exodus 17:6, and this appearance of Jesus is called a "theophany"—a pre-incarnate appearance.

      Underline John 4:14 in your Bible.

3. **The Testimony of Peter.**

   a. Peter, the little stone, testified that the church is built on Jesus Christ.

      Write in I Peter 2:3-4: _____

      _____

      _____

      Here Peter calls Jesus a Living Stone. The Greek word for "stone" is "LITHON" meaning a large stone (singular).

   b. Peter never claimed that he was the rock on which the church is built but was the first to admit that he was a little stone in the great structure of the church.

      Write in I Peter 2:5: _____

      _____

      _____

      Here the word translated stones (plural) is "LITHOI," indicating many stones. Christ, according to Peter, is the "Lithon," the One foundation Rock; and we are "lithoi," many living stones built upon the one foundation, Jesus Christ.

D. THE CHURCH IS THE BODY OF CHRIST

1. **The Church is a Body, an Organic Unity.**

   a. Write in I Corinthians 12:12: _____

      _____

      _____

      _____

      The body is an organism composed of many members. All members do not have the same function. Notice the last four words, "so also is Christ."

   b. Write in I Corinthians 12:13: _____

      _____

_____

Believers are made members of His body by one Spirit (the Holy Spirit). This is the act of regeneration which God the Holy Spirit does in the heart. We are placed into the body of Christ by an act of the Holy Spirit.

  c. *Regeneration* is "son making." *Adoption* is "son placing."

Write in I Corinthians 12:18: _____

_____

_____

Write in I Corinthians 12:27: _____

_____

_____

God sets the members in the body of Christ. We do not place ourselves. As part of the body, each believer needs every other part of the body to function. If one part is sick, or missing, or withered, the entire body suffers.

The emphasis in I Corinthians 12:15-27 is the need for each part of the body to function properly. We have been set in the body of Christ by God. We have no right to change that position.

2. In God's Foreknowledge, He Saw the Church Complete.

  a. We have studied "free will and election" as well as "foreknowledge and predestination." There is no need to expand on God's foreknowledge. He saw the body as a complete body. He saw every member of that body from eternity. Underline Ephesians 1:3-6 in your Bible.

Write in Ephesians 1:4: _____

_____

_____

  b. God determined the body, the church, long before there were denominations and human differences. The true church is not a material building—it is a group of "living stones"—saved people—built upon the foundation Stone, Jesus Christ.

3. Jesus Christ is the Authority of the Church.

  a. The true church has one Head, Jesus Christ. Christ is the Head of the church and the only Head.

Write in Colossians 1:17-18: _____

_____

_____

_____

_____

  b. Jesus is both the foundation and the Head of the church. The position can never be claimed by man nor angel. As the foundation, He assures us, it is sound and sure and will never give way. As the Head of the body, He directs and guides. If our direction and guidance came from any other, we would be led astray.

4. Jesus Christ is the Chief Cornerstone of the Building.

    a. The church is the "household of God" made up of "saints," saved ones.

        Write in Ephesians 2:19: _____

        _____

    b. The church has a sure foundation—the prophets and apostles. They gave to us the Word of God which speak of Him. Jesus is the "Chief cornerstone."

        Write in Ephesians 2:20: _____

        _____

    c. The church is a temple.

        Write in Ephesians 2:21: _____

        _____

        The church is "a holy temple in the Lord." In the first temple all the materials were made beforehand and brought to be placed in the temple. So, the church was elected before the foundation of the world. Each stone was in the mind of God to be placed in a specific place of the household of God. Every believer is important—a part of the total body.

    d. Every believer is a part of the temple of God.

        Write in I Corinthians 3:16: _____

        _____

E. THE CHURCH IS THE BRIDE OF CHRIST

1. The Bride is Purchased by Christ.

    a. The beautiful intimacy of Christ and His church is revealed by Paul.

        Write in Ephesians 5:25: _____

        _____

    b. The marriage brings forth fruit unto God.

        Write in Romans 7:4: _____

        _____

2. The Bride is Cleansed by the Washing of the Word.

    a. Jesus died for His bride. He keeps the bride (church) clean by the Word of God.

        Write in Ephesians 5:26: _____

        _____

    b. Underline John 15:3 in your Bible.

3. The Destiny of the Church.

    a. Jesus, our Redeemer, has a destiny for His bride. Christ loves the church, nourishes the church, that He might present the church to Himself.

    Write in Ephesians 5:27: _____

_____

_____

    b. Believers are members of His body, His flesh, His bones (Ephesians 5:30).

    c. The church is a part of the last invitation of God. "And the Spirit and the bride (church) say, Come. And let him that is athirst come. And whosoever will, let him take the water of life freely" (Revelation 22:17).

V. WHAT THIS TRUTH TEACHES US TODAY

The church, the total body of Christ, which is made up of many members, may differ in many outward respects. However, all members bear the same marks of a true believer. They may worship in a great cathedral or in a tent, may have a ritualistic form of worship or a very simple form of worship. These things make no difference. The thing that makes the difference is their saving faith in Jesus Christ. They all believe in the finished work of Christ—His deity, His virgin birth, His atoning death and resurrection and His coming again. They believe in prayer and worship. Their denominational tag has nothing to do with their being a part of the body of Christ. They are to be found in every area of the earth, in hundreds of different named churches. They all worship God and draw their rules and precepts from the Word of God. Some will sing and get happy and emotional while others are quiet and serene; but all love the one Lord and worship Him. We are all a part of the true church, His body, if we have accepted Him as Lord and Saviour.

YOUR NEXT ASSIGNMENT:

1. Read Acts Chapters 2, 10, 15; I Corinthians 10:32; 12:13; II Corinthians 8:1-15; 9:1-8; Ephesians 2:15; I Timothy 3:1-13; 5:1-2; I Peter 5:1-4.

2. Review your notes on "The Church—The Body of Christ."

3. Mark your Bible where new truths are learned.

Lesson 48 "The Church — The Local Congregation"

(Where lines are provided, look up the Scripture and write in the Scripture or its main truth.)

I. INTRODUCTION

Every one who receives Christ by faith is a member of the body of Christ. But just as surely as you become a member of the one true church, you will immediately yearn for and seek the fellowship of other members of the body of Christ. This is the point where the local church, the local assembly, should become a part of your life. Even though the local churches are not perfect (as there will always be tares among the wheat), the true Christian will seek the fellowship of other believers. Every Christian should identify himself and join the fellowship of a local Bible believing church. There you should find the opportunity to study the Word of God and thereby grow in grace. You should be taught the purpose of the church, how to witness and how to worship our Lord. If you are saved, you should let your testimony be a part of a larger fellowship—the local church. The church may be small; it may be large, but size or prestige have nothing to do with one's personal growth. Jesus said, "Where two or three are gathered together in my name, there am I in the midst of them" (Matthew 18:20).

II. BASIC SCRIPTURES

Acts Chapters 2, 10, 15; I Corinthians 10:32; 12:13; II Corinthians 8:1-15; 9:1-8; Ephesians 2:15; I Timothy 3:1-13; 5:1-12; I Peter 5:1-4.

III. THE NUCLEUS OF THIS TRUTH

In the Bible there is the generic idea of "the church." We use the generic idea when we speak of "the state," "the home," "the school." There is also in the New Testament the word used to refer to the redeemed of all ages. In Hebrews 12:23 you find that thought, "To the general assembly and church of the first-born, who are written in heaven . . ." This is the great congregation of the redeemed; the body of Christ of which He is the Head (Ephesians 1:22-23). This is the church we studied in the last lesson (Number 47).

But the church that is referred to in Scripture over and over again is the local church. In the New Testament where we read of it, and in life when we have anything to do with it, the church is always the local congregation. The New Testament will speak of the churches (plural) of Judea, the churches (plural) of Galatia, the churches (plural) of Macedonia. Paul established local churches everywhere he went. John addressed the Revelation to the seven churches of Asia and he named them.

The *local assembly* is the physical body by which the *Body of Christ*, the church, is manifested.

IV. THE GREAT TRUTH: *"THE CHURCH—THE LOCAL CON-GREGATION"*

A. "ALL THAT JESUS BEGAN BOTH TO DO AND TEACH"

1. The Acts of the Lord Jesus Christ.

a. In our Bibles, the fifth book of the New Testament is entitled "The Acts of the Apostles." Some of the older manuscripts entitle the book "The Acts." This name includes "the Acts of the Apostles" and "the Acts of the Holy Spirit." More specifically, it presents "The Acts of the Lord Jesus Christ" which Jesus does in directing His work on earth from heaven.

b. Luke began by writing "The former treatise have I made (the book of Luke), O Theophilus, *of all that Jesus began both to do and teach*" (Acts 1:1).

c. Luke presented the works of the Lord Jesus while He was in the flesh in the third Gospel, the book of Luke. The book of Acts presents a continuity of what the Lord is doing from heaven of that which He began on earth.

d. In Acts 2, after Peter had preached, 3,000 souls were *added*. To what? To the church. The Lord did the adding and He is still adding to the church.

Write in Acts 2:47: _____

_____

_____

e. The book of Acts has no formal ending. There is no ending because the work of the Lord goes on, in and through the church. Luke finished what the Holy Spirit allowed him to write.

f. "All that Jesus began both to do and teach" will continue until the "fulness of the Gentiles be come in" (Romans 11:25). One of the most amazing things the Lord ever said is recorded in John 14:12: _____

_____

_____

We, the "called out assembly" are to do greater works than those Jesus began both to do and teach.

2. The Outline of the Lord Given to the Church.

a. In the book of Acts, one can see the Lord's outline (Acts 1:8). Everything He does is orderly and properly done.

b. Luke follows the outline as he writes the Acts. The Gospel is to be preached:

- in Jerusalem (Acts 2:1).
- in Judea and Samaria (Acts 8:1, 5).
- to the uttermost part of the world (Acts 8:26; 10:1).

B. THE PROMISE OF THE HOLY SPIRIT

1. The Promise of God the Father.

a. Out of more than 3,000 promises in the Bible, there is only one that is called "*the* promise of the Father."

b. Jesus spoke of "the promise of the Father."

Write in Acts 1:4: _____

_____

_____

Underline Luke 24:49 in your Bible.

c. Write in John 14:26: _____

_____

_____

Underline John 14:16 in your Bible.

These Scriptures refer to the Holy Spirit, to be given in the name of Jesus, to give comfort and help in doing His work.

2. The Holy Spirit Came in Power.

a. The group Jesus had told to wait for "the promise of the Father" were also told, "Ye shall receive power after the Holy Spirit is come upon you; and ye shall be witnesses unto me both in Jerusalem, and in all Judea, and in Samaria, and to the uttermost part of the earth" (Acts 1:8).

b. The Holy Spirit came in the name of Jesus (John 14:26). Underline Acts 2:1, 4 in your Bible.

c. This was the power Jesus had promised. The little group Jesus had trained (basically the twelve) was to be the foundation of the church. The church was visibly established on the Day of Pentecost (the 120 brethren of Acts 1:15).

d. Peter preached on that day and 3,000 souls were saved (Acts 2:41). Notice the word "added."

C. THE MANDATE OF THE LORD TO THE CHURCH

1. The Commission of Jesus to the Church (Matthew 28:19-20).

a. We are to go into all the world and
   - make disciples, students, followers. The Bible says, "teach all nations." (Jesus used the word "matheteuo" meaning "to make disciples.")
   - "baptizing them in the *name* (singular) of the Father, and of the Son, and of the Holy Spirit"
   - "teaching them to observe all things whatsoever I have commanded you." (Jesus used the word "didasko" meaning to teach.)

2. Jesus Ascended With This Great Promise.

a. In Matthew, He said, "Lo, I am with you alway, even to the end of the age" (Matthew 28:20).

b. In Luke, He said, "Repentance and remission of sins should be preached in His name among all nations, beginning at Jerusalem" (Luke 24:47). Then, He promised the Holy Spirit and was carried into heaven (Luke 24:49-51).

c. In Acts, He promised the power of the Holy Spirit to preach to all the world (the outline of our Lord), and then, "He was taken up, and a cloud received Him" (Acts 1:8-9).

3. Was This For the Local Church?

a. Yes! When Jesus ascended into heaven, there was no New Testament, no writings of instruction, only the "assembly" waiting for "the promise of the Father," the Holy Spirit. Jesus gave to this "church" the ordinances, discipline and commission.

b. The group He empowered was a Church, an assembly, a visible local group. One could see them, hear them, join them. *The history of the development of the local church begins with that assembly in Acts 1 and 2.*

c. The remainder of the Acts and the Epistles are, in the main, written for the local church.

d. The sainted John, in the Revelation, saw Jesus in the midst of seven local churches and he names them (Revelation 2 and 3).

D. THE LOCAL CHURCH IS A FELLOWSHIP

1. The Center of the Fellowship is Jesus Christ.

a. In the book of Acts, the churches were exciting fellowships with Christ as the living center. As a fellowship, the church is formed from within; Christ is the Head and the church is the body. They are one in fact and in name, "Christians."

b. Literally, it is the "fellowship of Jesus Christ."

Write in I Corinthians 1:9: _____

_____

_____

2. The Local Church is a Fellowship of Believers.

a. The New Testament does not mention any Christians who were not attached to the church in their midst. In fact, fellowship with the brethren was a test of discipleship.

Write in I John 3:14: _____

_____

_____

Underline I John 3:16 in your Bible.

b. It is a precious fellowship based upon mutual love for Jesus Christ. We are to "keep the unity of the Spirit" (Ephesians 4:3).

c. We are to be at peace with the fellowship and esteem the leaders the Lord has placed in the church.

Write in I Thessalonians 5:13: _____

_____

_____

Underline I Thessalonians 5:12 in your Bible.

d. We are to walk in the light of Jesus Christ.

Write in I John 1:7: _____

_____

_____

3. The Fellowship of a Church Sustains Believers.

a. The New Testament teaches that Christians should comfort one another (I Thessalonians 1:18).

b. Christians should love one another (I Peter 1:22).

c. The church should teach the Word of God and praise Him.

Write in Colossians 3:16: _____

_____

_____

The fellowship of a church is vital for spiritual growth.

4. The Fellowship of a Church Should Win People to Christ.

a. *The local church is the visible manifestation of the unseen Christ.* The church is made up of "spiritual stones," Christians, who are the manifestation of Jesus Christ. It is never a building nor an organization that witnesses. It is always a person who shares his faith (I Peter 3:15).

b. The local church should be involved in missionary work at home and around the world. Underline Romans 10:14-15 in your Bible.

The local church should encourage young people who are called to be missionaries, and support them with prayers and money.

E. THE LOCAL CHURCH IN THE NEW TESTAMENT

1. The New Testament Refers to the Local Church Approximately 100 Times.

a. Jesus referred to the local church in Matthew 18:17: _____

_____

_____

b. Peter preached on the Day of Pentecost and 3,000 souls were *added* (Acts 2:41-42). This was the church as Jerusalem.

c. "The Lord added to the church daily" (Acts 2:47).

d. "Multitudes were added to the church at Jerusalem" (Acts 5:14, 42).

e. "The number multiplied in Jerusalem greatly" (Acts 6:7).

f. "There was great persecution against the church at Jerusalem" (Acts 8:1, 3).

2. Paul Was Converted and Became a "Chosen Vessel to the Gentiles." (Space will not permit all references to the local church, but we shall list as many as possible.)

a. Paul and some of his references to the local church in Acts.

- Acts 9:31 - The churches did not fear Paul any longer.
- Acts 11:19-26 - Paul at the church in Antioch (in Syria).
- Acts 14:23 - Paul ordained leaders in the churches of Acts 13 and 14.
- Acts 14:27 - Paul back at the church at Antioch, Syria.
- Acts 15:41 - Paul went through Syria and Cilicia confirming the churches.
- Acts 16:5, 6 - Underline these verses in your Bible.
- Acts 16:11-40 - The beginning of the church at Philippi.
- Acts 17:1-4 - The beginning of the church at Thessalonica.
- Acts 18:2 - The church at Corinth.
- Acts 19:8-10 - The church at Ephesus.
- Acts 20:7, 17 - The church at Troas.
- Acts 28:17-31 - The Gospel preached in Rome.

b. Paul writing to and about the local churches.

- Romans 1:7-8
- I Corinthians 1:2
- I Corinthians 4:17
- I Corinthians 7:17
- I Corinthians 16:19
- II Corinthians 1:1
- II Corinthians 8:1
- II Corinthians 12:28
- Galatians 1:2, 22
- Philippians 1:1
- Colossians 1:2
- Colossians 4:15-16
- I Thessalonians 1:1
- II Thessalonians 1:1
- I Timothy 3:15
- Philemon 2

c. Other references to the local church (not by Paul).

- James 5:14
- III John 6, 10
- Revelation 1:4, 11, 20
- Revelation 2:1, 8, 12, 18
- Revelation 3:1, 7, 14
- Revelation 22:16

We have omitted so many references to the local church. We have listed only 48 references, enough to show the student the importance of the local church.

V. WHAT THIS TRUTH TEACHES US TODAY

Have you ever thought of living in a world with no local churches? The local church is not perfect—far from it—but it is the instrument of God to spread the Gospel of Jesus Christ. There are many good Christian organizations with great causes, but they do not take the place of the local church. Most of them would fade away were it not for the support of Christians in local churches.

Jesus loved the church and gave Himself for it. He blesses the church that is true to the Word of God—in its teaching and preaching ministries. Paul says, "Christ also loved the church and gave Himself for it; that He might sanctify and cleanse it with the washing of water by the Word" (Ephesians 5:25-26). The word for "wash" is the same word used for "laver." In the Greek the word is "loutron"—in Hebrew "kiyor." In the tabernacle or the temple there was the laver where the priests washed before entering the sanctuary of God. That is the word Paul uses, the laver of the Word. Our Lord washes His church with the laver of the Word.

YOUR NEXT ASSIGNMENT:

1. Read Matthew 24:24; Mark 13:22; II Thessalonians 2:1-12; I John 2:18; Revelation 6:2; 12:12; 13:1-18; 14:9-10; 17:15.

2. Review your notes on "The Church—The Local Congregation."

3. Mark your Bible where new truths are learned.

Lesson 49
"The Antichrist and the False Prophet"

(Where lines are provided, look up the Scripture and write in the Scripture or its main truth.)

I. INTRODUCTION

The Bible speaks of a man whom Satan will control, and he shall rule the world for a limited time. He shall be known as the Antichrist. Many movies and books have been produced recently on this subject. The world is being exposed to things concerning the end of this age. The church, in the main, is not providing Biblical answers on this subject. The subject of the Antichrist and the False Prophet is a part of God's Word—a part of the "counsel of God." The church should be the source of truth to young people and adults on any Biblical subject. This lesson shall present Scriptural facts about two prominent figures who shall appear on the world scene—the Antichrist and the False Prophet.

II. BASIC SCRIPTURES

Matthew 24:24; Mark 13:22; II Thessalonians 2:1-12; I John 2:18; Revelation 6:2; 12:12; 13:1-18; 14:9-10; 17:15.

III. THE NUCLEUS OF THIS TRUTH

Satan indwells bodies, or tabernacles in bodies. The Holy Spirit indwells all who are saved. Christ is in us, the hope of glory. So, Satan uses personalities or bodies in which to dwell. He has appeared in the past in the serpent in Genesis 3, and in Simon Peter in Matthew 16:23. He is the one Christ saw when he fell from heaven (Luke 10:18). Jesus knew him well from eternity past. Satan is known as "the prince of the power of the air" (Ephesians 2:2). He still has access to the throne of God as the "accuser of the brethren" (Revelation 12:10). In a period of judgment and tribulation, yet future, Satan's access to the throne of God will be withdrawn (Revelation 12:7-12). He shall be cast out of the presence of God. He shall have access *only* to the earth. Read and underline Revelation 12:7-12 in your Bible. Notice in verse 10, "the accuser of the brethren is cast down, who accused them before our God day and night." He accuses us, believers in Christ, day and night, but in verse 11, "the blood of Christ" is the only thing that defeats Satan.

The nucleus of this lesson shall be with the activity of Satan from this point in the Bible. Yes, we shall look back to the Old Testament, but the main thrust shall be his future activity as he clothes himself with the humanity of the Antichrist.

IV. THE GREAT TRUTH: *"THE ANTICHRIST AND THE FALSE PROPHET"*

A. THE NAMES FOR ANTICHRIST IN SCRIPTURE

1. Names in the Old Testament.

a. "The little horn" (Daniel 7:8).

b. "Another shall arise . . . and speak against the most High" (Daniel 7:24-25).

    c. "The prince" (Daniel 9:26).

    d. "The desolater" (Daniel 9:27).

    e. "The king of fierce countenance" (Daniel 8:23-25). Here Daniel used the title for Antiochus Epiphanes to prefigure the Antichrist.

2. Names in the New Testament.

    a. "The abomination of desolation" - the "desolater" is named by Jesus who refers to Daniel.

       Write in Matthew 24:15: _____

       _____

       _____

    b. "The man of sin" (II Thessalonians 2:3).

    c. "the son of perdition" (II Thessalonians 2:3).

    d. "That Wicked" (II Thessalonians 2:8).

    e. "Antichrist."

       Write in I John 2:18: _____

       _____

       _____

       Underline I John 2:22; 4:3; II John 7 in your Bible.

    f. "The conqueror on the white horse" (Revelation 6:2). He is the first to be revealed when the judgments of God begin. When Jesus opens the first seal judgment, the Antichrist is seen.

    g. "The great dragon" (Revelation 12:3-4, 9).

    h. "That old serpent" (Revelation 12:9).

    i. "The Devil" (Revelation 12:9, 12).

    j. "Satan" (Revelation 12:9).

    k. "The beast out of the sea" (Revelation 13:1)

B. THE ANTICHRIST - THE BEAST OUT OF THE SEA

1. A Sketch of This Man.

    a. During the period of tribulation and judgment, Satan will control a man who will rule the world and be known as the Antichrist. We see him in Revelation 6:2 when the first seal is broken. He is on the scene at the beginning of the judgments.

    b. The Antichrist will break his covenant with Israel in the middle of the tribulation (Daniel 9:27), and will turn on God's people, Israel. That is described in Revelation 12. Satan gives all of his power to Antichrist and indwells him (Revelation 13:4).

    c. The time of his control will be short (Revelation 12:12). In Revelation 13:5 that time is limited to 42 months. The same period is known as "time, and times, and half a time" (Revelation 12:14).

       The same time period is known as "1,260 days" (Revelation 11:3; 12:6).

2. The Political Ruler of This World.

    a. The one described in Revelation 13:1-10 will be the political leader of the world. John, in his vision, sees a beast, a monster, rising out of the sea. Why out of the sea? John explains the figure of speech in Revelation 17:15: _____

_____

_____

Write in Isaiah 57:20: _____

_____

So, the beast rises out of the chaos of a troubled world.

b. John's description of the beast is in a vision in Revelation 13:1-2. He is to have great authority. This is a picture of the last political ruler on the earth. When he is destroyed in Revelation 19, there is none after him.

c. The vision of John also refers to the book of Daniel. Read Daniel 7:15-28 for an interpretation of the vision.

d. There shall be a one world government—one man in control.

Write in Revelation 17:13: _____

_____

_____

(You are now wondering if this is symbolism. Yes, it is a picture, a word picture of the Antichrist. In Revelation 12:3 you read, "And there appeared another wonder (a sign, symbol) in heaven." That sign, symbol is still being described in Revelation 13—except in human form. This is Satan incarnate, described in verses 1-10. The terms "wonders" and "signs" are used 7 times in Revelation—12:1, 3; 13:13, 14 (miracle is sign in margin); 15:1; 16:14; 19:29.)

C. THE ANTICHRIST IS A PERSON

1. He is a Particular Person.

a. In Revelation 13:1-10 you read God's delineation of that man. There is no kingdom without a king, no empire without an emperor. This man is the leader of the final world government.

b. Paul calls him "that man of sin."

Write in II Thessalonians 2:3: _____

_____

2. His Personal Attractiveness.

a. He shall be an intriguing personality. He shall be one of the most magnetic mortal men to ever live. We know this from Revelation 13:3, "and all the world wondered after the beast."

b. He shall be praised and even worshipped as is indicated in Revelation 13:4, "and they worshipped the beast, saying, who is like the beast? Who is able to make war with him?"

c. This man will be received with gladness by the world leaders, "for there is none like him."

3. He Will Have Miraculous Power.

a. The people shall worship Him after a miraculous thing which happens in Revelation 13:3.

b. Write in Revelation 13:3: _____

_____

c. His power shall be limited to 3½ years—42 months (Revelation 13:5). This is the last half of the tribulation.

d. He shall have power "over all kindreds, tongues and nations." He shall curse God and make war on those who believe in the Lord during that period (Revelation 13:6-7). The saints shall be victorious in the end. Underline Revelation 15:2 in your Bible.

4. The Book of Life.

a. "All that dwell on the earth shall worship him, whose names are not written in the book of life" (Revelation 13:8).

b. That is the "book of the Lamb, Jesus Christ, slain from the foundation of the world." Can you imagine his wrath against those whose names appear in the book of life?

5. The Encouragement From God.

a. In Revelation 13:9, the words are familiar from Revelation 2 and 3. However, something is missing. The missing phrase is "what the Spirit saith to the churches." Why isn't that phrase stated? Because the church is gone, but to those who turn to God in such a terrible hour, He says, "If a man have an ear, let him hear."

b. God is not forgetful of those who suffer for Him. Revelation 13:10 says, "Here is the patience and the faith of the saints." Write in Revelation 14:12: _____

_____

_____

c. According to Revelation 13:10 every antichrist who has ever appeared or shall appear endures only according to the permissive will of God. Underline the first part of verse 10 in your Bible.

D. THE FALSE PROPHET

1. The Beast Out of the Earth.

a. The false prophet is described in Revelation 13:11-18. In verse 11, he has "two horns *like* a lamb," but he is no lamb. When he speaks, he shall sound like a dragon (Satan).

b. He is called the false prophet in Revelation 16:13; 19:20; 20:10. Underline these references in your Bible.

2. The False Prophet is a Religious Leader.

a. The first beast, the Antichrist, is political. This man rises out of the earth and is an ecclesiastical leader.

b. This beast is "like a lamb" and exercises his power to deceive the whole earth in accepting the authority and self chosen deity of the first beast—the Antichrist (Revelation 13:12). One of the amazing facts in history is that it has never been possible to rule without some "religious" devotion—"religious," not Christian. The false prophet supports the Antichrist.

3. The Authority and Power of the False Prophet.

a. He is dangerous because he appears to be religious. Of the two, he is the more dangerous. Any man who proposes to guide and command the minds, hearts and souls of people has in his power an unbelievable authority over mankind.

b. He is able to perform miracles (Revelation 13:13-14).

c. He shall cause the people to make an image of the Antichrist. He shall promote idol worship. Those who do not bow down to the image of the beast shall be killed (Revelation 13:14-15).

The first great world kingdom was guilty of the same thing. Nebuchadnezzar made an image of gold (Daniel 3:1). When we turn to the last kingdom of the age, humanity repeats the same weakness.

d. Revelation 13:14-17 describes the terrible mandate of the false prophet. If one does not obey, he is killed.

4. **The Amazing Number—The Mark of the Beast.**

a. Write in Revelation 13:16: _____

_____

_____

The false prophet shall have that power and control.

b. Without the mark, one will not be able to buy or sell (Revelation 13:17).

c. The false prophet says, "here is wisdom. Let him that hath an understanding count the number of the beast; for it is the number of a man; and his number is 666" (Revelation 13:18). What does it mean? There are thousands of speculations, but according to other Scriptures, the number 6 is the number of man, and it means falling short of perfection (7). Man was created on the 6th day. He is to work 6 of the 7 days. The fields were to be planted for 6 years—rest the 7th. A Hebrew slave could not be a slave for more than 6 years, etc.

d. There is a trinity of 6's here—666. This is the *number of the man*—666. This is Satan trying to be triune in man's number—6. The most man will ever attain shall fall short of perfection—only 6. Those who worship Antichrist shall have the mark of the beast.

5. **The People Who Receive the Mark of the Beast.**

a. What will happen to the millions who accept the mark of the beast? The false prophet's threats shall be effective.

b. The answer is found in Revelation 14:9-10. Read and underline in your Bible.

E. THE DOOM OF THE ANTICHRIST AND FALSE PROPHET

1. **They Shall Be Cast into the Lake of Fire.**

Write in Revelation 19:20: _____

_____

_____

_____

2. **Satan is To Be Cast into the Lake of Fire.**

Revelation 20:10 reveals that the Antichrist and false prophet were cast into hell before Satan. This verse confirms Revelation 19:20, and the doom of all three is settled for eternity.

V. WHAT THIS TRUTH TEACHES US TODAY

The Antichrist shall be the ruler—the king of a kingdom. He will accept

301

the "kingdoms of this world" which Satan offered Christ, and Christ refused (Matthew 4:8-10). He shall "speak great things." He shall be a smart person with the ability to gain and control the minds of people as well as their finances. The false prophet shall exalt the Antichrist. He shall cause the people to worship the Antichrist. He shall perform great miracles—deceive the population—and kill anyone who does not conform. He will force the people to receive the mark of the beast.

The future, depicted in God's Word, is as real as the past has been. All of the prophecies which *have* been fulfilled are testimonies that the prophecies yet to be fulfilled shall come to pass.

The Christian will not go through the judgments of the tribulation and therefore will not receive the mark of the beast, the church having been caught up with Christ (II Thessalonians 2:2).

There shall be those who will not accept the mark of the beast—those who will believe in Christ even when it will cost them their lives (Revelation 15:2). They shall be killed (Revelation 13:15).

The time is short to do the work of Christ. The end time is always imminent. All signs point to the coming of the Lord—the calling out of His body, the church.

YOUR NEXT ASSIGNMENT:

1. Read Job 19:25-26; Psalm 2:4-6; Isaiah 9:6-7; Matthew Chapters 24 and 25; Mark Chapters 11, 12 and 13; Luke 17:26-28; Chapter 21; John 14:1-3; Acts 1:9-11; I Corinthians 15:51-57; I Thessalonians 4:13-18; Titus 2:11-13; I John 3:2-3; Jude 14, 15; Revelation 1:7; 22:20.

2. Review your notes on the Antichrist and the False Prophet.

3. Mark your Bible where new truths are learned.

Lesson 50 "The Second Coming of Christ"

(Where lines are provided, look up the Scripture and write in the Scripture or its main truth.)

I. INTRODUCTION

The Bible contains far more about the second coming of Christ than His first coming. A great deal of the Old Testament prophecy speaks of His second coming. In fact, there are eight verses concerning the second coming to every one verse concerning the first coming. Isaiah speaks of His glorious first coming, but there is far more about His second coming in Isaiah. The book of Ezekiel is, in the main, occupied with the glorious Kingdom at the second coming of Jesus. The same is true of the prophets, Daniel, Jeremiah, Joel, Amos, Hosea, Malachi and the other prophets of the Old Testament. There are *320 references in the New Testament* concerning the second coming of Jesus. Without the second coming, His first coming is incomplete. The second coming of Christ cannot be ignored by a student of the Word of God. The subject consumes a great portion of the Bible. God the Father, God the Son and God the Holy Spirit placed the emphasis on the subject, and man cannot avoid nor overlook its importance.

II. BASIC SCRIPTURES

Read Job 19:25-26; Psalm 2:4-6; Isaiah 9:6-7; Matthew Chapters 24 and 25; Mark Chapters 11, 12 and 13; Luke 17:26-28; Chapter 21; John 14:1-3; Acts 1:9-11; I Corinthians 15:51-57; I Thessalonians 4:13-18; Titus 2:11-13; I John 3:2-3; Jude 14, 15; Revelation 1:7; 22:20.

III. THE NUCLEUS OF THIS TRUTH

The Bible makes the second coming of Christ as sure as His first coming. He is coming back to take His church unto Himself and to set up upon this earth a kingdom, the Kingdom of Heaven. There will be peace and blessing for the world. Yes, just as surely as He came the first time in fulfillment of God's Word, just so surely and literally will He come again the second time. The second coming of Christ, the blessed hope, is the greatest incentive for righteous living, serving, evangelism and missionary work.

IV. THE GREAT TRUTH: *"THE SECOND COMING OF CHRIST"*

A. A RECURRING THEME OF THE BIBLE

1. The First Prophecy of Christ Announced His Second Coming.

    a. The very first promise God gave to man after he fell was the promise of the second coming of Christ. Most of us know that Genesis 3:15 is the first direct prophecy of Christ, but we stop there.

b. Write in Genesis 3:15: _____

_____

_____

_____

c. The verse reveals *two comings* of Christ:

- the first coming, "thou (the seed of the serpent) shalt bruise His (the Seed of woman) heel."

This happened when Jesus hung upon the cross.

- the second coming, "it (the Seed of woman) shall bruise thy head."

This will happen at the second coming of Christ. The serpent can be crushed only by injury to the head. Christ shall return as King and shall crush the forces of Satan.

2. Job Looked for the Coming of Christ.

a. This, the oldest book of the Bible, makes a definite statement about the second coming.

b. Write in Job 19:25: _____

_____

_____

Notice the words, "He shall stand at the latter day." Underline Job 19:26 in your Bible.

3. David Looked for the Second Coming of Christ.

a. The 2nd Psalm is about the coming King, Christ. The rulers of the world would be against such a King (Psalm 2:1-3).

b. When Jesus has returned and is King on Mount Zion, the world shall be in subjection to the *King*, Jesus.

Underline Psalm 2:4-6 in your Bible.

4. Isaiah Prophesied Both - the First and Second Comings.

a. Isaiah, the evangelical prophet, saw Christ as a child (Isaiah 7:14; 9:6a). This was the first coming of Christ.

b. He saw Christ on the throne of David over His Kingdom (Isaiah 9:7). This is the second coming of Christ.

5. Paul Preached the Second Coming of Christ.

a. Paul gives us a library of material about the return of the Lord. Read and mark these passages in your Bible:

- I Corinthians 15:51-53
- Philippians 3:20-21
- I Thessalonians 1:10; 4:13-18
- I Timothy 6:14-15
- Titus 2:13

b. Write in Titus 2:13: _____

_____

_____

6. Other Announcements of His Return.

a. "Behold the Lord cometh with ten thousands of His saints" (Jude 14).

b. "And when the chief Shepherd shall appear, ye shall receive a crown of glory that fadeth not away" (I Peter 5:4). Peter also spoke of His coming in Acts 3:20; II Peter 1:16.

c. James preached His second coming. Underline James 5:7-8 in your Bible.

d. The Apostle John preached His second coming.
Write in I John 3:2: _____

_____

_____

Underline I John 2:28 in your Bible.

John also wrote the Revelation which we shall consider in this lesson.

e. From Genesis to Revelation there is that recurring theme—
"Jesus is Coming Again."

B. THE INCOMPARABLE ANNOUNCEMENT

1. The Bible Always Presents His Coming With Clouds.

a. "Behold He cometh with clouds" (Revelation 1:7). This is the incomparable announcement—the text of Revelation.

b. As He went away so shall He return. Underline Acts 1:9 in your Bible.
Write in Acts 1:11: _____

_____

_____

_____

c. "I saw in the night visions, and, behold, one like the Son of Man came with the clouds of Heaven . . ." (Daniel 7:13).

d. In His sermon on the mount, Jesus said He would return in the clouds.
Write in Matthew 24:30: _____

_____

_____

e. Before the Sanhedrin, Jesus used the same terminology. Underline Matthew 26:64 in your Bible.

2. The Cloud is a Radiant Sign of His Second Coming.

a. John was present when our Lord ascended. He heard the angel's announcement in Acts 1:11. He wrote, "Behold He cometh with clouds" (Revelation 1:7).

b. In the wilderness, the people of God were led by a pillar of fire by night and a cloud by day (Exodus 13:21-22; 14:19-20). This same cloud is the radiant sign of our Lord's return.

c. The transfiguration is another example of this glorious sign. Underline Matthew 17:5 in your Bible.

d. As He went away in the clouds, He shall return in the clouds. His return is sure. In His return, we have the entire circle of God's elective purpose completed. What was begun in Genesis finds its completion and ultimate consummation in Revelation.

C. THE RETURN OF CHRIST SECRETLY

1. Jesus Shall Return as a Thief in the Night.

a. In Revelation 1:7, John says, "Behold, He cometh with clouds; and every eye shall see Him" It does not say that all shall see Him at the same time or in the same manner. There

305

will be those who will see Him when He comes as a thief in the night. There will be those who shall see Him come in power and judgment, but everyone will see Him. (There is no contradiction in Scripture about His coming, as we shall see.)

b. His secret return is to take unto Himself the "pearl of great price"—the church (Matthew 13:45-46). The most precious thing God has on the earth is the church—the saved ones—the bride of Christ.

c. Jesus shall come secretly as a thief—quietly. Underline Revelation 3:3 in your Bible. Notice, He comes as a thief and takes out a "few names." Read verses 4 and 5 and note the division. He takes those whom He can confess before the Father.

d. The same thought is expressed in Matthew 24:42-44.
Write in Matthew 24:43: _____

_____

_____

In Matthew 24:40-41, Jesus comes and takes some and leaves some.

e. The same description is found in I Thessalonians 5:1, 2, 4.
Write in I Thessalonians 5:2: _____

_____

_____

Underline verse 4 in your Bible. When Paul says, "Ye brethren," he is speaking to the church.

f. The same figure of speech is mentioned in Revelation 16:15, "Behold, I come as a thief in the night."

g. He is coming for His church, which is described in I Thessalonians 4:13-18. This rendezvous will be in the air. Only the redeemed will be called out of the grave. Believers who are alive shall join them, and meet Christ in the air. "Some are taken, others left." Only the believers are taken—only the unbelievers are left. Underline I Thessalonians 4:15-17 in your Bible.

Paul spoke "unto you by the Word of the Lord" (verse 15). What did Paul mean? He means what Jesus said in John 14:3, "I will come again, and receive you unto myself that where I am, there ye may be also." Jesus is speaking of His own—believers in Him—a part of Him.

2. **The Secret Call of Christ is Presented Through Types and Teaching.**

a. "By faith Enoch was translated that he should not see death; and was not found, because God had translated him: for before his translation he had this testimony, that he pleased God" (Hebrews 11:5).

b. So, the church is an "ecclesia," a "called out" body. The church is "the called out"—the "called away," like Enoch.

c. The same kind of picture is seen in the days of Noah. Underline Luke 17:26 in your Bible. While the world was drinking and scoffing, God called Noah into the ark and God shut the door (Genesis 6 and 7). God took Noah out *before* judgment.

306

d. The same thing happened in the days of Lot (Luke 17:28-30). God did not judge Sodom until Lot got out (Genesis 19:22).

So, the Lord shall come secretly for His own. He shall come, and no one knows when except God the Father (Matthew 24:36).

D. THE RETURN OF CHRIST OPENLY

1. The Return of Christ to the Earth With His Saints.

a. Jesus shall come openly. "Behold, the Lord cometh with ten thousands of His saints" (Jude 14). The saints are the ones He received when He came as a thief in the night. They are the church.

b. The first message, after the ascension of Christ, was delivered by the angels: "This same Jesus, which is taken up from you into heaven, shall so come in like manner as ye have seen Him go into heaven" (Acts 1:10).

c. The same Jesus, the One born of a virgin, the One who died on the cross, is coming back. He left from the Mount of Olives; He shall return visibly to the Mount of Olives and His feet shall stand in that place. Underline Zechariah 14:4 in your Bible.

2. Jesus Shall Return as King.

a. "He shall be King over all the earth in that day" (Zechariah 14:9).

b. Jesus speaks of His return in detail (Matthew 24:4-31).

The signs of His return:
- "false christs" (verse 5),
- "wars and rumors of wars" (verse 6),
- "famines, pestilances, earthquakes" (verse 7),
- "persecution of believers—false prophets—" (verses 9-11),
- "the Gospel of the Kingdom preached to the world" (verse 14),
- "The abomination of desolation spoken by Daniel" (verse 15).

These are the signs leading to the visible return of Jesus. The "abomination of desolation" speaks of the Beast, the Antichrist. (We studied this in the last lesson.) Here Jesus uses Daniel's account to teach them, and us, the truth of the Antichrist (Daniel 9:27). Jesus gives warning concerning the Antichrist and the beginning of "the great tribulation" (Matthew 24:15-26).

c. The coming of the "Son of Man" shall be as lightening from east to west (Matthew 24:27).

Underline verse 29 (of Matthew 24) in your Bible.

d. Then, *Jesus says* He is coming back.

Write in Matthew 24:30: _____

_____

_____

He has outlined the conditions and told us He was to return with power and great glory. We have no authority to question His words. Notice His order of events—the signs of His coming, the tribulation, His return to earth as King.

    e. Jesus shall return as "King of Kings, and Lord of Lords" (Revelation 19:16). His return is vividly portrayed in Revelation 19:11-16. Underline Revelation 19:11 and 16 in your Bible.

So, Jesus shall return as King over all the earth: "and every eye shall see Him, and they also which pierced Him: and all kindreds of the earth shall wail because of Him" (Revelation 1:7). We shall continue this study in Lesson 51. There is so much to present. We have only touched His coming again, but perhaps it will cause you to dig deeper in the Word.

V. WHAT THIS TRUTH TEACHES US TODAY

The second coming of Christ is a fact. The *first promise* after fall of man is concerning *His coming*. The *last promise* in the Old Testament (Malachi 4:2) is concerning *His coming*. The first announcement in the New Testament was given by the angel to Joseph (Matthew 1:18-23) and to Mary concerning *His coming* in the flesh: "the Lord God shall give unto Him the throne of His father David: and He shall reign over the house of Jacob forever; and of His Kingdom there shall be no end" (Luke 1:32-33). The last words of Jesus before the cross were, "I will *come again*" (John 14:3). The first announcement at the ascension of Christ was, "this same Jesus which is taken up from you into heaven, shall so *come in like manner* as ye have seen Him go into heaven" (Acts 1:11). The last promise of Scripture is, "Surely I come quickly" (Revelation 22:20).

He is coming secretly, as a thief, to take unto Himself His church, His body. He will come in the clouds—the sign of the glory of God.

He shall come openly to reign as a King over all the earth. The saints, believers, will come with Him to reign with Him in His Kingdom. (The subject of the next lesson.)

"Even so, come, Lord Jesus."

YOUR NEXT ASSIGNMENT:

1. Read Psalm 2:1-12; 72:1-10; Isaiah 2:1-5; 11:1-16; 35:1-10; 65:18-25; Jeremiah 23:5-8; 30:1-9; Zechariah 12:10-14; 14:9-21; Matthew 24:27-30; 25:31; Luke 1:32-33; Acts 3:20-21; I Corinthians 15:24-28; Revelation 19:17-21; 20:1-10.

2. Review your notes on The Second Coming of Christ.

3. Mark your Bible where new truths are learned.

Lesson 51 "The King and His Kingdom"

(Where lines are provided, look up the Scripture and write in the Scripture or its main truth.)

I. INTRODUCTION

The world is talking more about peace than ever before in its history. But as the governments of the world discuss peace, they are frantically preparing for war. Every newspaper and news program is filled with items concerning peace. The same news, written or spoken, is also filled with the arms build-up by nations all over the world. Then, we are left with the question in our minds—"Will there ever be a day when the world shall know and experience such a thing as real peace?" (Jeremiah 8:11, 15). There is an answer, and it will not be found in the United Nations nor in any government of the world. The answer is found only in the Word of God. The world will never experience real peace until the King, Jesus, establishes His Kingdom upon the earth.

The Kingdom of Heaven is the period of time discussed in Revelation 20. The Holy Spirit emphasized the length of time by repeating the term "one thousand years" six times in that one chapter. Some people call this the "millennium." That phrase is not used in Scripture but it is a Scriptural truth. The term comes from two Latin words, "mille," meaning one thousand and "annum," meaning years. The millennium means one thousand years. The word has been so abused by theologians and others that it has become a "red flag" to some students. The emphasis of the thousand years is in Scripture—six times—and regardless of preconceived views, the Bible student has to face the fact that God has emphasized it for a purpose. The more appropriate term for the thousand years is the "Kingdom of Heaven." This should not be a subject to be argued about for years or even for one moment. The Lord must have known that Satan would take a precious truth, such as this one, and cause people to fuss and divide over a word not used in Scripture—"millennium." That must be the reason He used the term "one thousand years" six times. We shall use the term "Kingdom of Heaven" in our study.

II. BASIC SCRIPTURES

Psalm 2:1-12; 72:1-10; Isaiah 2:1-5; 11:1-16; 35:1-10; 65:18-25; Jeremiah 23:5-8; 30:1-9; Zechariah 12:10-14; 14:9-21; Matthew 24:27-30; 25:31; Luke 1:32-33; Acts 3:20-21; I Corinthians 15:24-28; Revelation 19:17-21; 20:1-10.

III. THE NUCLEUS OF THIS TRUTH

The Kingdom of Heaven is used by Matthew some 32 times. This is appropriate because Matthew presents Christ as King. The Kingdom of Heaven is that period of time from the first coming of Christ to the end of His Kingdom. When Jesus was rejected as King at His first coming, the Kingdom of Heaven was postponed and He ascended into glory. Jesus talked of the "mysteries of the Kingdom of Heaven" in Matthew

13. When Jesus comes again He will return as King and shall reign over His Kingdom for one thousand years. There is a volume of Scripture, in both Old and New Testaments, which presents the Kingdom of our Lord.

IV. THE GREAT TRUTH: *"THE KING AND HIS KINGDOM"*

A. THE BIBLE DECLARES THE KINGDOM OF HEAVEN

1. **The Testimony in the New Testament of the Kingdom of Heaven.**

   a. Many Scriptures are given to the subject of the return of Christ and His reign over the earth in an age of peace. More than *350 references* in the Old Testament and *320 references* in the New Testament deal with the subject of His second coming and establishing a reign of peace and righteousness upon the earth.

   b. John the Baptist announced the Kingdom of Heaven as "at hand."
   Write in Matthew 3:2: _____
   _____

   c. Jesus, Himself, announced the Kingdom of Heaven as "at hand."
   Write in Matthew 4:17: _____
   _____
   _____

   d. The twelve apostles announced the Kingdom of Heaven as "at hand."
   Write in Matthew 10:7: _____
   _____

   e. The seventy were sent out by the Lord Jesus and told to announce the Kingdom as "nigh unto you" (Luke 10:9).

2. **The Testimony in the Old Testament of the Kingdom of Heaven.**

   a. Jesus came the first time to be King over a Kingdom, as foretold by the Old Testament prophets. The King and the Kingdom were to be real, literal, actual. The announcements in the New Testament were made by *real* people talking about a *real* offer by Jesus, the *real* King, to Israel, a *real* people. The announcements were based upon God's revelation in the Old Testament and the incarnation of the Son of God.

   b. Isaiah described the Kingdom throughout his book. Underline Isaiah 2:2, 4 in your Bible.
   Write in Isaiah 9:7: _____
   _____
   _____

   Underline Isaiah 11:6-7 and 11 in your Bible.

   c. Jeremiah spoke of the Kingdom.
   Write in Jeremiah 23:5: _____
   _____
   _____

   Underline Jeremiah 23:3, 6 in your Bible.

d. Write in Habakkuk 2:14: _____

_____

_____

e. Zechariah spoke of such a Kingdom.
Write in Zechariah 14:9: _____

_____

These few Scriptures are sufficient to establish the purposes of God in Jesus Christ coming as a King to Israel.

B. THE PRESENTATION OF THE KING

1. Who is the King Who is Presented in Scripture?

a. As we look at the Word of God, there is a revealed purpose of the Lord God to build here on the earth a Kingdom. God never deviates from this purpose—it is all through the Bible.

b. In the Old Testament there is a *prophetic* portrait of the Messiah King. In the New Testament you have an *historic* portrait of that Messiah King.

c. He is none other than the promised Seed, the Messiah. In the Old Testament, He is presented vividly, clearly.

- In Genesis 3:15, He is to be the Seed of woman.
- In Genesis 9:26, He is to come through the line of Shem.
- In Genesis 12:1-3, He is to be of the seed of Abraham
- In Genesis 17:19, He is to be of the seed of Isaac.
- In Genesis 28:14-15, He is to be of the seed of Jacob.
- In Genesis 49:10, He is to belong to the tribe of Judah.
- In II Samuel 7:12, 16, He is to be the Son of David.
- In Psalm 89:3-4, 35-37, the Son of David is established on the throne forever and is unconditionally reiterated.
- In Jeremiah 33:17-26, that unconditional promise is reaffirmed.
- In Isaiah 11:1, 2, 10, it is reaffirmed again.

2. The King Presented is the Son of God.

a. The Bible clearly speaks of Jesus as the King.

- In Isaiah 7:14; 9:6-7, He is to be of divine heritage.
- In Luke 1:31-33, 35, that prophecy of Isaiah came to pass.
- In Micah 5:2, His birthplace is announced in advance.
- In Matthew 2:1-2, that prophecy of Micah came to pass. He was born "King of the Jews."
- In Daniel 9:26, He was to be cut off, but not for Himself—He was to die as an offering for sin.
- In Psalm 22, that death is described in detail.
- In Isaiah 53, the death of Christ is again described.
- In Psalm 16, there is a prophecy of His resurrection from the dead.
- In Acts 2:25-28, Peter quotes the prophecy and affirms His resurrection and exaltation.
- In Luke 19:11-15, Jesus spoke a parable and revealed the fact of His going away—"because they thought the Kingdom should appear immediately."

- In Acts 15:13-18, His Kingdom and His return is affirmed.

b. The King in all of these Scriptures is Jesus Christ our Lord. He is to be a real King, an actual King. He will be a visible King—not a symbolic character.

C. THE PRESENTATION OF THE KINGDOM OF HEAVEN

1. The Kingdom of Heaven is a New Testament Term.

a. The Kingdom of Heaven is used only by Matthew, where it is used 32 different times. For example:
- Matthew 4:23; 5:19, 20, 35; 6:10; 7:21; 8:11; 9:35; 10:7; 11:11; 13:11, 19, 24, 31, 33, 38, 44, 45, 47, 52; 16:19, 28; 18:1, 3, 4, 23; 19:12, 14, 23, 28; 20:1, 21; 22:2 and on through Matthew.

b. The Kingdom of Heaven is limited to time and sphere. The time is from the first coming of Christ to the end of Christ's Kingdom. The sphere is all Christendom. Now, let us explain.

Jesus came as a King. The Jews rejected Him as King (John 1:49; 18:33; 19:19-22). He died as a King—a rejected King—a King buried and resurrected.

The Kingdom was postponed and Jesus talked of the mysteries of the Kingdom of Heaven in Matthew 13. He knew that He would have to go back to the Father. In this period between His ascension and His return is that "musterion"—the "mystery of the church." (This was covered in Lesson 46.)

2. God's Purpose on the Earth.

a. Is there to be a Kingdom? In Acts 1:6 the disciples ask the Lord, "Wilt thou at this time restore the kingdom to Israel?" Jesus said, "It is not for you to know the times or seasons" (Acts 1:7).

b. The Bible does declare that Jesus will return and set up His Kingdom and we (the church—the saved ones) shall reign with Him (II Timothy 2:12; Revelation 1:6; 5:10).

c. We, the bride of Christ, shall be "heirs of God and joint heirs with Christ" (Romans 8:17).

D. THE DURATION OF THE KINGDOM OF HEAVEN

1. The Events Leading to the Kingdom of Heaven.

a. Jesus returns to the earth as "King of Kings and Lord of Lords" (Revelation 19:11-16).
Write in Revelation 19:16: _____

_____

_____

b. He shall come "in the clouds of heaven with power and great glory." At the conclusion of the Battle of Armageddon, Jesus will occupy the throne of David. This battle is described in Matthew 24:27-31; Joel 3:9-13; Zechariah 14:1-4; Revelation 16:13-16; 19:17-19. This battle is the conflict between Christ and the Antichrist. This is the seed of the serpent fighting the Seed of woman (Genesis 3:15).

c. The doom of the Antichrist and False Prophet (Revelation 19:20). Notice they were "cast alive into the lake of fire."

d. The judgment of the Gentile nations (Matthew 25:31-46)—and the judgment of Israel (Ezekiel 20:33-38).

e. Satan shall be bound in the bottomless pit 1,000 years.
   Write in Revelation 20:2: _____

   _____

   _____

2. **The Time of the Kingdom and the Repetition in Scripture.**

   a. The Kingdom of Heaven shall last 1,000 years. The Holy Spirit, knowing how people would deny this truth, repeats the length of time 6 times in Revelation 20:
      - in Revelation 20:2
      - in Revelation 20:3
      - in Revelation 20:4
      - in Revelation 20:5
      - in Revelation 20:6
      - in Revelation 20:7

      Underline these verses in your Bible.

   b. The Kingdom of Heaven is that period of time of 1,000 years when Christ shall personally be King of Kings. The only way the world will ever know peace is for the Prince of Peace to return to the City of Peace, Jerusalem. Jerusalem means "foundation of Peace." We are to pray for the peace of Jerusalem (Psalm 122:6-8). Peace shall come to Jerusalem and the world when He has come again.
      Write in Psalm 2:6: _____

      _____

      Underline Psalm 2:7-9 in your Bible.

   c. The King will have absolute obedience and "every knee shall bow to Him and every tongue confess that Jesus Christ is Lord" (Isaiah 45:23; Romans 14:11; Philippians 2:10-11).

   d. Christ shall rule with a rod of iron (Psalms 2:9; 46:9; Isaiah 2:4).

E. THE CONDITIONS DURING THE KINGDOM AGE

   1. *Israel* **Shall Become the Head of all Nations.**

      Israel shall be the head and not the tail as she is today (Deuteronomy 28:13; Isaiah 61:5; Zechariah 8:23).

   2. *The Church* **Shall Reign With Christ During the Kingdom of Heaven (II Timothy 2:11-12; I Thessalonians 4:17; I Corinthians 6:2-3).**

      Wherever the Lord shall be, there we, the church, shall be with Him. We shall reign and judge over the angels and the world. Underline the Scripture above.

   3. *Satan* **Shall Be Bound for the 1,000 Years (Revelation 20:2).**

      The Antichrist and the false prophet were cast into the lake of fire before Satan (Revelation 19:20).

   4. *The Nations* **of the World Shall Worship the Lord or Receive no Rain (Zechariah 14:16).**

   5. **The** *Spiritual Condition of Mankind* **During the Kingdom Age.**

      Human nature never changes. There will be universal adoration of Christ, but it will be pretended obedience on the part of some people. If the Kingdom is made up of only believers in Jesus Christ, where will sin come from during this period? (Remember, Satan is bound during this time.) They will have been born to saved parents who came out of the tribulation alive (Hebrews 2:14; 8:11).

When Satan is loosed after the 1,000 years for a season (Revelation 20:2-3), he will be the head of a final effort to defeat Christ. The ones who had pretended to adore the Lord will follow Satan. Defeated in his effort, Satan shall be cast into the lake of fire, his final doom (Revelation 20:10).

6. **The *Physical Condition of Mankind* During the Kingdom Age.**

Life shall be lengthened and some shall live as long as Methuselah (969 years) or longer. There will be good health, long life, no suffering (Isaiah 35:5-6). No one will die during this age except those with an open rebellion against the Lord. When such a person becomes 100 years old and still rejects Christ as King, he shall die (Isaiah 65:20).

7. **The *Physical Creation* During the Kingdom Age.**

Creation shall be restored. No more famines, pestilences, earthquakes. Underline Isaiah 32:15; 35:1; 65:18-25 in your Bible.

Notice the animals shall revert back to the way the Lord made them (Isaiah 11:6-9; 65:25).

F. THE KINGDOM OF HEAVEN DELIVERED UP TO GOD

1. **The Kingdom of Heaven is to be Presented to the Father.**

   a. At the end of the Kingdom Age, Christ, having put all things under His feet, shall "deliver up the Kingdom to God, even the Father" (I Corinthians 15:24).

   b. "That God (the triune God-Father, Son and Holy Spirit) may be all in all" (I Corinthians 15:28).

2. **The Kingdom of God is Forever.**

   a. The Kingdom of God is everlasting (Psalm 103:19; Daniel 4:3).

   b. The eternal throne is that "of God and of the Lamb"—Jesus Christ (Revelation 22:1).

V. WHAT THIS TRUTH TEACHES US TODAY

The King, Jesus, and His Kingdom are real, actual, literal. The Kingdom of Heaven is the Kingdom of Jesus Christ upon the earth. He shall reign and rule as King of Kings and Lord of Lords. The Old and New Testaments present the Kingdom Age. There is no way for us to explain it away when we compare Scripture with Scripture.

The church shall be called out before Jesus literally comes to the earth (I Thessalonians 4:13-18;II Thessalonians 2:1-7). Read again Zechariah 14:4-7.

The church, the bride of Christ, shall return with Christ when He comes to set up His Kingdom. We, the church, shall reign with Him (II Timothy 2:12; Revelation 5:10). Read Zechariah 14:5. Notice in that prophecy "all the saints" shall return with Jesus to the Mount of Olives.

If you are saved, you are an heir of God and joint heir with Christ. If you are "born again," you are in the Kingdom of God. If you are not "born again," you face eternal doom and judgment. In Revelation 22:17 you read, "The Spirit and the bride say, come." This last invitation is from

God the Holy Spirit and the bride, the church. The triune God and all the members of the body, the bride of Christ, say, "Come."

YOUR NEXT ASSIGNMENT:

1. Read Isaiah 65:17; 66:22-24; II Peter 3:7-13; Revelation 21 and 22.

2. Review your notes on the King and His Kingdom.

3. Mark your Bible where new truths are learned.

Lesson 52 "The New Heaven and New Earth"

(Where lines are provided, look up the Scripture and write in the Scripture or its main truth.)

I. INTRODUCTION

In Acts 7:49, Stephen quotes the Prophet Isaiah and tells the Sanhedrin that the Lord God says, "Heaven is my throne, and the earth my footstool." The very word "heaven" causes us to think of joy, bliss, peace, harmony and the delights of glory. In our minds Heaven is associated with everything which stands for happiness, reunion, expectation and tranquility. When we wish to express the superlative of joy and beauty, we call it heavenly. The word "heaven" is used in the Bible almost 600 times. Of the 600 times the word occurs in the Bible, comparatively few refer to the heaven of heavens, the third heaven, the dwelling place of God. The Bible has little to say about the heaven of heavens.

There are some things that God has not revealed to us in His Word. We would not be able to stand the revelation of the glories of heaven. Heaven is so glorious, so wonderful, that in these earthly temples (physical bodies) we could not bear the full description of our heavenly home. It would overwhelm us. "The secret things belong unto the Lord our God: but those things which are revealed belong unto us and to our children forever, that we may do all the words of this law" (Deuteronomy 29:29).

II. BASIC SCRIPTURES

Isaiah 65:17; 66:22-24; II Peter 3:7-13; Revelation 21 and 22.

III. THE NUCLEUS OF THIS TRUTH

All individuals will spend eternity somewhere, in one of two places prepared by Almighty God. According to the Bible every person will live forever, either in heaven or in hell, either with the Lord or with Satan. This being so, it is the better part of wisdom that we should learn everything we possibly can about our future abode. We have a Book which tells us what God wants us to know about heaven and hell. This study shall focus on heaven.

IV. THE GREAT TRUTH: *"THE NEW HEAVEN AND NEW EARTH"*

A. THE NEW HEAVEN (REVELATION 21:1-8)

1. The Bible Speaks of Three Heavens.

    a. In the original Hebrew there are three words used for "heaven." In the Greek there are three words for "heaven." These six words are translated in our Bible by one word - "heaven."

    b. The three Hebrew words and the three Greek words refer to:

       • the atmospheric heaven, where we live.

- the planetary heaven, the sun, moon, etc.
- the heaven of heavens, the dwelling place of God.

2. A Glimpse of Heaven.

a. Only a few men have had the privilege to see a glimpse of heaven. In each case, they were overcome and overwhelmed by the vision.

b. Paul caught a glimpse of the third heaven and describes that vision in II Corinthians 12:1-9.

Write in II Corinthians 12:2: _____

_____

_____

c. *Stephen* caught a glimpse just before he entered into heaven. That vision of heaven, with Jesus standing to greet him, transformed Stephen's whole being. What the Sanhedrin (council) saw in Stephen is recorded in Acts 6:15: _____

_____

_____

What Stephen saw in glory is recorded in Acts 7:54-60. Underline verses 55 and 56 in your Bible.

d. *John*, the beloved apostle, had more than one glimpse of heaven. In his revelation, John saw Jesus Christ and "fell at His feet as dead" (Revelation 1:17).

John was called up to heaven and there he saw the throne and the One on the throne, the beauty of heaven, the 24 elders, the angels of the Lord. Read Revelation 4:1-11.

Write in the key verse of the context:
Revelation 4:1: _____

_____

_____

Again, John saw the door of heaven open, and he saw Jesus as He was leaving heaven to come as King of Kings and Lord of Lords (Revelation 19:11-16).

3. Heaven is a Place.

a. Heaven is a definite place, and not merely a condition or sentiment or figure of speech. It is an actual, literal place. It is the place Jesus spoke about before He went to the cross.
Write in John 14:2: _____

_____

_____

b. The "citizenship" of believers is in heaven.
Write in Philippians 3:20: _____

_____

_____

4. The Library of Heaven.

a. Heaven contains a library of many books of one kind, and one book altogether different. The many books (plural) contain the record of every word and deed of the unsaved individual. Jesus indicated this fact in Matthew 12:36 and

318

Luke 12:2-3.

b. The book (singular) is the "book of life." In this book are the names of all of the redeemed.

Write in Revelation 20:12: _____

_____

_____

_____

5. Heaven is a Place of Rest.

a. Heaven is a place of rest and peace. Underline Luke 19:38 in your Bible.

b. It is a place of perfect rest. Rest from all the trials and labors of this life.

Write in Revelation 14:13: _____

_____

_____

6. Heaven is a Place of Total Satisfaction.

a. Every care is forgotten, every need is supplied because God and Christ are there.

b. There are seven things God does for His own in glory (Revelation 21:3-4):

- "God Himself shall be with them"
- "and be their God"
- "and God shall wipe away all tears from their eyes"
- "there shall be no more death"
- "neither sorrow"
- "nor crying"
- "neither shall there be any more pain: for the former things are passed away."

(In our study of the new heaven and the study of the new earth, we should find out how the earth and the heaven are to become new.)

B. THE NEW EARTH, A REDEMPTION, A RENOVATION

1. Does John Mean Extinction of the First Heaven and Earth?

a. John says, "And I saw a new heaven and a new earth: for the first heaven and the first earth were passed away" (Revelation 21:1).

b. Does John mean that the heaven above is to be destroyed and this planet is to be swept away—with God creating another heaven and another earth?

Or does John mean that God will redeem, renovate, purify the same earth and the same heaven?

2. The "New" is a Redemption, a Renovation.

a. Why would anyone believe that statement? First, because of the meaning of certain words in describing these things of God. In Revelation 21:1 we read, "the first heaven and the first earth were *passed away*." The same word is used often in the New Testament. In Greek, the primary meaning of the word, "parerchomai," is not annihilation nor extinction—rather, it refers to a change of one place or kind to another.

319

b. The primary meaning of the Greek word can be illustrated. For example, a ship would "parerchomai" through the seas—that is, "pass through" the sea over the horizon. It does not refer to extinction nor annihilation of the ship.

For example again, a man may "pass through" a door and one can't see him any longer. It does not mean annihilation of the man. So it is with the primary meaning of the word. When John says, "the first heaven and the first earth were *passed away*," he does not mean that they shall be annihilated, but rather that they change from one condition to another. The heaven and the earth are here, but changed, redeemed, regenerated.

3. The Testimony of Peter.

a. "Whereby the world that then was, being overflowed with water, perished" (II Peter 3:6). Peter is talking about the terrible days of the flood. In that judgment of God, the "kosmos," the civilized order of man, overflowing with waters, perished. The fashion of that civilized order and culture ceased to exist.

b. One word in that Scripture must be understood. The word is "perished." The earth *did not* perish, the planet did not undergo annihilation. Yet Peter says, "The world overflowing with water, perished." The meaning is—the civilized order, the "kosmos," which means "beauty and adornment," ceased to exist.

c. "But the heavens and the earth which are now, by the same Word (of God) are kept in store, reserved unto fire (the cleansing fire) against the day of judgment and perdition of ungodly men" (II Peter 3:7).

Peter says this great cleansing fire will be in the day of judgment and perdition of ungodly men.

d. The method of purification is given by Peter in verse 7. In that verse Peter gives what probably is the most thorough description of how God is going to make the new heaven and new earth. This is the most advanced and scientific statement made in Scripture about this subject. A free and literal rendering of the verse could be:

"But the present heaven and earth are held in check by the same Word of God, stored up with fire, reserved unto the day of judgment and perdition of the ungodly."

e. The statement "stored with fire" is to be found within the earth. We know it to be true scientifically, while Peter knew all of this 1,900 years ago.

f. God shall purify, cleanse, redeem everything that has been defiled by Satan and sin. Since the earth was defiled by sin, it shall be purified. Since the atmosphere of the air is the present domain of the "prince of the power of the air," it shall be purified by fire.

4. The Testimony of Scripture.

a. The Scriptures declare that we shall inherit the earth.

- Psalm 37:9, 11, 29; Matthew 5:5

b. Underline Isaiah 65:17 in your Bible.

C. THE NEW JERUSALEM (REVELATION 21:9; 22:5)

1. The Heavenly City of God—Outside.

a. First, John gives a description from the outside as he saw it descend *"from God out of heaven."* The description of the outside is recorded in Revelation 21:9 on through the first half of verse 22.

b. John was called by an angel to a great high mountain and there he saw the Lamb's wife (Revelation 21:9-10). The wife is the church, the bride of Christ.

c. The city is the home of the redeemed of all time. We know this is a truth because that city has some names written on the 12 gates—the names of the 12 tribes of the children of Israel (Revelation 21:12). The 12 names represent all of the saved of the Old Covenant.

d. John saw the 12 foundations of the wall and the 12 names of the apostles of the Lamb in the foundation (Revelation 21:14).

e. John describes the size of the city (Revelation 21:15-17). To us, the measurements would be 1,500 miles each way and 1,500 miles high. The wall of the foundation would be 250 feet high.

2. **The Heavenly City of God—Inside.**

a. As John entered the city (middle of verse 21 of Revelation 21), he saw the streets of gold as it were transparent glass.

b. John saw no temple. The Lord God and Christ are the temple (Revelation 21:22). There is God's presence and there is no need for veils, curtains or ceremonies.

c. The illumination of the city is provided by the glory of God and Jesus, the Lamb (Revelation 21:23-25; 22:5). There will be no night, no darkness in that city.

d. The water of life proceeds from the throne of God (Revelation 22:1).

e. The fruit of the tree of life is on either side of the river (Revelation 22:2).

f. The servants shall serve God and the Lamb (Revelation 22:3). We will be doing—not sitting. In the garden of Eden God placed man to keep and care for the garden. In like manner we shall do what God gives us in that heavenly city.

g. His name shall be on our foreheads when we see Him (Revelation 22:4). Gates of pearl are incidental; the streets of gold are incidental; walls of jasper, all great—but the dearest of all is to be with the Lord forever.

h. It is impossible to describe the city of God except in the words John gave to us.

D. EVEN SO, COME, LORD JESUS

1. **The Avowal of the Lord.**

a. "Behold, I come quickly, and my reward is with me" (Revelation 22:12).

b. Underline the Lord's avowal in Revelation 22:16.

c. Write in His blessed invitation in Revelation 22:17: _____

_____

_____

_____

2. The Response of God's People.

    a. Again, Jesus says, "Surely I come quickly."

    b. The response of all who love Him, all of us who are saved should respond with—"Even so, come, Lord Jesus" (Revelation 22:21).

V. WHAT THIS TRUTH TEACHES US TODAY

Heaven is the place Jesus has prepared for all who trust Him. It is actual, literal, eternal. It is indescribable in the English language. The Lord God will redeem the heaven and the earth—renovate it, change it, purify it—just as He has done before. The church, the bride of the Lord Jesus, will have a vital role in heaven. There, Jesus will let us be a part of the great invitation to the last to "come." We shall serve Him. We shall be busy. The last words of Jesus on the earth are in Revelation 22:20. The next time we hear the voice of the Son of Man will be when He comes secretly, as a thief in the night, to take out His pearl of great price.

The final benediction: "The grace of our Lord Jesus Christ be with you all. Amen."

(As we conclude this study, it is our prayer that the Lord will use the 52 lessons to make you fall in love with the Bible. When you reach that point of excitement about His Word, you will become a witness, a helper, a teacher, a worker for the Lord. Let the Holy Spirit teach you and guide you as you grow in grace.)

ENERGIZE, REVITALIZE, REVOLUTIONIZE
YOUR BIBLE STUDY WITH ANOTHER SELECTION
FROM HENSLEY PUBLISHING

Through the Bible in One Year
Alan B. Stringfellow • ISBN 1-56322-014-8

God's Great & Precious Promises
Connie Witter • ISBN 1-56322-063-6

Preparing for Marriage God's Way
Wayne Mack • ISBN 1-56322-019-9

Becoming the Noble Woman
Anita Young • ISBN 1-56322-020-2

Women in the Bible — Examples To Live By
Sylvia Charles • ISBN 1-56322-021-0

Pathways to Spiritual Understanding
Richard Powers • ISBN 1-56322-023-7

Christian Discipleship
Steven Collins • ISBN 1-56322-022-9

Couples in the Bible — Examples To Live By
Sylvia Charles • ISBN 1-56322-062-8

Men in the Bible — Examples To Live By
Don Charles • ISBN 1-56322-067-9

7 Steps to Bible Skills
Dorothy Hellstern • ISBN 1-56322-029-6

Great Characters of the Bible
Alan B. Stringfellow • ISBN 1-56322-046-6

Great Truths of the Bible
Alan B. Stringfellow • ISBN 1-56322-047-4

Inspirational Study Journals
A FRESH APPROACH
TO INDIVIDUAL AND SMALL-GROUP STUDY

In His Hand
Patti Becklund • ISBN 1-56322-068-7

In Everything You Do
Sheri Stout • ISBN 1-56322-069-5

Rare & Beautiful Treasures
Nolene Niles • ISBN 1-56322-071-7

Love's Got Everything To Do With It
Rosemarie Karlebach • ISBN 1-56322-070-9

AÑADE ENERGIA, REVITALIZA Y REVOLUCIONA
TU ESTUDIO BIBLICO CON OTRAS SELECCIONES
DE PUBLICACIONES HENSLEY

A Traves De La Biblia En Un Año
Alan B. Stringfellow • ISBN 1-56322-061-X

*Preparando El Matrimonio
En El Camino De Dios*
Wayne Mack • ISBN 1-56322-066-0

Mujeres En La Biblia
Sylvia Charles • ISBN 1-56322-072-5